TRANSGRESSION
IN ANGLO-AMERICAN CINEMA

TRANSGRESSION
IN ANGLO-AMERICAN CINEMA

Gender, Sex and the Deviant Body

Edited by Joel Gwynne

WALLFLOWER PRESS
LONDON & NEW YORK

A Wallflower Press Book

Wallflower Press is an imprint of
Columbia University Press
Publishers Since 1893
New York   Chichester, West Sussex
cup.columbia.edu

Copyright © 2016 Columbia University Press
All rights reserved

Wallflower Press® is a registered trademark of Columbia University Press

A complete CIP record is available from the Library of Congress

ISBN 978-0-231-17604-0 (cloth : alk. paper)
ISBN 978-0-231-17605-7 (pbk. : alk. paper)
ISBN 978-0-231-85098-8 (e-book)

Columbia University Press books are printed on permanent
and durable acid-free paper.
Printed in the United States of America

Cover image: *Little Children* (New Line Cinema/Bona Fide Productions, 2006)

Contents

Notes on Contributors vi

Introduction Queering Heterosexuality in New Transgressive Cinema 1
JOEL GWYNNE

PART I: EXTREME BODIES, EXTREME DESIRE

Chapter 1 The New Anglo-American Cinema of Sexual Addiction 9
ALISTAIR FOX

Chapter 2 Carnotopia: The Culture of Sadism in *Nymphomaniac*, *Shame*
and *Thanatomorphose* 25
MARK FEATHERSTONE

Chapter 3 *Feed*: A Representation of Feederism or Fatsploitation? 43
NIALL RICHARDSON

Chapter 4 Proving their 'Virility'? Steve McQueen's *Hunger* and Transgressive Masculinity 57
ALISON GARDEN

Chapter 5 Male-Nutrition: Extreme Weight Loss, Socio-Cultural Transgression
and the Male Body in Recent American Cinema 73
TOM STEWARD

Chapter 6 Surgery, Blood and Patriarchal Sex: *Excision* and *American Mary* 89
ALICE HAYLETT BRYAN

PART II: ADOLESCENCE, AGEING AND QUEER AGENCY

Chapter 7 A Child is Being Raped! Homosexual Panic in *Mystic River* 103
VULCAN VOLKAN DEMIRKAN-MARTIN

Chapter 8 Crash-and-Burn Girls and Culpable Parenthood: Negotiating
Sexualisation Discourses in Independent Cinema 119
JOEL GWYNNE

Chapter 9 'Please be a good boy': Challenging Perceptions of Paedophilia
in Contemporary US Cinema 131
AMY C. CHAMBERS

Chapter 10 Nowhere Teens: Following Gregg Araki's Queer Adolescents through
the End of a Century 147
ARNAU ROIG-MORA

Chapter 11 Unsettling Heteronormativity: Abject Age and Transgressive Desire
in *Notes on a Scandal* 161
EVA KRAINITZKI

Index 177

Notes on Contributors

Amy C. Chambers is a Wellcome Trust Research Associate in Science Communication and Film Studies at the Centre for the History of Science, Technology and Medicine at the University of Manchester. She researches and publishes on religious audiences and science-based cinema, domestic horror, science fiction cinema, participatory cinema and transmedia storytelling.

Vulcan Volkan Demirkan-Martin is a Lecturer at Nisantasi University, Istanbul, where he teaches courses on social and new media. He completed his PhD in Cultural Studies at the University of Canterbury. He has previously lectured on feminism, psychoanalysis, queer studies and film studies.

Mark Featherstone is Senior Lecturer in Sociology at Keele University, UK. He teaches modules focused on social and cultural theory, the history of the idea of globalisation, and psychoanalysis from Freud to Žižek. He is author of *Tocqueville's Virus: Utopia and Dystopia in Western Social and Political Theory* (Routledge, 2007), *Planet Utopia: Utopia, Dystopia, and the Global Imaginary* (Routledge, 2015) and a range of articles in journals including *Cultural Politics* and *Ctheory*. He is currently working on a book focused on carnographic culture in contemporary cinema and a study of the relationship between psychoanalysis and processes of globalisation.

Alistair Fox is Professor Emeritus at the University of Otago, New Zealand. He has written extensively on topics ranging from Renaissance literature to issues of national and gendered identities, the psychodynamic processes involved in authorship, and the nature and effects of fictive representation as a phenomenon in human life. His major books include *Thomas More: History and Providence* (Blackwell/Yale University Press, 1982), *The English Renaissance: Identity and Representation in the Reign of Elizabeth I* (Blackwell, 1997), *The Ship of Dreams: Masculinity in Contemporary New Zealand Fiction* (Otago University Press, 2008), *Jane Campion: Authorship and Personal Cinema* (Indiana University Press, 2011), *New Zealand Cinema: Interpreting the Past* (Intellect, 2011), *A Companion to Contemporary French Cinema* (Wiley-Blackwell, 2015) and *Speaking Pictures: Neuropsychoanalysis and Authorship in Film and Literature* (Indiana University Press, 2016).

Alison Garden is a Leverhulme Postdoctoral Fellow at University College Dublin, where she is conducting research on the literary afterlives of the Irish nationalist and human rights campaigner, Roger Casement. She has forthcoming publications in

The Canadian Journal of Irish Studies and *Critique: Studies in Contemporary Fiction* and is co-editing special issues of *Symbiosis: A Journal of Transatlantic Literary and Cultural Relations* (2015) and the *Irish Review* (2017).

Joel Gwynne is an Associate Professor of English and Cultural Studies at the National Institute of Education, Nanyang Technological University, Singapore, where he teaches courses on literature and cultural studies. He is the author/co-editor of *Erotic Memoirs and Postfeminism: The Politics of Pleasure* (Palgrave Macmillan, 2013), *Postfeminism and Contemporary Hollywood Cinema* (Palgrave Macmillan, 2013) and *Ageing, Popular Culture and Contemporary Feminism* (Palgrave Macmillan, 2014). His essays on gender, cultural studies and cinema have appeared in journals such as *Women's Studies International Forum*, the *Journal of Gender Studies*, the *European Journal of American Culture*, the *Journal of Contemporary Asia*, *Feminist Media Studies*, *Critical Studies in Television*, *Film International* and *Feminist Theory: An International Interdisciplinary Journal*.

Alice Haylett Bryan is a PhD candidate and Graduate Teaching Assistant at King's College, London, where she recently submitted a thesis on womb phantasies in international horror and extreme cinema. Her current research areas include the representation of sexuality in American independent horror, and contemporary French horror cinema.

Eva Krainitzki is a Postdoctoral Researcher at the Centre for Women, Ageing and Media (WAM), at the University of Gloucestershire, Cheltenham, UK, where she researches in the areas of Age/ing Studies, Gender and Sexuality, with a specific interest in the representation of lesbian identities in popular culture. She also teaches on film studies and research methodologies. She has published in the *Journal of Aging Studies* and the *Journal of Lesbian Studies*.

Niall Richardson is Senior Lecturer in Film Studies at the University of Sussex where he convenes the MA in Gender and Media. He is the author of several books on gender, sexuality and the body including *The Queer Cinema of Derek Jarman* (I.B. Tauris, 2009), *Transgressive Bodies: Representations in Film and Popular Culture* (Ashgate, 2010), *Studying Sexualities* (Palgrave, 2013), *Gender in the Media* (Palgrave, 2014) and *Body Studies: The Basics* (Routledge, 2014).

Arnau Roig-Mora is a PhD candidate in the Institute of Communications Research at the University of Illinois and an Instructor at ESERP Business School and Universitat Autònoma de Barcelona, where he teaches courses on communication and gender studies. He has published chapters on queer cinema, including in *Thinking Dead: What the Zombie Apocalypse Means* (Lexington Books, 2013).

Tom Steward is an Instructor in Film and Society at Platt College in San Diego, where he teaches courses on film history and analysis. He previously taught Film and Television Studies at several UK universities, including the University of Warwick and the University of Nottingham. Journals in which his work has appeared include *Continuum: Journal of Media and Cultural Studies* and the *Journal of Screenwriting*.

Introduction
Queering Heterosexuality in New Transgressive Cinema

JOEL GWYNNE

In its most simple definition, transgression is 'the act of breaking a law, committing a crime or sin, doing something illegal, or otherwise acting in some manner proscribed by the various forms or institutions of Law in societies, whether secular or religious, all of which have histories and which themselves are mutable, self-translating' (Wolfreys 2008: 3). By this definition, parking illegally is clearly transgressive, and yet any claim to political subversion and subcultural rebellion made by such an act would undoubtedly be absurd. What constitutes social transgression and legal transgression are markedly different, and it is my interest in the former that binds the chapters in this collection. The films discussed in this book concern themselves with crossing social boundaries and moving beyond convention in both narrative form and narrative function. While transgressive art such as Cedric Chambers' *The Prophet* or Robert Mapplethorpe's photography might be understood as that which sets out to consciously flaunt social and cultural mores, to violate tradition and to obfuscate boundaries, it could also be reasonably asserted that transgression can be motivated by a desire to resist oppression and to address inequality; it can be both utopian and democratising in its aims and intentions, if not its operation. The most confrontational and abrasive of films may have utopian imperatives, and as a heterosexual scholar of sexuality studies it is in this spirit that I approach cinema. I hope to find libertarian articulations of queer heterosexuality which celebrate a deviant conception of heterosexuality premised on gender fluidity, non-reproductive sex, the recognition of pleasure as a fundamental human need rather than an expendable luxury, and an understanding of heterosexuality as merely one configuration among others. My interest in taboo representation is also attentive to more practical considerations. Examining controversial images and content within cinema is important in terms of understanding media production more discursively, since it exposes the mechanisms of censorship and regulation and the limits and conventions of media forms; how they are challenged and overturned. This is not always an easy task since serious exploration of sexual taboos is often difficult to find within mainstream cinema. While sex is frequently and fleetingly an aspect of most cinematic narratives regardless of genre, sexuality as a serious subject of enquiry and exploration is almost non-existent in Hollywood.

Genre is a pertinent issue here. Caroline Ruddell has observed that in some respects horror and pornography have 'similar modes of address and affect, in that they incite particular responses from their audiences' (2013: 160), while other genres may move the body in less visceral and inflammatory ways. Genre is certainly significant where sexual exploration is concerned. Within mainstream cinema sexuality features primarily in comedy or rom-com genres, where lightness of tone allows audience engagement with what would otherwise, perhaps, prove to be difficult affective terrain. Independent cinema has, of course, been more willing to take sex seriously, commensurate with its status as a genre that marks itself against mainstream audience expectations and textual practices. Both critics and audiences have come to associate independent filmmaking with the empowerment of the marginalised and a defiant stance towards tradition in both culture and cinematic convention. This was, after all, one of the founding tenets of avant-garde movements such as New Queer Cinema and the films of Gregg Araki, Jennie Livingston, Gus Van Sant and Todd Haynes – appropriating genres like the teen movie and documentary film, and subverting conventional linear narrative modes to provide queer alternatives to classic cinema. And yet, despite these examples, independent productions do not always demonstrate progressive views of sex. Many, in fact, gesture towards an imperceptibly reactionary understanding of sex as compulsive and usually destructive to self and others, precipitating feelings of shame, humiliation and despair. Sex is frequently understood as a problem that requires intervention, and even in films where intervention is not achieved, it is nevertheless implicitly sought through redemption. Examples of such films include *Shame* (Steve McQueen, 2011), *Thanks for Sharing* (Stuart Blumberg, 2012) and *Nymphomaniac* (Lars von Trier, 2013).

This is a collection of essays which focuses on the 'problem' of sex, the gendered dynamics of sex and the body and particularly its deviation from normative cultural and gendered scripts. It works to understand the ways in which corporeality inscribes not only gender discourse but also reflects culture more discursively. In charting the manner in which, for example, bodies refuse to legitimise male power, many of the chapters in this book queer and problematise our cultural understandings of gender boundaries and what constitutes 'healthy' sex/sexual identity. Quite frequently, the contributions serve to illustrate how cinema renders the body as a cultural artefact which should be read pluralistically as a site of both gender and political subversion. The chapters figure the transgressive body in a number of ways. While all explore the depiction of the eroticised body in some form, many examine those which are seldom depicted on the cinema screen, particular the naked bodies of men, older women and those in states of extreme weight loss or gain. Eva Krainitzki's chapter on *Notes on a Scandal* (Richard Eyre, 2006) draws our attention to the erotic, disruptive potential of ageing femininity, suggesting that if mainstream cinema perpetuates the shame of ageing in its preoccupation with the desirable bodies of young women, then transgressive cinema refuses to define the ageing female body as unwatchable, unsettling the structures of heteronormative desire. Alison Garden's on *Hunger* (Steve McQueen, 2008) navigates the hypermasculinity of the stripped male form under duress, codified for scopophilic pleasure; while Tom Steward's chapter on *Fight Club* (David Fincher, 1999), *The Machinist* (Brad Anderson, 2004) and *Dallas Buyers Club* (Jean-Marc Vallee, 2013) positions the underweight male body as not only a subversion of hegemonic masculinity, but also a product and rejection of late capitalism and its excesses. Moving away from the adult body and focusing our gaze upon the stripped child, other chapters are interested in disrupting received cultural understanding of childhood sexual agency, and the power dynamics between children and adults. Amy C. Chambers' analysis of *Mysterious Skin* (Gregg Araki, 2004) demonstrates how film positions abuse as sexual enlightenment, while her examination of Hayley in *Hard Candy* (David Slade, 2005) illustrates the agentic liminality of teen girls, moving between maturity and innocence. Both of these films join others, such as *L.I.E.* (2001), *Birth* (Jonathan Glazer, 2004) and *The Woodsman* (Nicole Kassell, 2004), offering contentious representations of relationships between adults and their 'victims'. Such films provocatively challenge binary constructions of child and child abuser, confront the presumption that children cannot experience sexual desire except as trauma, and advocate a wider discussion of culturally rejected forms of taboo love, desire and sex.

This book hopes to extend the growing body of scholarship on sexuality, gender and the non-normative body in contemporary cinema. Treading similar thematic and conceptual terrain as Robin Griffiths' *British Queer Cinema* (2006) and Nick Rees-Roberts' *French Queer Cinema* (2014) and Darren Kerr and Donna Peberdy's *Tainted Love: Screening Sexual Perversities* (2016) the chapters that follow seek to broaden our discussion of sexual transgression by encompassing gay sexuality but also focusing on queer heterosexuality. The chapters are divided into two sections. The first, 'Extreme Bodies, Extreme Desire', examines the body in states of pathology and excess; bodies suffering from extreme and compulsive sexual desire and those under extreme forms of physical duress. Exploring the former, and noting the emergence of a cycle of indie-auteur movies on sexual addiction both in the UK and the US, Alistair Fox's chapter locates this phenomenon as a consequence of the sexual revolution and, in more immediate terms, the 'pornographication' of the media. Through an examination of *I Am a Sex Addict* (Caveh Zahedi, 2005), *Choke* (Clark Gregg, 2008), *Shame*, *Thanks for Sharing*, *Don Jon* (2013), *Nymphomaniac* and *Welcome to New York* (Abel Ferrara, 2014), this chapter studies what these films reveal about the causes, dynamics and outcomes of sex addiction as this newly foregrounded phenomenon, and speculates on where their representations may be leading.

Remaining on the topic of compulsive sexuality, Mark Featherstone's chapter navigates the image of the transgressive, hyper-sexualised body in three recent films: *Shame*, *Nymphomaniac* and *Thanatomorphose* (Eric Falardeau, 2012). In analysing these texts, Featherstone suggests that Anglo-American culture has, since the late twentieth century, transmuted into a sadistic, 'carnographic' space, as testified by films such as *Nymphomaniac* in which Charlotte Gainsbourg's character, Joe, seeks to replace emotional connection with the pursuit of sexual non-relations, culminating in psychological collapse. Likewise, in *Shame*, the central character, Brandon, is a sex addict who consumes hardcore porn on screen, hires prostitutes and works his way through an endless chain of one night stands with a relentlessness suggestive of Freud's concept of the death drive. Finally, the author explores the body horror of *Thanatomorphose* in order to show how the transgressive, drive-based body eventually consumes itself in a carnographic orgy that is representative of the state of Western culture in its contemporary neo-liberal phase.

Moving away from sexual compulsion, the other chapters in this section are concerned with examining bodies under conditions of physical duress. Beginning with the topic of feederism – a practice that eroticises both the act of excessive feeding/eating and subsequent gaining of body fat – Niall Richardson's chapter considers its representation in the horror film *Feed* (Brett Leonard, 2006), and argues that while it may appear to be interested in investigating the psycho-sexual dynamics of feederism, it instead codes the excessive fat of the feedee as the most horrific visual element of the text. In this respect, the film fails to offer a nuanced consideration of a transgressive psycho-sexual activity, and instead acts as a vehicle to articulate contemporary fat-phobia.

If *Feed* fails to politicise non-normative desire and the eroticisation of the extreme body, then Alison Garden's chapter on *Hunger* can be positioned as a useful counterpoint. Dramatising the 1981 Long Kesh/Maze hunger strike, Garden asserts that the film exposes a complex nexus of cultural ideas about gender and the transgressive body within an Irish colonial context. The film's visual vocabulary, she argues, with its focus on somatic suffering, moments of male nudity and lingering shots over disembodied male body parts, inverts the filmic language of the male gaze often used to police and objectify the female body. The chapter suggests that the unclothed male body unsettles the scopophilic pleasures associated with traditional Hollywood cinema, and that by presenting his male leads as eroticised in the first sections of the film, and passively suffering by the conclusion of the film, director Steve McQueen feminises the bodies of these paramilitary prisoners. Garden persuasively argues that the film's gender 'transgression' is thus complexly wrought; *Hunger* does not sustain genuinely subversive gender politics and McQueen's appropriation of the feminine works only to absolve his male subjects of their violent pasts.

Tom Steward's chapter also analyses the suffering, starving male body. Noting that several high-profile male film actors have lost an unhealthy amount of weight in preparation for roles and appeared underweight onscreen, Steward turns his attention to Edward Norton and Brad Pitt in *Fight Club*, Christian Bale in *The Machinist* and Matthew McConaughey in *Dallas Buyers Club*. He argues that these bodily transformations transgress cultural discourses of male health and beauty, and yet invest the actors with greater cultural standing and celebration. The chapter explores the social transgressions of the actors' weight loss and evaluates how effective, and yet unhealthy, weight loss manifests itself in the actors' portrayals of their characters' social transgressions, demonstrating how these stars' acts of bodily transgression enhanced their status in the film establishment and acting community.

Turning away from the malnourished body, but remaining on the topic of how gender transgression is an embodied practice, Alice Haylett Bryan focuses on two North American independent films which feature female protagonists carrying out surgical procedures in contemporary interpretations of the mad-doctor horror subgenre: *Excision* (Richard Bates Jr, 2012) and *American Mary* (Jen and Sylvia

Soska, 2012). This chapter makes a case for the potential of these films to challenge issues of control and heteronormativity in contemporary sex and society, arguing that the depiction of women as surgeons in these works allows for a dissection of white, male, middle-class values. It examines what occurs when women pick up the surgical scalpel and begin to penetrate instead of being penetrated, asking whether this act still operates within a hetero-normative structural logic, or whether it allows for a potential queer interpretation of the penetrating female protagonist. Building on the work of Jack Halberstam, the chapter surveys the representation of violence, control and desire in these films, and asks whether the actions of these women could be seen to present a fissure in the patriarchal heterosexual system.

The second section of this book, 'Adolescence, Ageing and Queer Agency', is particularly interested in the polarised periods of youth and old age, and how cinema may be engaged in a process of queering these categories. The queering of childhood is especially significant not least because, as Henry Jenkins asserts, our culture imagines it as a 'utopian space, separate from adult cares and worries, free from sexuality, outside social divisions, closer to nature and the primitive world, more fluid in its identity and its access to the realms of imagination, beyond historical change, more just, pure, and innocent, and in the end, waiting to be corrupted or protected by adults' (1998: 3–4). Jenkins goes on to assert that this conception of childhood 'dips freely in the politics of nostalgia' (1998: 4). Films which are invested in a 'politics of nostalgia' characteristically refuse to challenge the mythology of childhood innocence, and in order to appreciate the agency inherent in transgressive depictions of childhood in independent filmmaking, it is important to begin with an analysis of mainstream cinema.

In his chapter on Clint Eastwood's *Mystic River* (2003), Vulcan Volkan Demirkan-Martin asserts that through the figure of child abuse victim Dave Boyle, homosexuality, paedophilia and child abuse are extravagantly conflated in ways which position both Dave and his abusers as monsters. Relating Dave's monstrosity to the pollution represented by the cellar in which the rape takes place, this chapter defines the space of the cellar as a symbolic space of exclusion. In so doing, *Mystic River* can be read as typical of a mainstream film which parallels the construction of paedophiles and victims in mass journalism – as inflexibly positioned in the categories of 'monsters' and 'victims'. In this way, the film shores up cultural understandings of childhood as a space to be protected.

Likewise, in my chapter on *Thirteen* (Catherine Hardwicke, 2003) and *Trust* (David Schwimmer, 2010), I focus on the manner in which these films *appear* to be invested in problematising childhood, only to reify notions of childhood innocence and, in doing so, strip their teen protagonists of agency. While ostensibly offering 'edgy' representations of girlhood, I argue that these films emphasise the role of parents in protecting children from harm, rendering their depiction of childhood conventional. Furthermore, in attempting to understand the causes of teen transgression, complex cultural and interpersonal determinants such as poverty, familial conditions, curiosity and, perhaps most importantly, desire, give way to a simplistic commitment to the all-encompassing power of the mass media and commodities.

In contrast to these chapters, Amy C. Chambers and Arnau Roig-Mora focus on films which problematise normative depictions of childhood and adolescence. In her chapter on *Mysterious Skin*, *Hard Candy* and *Little Children* (Todd Field, 2006), Chambers highlights how these films can be read as part of cycle of independent films which challenge perceptions of paedophilia by subverting the traditional cinematic discourse of 'monstrous' paedophiles and 'innocent' child victims. Her chapter analyses how previously under or entirely un-represented figures are given visibility through cinematic form and style. Both children and paedophiles are given a voice that allows for an exploration of the complexities of their character that extends beyond monstrosity and innocence. Paedophiles are presented as sympathetic, caring, broken and even as victims, and children are active figures often with burgeoning sexual awareness. These complex meditations upon child sexuality and agency, and adult culpability are, Chambers argues, indebted to their independent production context that allows for these films' controversial moral ambiguity. Similarly, in complicating the identity of the queer teenager against heteronormative depictions, Arnau Roig-Mora examines the cinema of Gregg Araki, focusing primarily on his trilogy *Totally Fucked Up* (1993), *The Doom Generation* (1995) and *Nowhere* (1997), but also *Kaboom* (2010). By following queer teenagers into the new century, the chapter shows how Araki denounces their precarious situation and the structural violence exerted on their queer bodies, as well as how he succeeds in giving a space to minority sexualities often underrepresented in the media.

The final chapter in this section moves away from childhood and adolescence, and instead considers how transgression manifests itself in the depiction of ageing womanhood. This chapter considers Barbara Covett (Judi Dench) in *Notes on a Scandal*, taking an age/ing studies approach to queer transgression. In the tradition of feminist and queer appropriations of stereotypical portrayals of non-normative female sexuality, such as the older predatory lesbian, it proposes an alternative reading of abject-ageing characters, inviting viewers to identify moments of resistance where normativity is unsettled by queer desire and/or a refusal to age appropriately. Employing Halberstam's concept of 'queer failure', this chapter challenges the notion of 'unsuccessful' ageing, casting Barbara as purposefully disgraceful, queer and, thus, transgressive of normative structures.

Bibliography

Griffiths, R. (2006) *British Queer Cinema*. London: Routledge.
Jenkins, H. (1998) 'Introduction: Childhood Innocence and other Modern Myths', in H. Jenkins (ed.) *The Children's Culture Reader*. New York, NY: New York University Press, 1–40.
Kerr, D. and D. Peberdy (2016) *Tainted Love: Screening Sexual Perversities*. London: I.B. Tauris.
Rees-Roberts, N. (2014) *French Queer Cinema*. Edinburgh: Edinburgh University Press.
Ruddell, C. (2013) 'Cutting Edge: Violence and Body Horror in Anime' in F. Attwood, V. Campbell, I.Q. Hunter and S. Lockyer (eds) *Controversial Images: Media Representations on the Edge*. New York, NY: Palgrave Macmillan, 157–69.
Wolfreys, J. (2008) *Transgression: Identity, Space, Time*. Basingstoke: Palgrave Macmillan.

PART I
EXTREME BODIES, EXTREME DESIRES

Chapter 1
The New Anglo-American Cinema of Sexual Addiction

ALISTAIR FOX

Film critics have recently been noticing the emergence of a cycle of indie-auteur movies on sexual addiction, both in the United States and also in the United Kingdom (sometimes with financial input from European countries such as France and Germany). Indie cinema, which has become a cultural genre and cultural category in its own right, defines itself against mainstream Hollywood cinema in terms of audience expectations, textual practices and genre preferences (see Newman 2011). Being character-centered, often marked by socially engaged realism, frequently inspired by the auteur-director's personal experience and aimed primarily at festival and art-house audiences, it has much greater freedom to explore marginal and alternative spheres than mainstream Hollywood genre films. Unsurprisingly, therefore, indie-auteur films have been a prime site for the exploration of sexual dysfunction since *sex, lies, and videotape* (Steven Soderbergh, 1989), the success of which was instrumental in fuelling the boom of independent filmmaking in the 1990s.

The cycle of sex addiction films I wish to discuss represents a continuation of this preoccupation, updated to reflect awareness of what is being experienced or perceived as a growing personal and social problem. As Tom Shone, an American film critic who writes for *The Guardian* puts it: 'For the indie-auteur sphere, the figure of the sex addict has become what the serial killer was for mainstream thrillers in the 1990s: a repeat offender, plot-driver and sensation source, drawing audiences with a mixture of curiosity, skepticism and astonishment' (2014). Among the films that have appeared on the American circuit may be listed *I Am a Sex Addict* (Caveh Zahedi, 2005), *Choke* (Clark Gregg, 2008), *Thanks for Sharing* (Stuart Blumberg, 2012), *Don Jon* (Joseph Gordon-Levitt, 2013) and *Welcome to New York* (Abel Ferrara, 2014). To these may be added the British-made *Shame* (Steve McQueen, 2011) and *Nymphomaniac* (Lars von Trier, 2013), the two volumes of which were funded as a co-production involving the United Kingdom and a variety of European countries. Why should a rash of such films suddenly be appearing now, and why should they have become a preoccupation of indie-auteur filmmakers? To find an answer, one needs to take a look at the evolution of the post-World War II sexual revolution and its aftermath.

The Sexual Revolution, the Media and the Screening of Sex

The story of the sexual revolution is by now well known. Starting in the 1950s, and accelerating in the 1960s and 1970s, Western societies experienced a powerful reaction against traditional normative constraints in many spheres of life. In the domain of sexuality, this was manifest in a movement aimed at legitimising premarital and extramarital sex, promoting acceptance of homosexuality and alternative forms of sexuality and privileging the visceral pleasure to be derived from sex as a valid form of self-gratification and fulfillment (see, for example, Allyn 2001). In America, in particular, this liberation into relatively unconstrained sexuality was celebrated as consonant with the country's neo-liberal commitment to 'freedom' in other areas of life, as manifest in the conflation of sexual gratification with the personal gratification derived from indulgence in consumer culture (see Radner 2010). In terms of behaviour, it produced a 'hook-up culture'.

This cultural shift can be ascribed to the convergence of three factors: political change, leading to a 'transformed political economy of desire'; the emergence of digital communication technology, which has transformed the consumption and production of sexual culture; and familiar economic factors, such as the profit imperative and efficiency of the market as a distribution mechanism, that has led to the 'commercialisation' and 'commodification' of sex (see McNair 2013: 4–6). The sexualised culture that has resulted has been characterised as involving

> a preoccupation with sexual values, practices and identities; the proliferation of sexual texts; the emergence of new forms of sexual experience; the apparent breakdown of rules, categories and regulations designed to keep the obscene at bay; a fondness for scandals, controversies and panics around sex. (Attwood 2006: 78)

From the outset, cinema was centrally involved in what sociologist Brian McNair has described as 'pornographication' – 'the colonisation of mainstream culture by texts in a variety of forms, genres, and styles which borrow from, refer to, or pastiche the styles and iconography of the pornographic' – leading to a commensurate enlargement of 'the pornosphere' (the cultural space in which sexually explicit texts circulate) (2013: 36, 3). Eric Schaeffer, the editor of a recent volume on this topic, proposes that 'a rapidly and radically sexualized media accounts for what we now think of as the sexual revolution', owing to the fact that 'sex was no longer a private matter that took place behind closed doors' (2014: 3). Linda Williams has also argued that cinema, along with its extension into television, advertising and pornography, has played a crucial role in propagating the liberation of the modern individual into a desirable capacity for eroticism: when we watch sex on screen, she writes, 'we are disciplined into new forms of socialized arousal in the company of others' (2008: 18).

For some, including McNair and Williams, sexualisation in the media is to be welcomed. Williams, for example, asserts that 'the very act of screening is desirable, sensual, and erotic in its own right' (2008: 326), and therefore to be celebrated, along with pornography. For his part, McNair has argued that the sexualisation of culture through pornography, porno chic and sexually transgressive art has been instrumental not only in driving 'the transformation of patriarchal and heteronormative structures, as well as authoritarian governance in general', but also in giving millions of people 'access to sexual pleasure they would not otherwise have had', thereby increasing the 'stock of human happiness' (2013: 157, 158).

Others, however, are not so sure, or else are emphatically convinced of the opposite. McNair himself notes that 'somewhere around 2003 commentators began to identify cultural sexualisation as a major social problem' (2013: 56), citing an article in *The Guardian* in which Edward Marriott identified pornography, 'like drugs and drink', as 'an addictive substance' (2003). Even earlier, Patrick Carnes had introduced the idea of sex addiction into popular culture with his groundbreaking book, *Out of the Shadows: Understanding Sexual Addiction* (1983). Since then, there has been a veritable explosion of self-help and clinical books on sexual addiction, especially since 2005, along with the highly publicised entry of celebrities such as Michael Douglas, David Duchovny and Russell Brand into clinics for sex addiction therapy.

Clearly, then, a backlash is in process, arising from a growing anxiety about sexual addiction as a dysfunction. This is reflected, for example, in the alarm expressed by the psychologist and social commentator Philip Zimbardo in *The Demise of Guys* (2012), who warns about the growing danger of cyber-porn addiction (see Zimbardo and Duncan 2012). The statistics Zimbardo presents, citing a University of Alberta study, are startling: in America, which is the top producer of pornographic web pages, 'one in three boys is now considered a "heavy" porn user, with the average boy watching nearly two hours of porn every week' (loc. 553). Zimbardo also draws attention to how addiction to Internet porn is beginning to damage the ability of young men to form healthy sexual relationships. Quoting Leonard Sax, another psychologist who has conducted a parallel study of a new crisis facing girls, he observes:

> Given the choice between masturbating over online pornography and going out on a date with a real girl – that is to say, a girl who doesn't look like a porn star and isn't wearing lingerie – more and more young men tell me that they prefer online porn. 'Girls online are way better looking', one young man said to me, with no apology or embarrassment. (loc. 553)

Zimbardo's anxiety over internet porn is merely one manifestation of a larger concern with sexual addiction more generally, defined as involving 'people whose lives worsen in direct proportion to self-destructive patterns of sexual behaviors over which they appear to have little control' (Weiss 2013: loc. 457).

The cycle of films in this chapter has self-evidently been generated in response to this relatively new cultural context – one in which a hyper-sexualisation of culture has given rise to sexual addiction as a dysfunctional version of sexuality that is causing concern. It might be argued that the production of these films is simply an attempt to jump on the commercial bandwagon to participate in the commodification of sex, but the content of the films themselves would argue against this. McNair defines pornography in terms of 'its intention to sexually arouse the user through the explicit, transgressive representation of sex' (2013: 17). Virtually without exception, the films in the sex addiction cycle are devoid of titillation; to the contrary, the compulsive sexual behaviours of the protagonists are depicted as self-destructive and destructive of relationships, humiliating and shameful, and a cause of misery and despair. They are thus very far from the joyful pleasure, self-gratification and personal satisfaction that is extolled by the likes of McNair and Williams as an outcome of healthy sexuality.

In the rest of this chapter, I shall explore in detail what these films show about the causes, dynamics and outcomes of sex addiction as this newly foregrounded phenomenon, and where their representations may be leading.

Variations of Tone and Genre

Upon inspection, the films in this cycle display such a high degree of congruence in their representation of the manifestations of sexual addiction that they can be viewed collectively as a 'theme and variations', to speak in musical terms. In music, a 'theme and variations' begins with a motif that provides the main melody, which is then followed by one or more variations of that melody, achieved by changing the music melodically, harmonically or contrapuntally. In other words, the same material returns, but it is slightly or substantially varied through an application of the principles of repetition or contrast.

In the sex addiction movies, this theme-and-variation principle is apparent in the range of genres, tones and moods that are used variously to address the central problem – or 'theme' – and in the relative extent to which each film focuses on the causes relative to the effects. To generalise, one can say that whereas the films in the American cycle are predominantly comic, or, at the very least, mix elements of comedy with more serious elements, those produced in Europe tend to be unrelievedly grim and harrowing. In other words, there is a continuum along which all the films under discussion can be ranged, depending upon the relative disposition of tone, narrative perspective and story arc in each.

At one end of this continuum, one can situate *I Am a Sex Addict* and *Don Jon*, both of which are consistently light-hearted in tone, and comedic in their outcomes. In each, following a series of promiscuous encounters that provide the protagonist with no lasting satisfaction, the hero masters his sex addiction (to a greater or lesser degree) and is rewarded with the love of a woman who not only understands him, but also has a beneficial, ameliorating effect on him. As far as filmic techniques are concerned, both of these films maintain their comic tone by interposing a distance between the spectator and the action to maintain a degree of evaluative detachment. Both films use a voice-over delivered by the protagonist, and both broach the fourth wall by having the hero directly address the spectator.

Fig. 1: Caveh (Caveh Zahedi) addresses the spectator in *I Am a Sex Addict* (2005).

Caveh Zahedi in *I Am a Sex Addict* goes still further by presenting himself explicitly, and without overt fictionalisation, as the main character (he appears in the film under his own name) and by including extra-diegetic inserts (such as cartoons) and real-life footage into the depiction of past episodes – which has the effect of emphasising the constructed nature of the fictive reenactment. This ensures that it remains situated at an affective remove from the spectator, who implicitly is invited to share the more discriminating perspective of the older and wiser character in present time.

At the other end of the spectrum is *Nymphomaniac*, with its scenes of sado-masochism, physical violence and crime, eventuating in murder, and *Shame*, a film which, while stopping short of the biological destruction of its main characters, concludes with the attempted suicide of the hero's sister and the abjection of the hero himself, who ends up in a state of extreme degradation, grief and despair. Thus, whereas the comic films are given an upwards narrative arc, the arc in the latter two films moves relentlessly in a downwards direction, making use of close-up shots rather than distancing techniques, so that the spectator is compelled to confront the full horror of what is taking place with a high degree of immersive intensity that deprives him or her of any reassurance to be gained through the interpolation of light relief.

In between these two extreme poles, the other three films occupy a middle ground that is best described as that of 'comedy-drama' – although the relative proportions in each individual film differ, along with the effects of the combination. In *Choke*, even though Clark Gregg, like Zahedi and Gordon-Levitt, uses an ironic, facetious voice-over as a device to establish some degree of comic detachment, in between the scenes in which this comic perspective is uppermost, he interposes flashbacks that recreate episodes in the traumatic childhood of Victor (Sam Rockwell), the film's protagonist, exploiting a mode of high seriousness in order to show that there are disturbing psychological reasons for Victor's sexual addiction that have their roots in his past. Furthermore, Gregg depicts, in present time, the distressing dementia of Victor's mother, Ida (Angelica Huston), who is now effectually incarcerated in a hospital for the mentally ill.

Similarly, in *Thanks for Sharing*, Stuart Blumberg, while he includes a character, Neil (Josh Gad), a backsliding trickster who functions like a comic clown, he also incorporates other plot lines – especially that involving Mike (Tim Robbins), an older addict – that exemplify how destructive the effects of addiction can be on other members of the family, even in the case of those who believe that they have recovered.

Yet another variation in the relative deployment of comic, as against dramatic, elements can be seen in *Welcome to New York*, which, as Peter Labuza observes, is sometimes as 'absurdly funny' as it is 'horrifying' (2014). *Welcome to New York* differs from the other mixed-genre films, however, in that the audience laughs *at* Devereaux (Gérard Depardieu), the arrogant, self-entitling protagonist (based on the real-life Dominique Kahn-Strauss), rather than *with* him, as is the case with Victor and Neil. Abel Ferrara, the director, ensures that the spectator maintains a satiric distance from the fiction by commencing the film with a non-diegetic prologue consisting of an interview with Gérard Depardieu in which the actor describes his own personal inability to feel close to the character he is about to assume. Then, when the film successively undergoes a series of generic transformations, as it moves from being a softcore fiction at the beginning (in scenes showing Devereaux's sex parties and exploitation of prostitutes) into a crime procedural (once Devereaux is arrested on a charge of rape) and finally into a chamber drama (once his wife Simone [Jacqueline Bisset] enters the scene) (see Furtado 2014), the humour disappears completely. In Ferrara's grim film, the broaching of the fourth wall, the two occasions when Devereaux addresses the camera directly, serves not to humanise him in the eyes of the spectator, but to induce revulsion: as when this brute, defiant in his lack of remorse, directly says to the audience, 'Fuck you all!' – thus intensifying the spectator's sense of alienation.

Undoubtedly, one reason for the adoption of a comic mode in the majority of American sex addiction films is a concern to create a movie with potential crossover appeal – on the model of films like *Juno* (Jason Reitman, 2007) and *My Big Fat Greek Wedding* (Joel Zwick, 2002) that ended up being very successful at the box office. In general, serious films on this topic have not done well, in contrast to those which have tapped into popular comedic genres. Von Trier's *Nymphomaniac* garnered a mere $785,896 in the USA for Volume I, and even less ($327,167) for Volume II, whereas Gordon-Levitt's *Don Jon* achieved $24,477,704 – partly because it poured its representation of sex addiction elements into a conventional rom-com mold, enhanced by the pulling power of Scarlett Johansson in the lead female role, and partly because the director changed the film's title, which had originally been *Don Jon's Addiction* when screened at the Sundance Festival, simply to *Don Jon*, which had the effect of appearing to align it with the popular 'slacker-striver' genre represented by such hits as *Knocked Up* (Judd Apatow, 2007), which accrued a domestic box office take of $148,768,917.[1]

There is a further reason for the choice of comedy, however, which is summed up in comments made by Clark Gregg, the director of *Choke*. It was precisely the comic treatment that drew him to Chuck Palahniuk's novel, upon which the film is based, in the first place:

If you kind of describe what goes on for the people [in the film], it makes you want to put a bullet in your head, yet when you read it, it's screamingly funny, and there's a reason why it's funny – that there's something very cathartic about going in to those places and finding the humour in it, that you're able to look at these things in a way that doesn't make you give up hope, but which allows you to absorb something in a way that perhaps is digestible and meaningful.[2]

For Gregg, therefore, the choice of a comic mode was essential to the achievement of the kind of response to the movie that he hoped to elicit, which was one of compassionate understanding of a sort that could facilitate the functioning of the film as a regenerative instrument.

With films at the more serious end of the continuum, a functional relationship is equally apparent between genre, tone and mood on one hand, and the evaluative perspective the spectator is invited to share with the filmmaker, on the other. We can clearly see this in the case of *Welcome to New York*. Instead of inviting the spectator to experience catharsis through empathic identification with the protagonist, the satiric mode of the film ensures that the spectator will remain aligned with the critical perspective of the filmmaker. Ferrara has been candid about the nature of his own personal relationship to the film. Making films, he says, 'is my personal therapy' (in Shoard 2014). His concern in *Welcome to New York* is to address the protagonist's 'addictive nature': 'The self-destruction, the destruction he does to his family, the destruction he does to his life, where it gets him', and the fact that 'he doesn't see it' because 'he's not confronting himself'. Devereaux's problem is one that Ferrara himself has shared: 'Have I been where this guy's been? Yes.' The difference, though, is that whereas Devereaux, his fictive alter ego, asserts that 'no one wants to be saved', Ferrara, for his part, says: 'Well, let him speak for himself, because I do! I got news for you. I want to be saved and I'm trying to be saved' (in Kasman 2014). On the basis of these comments, one can infer the function of the comic-satiric-dramatic mode Ferrara has chosen: it is designed to enable the projection of a shadow-self that the filmmaker would like to feel he has repudiated, and would like the spectator, sharing his recoil, to abhor. The film has thus been designed to function as an instrument for protective self-reinforcement and self-assertion to bolster a rejection of the mindset within which the protagonist, Devereaux, is shown to be stuck – in contradistinction to the filmmaker who has created him.

Manifestations of Dysfunction

Even though the sex addiction films display a range of tones and generic choices, they all share one constant theme: that sexual addiction is involuntary, involves compulsive repetition, withdrawal and cravings, and is harmful to the individual who suffers from it. Between them, these films expose the dynamics of sex addiction with almost clinical precision. The compulsive nature of the disease is vividly exemplified in the behaviours of all of the addicted fictive protagonists. Several of them are shown compulsively masturbating, often in inappropriate places: Brandon in the toilets at work; Neil in *Thanks for Sharing* on a subway train (in the form of frottage)

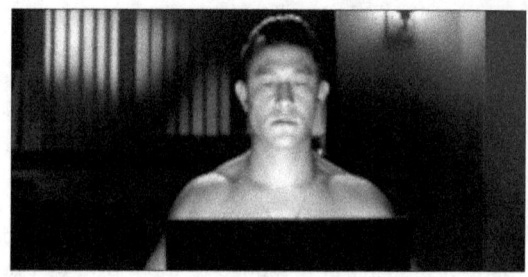

Fig. 2: Jon (Joseph Gordon-Levitt) masturbates to Internet porn in *Don Jon* (2013)

and, most extremely, Jon (Joseph Gordon-Levitt), who, even after having sex with a real girl, is shown on two occasions getting out of bed in order to masturbate to porn on his computer. Manifesting a different impulse, Caveh (Caveh Zahedi) is depicted as having an obsession with prostitutes – an obsession that leads to the failure of two earlier marriages.

All of these addicts are portrayed as engaging in excessive risk-taking: Neil films up his boss's skirt, which causes him to lose his job; Caveh masturbates in a confessional; Victor has sex in the toilet of an airplane; Devereaux, believing in the impunity that his wealth and political power gives him, recklessly forces himself on a hotel maid and a young female journalist, in spite of their protests; and Brandon (Michael Fassbender) in *Shame* audaciously and insolently caresses the vagina of a woman while her boyfriend is sitting next to them in a bar, which leads to him being savagely beaten.

To make matters worse, these films depict a pattern of intensifying escalation in the compulsion that drives its victims. Caveh finds that the more he indulges his fixation on having sex with prostitutes, the more powerful his urge to do it becomes. Brandon, discovering that his sexual activities involve a law of diminishing returns, escalates them from masturbation, to one night stands, to the use of prostitutes, to sex in public view, to engaging in a threesome, to indulging in gay sex in a club – all in a search for visceral pleasure that he hopes will be sufficiently powerful to supply the numbing of mind and emotions that he is seeking. Generally, these protagonists resort to sex as a response to their problems: Brandon's most extreme encounters occur after he has problems at work, and when he discovers his sister, Sissy (Carey Mulligan), with her wrists slashed; Adam (Mark Ruffalo) in *Thanks for Sharing* falls off the wagon when he breaks up with Phoebe (Gwyneth Paltrow), after five years of sobriety; Victor takes refuge in Internet porn when Paige (Kelley Macdonald) breaks up with him, and hires himself out as a gigolo, determined to 'reclaim [his] booth at the café of diminished expectations', by doing 'what Jesus would *not* do'.

Almost all these heroes suffer from an intimacy disorder when they meet a woman whom they like at a personal level. In *Choke*, when Victor finally has a chance to make love to the girl to whom he is attracted – Paige Marshall, whom he thinks is a doctor, but who is really a patient in the mental hospital that cares for his demented mother – he is unable to maintain an erection, confessing, 'I think maybe I can't fuck you because I want to like you'. Later in the movie he explains: 'I have sex with strangers because I'm incapable of doing it with someone I actually like … I kept myself numb for so long that now I want to feel something, I can't.' Similarly,

Adam, in *Thanks for Sharing*, is reluctant to have sex with Phoebe in an inverse ratio to the deepening of their emotional relationship. When, after having tried to instigate love-making, only to have her advances rejected, Phoebe complains that she feels he is 'pulling away', Adam explains that sex, for him, was a 'secretive chase' for such a long time that now it is hard for him 'to connect with something that's a lot more intimate and real'. Brandon, too, suffers erectile dysfunction when he tries to make love to a woman for whom he has genuine feelings. For these men, addictive sex has become a substitute for intimacy, being used as a drug or antidepressant to avoid feelings of loss and grief that derive from other, deeper causes.

This similarity between sex and other forms of drugs is underlined in several of these films by the fact that certain characters have suffered from them in combination. Chief among these is Mike in *Thanks for Sharing*, an older mentor in the twelve-step programme for sex addicts, who has been sober from alcohol addiction for fifteen years. Caveh, too, comes to realise that his sexaholism is merely a mirror image of the alcoholism from which Devin (Amanda Henderson), one of his girlfriends, suffers.

Generally, then, there is a remarkable concordance between the films in this sex addiction cycle: all of them show their protagonists facing the danger of a downwards spiral capable of leading them to self-destruction unless they can find some way of arresting and reversing it.

The Ascription of Causes for Addiction

While not all of the films in this sex addiction cycle ascribe causes to the dysfunctions they depict, several of them do – specifically, by establishing a link between a past marked by childhood trauma and the compulsive behaviours and suffering of the protagonists in the present.

In *I Am a Sex Addict*, Caveh acknowledges the lasting impact on him of his parents' dysfunctional relationship. When he was eight years old, he reveals, his mother discovered that her husband was unfaithful, and took the boy with her when she confronted the former at the scene of one his assignations. When they subsequently divorced, leaving Caveh feeling unloved, he came to the conclusion that sex had been responsible, and began to hate his father. Elaborating upon this episode in a subsequent interview, Zahedi confesses that 'I knew it was "bad" and I felt I had to do the opposite of that', particularly given that his parents were both Iranian, and observants of a very strict religion. Paradoxically, however, he discovered that despite his awareness of the 'sinfulness' of illicit sex, he found himself irresistibly drawn toward it: 'It turns me on, to think that I'm sinning: to transgress' (in Hundley 1996). In the movie, this thrill of transgression associated with illicit sex is represented in a number of episodes: for example, when Caveh reveals how he masturbated in a confessional because it appealed to his 'sense of transgression', or when he is 'turned on' during an encounter with a prostitute who says 'rape me!' – 'It was suddenly as if I had no choice'. Caveh's prostitute fetish and transgressive acting-out suggest that his addiction arises from an unconscious desire to reunite with his father – by replicating the illicit behaviour that he viewed as responsible for his abandonment in the first place. Caveh's sexual addiction is thus presented simultaneously as an attempt to numb the pain of loss, and also as an attempt to restore the lost relationship.

In *Choke*, it is the mother, rather than a father, who is identified as being at the root cause of the hero's problems. Victor's mother, having stolen him as baby from a stroller, is constantly on the run from the law, periodically in prison, and therefore unable to provide the growing boy with the security and stability he needs. Furthermore, she spousifies him to a degree that amounts to emotional incest, as we are shown in one flashback in which she forces young Victor (Jonah Bobo) to say: 'I'm yours forever and ever!' The effect on the adult Victor is twofold: on one hand, this maternal invasion leaves him fearful of any form of intimacy with a woman; on the other, it renders him completely dependent on her, leaving him unable to cope with the realisation that she is going to die. His response is to take refuge in depersonalised sex acts, as he explains in a voice-over at the beginning of the film, as he is about to have furtive sex in a public washroom:

> Sex addicts become literally dependent on the rush of constant sex. Orgasms release endorphins, endorphins kill pain. I'm all for that.
>
> I'm not thinking about that now, because at any moment I won't have a problem in the world – no bills, no stupid job, no crazy mother – all I'm going to feel is perfect, beautiful, nothing!

Victor's other way of dealing with the pain of narcissistic deprivation is to pretend to have choking spells in restaurants. Ostensibly, his motive is to gull rich patrons into 'saving' him, so that they feel sufficiently invested in his wellbeing to continue supplying him with gifts and money. A deeper, unconscious motive is revealed, however, in a flashback that shows the first occasion when, as a boy, he choked, for real. His mother, having told young Victor that he could not go to a park to play, given that they needed to hurry to make the State line, urges him to hurry up and eat his hot dog, whereupon he chokes. His mother's anxious concern, as she gathers him in her arms, gives him a feeling of security that is lacking at other moments in his life, and it is this childlike security that he is attempting to regain, as an adult, by choking to gain the attention of older diners: 'Before you know it, you're their child, you belong to them. You see this, this is my favorite part.' Significantly, Victor is only able to start on the road to recovery when Ida, in a fleeting moment of lucidity shortly before she dies, recognises that Victor's inability to reciprocate Paige's love derives from his excessive attachment to *her*, and tells him that he needs to 'break up' with her, his own mother, 'now'.

Other films focus on further causes of sexual addiction – the effect of media images and societal expectations on the way we see the world and ourselves, both of which impinge upon the formation of a healthy sense of identity and self-worth. The prime exemplar of this syndrome is Jon in *Don Jon*. As Gordon-Levitt explains:

> Both the Jon character and the Barbara character are people who are very intent on fitting into the conventional idea of what a masculine man is supposed to be and what a feminine woman is supposed to be. They are both very concerned with their looks and they put a lot of effort into their looks. They use their looks to get

what they want, and are disappointed with life because if you are so busy trying to fit yourself into a mold, you're going to miss what's actually beautiful about life, which is what makes people unique, not what makes everybody the same. (In Minow 2013)

Jon and Barbara (Scarlett Johansson) exemplify the painful truth of this observation. Jon chooses Barbara because she looks most like the stereotypical sexy beauties displayed through the media – but the reality of sex with her disappoints him because it does not live up to what he sees on his pornographic websites. Similarly, Barbara ridicules Jon for cleaning his own apartment, because it does not conform to her romantic image of what a lover should be like – 'it's not sexy'. Jon's response to his disappointment is to seek compensation in the intense pleasure he derives from masturbating to Internet porn: 'For the next few minutes, all the bullshit fades away, and the only thing in the world is those tits, that ass, the blowjob, the cowboy, the dog, the money shot ... I just fuckin' lose myself.'

Although in *Welcome to New York*, Devereaux's sexual activities take a far more sinister turn, the underlying pressures that motivate them are depicted as being generically similar in kind, even though they are situated in another class and social sphere. Seeking to evade responsibility for the 'little disease' – a euphemism for his sex addiction – that has got him into trouble, Devereaux locates the blame with his wife, for wanting to make him conform to her 'plans'. Those plans include her ambition to have him become President of France, with the assistance of her enormous wealth. The gap between her aspirations for him (and, by extension, her) and his ability to fulfill them eventuates in his telling her, with extreme bitterness, that she has succeeded in making him 'hate' himself. Nevertheless, Ferrara, while recognising the part such pressures might have played in damaging Devereaux's sense of self, does not allow them to exculpate him, owing to the fact that Devereaux remains obstinately perverse:

> I'm not defending the guy, I see his suffering and I feel for it, but you come and gotta make the attempt. He's got to feel, Devereaux's got to come back to the world. Otherwise, where is he? He's railing against God, he's railing against his mother, he's railing against his wife, he's railing against the world. It's all this fucking drunkin' shit, man, it's really bullshit. He's in pain, he's in agony, the guy ends in agony, and for what, for what? Pursuit of what? (In Kasman 2014)

In Ferrara's view, there is no absolution to be gained from remaining in denial or disavowal, even if the expectations of others are partially to blame.

The Prospects: Salvation, Damnation or Limbo?

As far as the prospects of recovery for these fictional sex addicts are concerned, the films once again range themselves along a continuum – one that is not unrelated to the choice of genre, tone and mood.

The most optimistic is *Don Jon*, in which a solution is clearly in sight. Jon, after reaching a low point when he tries to stop masturbating to porn, but finds he is unable to do so, is rescued by an older woman who functions like a guardian angel, Esther (Julianne Moore), whom he meets when he goes back to school. She instructs him that if he wants to lose himself – an effect he tries to get from porn – he needs to 'lose' himself in another person, 'and she has to lose herself in you'. Instead of being one-sided, she explains, it is a two-way thing. When Esther reveals that the reason she cries is because her husband and son died fourteen months earlier, Jon begins to connect with her at a personal, human level, so that when they make love, Jon experiences an intensity of feeling that is a revelation for him. The effect on him is transformative: he no longer puts junk in his hair, no longer kindles with road rage when he drives his car, and when he goes to the gym, instead of going to the weights room to build a shredded, muscular body, chooses instead to join in a game of basketball with other young men. Jon is thus able to break out of his old cycle, turning his back on porn – as a consequence of which he finds that 'all the bullshit does fade away', as his relationship with Esther develops, and they become 'lost together in each other'. In Gordon-Levitt's vision, therefore, relational sex is presented as the alternative to, and remedy for, the impersonal sex that constitutes sexual addiction.

I Am a Sex Addict, *Choke* and *Thanks for Sharing* are much more ambivalent. In all three cases, their respective heroes, after reaching a low point similar to that which Jon in *Don Jon* encounters, decide to attend a twelve-step programme for sex addicts. Caveh, after he has broken down and cried at one such meeting, is eventually able to stop having sex with prostitutes and gets married again. He relapses, however, and his second wife divorces him. When the film ends, he is in the process of marrying his third wife, Mandy, with whom he has been in a relationship for seven years. Will he relapse again? The film concludes without any prediction of the future outcome.

In *Choke*, Victor arrives at the same low point after his inability to reciprocate the love of Paige, and, like Jon and Caveh, joins a support group for recovering sex addicts. Although his condition ameliorates to a certain degree, Victor confesses at the end of the movie that he 'didn't leave the circuit entirely behind'. Indeed, the closing shot shows him engaged in sex with Paige in an aircraft's toilet, which suggests a desire to retain the best of both worlds by combining relational sex with a sense of transgression. On the other hand, any doubts we may have about Victor are offset by the presence of Denny (Brad William Henke), who, much earlier than his friend, has been able to form a genuine relationship with a former stripper

Fig. 3: Mike (Tim Robbins) and Adam (Mark Ruffalo) attend a twelve-step programme in *Thanks for Sharing* (2012).

named Cherry Daiquiri (Gillian Jacobs) – whose real name, he discovers, is actually Beth. The presence of this couple suggests the possibility of achieving a recovery that is much more lasting and substantial.

Like the characters in *I Am a Sex Addict* and *Choke*, those in *Thanks for Sharing* enter a twelve-step programme. When the film commences, they are already attending meetings, which means that the story can focus on their efforts to maintain sobriety and develop a life for themselves that excludes compulsively addic-tive sex.

What the film shows, however, is the precariousness of that sobriety. The main character, Adam, does relapse, when the love relationship he is trying to develop appears to fail because of his fear of intimacy. Although Phoebe, his girlfriend, gives him a second chance, he has to begin the process of regaining sobriety all over again. Mike teeters on the verge of a relapse, but is saved by a telephone call informing him that his son Danny (Patrick Fugit), whom he has wronged, has been badly injured in a car accident. Neil is similarly threatened with a relapse when he finds his bike stolen, prompting him to re-enter the forbidden subway – the site of his frottage – but saves himself at the last minute by running to the apartment of Adam, his sponsor. All of these characters are presented as needing support at a personal level, in addition to that provided by the twelve-step group. As the movie ends, a song is heard which encapsulates the message: 'Brothers in arms, in each others' arms', they go their separate ways, to continue the struggle.

The remaining three films are much more pessimistic. In *Shame*, Brandon and Sissy, who suffers from a love addiction that is a corollary to her brother's sex addiction, appear locked into a vicious spiral from which there appears to be no exit. Sissy slashes her wrists, and the film concludes with Brandon encountering on a subway train the same girl he tried to seduce at the beginning. This time, she is wearing an engagement ring, which shows that she has been able to move on, whereas Brandon is left trapped in his despair as the train enters (symbolically) a dark tunnel. No explanation is given as to why he is trapped in this addicted condition; the closest we get is Sissy's observation that 'We're not bad people. We just come from a bad place.'

Welcome to New York and *Nymphomaniac* are even more pessimistic. Devereaux in the former is so desensitised that he 'feels nothing', and is incapable of feeling guilt or remorse. He refuses to believe that people 'can be saved' – the poor will remain poor – and he, personally, unlike Brandon, does not *want* to be saved. He is completely stuck in his addiction, and accepts the fact he is so. In *Nymphomaniac*, the heroine, Joe (Charlotte Gainsbourg), attempts to find a solution by attending a sex addicts anonymous group – but only at the prompting of her boss, after being threatened with the loss of her job. After three weeks, however, she drops out of the group, and ends up being savagely beaten, nearly losing her life, and committing murder as an act of rage born of despair.

As a group, then, these sex addiction films present a range of possibilities, but whereas their presentation of the problem is remarkably congruent, there is no such congruence concerning their sense of a solution, or even whether any solution is even possible.

Conclusion

It is too soon to say whether the concern that prompted this wave of sex addiction films has already exhausted itself, being a momentary blip on the sonar radar, or whether the impulse to make such film will expand and resonate to a greater extent. Even though sex addiction has frequently been explored in gay literature – as, for example, in John Rechy's *Numbers* (1967) – there has, as yet, been no comparable cinematic exploration of the issue as a problem in queer culture – although the appearance of films like *I Want Your Love* (Travis Mathews, 2012), which portrays a desire for intimacy as well as impersonal visceral sex, may be the precursor for such a movement.

There are signs, too, that even though the films I have discussed are not part of general 'pornographication' of culture identified by McNair, the film industry may be about to jump on the bandwagon in order to mine the sex addiction theme precisely for its titillating, and hence box-office potential. The latest sex addiction film to be announced is *Addicted* (Bille Woodruff, 2014), made by CodeBlack Entertainment, an American entertainment conglomerate founded and run by the African-American entrepreneur Jeff Clanagan to facilitate positive presentations of African-Americans in film – a company that has a strategic business alliance with 20th Century Fox. Based on a novel by Zane, the author of erotic fiction novels, *Addicted* has all the hallmarks of a 'sexploitation movie': it is cast in the form of an erotic thriller, with the addiction theme providing a pretext for soft-core scenes of sexual titillation enacted by highly eroticised actors, while the 'thriller' element licenses the inclusion of gratuitous violence and sensational plot surprises.

Does the appropriation of sex addiction cinema for purposes of erotic arousal and sensation, rather than for the exploration of issues of serious concern, mark the end of the epochal impulse that produced the cycle of films discussed in this essay? In other words, is the genre about to become absorbed into mainstream filmmaking without having been developed into the realisation of a greater potential? Or is it the case, to the contrary, that the topic is about to be taken up by other groups, in other domains? Only time will tell.

Notes

1. Figures cited are taken from Box Office Mojo.
2. 'A Conversation with Clark Gregg and Chuck Palahniuk', *Choke* (Twentieth Century Fox, 2009), DVD extra.

Bibliography

Allyn, D. (2001) *Make Love Not War: The Sexual Revolution, an Unfettered History*. New York: Routledge.

Attwood, F. (2006) 'Sexed-up: Theorising the Sexualisation of Culture', *Sexualities*, 9, 1, 77–94.

Carnes, P. (1983) *Out of the Shadows: Understanding Sexual Addiction*. Minneapolis, MN: CompCare Publications.

Furtado, F. (2014) *Letterboxd*, 21 July; http://criticsroundup.com/film/welcome-to-new-york/ (accessed 11 August 2014).

Hundley, J. (1996) 'Caveh Zahedi: Life as a Film – A Conversation with Caveh Zahedi', *Mommy And I Are One*, Summer; http://www.cavehzahedi.com/#!i-am-a-sex addict/c1zcq (accessed 11 August 2014).

Kasman, D. (2014) 'The Pursuit of Freedom: Abel Ferrara Discusses "Welcome to New York"', *Notebook*, 7 June; https://mubi.com/notebook/posts/the-pursuit-of-freedom-abel-ferrara-discusses-welcome-to-new-york (accessed 11 August 2014).

Labuza, P. (2014) 'Welcome to New York, Cannes 2014 Review', *The Film Stage*, 18 May; http://thefilmstage.com/reviews/cannes-review-welcome-to-new-york/ (accessed 10 August 2014).

Marriott, E. (2003) 'Men and Porn', *The Guardian*, 8 November.

McNair, B. (2013) *Porno? Chic! How Pornography Changed the World and Made It a Better Place*. London and New York: Routledge.

Minow, N. (2013) 'Joseph Gordon-Levitt Discusses "Don Jon"', *Roger Ebert*, 26 September; http://www.rogerebert.com/interviews/joseph-gordon-levitt-discusses-don-jon (accessed 11 August 2014).

Newman, M. Z. (2011) *Indie: An American Film Culture*. New York: Columbia University Press.

Radner, H. (2010) *Neo-Feminist Cinema: Girly Films, Chick Flicks, and Consumer Culture*. New York: Routledge.

Rechy, J. (1967) *Numbers*. New York: Grove Press.

Sax, L. (2011) *Girls on the Edge: The Four Factors Driving the New Crisis for Girls – Sexual Identity, the Cyperbubble, Obsessions, Envy*. New York: Basic Books. Kindle edition.

Schaeffer, E. (ed.) (2014) *Sex Scene: Media and the Sexual Revolution*. Durham, NC: Duke University Press.

Shoard, C. (2014). 'Abel Ferrara at Cannes: "You gotta be careful what you say ... but I'm not"', *The Guardian*, 23 May; http://www.theguardian.com/film/2014/may/23/abel-ferrara-interview (accessed 11 August 2014).

Shone, T. (2014) '*Nymphomaniac, The Wolf of Wall Street* and Cinema's Bad Sex Renaissance', *The Guardian*, 19 March; http://www.theguardian.com/film/2014/mar/19/nymphomaniac-wolf-wall-street-cinemas-bad-sex-renaissance?CMP=fb_us (accessed 8 August 2014).

Weiss, R. (2013) *Cruise Control: Understanding Sex Addiction in Gay Men*, second edition. Carefree, AZ: Gentle Path Press. Kindle edition.

Williams, L. (2008) *Screening Sex*. Durham, NC: Duke University Press.

Zimbardo, P. and N. Duncan (2012) *The Demise of Guys: Why Boys Are Struggling and What We Can Do About It*. New York, NY: TED. Kindle edition.

Chapter 2
Carnotopia: The Culture of Sadism in *Nymphomaniac*, *Shame* and *Thanatomorphose*

MARK FEATHERSTONE

In this chapter I propose to explore three contemporary cinematic representations of sex and sexuality through the lens of the concept of utopia, where sexual pleasure is necessary, obligatory and always available, and dystopia, where absolute availability of sex pushes the sexual subject beyond the pleasure principle towards the horror of drive, and its manifestations in addiction, decay and finally death. Although I confine my main analytic points to the discussion of three films – Lars on Trier's *Nymphomaniac* (2013), Steve McQueen's *Shame* (2011) and Eric Falardeau's *Thanatomorphose* (2012) – I argue that taken together these cinematic texts capture three important moments in the evolution of what I want to call carnographic culture, following *Time*'s Jon Skow's use of the term 'carnography' to describe David Morrell's novel *First Blood* (1972). While Skow employed the term to refer to graphic depictions of violence, and the idea has since been taken up by writers looking to capture the obscenity of torture porn cinema (see Kattelman 2010), I want to use the concept of the *carnal*, and the related idea of carnality, to focus on the hyper-sexualisation of contemporary culture articulated in *Nymphomaniac*, *Shame* and *Thanatomorphose*, but also a range of other recent films, including Joseph Gordon-Levitt's *Don Jon* (2013).

Centrally, my use of the term 'carnal' in order to capture the cultural condition of hyper-sexualisation is not simply about reference to a sexy illustrative adjective, but rather relates to the conclusion of the utopian-dystopian psycho-sexual trajectory I want to trace through the three films under consideration. Here, the term carnal refers to the sexual, but most importantly the sexual torn out of human context, where sexual pleasure is mediated by desire, emotion and fantasy. While it is possible to understand carnal experience, and the separation of sex from the practice of human symbolisation found in desire, emotion and fantasy, in terms of a return to a base, or animalistic, form of sex, my use of the term in this chapter understands the carnal through the idea of a mode of dehumanisation that is less pre-human and more post-human; more rational, mechanised, technological and nihilistic than a properly human sexual experience, which I would argue must include both material and ideal interactions.

The purpose of my analysis of *Nymphomaniac*, *Shame* and *Thanatomorphose* is, therefore, two-fold. First, I seek to interpret and explain the films on their own terms. Second, I look to employ them to form a story of the progressive rationalisation of sexual experience, which I suggest has come to dominate contemporary Western culture and led to the creation of what I call a *carnotopia* – a hyper-sexualised space where sex is transformed into a base commodity, devoid of the symbolic dimension found in human desire, emotion and fantasy where we must imagine and relate to the other in ways that mediate corporeal intercourse. My reference to the psychoanalytic concept of hyper-sexualisation is important here because my use of the prefix *hyper* suggests a form of sexual experience that is simultaneously 'more than', and 'beyond', human sex, in respect that contemporary culture is saturated by sex and sexual imagery, but also 'less than', or 'a reduction', of the human sexual relation to base objective exchange.

In my analysis of Steve McQueen's *Shame* I suggest that it is possible to understand this reduction of the human sexual relation to soulless, base, commodity exchange in terms of the expansion and globalisation of neo-liberal culture where everything is an object to be bought and sold and the vulnerability implicit in the sexual relation which opens self to other becomes more or less impossible to tolerate because of the necessity of taking every other person for a competitor or obstacle to self-realisation. Under these conditions, which *Shame* locates in the centre of neo-liberal power, 'New York, New York', sex becomes a horrific non-relation where the other is simply one more object. Akin to Mary Harron's *American Psycho* (2000), which also captures the frozen dialectic of sexual desire and revulsion, the horror of McQueen's *Shame* resides in its depiction of the main character, Brandon's (Michael Fassbender), simultaneous desperate desire for and allergic reaction to intimate relations with others. Unfortunately, his resolution of this bind, which is also the resolution of neo-liberal carnal culture – base sex with faceless others, so many objects – only serves to remind him, and the viewer, of the meaninglessness and nihilism of his project. The desperation of *Shame* resides in this recognition.

If *Shame* captures the transformation of sexual experience into the fatality of drive, and the vicious circle of addiction, where the endless search for others is always thwarted by an embodied, ideological commitment to ontological security, freedom and the independent self, my reading of Falardeau's *Thanatomorphose* shows how this repetitious cycle resolves itself in the Freudian death drive, or Thanatos, where the failure to reach the other in a proper human manner results in psychological and corporeal decay, destruction and death (see Freud 2001a). The reason I close my chapter with discussion of this film is because what Falardeau seeks to show in his story is how psychological and emotional collapse (which we see played out in McQueen's *Shame*) forms a dystopian counter-point to the utopian image of the happy, desiring, sexed subject that represents the dominant ideological text of contemporary neo-liberal culture (see Williams 1999; Atwood 2009). Against this utopian story, which we find in high-end, hard-core Californian porn where bodies are shiny machines designed for hard fucking and the viewer has no sense of the human ruination taking place off screen, Falardeau's gloomy dystopia projects the ruination, emotional despair and endless loneliness of its main character, Laura (Kayden Rose), into corporeal decay, destruction and death. By contrast to the pumped up, cybernetic bodies of the San Fernando Valley scene, where sex between human objects is big business and there seems to be no human damage, in Falardeau's story there is only human damage, and the utopia of open, promiscuous, sex reverses into a horror story of desperation, misery and pain manifest in the slow decay and eventual collapse of the body.[1] In this situation the utopia of open, promiscuous sex transforms into a dystopia of cold, emotionless, abusive fucking. It is this gloomy, post-human world which leads to the transformation of Laura into a monstrous walking cadaver – a female version of Kafka's Gregor Samsa from *The Metamorphisis* (1915) or David Cronenberg's Seth Brundle from his classic film, *The Fly* (1986) – confined to her small, empty apartment that symbolises her isolation, loneliness and deep damage.

Where *Thanatomorphose* – or transformation through decline, decay and despair – marks the final moment or the realisation of the contemporary sexual dystopia, what I am calling *carnotopia*, I begin my argument about the emergence of the hyper-sexual society through reference to Lars von Trier's two-part *Nymphomaniac*, which itself forms the final part of his 'Depression' trilogy (*Antichrist*, 2009; *Melancholia*, 2011; *Nymphomaniac*, 2013). Against the horror of *Thanatomorphose*, which depicts transformation and the transgressive body in terms of decay and destruction, what we see in *Nymphomaniac* is a vision of transformation through hyper-sexualisation that is, initially at least, symbolic of liberation and escape from Oedipal structures concerned with repression, monogamy, and so on. In this respect it is possible to read the early scenes of *Nymphomaniac*, where Joe discovers her sexual powers, as a dramatisation of Deleuze and Guattari's (1983) late-1960s figure of Anti-Oedipus who opposed the repressed, regimented body of the 1950s with the new liberated body without organs where desire runs free and is no longer constrained by Freudian repression. However, what *Nymphomaniac* achieves across its two parts is a critique of this liberatory strategy and the gradual transformation of desire into drive which eventually finds form in something akin to the desperate addiction of Brandon in *Shame*. Basically *Nymphomaniac* achieves this reversal – where the transformation of the nymph shifts from being concerned with the transgression of repressive social norms to revolving around a viscous cycle of abuse in search of feeling itself – through Joe's loss of orgasm. It is this traumatic loss, which first occurs when she tries to make love to Jerome (Shia LaBeouf), that sets Joe on an ever more desperate search for pleasure which ultimately she never finds, primarily because this resides in relatedness beyond base corporeality in the connection between minds and bodies.

My conclusion is, therefore, that the final moment of *Nymphomaniac*, where Joe shoots her 'friend' Seligman (Stellan Skarsgard), signals the shift towards the condition illustrated in *Shame* because this point symbolises the end of friendship, the rise of generalised enmity and the transformation of sex into a desperate, commodified, non-relation. We see this trajectory played out in *Shame* through Brandon's story, and in particular his desperate attempt to avoid relating to this sister, Sissy (Carey Mulligan), through endless empty sexual encounters, and conclude in *Thanatomorphose* where Laura literally falls apart because of the violence, coldness and emptiness of her sexual relationships. Thus my thesis is that this desperate *ménage à trois* (*Nymphomaniac*, *Shame* and *Thanatomorphose*) tells a psycho-sexual story that takes in the grand sweep of a women's sexual life history/narrative, moves through a tale of sex addiction in contemporary New York and concludes in a depiction of psycho-sexual-corporeal collapse in a gloomy apartment that could be located anywhere. Moreover, I want to suggest that this threesome also talks to the development of the contemporary utopia/dystopia of carnotopia *and* creates a space to enable a critical understanding of the hyper-sexualisation of Western culture. The spatial symbolism working through these films, which is also the spatial symbolism of carnotopia itself, is enough to demonstrate why we need this critical understanding of Western sexual culture today. While *Nymphomaniac* takes in the wide open spaces of a woman's sexual life, and *Shame* takes place against the backdrop of New York, *Thanatomorphose* leaves Laura to her lonely apartment, a gloomy prison cell. What is this if it is not a symbol of the desperation of the carnotopic condition – sexual life reduced to the meaninglessness of empty rooms, bare walls, a functional mattress, and cold, empty, fucking?

Coitus Interruptus: The Sexual Non-Relation

Lars von Trier's *Nymphomaniac* tells the story of Joe (Stacy Martin / Charlotte Gainsbourg), a self-confessed nymphomaniac, and her struggles with sex and sexuality. The story itself is essentially a Freudian one, which begins with Joe's refusal of repressive patriarchal codes around sexual behaviour, tracks her through her Anti-Oedipal adventures, and concludes in her exhaustion and realisation that her project is unsustainable. The narrative itself begins when Seligman, who is apparently entirely asexual, finds Joe beaten, lying in an alley. She refuses medical attention, so he takes her into his apartment, where she recounts her life story. The narrative of the film develops on the basis of the conversation between Seligman and Joe and is essentially dialogic in style. The discussion between the two main characters carries Joe's story and recalls the style of both Plato's Socratic dialogues, where truth is the product of dialogic interrogation, and Freudian psychoanalysis, where truth results from reflection in the mirror of the therapist. The identity of the two main characters is key and von Trier structures his story around their relationships to sex. While Seligman's name stems from the German word *selig*, meaning blessed, blissful and beatific, and suggests a state of satisfaction and equilibrium, Joe's name, presumably from Josephine, means *the Lord increasing* and creates the impression that her journey is concerned with religious conversion and an eventual rejection of the flesh. Upon the film's conclusion, this is exactly what happens – Joe rejects her attachment to sexuality, while Seligman experiences the fall from his blissful state into desire. However, before we reach the point where we discuss the conclusion of the film, it is crucial to consider the details of Joe's nymphomania.

Joe's story begins with an account of her family relationships. She is the daughter of a loving father and a cold, distant, mother (played by Christian Slater and Connie Nielsen, respectively). She calls her mother a 'cold bitch'. By her late teens we see that Joe's obsessive relationship to sex has begun to manifest itself. Although the relationship between her sexuality and parental relationships is not explained by the explicit narrative of the film, and her mother barely appears in the story itself, consideration of Freud's female Oedipus sheds some light on the origins of Joe's nympho complex. In his work on feminine sexuality, Freud (2001b) explains that the female Oedipus complex emerges out of the young girl's initial attraction to her mother, who provides love and security. Akin to the male Oedipus complex, where this initial attraction is based in polymorphous sexuality, the same is true in this instance. However, whereas in the case of the male child the mother threatens to suffocate the child and it takes Dad to cut the apron strings and individualise his boy, in the case of the female child Mom rejects her daughter and pushes her towards independence. Upon her rejection, and realisation that Mom does not possess phallic power, Juan-David Nasio (2011) explains that the young girl experiences the pain of privation – she is deprived. As a result of this she turns to Dad, who has what she wants – phallic power, security, and so on. Of course, Dad keeps his daughter at arm's length, and the successful conclusion of the complex results in the idealisation of both parents through a process of identification. The young girl desires Daddy in symbolic form – other boys and, later, men – and realises that the way to boys is to be like Mommy, with who she identifies, and becomes her ideal. What we see in *Nymphomaniac* is that Joe becomes a Daddy's girl, but she fails to identify with her Mom, who is cold and distant.[2] The result of this is that Joe desires the phallus, power and pleasure, but without the Freudian model of wife, mother and the disciplined woman to ground her behaviour. The result of this lack is that she turns away from the idea of love, and the patriarchal model of the family, and becomes a sexual revolutionary. Thus Joe becomes Deleuze and Guattari's 'ideal woman' – a woman defined by the free flow of desire.

Joe's first sexual relationship occurs with Jerome, who reappears throughout the film. Joe asks Jerome to take her virginity and he fucks her in-between working on his motorbike. The bike serves an important purpose in this initial sex scene because it provides a backdrop to the cold, mechanical sex between Joe and Jerome. Jerome pushes into Joe eight times and von Trier counts his thrusts on screen. The effect of keeping count is to simultaneously rationalise this vision of sex and set up Joe's coming adventures which are concerned with the consumption of men – what matters here is less the quality of her sex, which is often marked by her very clear apathy, and more the quantity of her sexual encounters with a range of partners in a variety of places. In the next key scene Joe boards a train with a friend in order to play a sex game. The aim of the childish 'train game' is to have sex with as many men as possible in order to win a bag of sweets. Again, the numerical dimension of Joe's relationship to sex is foregrounded and the girls keep score on screen. Following Joe's initial experience in front of Joe's bike, the situation of the game is important. In his *The Logic of Sense* (2004), Deleuze explains that the train is the classic symbol of the death drive because of its cold, relentless, mechanisation. Akin to Freud's Thanatos, which is endlessly repetitious upon pain of death, the train simply works. It recalls Joe's approach to sex in the sense that its progress is mindless and defined by motion without end. Later Joe forms a revolutionary group – the Little Flock – which opposes sex to love in order to undermine bourgeois morality. The group's motto is 'Mea Vulva, Mea Maxima Vulva' and they eject members who fuck the same man twice or show any form of attachment. In this respect, sex becomes a political tool concerned with the rejection of Oedipal structures, and the embrace of female sexual emancipation. Again, we can see how Joe is a classic Anti-Oedipal figure – a sexual terrorist, Deleuze and Guattari's 'becoming-woman', who grows through the free pursuit of desire and resistance to patriarchal repression.

However, the downside of Joe's voracious consumption of men is that keeping track of her various non-relations becomes work in itself. She explains that she could no longer easily decide who to fuck and so organised her relationships on the basis of the throw of a dice. Thus the meaninglessness of chance and fate takes precedent over the meaningful dimension of sex and relationships and this is thrown into sharp relief when Joe is confronted by the wife of one of her conquests, Mrs H. (Uma Thurman). Although Joe's conquest, Mr H. (Hugo Speer), imagines he will become a significant other in her life, it is clear that Joe feels nothing, and that he is simply one of many. The main casualty of this situation is Mrs H. and her family. This is an important scene in the first part of the film because it leads to Joe's confession of her desperate loneliness – she explains that 'she has always felt that her body is filled with tears' – that opens out onto her loss of her father. Von Trier titles this chapter 'The House of Usher' and events follow Edgar Allen Poe's (1839) tale of sickness and psychological collapse. Where Roderick Usher buries Madeline and then cracks up, Joe watches her father's slow death and tries to escape herself in mindless, soulless, sex. However, collapse is very close and occurs in her description of her sexual polyphony. Here, she explains her relation to three different men – F., who pleases her, G., who pleases himself, and Jerome, who reappears on the scene, and forms the dialectical synthesis of F. and G. Of course, this should result in the emergence of a proper relationship, which involves two people who interact through minds and bodies, but it is precisely now that Joe's nymphomania takes a dark turn. In the middle of what appears to be passionate sex, Joe calls out, 'I can't feel anything', and we later learn that she has lost her orgasm.

The second volume of *Nymphomaniac* starts with Joe's reflection on her lost orgasm. She compares this experience with a childhood memory of spontaneous orgasm which she describes in terms of religious ecstasy. This description leads her to take up her story through Seligman's religious frame. Whereas the first part of her story was the narrative of what he calls 'the eastern church' concerned with joy and love, the second part of her history reflects her experience of 'the western church' where sin and punishment run the show. She starts off by explaining that her loss of orgasm led to the domestic period of her life. She became pregnant, gave birth and lived in a family unit. However, she explains that she insisted upon a caesarean birth in order to save her sexual life and rejects her bourgeois family life in pursuit of her orgasm. This leads her to meet the black African 'dangerous men' who proceed to argue over her orifices, ultimately leaving her unsatisfied, before she turns to K. (Jamie Bell), a sadist for hire, in search of sexual fulfilment. In her desperate state Joe visits K., and leaves her young son Marcel alone in their apartment, which leads to a partial re-run of the balcony scene from *Antichrist*. While the child falls from the balcony in *Antichrist*, Jerome returns to catch his son in *Nymphomaniac*, and father and son end up leaving Joe. Unfortunately, Jerome is no heroic father, willing to live for his son, and we later learn that Marcel has been placed in foster care. Following the dominant theme of *Nymphomaniac*, where human relations are always cold, even the relationship between father and son fails to hold. Joe's own life is in terminal decline now. After several brutal sessions with K., her boss insists that she visits a therapist in order to overcome her addiction to sex. Joe's therapist explains that she needs to take away her motivation and opportunity for engaging in sexual activity leading her to transform her apartment into a Spartan cell. It turns out that almost every object in Joe's life had become sexualised and her entire existence was infused with libidinal energy. As Joe lays on her bed, fully clothed, buried in a winter coat, we realise that her desire cannot be contained, and her body transgresses the constraints of the Freudian law. Ironically, she experiences a spontaneous orgasm on the basis of her efforts to control her desire.

The final passage of the second volume of *Nymphomaniac* starts with Joe's refusal of the Freudian law of repression. She tells her therapy group that she is a nymphomaniac and that she will not abandon her desire which eventually leads her to a life of crime. She explains this situation to Seligman in terms of his desire for books, which she says he could never give up, before moving into the final chapter of her story concerned with her criminal life. The origin of Joe's criminal life resides in her realisation of her inability to conform and her transformation into Deleuze and Guattari's (1987) nomadic subject who lives outside of the structures of the law. In Joe's new line of work, extortion, the realisation or exposure of desire becomes central. Here, desire is no longer simply outside of the law, but becomes criminal currency itself, and Joe's expertise in this field means that she is perfectly suited to the revelation of her subjects' every want.[3] This is illustrated by her interrogation of a man she eventually reveals to be a paedophile, who she proceeds to fellate in the name of the horror of unrealised desire. Essentially, this is the position Joe herself now occupies because her broken body is no longer fit for sex. Enter her successor, P. (Mia Goth), who she trains to take over her extortion business. After following Joe's lead, P. is thrust centre stage when the focus on their sting turns out to be Jerome, who proceeds to have a relationship with the new recruit. At this point Joe realises her outcast position, which she now no longer controls. Throughout the story Joe had maintained control of her non-relations and it is only when she sees P. and Jerome together that she realises she has been side-lined by others. Seeking escape, she climbs a mountain and discovers her 'soul tree' – a broken, twisted, barren oak. In the first part of the film she explained that her father spoke of his 'soul tree' – a proud oak – which symbolised his identity, but that she had never found her own special tree. Throughout the story nameless others stood in for Joe's tree, her self, and she based her identity upon their consumption. She *was* her orgasm, which was an embodied symbol of her self-affirmation, her very existence. But she finds herself beyond others in this broken tree which is importantly rooted in the phallic, paternal, symbol of the mountain. In recognition of her identity, Joe renounces her prison of desire, but not before she seeks revenge on Jerome.

Fig. 1: Joe (Charlotte Gainsbourg) discovers her soul tree in *Nymphomaniac* (2013).

Although she had renounced violence in the name of sex earlier in the story, freed from sex she takes up violence and attempts to kill her former lover. She fails and Jerome beats her. P. urinates on her before Jerome fucks his younger model in a repetition of his first contact with Joe – eight thrusts symbolise the start of P.'s story of cold, meaningless, sex.

Joe concludes her story and tells Seligman that she realises that she must escape her desire. She explains that she wants to conquer her sexuality and free herself from the curse of her nymphomania. At this point Seligman, who she calls her only friend, leaves her to sleep. He returns seconds later in order to fuck her – he explains that she 'must have fucked thousands of men' – before Joe reaches for her gun. The film cuts to black, we hear a gun shot, what we assume to be a body fall to the floor, and finally footsteps leaving the apartment. We assume that Joe has shot Seligman and fled the scene. *Nymphomaniac* ends in this strange, ambiguous, way. We must conclude that Joe shoots Seligman in self-defence. Throughout the film she had chosen to fuck, whereas at the end *he* decides she is easy meat, and believes she is open to be taken. Whereas she was in control of her sexuality, Seligman transforms her into an object to be fucked. In an early scene he tells her that nymphomania is concerned with transformation, and cites the growth of insects that form cocoons to make his point, but here he makes her his object. She responds and resists his objectivity on the basis of her realisation of her identity in her soul tree. However, Joe's self-defence is not simply concerned with empowerment, because her use of the gun essentially symbolises her identification with the Freudian law and transformation into a 'chick with a dick'. Regardless of this reading, however, we must also recognise that the violent final scene of *Nymphomaniac* results in the end of Joe's only real relationship and the collapse of the dialogue between friends, which we had imagined was based on a Socratic, Platonic meeting of minds around the issue of sexual life. The deeply depressing conclusion of *Nymphomaniac* is, therefore, that anonymous sex, which is about intercourse in the context of a non-relation, always fails, leading to endless repetition. But even worse, perhaps, it also suggests that the pure, Socratic, Platonic relationship defined by the meeting of minds is fatally flawed and always likely to explode in sexual violence, primarily because human beings cannot escape their desire in the way that Seligman imagines. Thus, the utopian solution to this situation, which *Nymphomaniac* suggests *negatively*, is a sexual relationship based in a holistic interaction between minds and bodies. This solution is, however, a pure fiction, a spectre that the film generates out of despair, because nowhere in the narrative is this interaction of minds and bodies present. Instead what we find is a story of empty relationships, defined by either a lack of care or, in the case of Joe and Seligman, the looming threat of sexual violence. This is the human condition in *Nymphomaniac*, a desperate state of existential loneliness, which is also played out in 'New York, New York' in *Shame*.

Shame projects the desperate conclusion of *Nymphomaniac* onto contemporary New York and explores the horror of the empty relationship, or relationship established within the context of a commitment to individualism and separation from others. While *Nymphomaniac*'s Joe began her sexual adventure from the position of Deleuze and Guattari's becoming-women, a sexual terrorist, who refused patriarchal law, only to end the story lonely and broken, *Shame*'s main character, Brandon, symbolises what happens in the wake of sexual liberation – he is a successful but deeply lonely man who struggles to survive the neo-liberal city (New York), where everybody is an individual and all relationships are entirely contingent on and based around work schedules. In order to manage this situation, and relate to others in a context where deep relationships are barred by the nature of the neo-liberal city, Brandon falls into sex addiction. Unlike *Nymphomaniac*, where we witness the evolution of Joe's condition, in *Shame* Brandon appears fully (de)formed, and we have no sense of his back story. Instead, we plunge into his routines and rituals. We watch him move around his apartment in silence, see him masturbate in the shower, follow his commute to work, making eye contact across the train with unknown women, and visit bars with his friend, who is also his boss, looking to pick up women. While his boss is loud and brash, Brandon is largely silent, and makes little overt attempt to engage the women they meet. He seems entirely dis-interested. This silence, and social withdrawal, is indicative of his behaviour throughout the film, and symbolises his sense of alienation from others. It turns out that he cannot communicate. However, this lack of social relation does not impact Brandon's ability to find meaningless sex, which finds *him* in the early bar scene, where he ends up fucking one of the women from the bar in a dark alley. In many respects this scene is key and sets the tone for the rest of the film. It shows the unknown woman (played by Elizabeth Masucci) give Brandon's far more enthusiastic boss the brush off and leave the bar, only to pick up Brandon later on the street. There is no social interaction between the woman and Brandon in the bar, and we never see their interaction in the car, but only witness the conclusion of their short relationship. What we see here, then, is a reflection of Brandon's life, where the prelude to sex, the establishment of a social relationship, never takes place, which essentially means that his sexual encounters are largely empty and vacuous. There is nothing beyond the fuck itself. In this early scene, however, there is little sense of Brandon's desperate situation, and it is easy to understand his lifestyle through the lens of the male fantasy of a sexual utopia, where women are free and easy and sex always comes with no strings.

In this respect it is possible to imagine that Brandon is the outcome of Joe's sexual revolution. He is the male partner who enjoys the sexually liberated woman.

Fig. 2: Sissy (Carey Mulligan) sings Sinatra in *Shame* (2011).

The unknown woman picks *him* up on the street in a parody on the curb crawler who looks for street walkers and then lets him fuck her in an alley. This idea of the sexually liberated woman is, of course, a naïve male fantasy, where she wants and takes sex, and requires absolutely no commitment, and in this early phase of the film McQueen leads the viewer towards this conclusion. It is easy to think that Brandon is living in utopia. However, while *Nymphomaniac* explores the collapse of Joe's revolution, what we see in *Shame* is the horror of Brandon's sexual utopia, where the male fantasy of the urgent, no-strings-attached fuck becomes a desperate, meaningless void, a collision of bodies whose only purpose is escape from the emptiness and loneliness inside. In this respect, it is possible to read *Shame* as a kind of ghoulish response to the early 1990s sexual utopia of New York singles, *Sex and the City* (1998–2004). McQueen refuses the fantastical vision of *Sex and the City* and drops his viewer into a sexual black hole. Following his construction of the male utopia of the easy lay, McQueen establishes the horror of Brandon's emotional state through the introduction of his sister, Sissy, who appears at his door. Brandon is reluctant to allow Sissy to stay at his place, but grudgingly agrees, so long as she does not disrupt his life. This is, of course, precisely, what happens, and Brandon's life quickly unravels. The horror begins when he visits a high-end bar with his boss and watches Sissy transform Sinatra's 'New York, New York' into a hymn to loneliness, loss and despair. The effect of this scene – which reveals the desperate splendour of the primal scene of neo-liberal capitalism, New York City – is devastating and Brandon realises his emptiness. It turns out that Sissy is desperately alone too and needs her brother, or someone.

Of course, caught up in the same horror show, Sissy ends up fucking Brandon's boss back at Brandon's place, and he can't cope, mainly because his life, his routine, his defensible space, set up to shield him from his own emptiness, is shattered by her appearance and her sex. Ironically, Brandon, the sex addict, cannot cope with the introduction of sex into his home as it fractures his carefully constructed fortress of solitude and reminds him of the barren wastes of his life. At this point it becomes clear that Brandon's sexual life, his relationship to empty sex, is not about sexual relations but rather the endless repetition of orgasm, which can numb him from his loneliness. His orgasm is safe, and secure, and saves him from others who are intolerable because of their emotional depth. He wants, and needs, the little death in order to stay alive. This is precisely why media, and especially the Internet, plays such an important role in Brandon's life; it allows him to consume so many images of others without ever having to relate to anybody. The problem is, however, that this coping mechanism, which Brandon uses to live with himself, collapses under the pressure of Sissy's proximity. She opens his laptop to find his always-on connection to a webcam sex show. Around the same time Brandon's boss tells him that his work machine, which had been taken away to be serviced, was full of hard-core porn. There are no obvious consequences and neither Sissy nor his boss pursue Brandon's use of online sex sites, but Brandon comes to see the horror of his own neo-liberal sex life in the reflection of its exposure. In his realisation he confronts the misery of the carnotopia, where everybody is available and everything is permissible, on the basis that the cold, glacial, self remains pure, pristine and untouched by the emotional lives of others who cry, feel pain and need care.

There is no way to confuse *Shame*'s Brandon with *Nymphomaniac*'s Joe, especially in her early exploration of the 'eastern church', as there is no sense or pretence of development about Brandon. Whereas Joe thought she was on some kind of journey, Brandon is a sex addict who relies on repetition and orgasm in order to hide away from both himself and others. Sex is, therefore, a survival strategy. But Brandon is not a complete lost cause and he attempts to save himself from his existence by establishing a relationship with his co-worker, Marianne (Nicole Beharie). He throws out his pornography and attempts to make love to her, only to find that he cannot perform, precisely because he knows her, and there is no relationship between sex and social interaction in Brandon's world. At this point Brandon embodies Lacan's famous line from his seminar on sexuality, 'there's no such thing as a sexual relationship' (2000: 12), but he cannot escape this lonely situation because it is a reflection of the neo-liberal context in which he lives, where everybody is an object to everybody else. In his deep despair, he calls a prostitute and fucks her in the apartment where he had attempted to have sex with Marianne, but this meaningless lay is no help. On return to his apartment Brandon argues with Sissy – he says 'you're trapping me' – and he cannot stand her proximity because it reveals his own emptiness. He leaves her on her own, and, face to face with his loneliness, seeks to lose himself in a bar fight, gay sex and a threesome with two prostitutes. Against the backdrop of this orgy of meaningless sex, Sissy makes a desperate attempt to reach her brother, but he is caught up trying to lose himself in his own orgasm.

In the climactic scene of the film, Brandon realises that he cannot escape himself in sex – his orgasm plunges him further into the reality of despair – and he rushes to find Sissy following what turns out to be her suicide attempt. After his attempt to escape reality through his orgasm, and Sissy's comparable attempt to escape herself by taking her own life, Brandon holds his sister and appears to overcome his phobia of intimacy. As she lies in a hospital bed, he crumples to the floor, cries in anguish and expresses the pain of his loneliness. However, McQueen realises the force of the Freudian compulsion to repeat and throws doubt upon Brandon's recovery in the final scene of the film. Brandon sits on a train, Deleuze's classic symbol of the death drive, catches the eye of an unknown woman (played by Lucy Walters), and notices her wedding ring. It is clear she wants to escape into the excitement of a new man, but Brandon must decide whether to escape himself into a new relationship based upon emotional distance, or resist and insist upon sex founded upon intimacy. Essentially, this is the horror of the human condition, which McQueen presents to his viewer. This horror of meaningless sex and frozen emotions revolves around the terror of vulnerability and the easy choice of the empty relationship in an urban context that encourages anonymity. Where *Nymphomaniac* starts off with the transformation of Joe, who grows like a nymph inside a cocoon, and concludes in her fall into objectivity and abjection, *Shame* picks up the story of carnotopia in the/an abyss of abjection, locates it in a hyper-urban context where objectification is normal and follows the unfolding horror through Brandon's desperate attempts to escape himself in meaningless sex.

Ironically, the representation of sex in McQueen's film is never really concerned with pleasure, and more, I would suggest, about psychological survival. Sex is, of course, in the first place focused on biological reproduction and species survival, but in McQueen's neo-liberal 'New York, New York' (so bad, they named it twice) there is no biological element to sexual relations because nobody has children. There is no family. Instead, sex is only ever about the desperate need to simulate connection in the context of the world where others are strangers. In this respect sex is psychological survival, the simulation of social support without the emotional risk, since it is impossible to live without others in a world where everybody is an object, a competitor and a potential threat to the fragile ontological security of the independent self, which is a kind of utopian principle in the desperate dystopia of the carnal society. Thus McQueen ultimately shows that the Sadean fantasy – where everybody is an object for the use of everybody else – is unliveable for humans and can only really ever work for the sadist who imagines they will always be the fucker and never the fucked. However, even in this instance, where the sadistic fucker is never fucked, the problem is that the sadist fucks himself through the other and ensures that he can never escape the black hole of loneliness, despair and hurt that characterises his condition. As Wilhelm Stekel showed in the late 1920s, the violence of the sadist is always premised on some basic, and profound, trauma. The key theme of *Shame*, therefore, revolves around an exploration of how humans live, endure and ultimately survive, and Sadean sexual utopia, what I call carnotopia, where people are so many objects. How can humans survive the Sadean Thanatos and a world where there are no others who care? The final film of my carnotopic threesome suggests that there is no way to survive this situation and it is through a discussion of Eric Falardeau's sexual body-horror *Thanatomorphose* that I propose to conclude.

After Sex ... or Sade with Kafka

Whereas *Nymphomaniac* paints the psycho-history of a woman from her teens through to middle age, and *Shame* explores the psychological collapse of a man against the backdrop of a global city, *Thanatomorphose* compresses the historical sweep and spatial span of these two films into the narrow space of a gloomy apartment where time is meaningless outside of the horror of psycho-sexual-corporeal decay. Falardeau's film tells the story of a violent, abusive, sexual relationship and its catastrophic effects on a young woman, Laura, who cannot survive the Sadean society and literally rots away until she resembles a walking cadaver. While *Nymphomaniac* makes sex central to the narrative, and *Shame* shows how sex stands in for Brandon's barren emotional life, *Thanatomorphose* completes the cycle and suggests that there is very little that is sexual about the hyper-sexual, Sadean, society, which is really a rational fucking machine. Apart from the first nightmarish moments of the film where sex is shown in garish colours and obscene close-up, depictions of intercourse in *Thanatomorphose* are short, hopeless and violent. Here, sex fails, and simply throws the loneliness of existence into relief, making it truly unliveable. Indeed, Falardeau's exploration of the thanatological world is deeply depressing in its reversal of *Nymphomaniac*'s early story of sexual revolution. In the first volume of von Trier's film sex was about evolution, and Joe believed that she could grow through sexual adventure, only to later find that she had herself become an object of the Sadean master, Jerome. Following Joe's realisation of her broken identity, *Shame* shows how Brandon struggles to survive in a world where sex is a narcotic to numb the pain of loneliness. But there is no survival in *Thanatomorphose* – there is only the slow transformation through decay towards death. Falardeau's story starts by founding the primal scene of decay, and eventual death, in mechanical fucking, and, while Freud and others have made this equation between sex and death, *Thanatomorphose* pushes this connection towards its nightmarish limits. The opening, primal sex scene of the film is truly post-human, mechanical, alien, and sets the Kafka-esque tone for the story that follows.

In the wake of the sexual nightmare that opens *Thanatomorphose* the story follows Laura's movements about her cold, empty apartment. The space of the film is claustrophobic, spartan, silent, and loneliness haunts Falardeau's representation of Laura's life. We see Laura wake up, make breakfast, shower and apply her make up. She notices bruises on her arm, and soreness around her vagina, and we assume these injuries are the result of rough sex. However, her injuries spread and she loses a fingernail in the shower. The bruises on her body fail to heal and instead spread. Soon her arms and back are covered in deep purple bruises which symbolise the emotional and psychological wounds inflicted upon her by her non-relation with Antoine (David Tousignant), the man who presumably fucks her in the nightmarish first scene of the film. Following this scene Laura's next interaction with Antoine confirms the violence of their relationship. Laura throws a small party, which is broken up by her landlord who informs her that parties are prohibited by her tenancy agreement, and ends up fighting with Antoine. There is no 'kiss and make up' in the wake of their fight, but only more violent sex. But Laura shows no interest. She allows herself to be fucked while staring into space. Against this backdrop, Laura continues her slow decay. She wakes in the middle of the night and throws up over Antoine. He complains and leaves. In an early scene in the film Antoine steps on a nail in Laura's apartment, which leads her to bandage his foot, but he fails to care for her in return. Alone, her body blackens, bruises and rots. In a state of shock about her decay, she collapses and cracks her head. She wakes in a pool of blood and bandages her head. At this point Laura is less than human and resembles a walking cadaver. Her desperation is simultaneously corporeal, psychological and emotional.

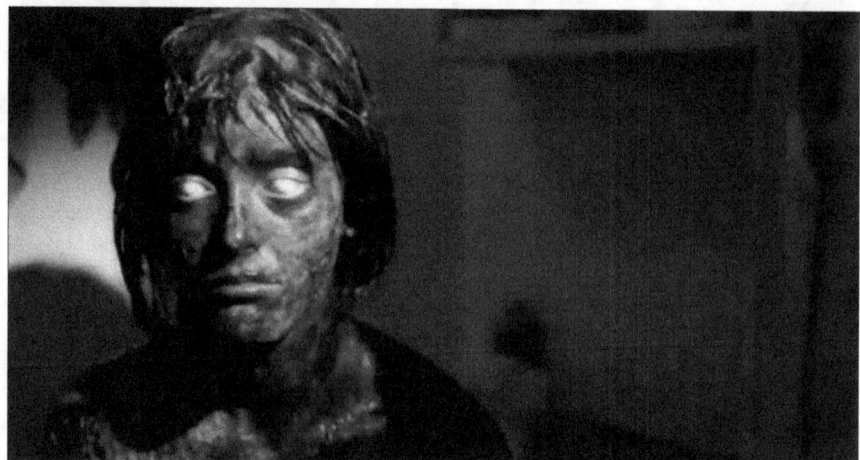

Fig. 3: Laura (Kayden Rose) rots in *Thanatamorphose* (2012).

When her friend Stephan (Roch-Denis Gagnon) visits she never mentions her decay, but performs oral sex on him in the corridor in a desperate attempt to find emotional support. But there is no support and Stephan leaves without a word. She sleeps and her dreams confirm her desperation – she imagines her own death and her corpse torn to pieces by ravenous men. Her life is now vomit, rot and decomposition and she survives in bandages. She festers in bed and her apartment reflects her abjection. Walls blacken with stains, cracks appear and a heavy gloom hangs over her place. Now her body starts to collapse, fingers falling off, and she collects her flesh in jars, labelled in a ghoulish record of her decay. At this point, Laura recalls Lacan's famous 'body in pieces' (2007a), which describes the self prior to imaginary identification, with the qualification that her corporeal fragmentation is representative of a psychotic collapse in the context of psycho-sexual maturity.

Apart from Lacan's torn body, Laura's state also references Cronenberg's Seth Brundle, or perhaps more clearly Kafka's Gregor Samsa, who became a monster under pressure of a cold, post-human, bureaucratic machine. In the early 1960s Lacan wrote his famous essay 'Kant with Sade' (2007b) in order to show how Kantian rationalism was in many respects identical to Sadean torture, and I would suggest a similar coupling of 'Sade and Kafka' would be useful to explain Laura's transformation through decomposition. In Lacan's story the idea is that Kant's philosophical reason is hyper-rational with the effect that it produces a space of post-human violence that sexualises precisely because sex is no longer in view. In turn Sade's philosophy of pleasure and torture is hyper-sexual with the result that it slides into a form of cold, hard, rationality which is very close to Kantian reason. While Sadean perversion worms its way into the Kantian machine by virtue of its exclusion, Kantian reason overtakes the Sadean philosophy of pleasure and sex falls by the wayside to be replaced by a kind of mechanisation of punishment that has no sense of humanity. In order to understand Laura's plight I think we need to recognise that her life in carnotopia is in effect organised around this Kantian-Sadean system where neo-liberal reason is simultaneously absolutely defined by the weighing of costs and benefits, and everything and everybody has a price, *and* a kind of cold, hard, mechanical, sexualisation characterised by power, where one is either fucker or fucked, and relationships are entirely devoid of affection, care and love. Once we reach this conclusion, which also applies to the second volume of *Nymphomaniac* and *Shame*, we can explain Laura's transformation by setting up a coupling between Sade and Kafka, which shows how the cold, hard, mechanical sex of the neo-liberal carnotopia results in the kind of decline, decay, decomposition and eventual collapse that we find in Kafka's *The Metamorphosis*.

While cold, post-human reason transforms Gregor Samsa into a monstrous beetle – which recalls *Nymphomaniac*'s story of insectoid development – the cold, sexual, rationality of neo-liberal life, where sex is about results (the individual's orgasm), leads Laura into a process of *thanatomorphosis* – decomposition towards death. In this respect what the coupling of Sade and Kafka reveals is that the Sadean fantasy, which is that cold, hard, mechanical sex is liveable for humans, is a patriarchal utopia premised on post-human reason, and that the dystopic truth of this fantasy is Kafka's story of monstrous metamorphosis, which we find reflected in *Thanatomorphose*. While de Sade (1787) leads his reader to believe that the fucker and the fucked never tire, and can literally keep fucking forever like the fantastical sexual superheroes of hard-core porn, Kafka's truth is that endless repetition, drive and addiction are never sustainable, and cast both fucker and fucked into a story of metamorphosis, which is also a story of dehumanisation, decline, decay, decomposition and death. In much the same way that Lacan thought that de Sade reflected the secret truth of Kant, I think that Kafka represents the hidden other side of de Sade, and that this is important in order to understand that the sexual utopia, the neo-liberal carnotopia, is entirely unsustainable and unliveable for humans. This is what I think *Thanatomorphose* explains, especially in the final scenes of the film, which results in Laura's murder of Antoine and Stephan and her own eventual collapse and death. Where *Nymphomaniac* structures its narrative around the sexual history of Joe, and *Shame* bases its story in the urban alienation of New York, the central plot device of *Thanatomorphose* is Laura's blackening, bruising and decay. There is nothing else.

In this respect, I would suggest that Laura's story reflects the psychological and emotional collapse of Joe and Brandon played out in corporeal terms and thus captures the holistic nature of the ideal sexual relationship, where minds and bodies meet in a purely negative form. Here, there is no ideal meeting of minds and bodies, but rather a representation of emotional despair and psychological breakdown reflected in a story of corporeal decay. My conclusion is, therefore, that this desperate threesome – *Nymphomaniac*, *Shame* and *Thanatomorphose* – can be taken together to tell the story of neo-liberal carnotopic culture. These films represent three codings of the body – the body as resistance, the body as object and the body as death – which, I would suggest structure the transformation of the neo-liberal sexual utopia into a dystopia of desperate, hopeless need. While I have sought to suggest that this trajectory may be a historical phenomenon, which we see played out across *Nymphomaniac*'s historical sweep, *Shame*'s contemporary situation and *Thanatomorphose*'s apocalyptic focus on endings, there is also a sense in which the translation from *Nymphomaniac* through *Shame* to *Thanatomorphose* captures the psycho-sexual bind of the human condition, which is that the ideal sexual relationship is impossible and there can be no perfectly symmetrical fusion of minds and bodies. However, what my *ménage à trois* also suggests is that even though, or perhaps precisely because, humans lack in this way, and are forever fated to want and desire their ideal other in the way that Plato first articulated in his *Symposium*, sexual culture needs to resist the temptation to coldness, carelessness and, what has become under the neo-liberal carnotopia, a Sadean view of the human object able to satisfy a hunger for flesh. The body will always have drive, but the role of culture must sublimate this base materialism and transform drive into desire, where the true sexual relationship is concerned with minds, bodies, affection, care, love, eroticism and fantasy. In my view, then, what the three films analysed here show is that this symbolic-sexual space, where humans can be creative, imagine, fantasise about, communicate with and care for others, must be kept alive in the face of the Sadean space of neo-liberal carnotopia, where we objectify, fuck, despair, breakdown and collapse.

Notes

1 My use of the term 'promiscuous' is not employed in order to indicate a moral judgement, but rather to indicate free, open sex outside of the bounds of monogamy. In connection to the ideas of utopia and dystopia, promiscuity indicates *either* a utopian state of easy sex or a dystopian condition where the consequence of easy sex is loneliness and alienation.
2 I use the colloquial 'Mom and Dad'/'Mommy and Daddy', rather than 'Mother and Father', in order to indicate the child's position, because desire and identification is less with 'Mother/Father', and more the child's vision of the parent, 'Mommy'/'Daddy'.
3 I employ the term 'revelation' to indicate both Joe's ability to 'reveal' her targets' desires, but also to indicate the religious dimension of this practice, which is explored through Joe's own sexual history concerning first the 'eastern' and second the 'western' church.

Bibliography

Atwood, F. (2009) *Mainstreaming Sex: The Sexualisation of Western Culture*. London: I.B. Tauris.
Deleuze, G. (2004) *The Logic of Sense*. London: Continuum.
Deleuze, G. and F. Guattari (1983) *Anti-Oedipus: Capitalism and Schizophrenia: Volume I*. Minneapolis, MN: University of Minnesota Press.
____ (1987) *A Thousand Plateaus: Capitalism and Schizophrenia: Volume II*. Minneapolis, MN: University of Minnesota Press.
De Sade, M. ([1787] 1990) *Justine, Philosophy in the Bedroom, and Other Writings by Marquis de Sade*. New York: Grove Press.
Freud, S. (2001a) 'Beyond the Pleasure Principle', in *Complete Psychological Works of Sigmund Freud. Volume 18: Beyond the Pleasure Principle, Group Psychology, and Other Works*. London: Vintage, 3–67.

____ (2001b) 'Female Sexuality', in *Complete Psychological Works of Sigmund Freud. Volume 21: The Future of an Illusion, Civilization and Its Discontents, and Other Works*. London: Vintage, 225–47.

Kafka, F. (1915; 2007) *Metamorphosis and Other Stories*. London: Penguin.

Kattelman, B. (2010) 'Carnographic Culture: America and the Rise of the Torture Porn Film', in M. Canini (ed.) *The Domination of Fear*. Amsterdam: Rodopi, 3–17.

Lacan, J. (2000) *On Feminine Sexuality, the Limits of Love and Knowledge, 1972–1973. Encore: The Seminar of Jacques Lacan: Book XX*. New York: W. W. Norton.

____ (2007a) 'The Mirror Stage as Formative of the I Function as Revealed in Psychoanalytic Experience', in *Ecrits*. New York: W. W. Norton, 75–82.

____ (2007b) 'Kant with Sade', in *Ecrits*. New York: W. W. Norton, 645–71.

Nasio, J.-D. (2011) *Oedipus: The Most Crucial Concept in Psychoanalysis*. Albany, NY: State University of New York Press.

Plato (2008) *Symposium*. Oxford: Oxford University Press.

Poe, E. A. (1839; 2003). *The Fall of the House of Usher and Other Writings*. London: Penguin.

Stekel, W. ([1929] 2011) *Sadism and Masochism: The Psychopathology of Sexual Cruelty*. Chicago, IL: University of Chicago Press.

Williams, L. (1999) *Hard Core: Power, Pleasure, and the 'Frenzy of the Visible'*. Berkeley, CA: University of California Press.

Chapter 3
Feed: A Representation of Feederism or Fatsploitation?

NIALL RICHARDSON

The association between eating and sexual activity has long been acknowledged in Western culture. Both sex and food share a common linguistic discourse so that not only are foods used as terms of endearment ('honey', 'pumpkin', 'sugar', 'sweetie') but the same verbs and adjectives are used to describe both the pleasures of sex and consumption. A chocolate cake may be 'orgasmic' while a person may 'drool' over a loved one and we may all 'crave' both sex and food and seek to 'spice up' our sex life. Visual representation, especially cinema, has supported this connection – not least because the Hollywood Hays Code prohibited explicit representations of sexuality and so filmmakers had to invent metaphors to suggest sexual activity to the spectator. For example, dance was used to connote sex (Fred and Ginger were in heaven when dancing 'Cheek to Cheek' [see Dyer 1993]) while supernatural creatures (the vampire, in particular) symbolised unsanctioned sexual desires (see Dyer 2001). Eating as a metaphor for sexual activity, however, has continued since the decline of the Hays Code and thus more recent films such as *9½ Weeks* (1986), *Jawbreaker* (1999) and, most recently, *Woman on Top* (2000) have used the metaphors of food and eating to represent sexual activity in a playful, and often ironic, fashion. Arguably, the pleasure of watching sexual metaphors in contemporary representations is that they remind the spectator of an earlier era, prior to contemporary pornographied culture, in which flirtation and suggestion were the cinematic norm rather than explicit sexuality. Most recently, however, a sexual practice has been identified in contemporary culture in which eating is not simply a form of erotic suggestion or foreplay but is *the* sexual pleasure itself. This activity has been labelled feederism.

What is feederism?

Feederism is a practice that eroticises both the act of feeding/eating and subsequent gaining of body weight (see Giovanelli and Peluso 2006: 309). The person who is fed is identified as a feedee (or sometimes a gainer) while the participant who enables the feeding is called a feeder. Although, the media (especially the film addressed in this chapter) have focused on extreme representations of feederism, various critics have stressed that the practice of feederism 'exists on a continuum' (Terry *et al.* 2012: 250), which may range from people simply reading stories or fantasies about the activity, through to someone merely encouraging another person to gain weight, to the extreme cases in which someone may wish to (force)feed a person to gain weight to the point of immobility. Most importantly, Lesley Terry *et al.* argue that, although extreme versions of the activity might be taking place, many acts of feederism *may* be interpreted as little more than an exaggerated version of 'normative courtship behaviour' (ibid.) in which a man buys a woman dinner/food as part of heteronormative dating practices (see also Prohaska 2013a). In this respect, what *may* be eroticised is the theatricalisation of old fashioned courtship rituals where a male suitor is not only the active partner during the courtship rituals but the sole provider. Read this way, the practice is simply a reaffirmation of mainstream heteronormative dating practices which give agency for men in terms of initiating the process of courtship.

Other critics have emphasised that the activity *may* often be little more than Internet fantasy role play (see Richardson 2010; Prohaska 2013b) and, in this respect, have cautioned against literal interpretations of Internet messages/chatrooms which may simply be auto-erotic, elaborate fictions. It is also important to remember that feederism, although often featuring the male as the feeder and the submissive female as the feedee, may be enacted by same-sex couples (see Monaghan 2005) or indeed heterosexual couples in which the roles are reversed. It is also worth noting that although many people who engage in the activity of feederism have an erotic interest in the gaining of bodyfat, the practice can also exist, to some extent, within muscle-worship and muscle-growth scenarios in which the consuming of extra calories is deemed erotic because the nutrition is required for weight training and subsequent muscle growth (see Richardson 2008). A variation, or subsection, of feederism is the practice of stuffing in which the participants eroticise the act of feeding beyond the level of satiation so that the stomach is stuffed and stretched beyond its limit (see Richardson 2010).

However, most critical interest has been inspired by the more excessive feederist scenarios in which extreme, gendered power dynamics are evident. Samantha Murray, one of the leading critics within the discipline of fat studies, cautions that feederism is often a misogynistic, abusive relationship that 'involves women who allow themselves to be force-fed through a funnel by a dominant male master, who derives sexual excitement from watching his submissive servant grow fatter as he forces her to eat more and more' (2004: 244). This type of scenario described by Murray is upsetting on a number of levels. First, for humans 'food is not feed' (Douglas 1975: 124). As civilised humans we do not feed; we dine. Animals (livestock; household pets) are given 'feed' by their owners and these animals simply consume the nutrients as and when they feel hungry. By contrast, the disciplining and ritualising of dining is one of the main activities to distinguish civilised humans from beasts. Humans do not simply eat when they are hungry but adhere to a dining ritual which, like all cultural activities, is implicated in discourses of class, gender, race, ethnicity and religion. Depending on what we eat, what time of the day we eat, how we label the meals (dinner or supper) and what eating utensils we use, a great deal can be discerned about a person's socio-cultural-racial identification. Therefore, one of the ways to degrade a human being is to make that person feed like an animal, and so Hollywood representations of owners abusing slaves have often shown images of slaves being hurled 'feed' as if they are animals. Second, Murray's scenario is an image of a coerced activity in which the male body pushes something into the overpowered female body and, in this respect, is suggestive of forced penetration or rape. Given that the female feedee seems willing to submit to this ordeal suggests the terrifying misconception that women really do want to be overpowered no matter how much they may protest. Eventually, the female feedee will become totally immobile due to her size, and unable to offer any form of protest whatsoever.

This chapter will analyse a filmic representation which offers a scenario similar to the one described by Murray: the recent thriller *Feed* (Brett Leonard, 2006). *Feed* is a crime thriller (its aesthetics are obviously inspired by *Seven* [David Fincher, 1995] that represents the feederist relationship between Michael (feeder) and Deirdre (feedee/gainer) and the cybercrime cop Phillip who is investigating the activity. The film depicts the most extreme version of feederism, suggesting that this is the only manifestation of the activity – rather than an awareness that such scenarios are rare and often the domain of Internet fantasies. More worryingly, however, the film does not actually represent the psycho-sexual dynamics of feederism as its source of horror but instead codes the excessive fat of the feedee as the most terrifying visual element of the text. In this respect, the film is simply offering the thrill of fatsploitation but absolving the spectator's guilt for shuddering in horror at the fat-suited Deirdre through its claim to be investigating the moral and ethical issues of feederism. The chapter will conclude that far from offering a nuanced consideration of a transgressive body, and a complex psycho-sexual activity, *Feed* merely excuses contemporary fat-phobia and, as such, can be read as yet another example of contemporary media's return to 'Freak Show' politics (see Richardson 2010).

Feed

Phillip (Patrick Thomson) is a cybercrime cop who investigates illegal Internet activity. He was recently successful in discovering a case of cannibalism in Hamburg but, while making the arrests, he witnessed the activity of cannibalism taking place and was traumatised by the sight. He is now investigating a fetish website – feederex.com – which represents oversize women being (force)fed calorie-rich food. Phillip suspects that the site's heavy encryption may conceal a darker issue and, after investigation, discovers that the site is not simply a fat admiration or feeder site but that these women are being fed until they become so fat that they die. Participants in the site are able to wage bets as to when the women will actually do so.

The man running feederex.com is Michael Carter (Alex O'Loughlin) and the film's narrative represents the relationship he has with his latest model, Deirdre (Gabby Millgate). Phillip tracks Michael to Ohio to investigate the website and, after questioning various people including Michael's adoptive parents and his wife, finally tracks him to the cottage where he is holding Deirdre. There is a prolonged altercation in the final sequence before Michael is overpowered. The film's coda shows that Phillip now holds Michael captive and, in a punishment suitable for the irony of Hades, is starving Michael to death while he dines in front of him. Michael's final phrase is the very same plea that he instructed his models to say: 'Feed me.'

Feed continues director Leonard's particular interest in cyber deviancy and the politics of re-presenting the body that were addressed in his previous films, *Lawnmower Man* (1992) and *Virtuosity* (1995). Although the film is certainly a sensationalised horror, which aims to stir the spectator's emotions with a few scares and queasy retches, it is also attempting to be a type of morality play, very much in the legacy of *Seven*. Some rather lengthy discussions and soliloquies draw attention to the fine line that exists between consent and abuse. Indeed, in one of the most truly disturbing sequences in the film cybercrime cop Phillip intercepts the cannibalism that is taking place in the middle-class house in a Hamburg suburb. The man who has consented to having parts of his body cut off, cooked on the stove and then eaten both by himself and his partner, becomes hysterical when interrupted and screams, 'It's my body. I can do what I like. I want to be eaten! I WANT TO BE EATEN!' Any spectator who has ever been part of a civil rights movement (especially feminism and LGBT rights) will recognise the argument that a person *should* have the right to do as they wish with his/her own body.

Other interesting moments in the film, in which the issue of consent and abuse is questioned, include the debate between Phillip and his work colleague over who is the 'master' and who is the 'slave' in the feeder/gainer relationship. Phillip's colleague points out that although the feeder is active, while the feedee is passive, the feeder is servicing the gainer's every wish. Indeed, the use of the terminology of 'master' and 'slave' may remind the spectator of the regimes of ancient Mediterranean cultures in which the Roman masters reclined and were fed by their slaves. As Matthew Roller has examined in detail, the act of dining in ancient Roman culture was structured around highly specific socio-economic roles. The most privileged and powerful members of the society (the adult males) reclined at mealtimes and were fed by their slaves. By contrast, women dined in a seated position and 'were thereby marked as socially inferior to men who reclined' (2006: 2). In other words, assuming the position which appears to be the most passive (reclining and being fed) actually denoted the very opposite in Roman culture and signified the role of being the master. As Roller points out, physical activity and passivity may not necessarily be ascribed to power dynamics as 'the body that must move to take action in response to another body or bodies is inferior, while the body that does not move or act in response to the others is superior' (2006: 20).

Similarly, the lengthy soliloquies offered by Michael to defend his activity of feederism should make the spectator question just who is being abused in this relationship. In one rather eloquent speech Michael describes how he is liberating women from the tyranny of slenderness, allowing them to be curvaceous and volup-

Fig. 1: Michael returning home.

Fig. 2: Phillip returning home.

tuous, rather than compelled to aspire to the dimensions of the emaciated models of the contemporary catwalk.

Likewise, the film, through its parallel editing (a homage to the editing style of *Seven* [see Dyer 1999: 12]), makes the spectator question what is a 'normal' and consensual relationship. The initial sequences of the film represent the (seemingly) monogamous relationship between Deirdre and Michael as tender and affectionate while the debauched, open relationship between Phillip and his girlfriend Abbey (Rose Ashton) is aggressive and, on occasions, even violent. The opening sequence represents Michael returning home to Deirdre with a supply of calorific food to feed to his loved one. The camera offers a medium shot of the man of the house entering a dark hallway and strolling into a bedroom to wake up his snoozing partner. Similar editing and cinematography depict Phillip returning home to Abbey who is also dozing in front of the TV.

However, while Michael proceeds to answer Deirdre's request to 'Feed me!' and their relationship is represented as giving both partners a sense of satisfaction (Michael masturbates at the sight of Deirdre indulging her huge appetite while Deirdre makes orgasmic noises while she eats), the relationship between Phillip and his girlfriend is shown to be strained if not even abusive. Abbey taunts Phillip by telling him that she has fucked four guys and two girls since he's been away and to annoy him even more has even pierced her clitoris. What ensues between Phillip and his girlfriend is not so much love-making as aggressive, even violent, fucking which culminates in Phillip slamming his girlfriend against the mirror and fucking her from behind. Phillip's girlfriend consents to this violent act even though, in another context, this would be an act of sexual violence. The parallel editing between Phillip and his girlfriend's fuck-frenzy and the tender, affectionate relationship between Michael and Deirdre, in which Michael caresses Deirdre's fat and praises her beauty, is intended to raise the question of what is a 'normal' relationship and, most importantly, what is consensual love-making. This is further emphasised later in the film when Phillip's girlfriend calls him 'a pig' and shows that she has been extremely unhappy with the way she has been treated in their relationship.

In this respect, the film attempts to make the spectator question culturally constructed ideas of beauty, sexual normativity and the issue of what is deemed 'consent' in a romantic relationship. Indeed, the film presses this issue even further by demonstrating parallels between the hero (Phillip) and the villain/monster (Michael) by suggesting that they both suffer from similar feelings of inadequacy and an inability to perform successfully in the bedroom. Again, parallel editing between Phillip and Abbey fucking, and Michael and Deirdre having a feeding frenzy, culminates in both male partners failing to attain sexual satisfaction and both mirror each other's pose of curling into a ball and holding their head in their hands. At other points, it also becomes apparent that both men desire the rush of power and control. This is obvious in Michael's relationship with his gainer women but is also suggested to be an issue in Phillip's life as he insists that he be the first cop to arrest the Hamburg cannibals because he is not satisfied with having been the computer geek who cracked the case online but wants the physical dominance of arresting the men. Yet this desire for control is what causes Phillip to become traumatised when he witnesses the (auto)erotic act of cannibalism. Similarly, when Phillip meets Michael's fat sister, and lies to her in order to extract information about Michael and his location, he very clearly enjoys the control he exerts over her by suggesting that he (a classically handsome, relatively in-shape man) is attracted to a big girl like her. In this respect, the film is not unlike the theme of many action/thriller movies in that its leitmotif is a masculine battle for power and control waged over the bodies of women. However, where *Feed* is flawed is that, rather than focus on the psycho-sexual and socio-cultural issues of feederism (with an investigation into the terrifying dynamics of abuse and consent), the film represents the image of fat *itself* as the ultimate horror in the film.

Fatsploitation

The opening sequence makes it very clear that Deirdre's 600-pound body is the supreme source of horror in the film. The extended montage sequence, in which Michael returns home with some fast food, is a superb example of horror cinema suspense. The editing, which connects shots of Michael driving along at *both* night time and day time, not only suggests that this activity of buying fast food is something he does round the clock but the editing also increases narrative suspense by confusing temporal and spatial relations. When and where is this sequence taking place? Likewise, the montage of close-ups on various parts of Michael's body (back of his head, eyes, mouth, hands) is also another disorienting technique but, more

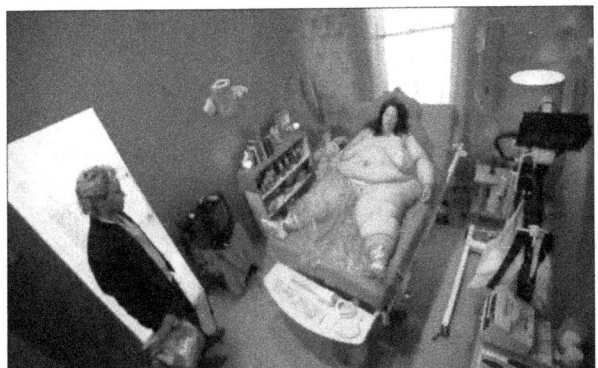

Fig 3: The spectator's first, clear view of the film's true horror: Deirdre's 600-pound body.

importantly, suggests that this film will set up a deliberate ambiguity as to how Michael should be 'read' by the spectator. Like the montage shots of Michael's body parts, the spectator should be struggling for a 'clear' view of Michael. Is he a monster or a hero? This sequence also increases suspense as the spectator has yet to be shown one body in its entirety – thus making the appearance of Deirdre, in all her 600-pound glory, even more shocking. Indeed, when Deirdre is finally revealed, the non-diegetic music stops – signalling that the grand moment has now arrived – and the camera tracks slowly to the left, gradually revealing the full extent of Deirdre's enormity. This is followed by the first in-focus shot in the entire film as Deirdre is represented from a high-angle to show the full size of her 600-pound body.

Given that all previous shots have either been extreme close-ups, or else deliberately out of focus, this image is now giving the horror fan the reward of pure terror (after teasing for such an elongated, build-up) and this horror is the vision of rolls and rolls of Deirdre's fat flesh. The image makes it clear: fat will be the true horror in *Feed* rather than the terror of one person manipulating and abusing another vulnerable human being.

This fatphobia is emphasised by the juxtaposition of the next two sequences in which Phillip's arrest of the Hamburg cannibals is succeeded by Michael's tender caresses of Deirdre. The Hamburg sequence follows the classic horror film suspense formula of the hero entering a house and ascending the staircase to discover the monsters in the room upstairs. All the standard horror conventions such as floating camera, the ambiguous noises (pleasure or pain?) coming from upstairs, the 'false' shock of a friend appearing outside the window to give the spectator a jolt and close-ups of suggestive images such as the body bits boiling on the stove (there appears to be a penis sizzling in the frying pan) help build up a suggestion of the horror that awaits upstairs. Of course, *Feed* does not disappoint the gore enthusiast as Phillip is greeted with the truly terrifying image of a romantic, candle-lit supper in which a man is consenting to have his body eaten.

However, the film then continues this horror by representing Michael and Deirdre in the next sequence. While the Hamburg scene is intended to make the spectator question the line between consent and abuse, and suggest that a similar relationship may be happening with Michael and Deirdre, the following scene does *not* represent obvious abuse of one person by another but instead represents one of the few tender, affectionate sequences in the whole film. In this scene, Michael caresses Deirdre, lovingly strokes her body and feeds her expensive chocolates. While the previous sequence represented mutilation of one person's body by another, this scene is the classic smooching of a loving couple. However, the horror of this scene is quite simply the folds of Deirdre's fat. While the previous sequence offered suspense and terror, this scene offers the 'pleasure' of retching in disgust as Michael plays with Deirdre's pasty, freckly, stretch-marked, cellulite pock-marked fat which, fresh from its sponge bath, now looks slimy. In a stomach-churning image, Michael sticks his index finger in Deirdre's belly button and there is a squelching, slurping sound. While the previous sequence represented a person being violated and mutilated, this sequence simply depicts highly normative rituals of affection between a man and woman. Yet it is coded as being as horrific, if not even more so, than the previous sequence of cannibalism. If the film were then to offer some form of meta-critical analysis as to *why* the spectator should be equally nauseated by an image of female fatness as by an image of 'consensual' torture then the sequence could be interpreted as interrogating fat-phobia in the same way it is questioning the line between consent and abuse. However, as it stands, this sequence is simply revelling in the accepted dynamic of fatphobia. The real horror of *Feed* is Deirdre's excessively fat body.

A similar point is made in the sequence where Phillip is making investigations about Michael and is questioning Michael's foster parent, a priest named Father Turner. Eventually Turner narrates how he discovered that Michael was a 'very troubled boy' – the montage accompanying Turner's story represents how he caught Michael in the act of masturbating to the image of his (adopted) fat sister sleeping in her bed. The interesting point is that this sequence is represented as evidence that Michael was 'very troubled'; yet what, exactly, is the basis for identifying someone as 'troubled' from this one incident? Parents catching teenage boys in the act of masturbation is a common occurrence and is often a standard joke in many low-brow comedy films. However, the key issue in the *Feed* sequence seems to be that Michael is not simply masturbating, but that he is masturbating to the sight of *fat* legs. In this respect, the sequence is suggesting that Michael's fat admiration is the reason he is identified as 'troubled'. The argument here is that, although *Feed*

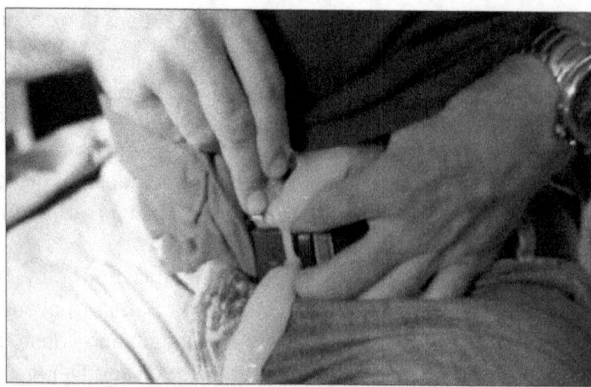

Fig. 4: Lancing the fat 'blister': fat represented as pus.

Fig. 5: Promotional poster

pertains to be an investigation of the horror of abuse that exists within a feederist relationship, it codes the 'true' horror as fat itself and, even more horrific, that any person could actually find fat to be erotic.

Indeed, a scene halfway through the film offers the most powerful image in asserting that fat itself is to be considered the ultimate source of horror. In this sequence Michael visits Phillip in his motel room and drugs him. When Phillip passes out, Michael produces a syringe filled with liquefied fat and injects this into Phillip's abdomen, thus forming a fat-filled blister under Phillip's skin. When Phillip wakes up, he immediately senses the blister and, grabbing his penknife, lances it so that the liquefied fat splatters out in an action that looks like pus exploding from an abscess or boil. In this scene, fat is not simply an unwanted element of bodily composition; here fat is coded as infection.

This coding of fat itself as the ultimate horror is also suggested by the film's poster, which represents abdominal fat folds, thus implying that, although the film is investigating the cult of feederism, it will offer the sensationalist pleasure of being permitted to gaze upon the 'horror' of fat.

Therefore, what the film, arguably, is offering is fatsploitation of the horror of fat in contemporary culture couched in a narrative which claims to interrogate consent/ abuse in alternative relationships. Yet this unashamed fatsploitation is excused by one key element – Deirdre is wearing a fat suit.

But it's only a fat suit?

The use of the fat suit in contemporary cinema has been the subject of considerable critical debate (see Mosher 2001; LeBesco 2005; Mendoza 2009; Richardson 2010). Indeed, a number of films/TV shows have delighted in representing lithe Hollywood stars in fat suits such as Gywneth Paltrow as Rosemary in *Shallow Hal* (Farrelly Brothers, 2001) and Courtney Cox as young, fat Monica in *Friends* (1994–2004). One argument that has been proposed is that the fat suit absolves the spectator of any guilt for laughing at the fat bodies. Rosemary is not really fat as underneath the fat suit is the svelte Gwyneth Paltrow (see Richardson 2010: 84), who, for most of the film, doesn't even appear in the fat suit. Indeed, on the occasions when Paltrow does appear as Fat Rosemary the pleasure afforded to the spectator is, arguably, the 'cinema of attractions' (Gunning 1986), the thrill in marvelling at the skill of the make-up department in creating such a believable fat body.

The case with Deirdre, however, is slightly different. The most important contrast is that, unlike *Shallow Hal*'s Rosemary or *Friends*' Monica, Deirdre is not played by a well-known actress. The only role for which Gaby Millgate is probably remembered is her small part in *Muriel's Wedding* (P. J. Hogan, 1995) where she played Muriel's slobby, lazy sister. The point is that, although Deirdre is represented as wearing a fat suit, there is no point of reference for the spectator beneath the fat suit. While the image of the svelte Courtney Cox and Gwyneth Paltrow is in the spectator's mind, while he/she marvels at the make-up department's magic in creating the fat suit, the same is not the case with Deirdre.

This enfreakment of Deirdre's fat is taken to an even greater level through comparisons and juxtapositions with the other bodies in the film. The narrative asserts that there is one other fat woman in the diegesis: Michael's adopted sister, Jesse. Jesse self-identifies as a 'big girl' and indeed it was her curvaceous thigh, exposed while she was sleeping, that first inspired Michael's lust for fat. Jesse is coded as one of the few *sympathetic* characters in the film. Although not very bright (Jesse asks if Sydney, Australia is near Japan) she is represented as kind hearted, unassuming and, as with most women in mainstream, narrative cinema, simply looking for the love of a good man. Like Deirdre, Jesse is also wearing a fat suit but, given its subtlety, the spectator may be forgiven for not noticing that it is prosthetic fat at all. The effect of this comparison is that *Feed* quantifies acceptable levels of fat. In order to assert that the film is not simply unbridled fatphobia, it represents the 'tolerable' amount of fatness in the character of the charming Jesse. Indeed, in a discourse that was often used to police gay culture, the film seems to say that fat is 'acceptable' provided it does not draw attention to itself and is not too 'excessive'.

The character of Jesse raises another key point in that *Feed* fails to represent any three-dimensional females. If Deirdre is the side-show 'freak' (the world's fattest lady has returned to the entertainment business with a vengeance), Jesse simply represents the 'dutiful daughter' stereotype who is juxtaposed with the 'whore' stereotype of Phillip's girlfriend, Abbey. The only other female character in the film is Michael's beautiful wife, Mary (Sherly Sulaimen). Although representing middle-class, educated femininity, Mary is the only non-Caucasian body in the film and her Asian-ness is highlighted by the way she performs the stereotypically Asian feminine 'cuteness' when she first appears on screen. Most importantly, Mary is represented as a fanatical Roman Catholic who refuses to acknowledge any problem with Michael's feederex.com website (even when Phillip forces her to look at the details online) and she proclaims Michael to be a 'child of God' whom Phillip will never be able to catch. In other words, Mary is not simply represented as a strange eclecticism (an Asian Roman Catholic) but as someone who is utterly irrational and unable to think critically, or even logically, about the issues in her life. Mary, therefore, represents the 'problem' with middle-class, post-feminist women (who have 'elected' to embrace domestic, pre-feminist, housewifery) and the danger of contemporary liberal society, which simply allows an extreme 'live and let live' philosophy. It is hardly surprising that Mary is killed off by the end of the narrative.

Feed, therefore, is hardly a film concerned with women's *actual* rights, despite Phillip's assertions that he is fighting to save the unfortunate victims of feederex.com, but instead is an extended altercation between two men who attempt to prove their masculinity by fighting over the bodies of incompetent, irrational women. What is taking place in *Feed* is a macho war between men in which the female victims of Michael's feederex.com are irrelevant and merely used as a justification for men proving their masculinity. The film itself does acknowledge this issue, articulated by Phillip's boss, Police Chief Richard (Jack Thompson), who accuses Phillip of needing to prove himself rather than being genuinely concerned for the plight of the female victims. This becomes very apparent in the film's final twist, when in the climax of the penultimate scene, Phillip actually shoots Deirdre in the head, killing her instantly. Whether Deirdre was rescued from Michael's clutches was irrelevant to Phillip as he was simply 'using' her case as an opportunity to prove his masculinity by capturing Michael.

However, this battle between Phillip and Michael is particularly interesting when we consider how both men are coded in the narrative. While Phillip represents archaic, macho, pre-feminist masculinity (Abbey, quite rightly, describes him as 'a pig'), Michael appears, at least initially, to embody the sensitivity of the New Man whose attention to personal grooming and compassion for women marks him as the opposite of Phillip. In a number of his soliloquies, Michael talks about how a woman should be honoured, cared for and loved as opposed to being treated as a sex object in the way Phillip does. Therefore, *Feed* may be read as an allegory in which the sensitivity of New Masculinity is exposed as not only fraudulent but as disguising psychotic tendencies. By contrast, the saviour of the day is the pre-feminist, macho man (although not British, Phillip is, in many ways comparable to the New Lad [see Whelehan 2000; Nixon 2001]) who swoops in and vanquishes the threat of 'deviant' New Masculinity.

An alternative ending to the film did provide a more satisfactory critique of the politics of masculinity by representing Phillip being shot by the Police Chief who, earlier in the film, had accused him of not actually being concerned about the female victims of feederex.com but merely wanting to use this case to prove his masculinity. However, this ending did not make the final cut of the film and so the end of *Feed* simply represents Phillip in a happy relationship with Michael's sister Jesse (the sweet-natured, simple, 'dutiful daughter'), who makes him his lunch and looks after their charming, little house.

Arguably, given the ending that made the final cut, the film *could* be read as not only fatphobic but highly misogynist as well. If the 'happy' ending is the old-fashioned, macho man living in domestic bliss with the pre-feminist housewife then there is a comment being made about the danger of 'alternative' relationships (Phillip and Abbey's; Michael and Deirdre's) and a suggestion that these 'emancipated' women, who choose unconventional lifestyles (such as being openly promiscuous like Abbey, or being a gainer like Deirdre) only bring extreme unhappiness upon themselves. Indeed, the 'horror' of the film may not only be the excessive feminine fat of Deirdre's body but also the subtle suggestion that women having the freedom to lead an alternative lifestyle is the path to absolute ruin. Deirdre, like all deviant women, is 'punished' with death for asserting her right to alternative, voracious desire. In this respect, rather than actually interrogating the psycho-sexual complexities of the practice of feederism, and questioning what is sexual consent and physical beauty in contemporary culture, *Feed* merely exploits the spectator's assumed horror of fat and, arguably, suggests that feederism is an example of the danger of women choosing an alternative sexual expression beyond the established domain of heteronormative domesticity.

Bibliography

Douglas, M. (1975) *Implicit Meanings: Essays in Anthropology*. London: Routledge.

Dyer, R. (1993) '"I Seem to Find the Happiness I Seek": Heterosexuality and Dance in the Musical', in H. Thomas (ed.) *Dance, Gender, and Culture*. London: Palgrave MacMillan.

―― (1999) *Seven*. London: British Film Institute.

―― (2001) *The Culture of Queers*. London: Routledge.

Giovanelli, D. and N. M. Peluso (2006) 'Feederism: a new sexual pleasure and subculture', in S. Seidman, N. Fischer and C. Meeks (eds) *Handbook of New Sexuality Studies*. London and New York: Routledge, 309–13.

Gunning, T. (1986) 'Cinema of Attraction: Early Film, Its Spectator and the Avant Garde', *Wide Angle*, 88, 3/4, 63–70.

LeBesco, K. (2005) 'Situating Fat Suits: Blackface, Drag and the Politics of Performance', *Women & Performance: A Journal of Feminist Theory*, 15, 2, 231–42.

Mendoza, K. (2009) 'Seeing Through the Layers: Fat Suits and Thin Bodies in *The Nutty Professor* and *Shallow Hal*', in E. Rothblum, S. Solovay and M. Wann (eds) *The Fat Studies Reader*. New York, NY: New York University Press, 280–8.

Monaghan, L. (2005) 'Big Handsome Men, Bears and Others: Virtual Constructions of "Fat Male Embodiment"', *Body and Society*, 11, 2, 81–111.

Mosher, J. (2001) 'Having Their Cake and Eating It Too: Fat Acceptance Films and the Production of Meaning' in J. Lewis (ed.) *The End of Cinema as we Know It: American Film in the Nineties*. New York, NY: New York University Press, 237–49.

Murray, S. (2004) 'Locating Aesthetics: Sexing the Fat Woman', *Social Semiotics*, 14, 238–47.

Nixon, S. (2001) 'Resignifying Masculinity: From "New Man" to "New Lad"', in D. Morley and K. Robbins (eds) *British Cultural Studies: Geography, Nationality and Identity*. Oxford: Oxford University Press, 373–85.

Prohaska, A. (2013a) 'Feederism: Transgressive Behaviour or Same Old Patriarchal Sex?', *International Journal of Social Science Studies*, 1, 2, 104–12.

____ (2013b) 'Help Me Get Fat! Feederism as Communal Deviance on the Internet', *Deviant Behaviour*, 35, 263–74.

Richardson, Niall (2008) 'Flex Rated! Female Bodybuilding: Feminist Resistance or Erotic Spectacle', *Journal of Gender Studies*, 17, 4, 289–301.

____ (2010) *Transgressive Bodies: Representations in Film and Popular Culture*. Farnham: Ashgate.

Roller, M. B. (2006) *Dining Posture in Ancient Rome: Bodies, Values, and Status*. Princeton, NJ: Princeton University Press.

Terry, L. L., K. D. Suschinsky, M. L. Lalumiere and P. L. Vasey (2012) 'Feederism: An Exaggeration of a Normative Mate Selection Preference?', *Archives of Sexual Behaviour*, 41, 249–60.

Whelehan, I. (2000) *Overloaded: Popular Culture and the Future of Feminism*. London: The Women's Press.

Chapter 4
Proving their 'Virility'? Steve McQueen's *Hunger* and Transgressive Masculinity

ALISON GARDEN

This chapter explores how Steve McQueen's *Hunger* (2008) exposes a complex nexus of ideas about gender, the body and transgressive masculinity within an Irish (post)colonial and 'post-conflict' context.[1] *Hunger* was McQueen's first full-length feature film, but he was already a critically acclaimed visual artist and had won the Turner Prize in 1999 on the strength of his short video installation, 'Deadpan' (1997). *Hunger* also met with great critical success: McQueen received the Caméra d'Or (first-time director) Award at Cannes in 2008 and numerous other awards. Subsequently, McQueen has gone on to direct *Shame* (2011) and *12 Years a Slave* (2013), both of which were commercial and critical successes. We can read *Hunger*, in many ways, as a transitional artwork in McQueen's career as he moves from short video installations to the full, narrative-driven drama of *12 Years a Slave*. Given *Hunger*'s potentially inflammatory subject material and McQueen's status as a first-time director, it is unsurprising that the film was an independent one; after failing to secure funding from the Irish Film Board, the film was financed by Film4 Productions, Channel 4, Northern Ireland Screen, Broadcasting Commission of Ireland and the Wales Creative IP Fund.

From McQueen's earliest video installation, 'Bear' (1993), we can trace preoccupations with corporeality – particularly the male physique – sexuality and violence, and *Hunger* is no exception. The film is, however, hard to place in terms of genre. In its focus on the endurance and suffering of a martyred male body for a higher cause, punished by a cruel, inhumane system, we could read *Hunger* in parallel with films such as Stanley Kubrick's *Spartacus* (1960), Martin Scorsese's *The Last Temptation of Christ* (1988) and Mel Gibson's *The Passion of the Christ* (2004). Indeed, the hagiographic dimension of *Hunger* is central: the film gestures towards the Catholic reverence of sacrifice that informs Irish Republican discourse but, further than this, McQueen's depictions of Bobby Sands (played by Michael Fassbender) and another prisoner, Davey Gillen (Brian Milligan) are transgressive – much like the hagiographic and iconographic depiction of saints' bodies. As I shall illustrate, the film's visual vocabulary, with its focus on somatic suffering, moments of male nudity and lingering shots over disembodied male body parts, echoes the filmic language of the male gaze often used to police and objectify the female body. In so doing, McQueen actively eroticises these bodies, which, given the political context of the film, works to appropriate the feminine and therefore negate the excessive, violent masculinity of these paramilitary prisoners.[2]

'Sacrificial martyrdom': Hagiography and Queer Masculinity

In his incendiary review of *Hunger* for *The Guardian*, David Cox labelled the film a 'Britflick hagiography of Provo [Provisional Irish Republican Army] hunger striker Bobby Sands' (2008). Although Cox's use of 'hagiography' is clearly intended as a derogatory slur on what he reads as the film's uncritical valorisation of Sands, the word is entirely appropriate. Hagiographic texts are accounts of the lives and trials of saints and, as documents that often emphasise the earthly sufferings endured by saints that led to their canonisation, they are texts that are overwhelmingly concerned with the body in pain. Whatever one's opinion of the film's politics, there can be no dispute that the central focus of the film is the male body under duress and the limits of endurance.[3] The prisoners' flesh is broken by beatings and their bodies penetrated by mirror searches of their anuses and mouths; by the end of the film, the emaciated body of Sands is riddled with bedsores. The porous nature of male bodies is further highlighted by shots of them 'bangling' contraband items and writings to smuggle them in and out of the prison – achieved by hiding them in their mouths, noses, anuses and foreskins. Of course, *Hunger*'s relentless depiction of this violence against the body furthers the hagiographic nature of the film, as it depicts Sands as a victim and therefore his fasting as an act of 'sacrificial martyrdom' (Kearney 1984: 61). Emilie Pine argues that Sands' 'abjected male body is elevated by virtue to the extent of its victimization to become symbolic of heroism' (2014: 166). 'Sacrificial martyrdom' has had an important role to play in the politics of both Irish Nationalism and Republicanism, and I argue that McQueen knowingly gestures towards this discourse in his film (see also Kearney 1984; Cullingford 1990; Harris 2002).

In addition to the visual depiction of Sands' suffering, which draws heavily on the iconography of hagiography, Enda Walsh and Steve McQueen's script paints Sands as a figure willing to suffer for the greater good and the Republican cause. The script is notoriously lean, with sparse dialogue:[4] we are asked to formulate our own ideas about character through meditative scenes of silence and repetitive motifs, such as the warder Raymond Lohan's (Stuart Graham) recurrent bathing of his knuckles, intersected with moments of warder brutality. The only extended piece of dialogue comes in the form of a scene in the middle of the film between Bobby Sands and Father Dominic Moran (Liam Cunningham), of which the first seventeen minutes was filmed as one long take. During this, Sands and Moran go back and forth over the logic for the hunger strike, and whether it is noble sacrifice (Sands) or selfish suicide (Moran). This scene – a medium shot backlit to create silhouettes – is largely an intellectual exercise that Sands uses to bolster his reasoning for the strike (or in Moran's words, as a 'sounding board' for it) and allows the audience to think through the e/affects that the strike will have for both local and national communities. It is evident that McQueen views Sands' strike as a form of martyrdom, and that he seeks to convince the audience of this too, when he moves, after seventeen minutes, from this medium shot into a close-up of Sands' face. This ensures that the ensuing scene, filmed entirely in close-up, feels more direct and emotional than the abstracted, theoretical discussion of the previous shot. In this scene, Sands recounts an anecdote from his childhood. He talks of a trip to Donegal with other Belfast boys from his running club for a race, run by the Christian brothers, and their encounter with a group of boys from Cork. The two groups of boys have gone on a warm-up run and, in the woods (which are out of bounds), find a dying foal, trapped in the rocks of the stream. The animal is in obvious pain, but none of the boys will kill it – their talk of ending its suffering is simply 'bravado'. A priest arrives and, immediately assuming that the boys are to blame for hurting the foal, threatens the boys with punishment. Sands then holds the foal's head under the water and drowns it. The priest, Sands tells us, is furious and beats Sands for his disobedience. McQueen/Walsh are not content to allow the viewer to deduce that Sands is obviously a man willing to make difficult decisions and suffer the consequences for his beliefs: they underscore this message by having Sands state: 'But I knew I did the right thing by that wee foal. And I could take the punishment for all our boys. I had the respect of them other boys now and I knew that.' McQueen's Sands is evidently an individual who is not only willing to endure suffering for his beliefs, but also one that takes a pride in proving the strength of his endurance for the witness of others, particularly men; his masculinity is, in part, a performance of stamina and sacrifice.

Within Catholicism, this rhetoric of martyrdom leads into prescriptive gendered performances, whereby men become active sacrificial heroes and women their passive mourners. Susan Harris notes that we can read these performances as 'continually recreat[ing] not only the crucifixion but also the pietà' (2002: 4). Curiously enough, because of the film's relegation of women to the sidelines, *Hunger* visually recreates both of these scenes, but with an important difference: the filmic gaze queers these images, rather than reproducing images that tally with the dominant, heteronormative male gaze that we associate with cinema. We are first introduced to Bobby Sands at about twenty-five minutes into the film: he is half-naked, clothed only in a towel wrapped around his waist, and his hair and beard are long. The resemblance to Christ is obvious. The Crucifixion scene begins with Sands being dragged by the hair up the corridor by warders to have his hair and beard cut in the bathroom. Sands resists and is subjected to severe beatings, including a direct punch to the face; the hair-cutting is particularly vicious and Sands' face is bloodied and bruised. Sands is then forced into a cold bath where he is scrubbed clean with a broom. After this, his naked, limp body is pulled out of the bathtub, with the camera at the level of Sands' buttocks; the paleness of his flesh is contrasted against the darkness of the prison uniforms worn by the warders who flank him on either side and so his skin demands our gaze. The next shot is of Sands' body as he is carried back up the corridor to his cell. The two warders have taken Sands under the armpits, with his arms pulled out to the side, imitative of a crucified body. Sands is framed by fluorescent lighting over his head, evocative of a halo; as the two warders carry him, Sands moves in and out of the light, revealing the swelling and lacerations to his face. At this point in the film, prior to his starvation, McQueen's depiction is highly gendered and his body is presented to us for scopophilic pleasure. Again, Sands is lit in a way that invites us to look upon the hyper-masculinity of his body: the play of light and shadow throws his silhouette into sharp relief and we are made to dwell upon the outline of the musculature in his shoulders and neck; the defined sinews and shape of his arms.

Later in the film, during the final third that charts Sands' fast to death, McQueen makes another reference to Christ through re-enacting the pietà. Sands lies in the bath, watched by a prison medic; the camera pans down to the medic's knuckles, to reveal the tattooed letters UDA (Ulster Defence Association), the loyalist paramilitary organisation. Sands, in an attempt to both show his contempt and prove his determined spirit, if weakened body, tries to get out of the bath unaided. The physical exertions of this cause him to collapse and lose consciousness. Following this, we see the warder carrying Sands' unconscious body down the corridor of the medical wing back down to his cell. The moment bears striking resemblance to Michelangelo's iconic sculpture of the pietà: the medic holds Sands' body under the armpit; Sands' head is thrown back, as in Michelangelo's sculpture; his body is similarly sinewy to the monumental Jesus and arranged in a near-identical pose; a white towel is positioned across his lap in an exact imitation of the sculpture. The parallels that the viewer is asked to make between Sands and Christ are blatant.

Visually recreating these motifs from the life of Christ asks the viewer to consider Sands in a similar light but, as mentioned earlier, these images are queer visions of the strictly heteronormative symbols from Catholic discourse. The potentially queer quality of Catholicism has been noted by various figures, including Eve Sedgwick, but I think it is more pertinent to think of McQueen's queering of these images as fitting with hagiographic depictions of queer and transgressive visual iconography.[5] Feminist scholarship has highlighted how medieval accounts of the lives and bodily punishments of female saints, represented in both literature (hagiographic) and visual culture (iconographic), 'opens a licit space that permits the audience to enjoy sexual language and contemplate the naked female body' (Gravdal 1991: 24). Robert Mills draws attention to the ways in which the lives of male saints, such as St. Sebastian and St. Lawrence, can be read in similar ways: 'Images of the saints were, it should be remembered, one of the few sanctioned spaces in which to depict the male nude in the Middle Ages' (2001: 25). In addition to the sanctioned (erotic) display of male flesh, a queer politics is at play in the gendered nature of these bodies, which occupy 'positions of gender ambiguity in their subjection to bodily torment'. Where 'male saints are visually de-phallicized by being decapitated, disembowelled and flayed ... female saints such as Barbara and Agatha are purportedly "de-sexed" by having their breasts removed' (Mills 2005: 173). Mills also argues that while the violated, tortured, beaten and unclothed bodies of saints could be read as feminised, in the focus on their fleshliness, the ability of these saints to withstand extreme violence actually works to reassert a potent form of endurance. We could read this endurance of suffering as a 'strengthening' undertaking and proof of an 'ultra-virile' masculinity (Mills 2001: 13). For ultimately, 'in the world of the martyr, *to be penetrated is not to abdicate power*' (Mills 2005: 171; emphasis in original).

How, one might ask, is a discussion about medieval hagiography relevant to our understanding of *Hunger*? I believe that it works towards explicating the conflicting messages that the film sends us about the bodies of the prisoners and notions of masculinity more broadly. Their corporeality is at once hyper-masculine – they are naturally armored by muscle – but, as will become apparent, in lingering on their (masculine) physical beauty, the camera stylises these bodies for scopophilic pleasure. Like iconographic depictions of St. Sebastian, McQueen's visual creation of the prisoners transforms them 'explicitly into exhibited, eroticized flesh' (Mills 2005: 166). While the nakedness of the prisoners befits the subject of the film, these bodies are represented in particularly striking ways: they are both violated and on display, befitting the 'feminised' role within film scholarship, following Laura Mulvey's seminal work on classic Hollywood cinema. I posit that the gaze of McQueen's film reflects the troubled and contradictory discourse surrounding Irishness and gender, particularly 'post-conflict' masculinity and, rather than attempt to categorise or delineate the film as emblematic of a particular way of seeing, we should instead ask what McQueen hopes to achieve with the disruptive and queer qualities of *Hunger*'s masculine bodies.

Male Beauty, Scopophilia and 'voyeuristic looking': *Hunger*'s Male Bodies

Mulvey's work on Hollywood cinema draws attention to the ways in which the female body is used to generate scopophilic pleasure: 'women are simultaneously looked at and displayed, with their appearance coded for strong visual and erotic impact so that they can be said to connote *to-be-looked-at-ness*' (2000: 40). Writing with specific reference to the work of Alfred Hitchcock and Josef von Sternberg, Mulvey argues that film 'builds up the physical beauty of the [female] object, transforming it into something satisfying in itself'; the female becomes 'a perfect product, whose body, stylised and fragmented by close-ups, is the content of the film and the direct recipient of the spectator's look' (2000: 42, 43). However, Steve Neale argues that male bodies can also be subject to this same 'voyeuristic looking', especially in cinematic genres dominated overwhelmingly with the relations between men, such as 'war films, westerns and gangster movies': or really 'any film ... in which there is a struggle between a hero and a male villain' (2000: 261). Neale contends that these films involve 'the repression of any explicit avowal of eroticism in the act of looking at the male' through 'narrative content marked by sado-mascochistic phantasies and scenes'; the archetypal example of one of these scenes, for Neale, is the shoot out, through which the pleasure of looking is 'displac[ed] ... from the male body as such and locat[ed] ... more generally in the overall components of a highly ritualised scene' (ibid.).

While *Hunger* is very much concerned with the struggle between two groups of men – prisoners and warders – the spectacular qualities of the sado-mascochistic scenes do not displace the gaze from male body to ritualised, stylised shoot outs, but actively place the male body at their centre. Where Neale suggests that these masculine genres allow us to 'see male bodies stylised and fragmented by close-ups' through an indirect gaze 'heavily mediated by the looks of the characters involved', *Hunger* is a film largely devoid of POV shots because the film is not sustained through a conventional narrative of dialogue and character relations (1981: 262). Indeed, some of the most overt gazing at male bodies is done through camera work that either knowingly disrupts natural patterns of vision, or through scenes that watch the solitary prisoners in their cells. The bodies of *Hunger*, unlike the examples that Neale discusses in his article, are 'displayed solely for the gaze of the spectator' (ibid.). What is more, at various points in the film, McQueen highlights the 'physical beauty' of these men's bodies in the manner that Mulvey argues is reserved for female subjects.

One such body that is stylised for our scopophilic pleasure is Davey Gillen, who partly facilitates our entry into the world of Long Kesh. As a new prisoner, we watch as he is inducted into the system. When presented to a prison officer for processing, Gillen refuses to wear the 'uniform of a criminal' and demands to wear his own clothes. The prison officer then notes Gillen's status as a 'non-conforming prisoner' in his ledger – enabling the audience to see quite how many of these there have been in recent weeks – and looks up at him with a slight smile, in silence, which prompts Gillen to start removing his clothes. Gillen does this slowly and fearfully; the camera sits just above the right shoulder of the prison officer, so the shot is one of the few that imitates POV, although keeping the prison officer slightly in frame highlights the voyeurism of the scene. In this sense, then, our watching of Gillen's undressing could be read, as Neale suggests, as 'mediated by the looks of the characters involved' but in more conventional cinema the (potentially erotic) spectacle of this moment would be diffused through rapid cutting across multiple POV shots. This scene, however, unfolds in one long cut. While the silence and palpable apprehension of Gillen fit the nature of this unclothing, we could also read this scene as one of uninterrupted erotic spectacle. The slow and careful nature of Gillen's movements heightens our sense of his vulnerability, but also of the exhibitionist quality of the scene, which unravels in an extended and delayed manner: it takes over one and half minutes for Gillen to remove his clothes, of which thirty seconds is spent with Gillen fingering the buttons of, and slowly removing, his shirt. Although the context of this scene negates a reading of it as a consensual 'striptease' – the 'leitmotif of erotic spectacle' associated with women in cinema – the watching of a man taking off his clothes slowly is strikingly unusual in film (see Mulvey 2000: 40). For example, in the similar scene from Terry George's *Some Mother's Son* (1996), when Gerard Quigley (Aiden Gillen) and Frank Higgins (David O'Hara) refuse their prisoners' uniform, they are already half-naked and the scene is meditated through close-up POV shots of the actors faces; there is no protracted gazing at the male body, or slow removing of clothes.[6] As noted above, the majority of Davey Gillen's scene is shot from the front of his body; however, when he goes to remove his trousers, McQueen knowingly moves the camera to Gillen's rear, so that one third of the frame is filled by Gillen's buttocks. This not only alerts the viewer to the dynamics of the double-voyeurism that structure the scene – we watch the prison officer watching Gillen undress – but this camera movement also disrupts naturalistic patterns of viewing. In so doing,

McQueen explicitly draws attention to the exhibited nature of Gillen's flesh: he is a body produced for our visual consumption in the manner more often associated with female bodies. This scene then cuts to that of a prison warder wielding a truncheon behind his back, which then cuts, again, to a shot of Gillen's naked buttocks as he is presented to this same prison warder as he hands Gillen his blanket: a montage that underlines the lament homoeroticism of the scene.

In addition to the shots of Gillen's disembodied buttocks, there are several other moments of what might be thought of as 'unnecessary' male nudity. And this nudity, rather than simple fidelity to historical accuracy (some Republican prisoners had been on 'Blanket Protest' since September 1976, whereby they refused to wear prison uniforms and were clothed only by a single blanket), or a desire to affirm the prisoners' vulnerability, is consistently and actively eroticised. McQueen does this through framing the bodies of Sands and Gillen by low-angle camera shots that emphasise their musculature and lighting that further contours their physiques, drawing our eye to their exposed flesh. Take, for example, the focus on Sands' arms in the scene that we spend with him in his cell: his chest, shoulders and arms are fully exposed. As with elsewhere in the film, discussed in greater detail below, the lighting of this scene highlights Sands' flesh in contrast to the darkness of the excrement-smeared walls of his cell. It is notable that Sands' arms, chest and shoulders, lit in a warm yellow light, are far more clearly visible than his face, which is shrouded in darkness and shadow. Some of the film's promotional material also featured images that concentrated on the musculature of Sands' arms. This focus on the natural, unclothed masculinity of Sands' body is curious, because in dwelling so consistently on his corporeality, McQueen actually constructs Sands' masculinity in a vein more usually associated with the male gaze's rendering of erotic female spectacle. This is also obvious in McQueen's decision to have Sands half-naked (though wearing trousers rather than a blanket) during the long dialogue scene in the middle

Fig. 1: Sands (Michael Fassbender) smoking in his cell in *Hunger* (2008).

of the film. Again, given the fixed position of the camera, the audience is asked to gaze upon Sands' exposed upper body because there is, quite simply, little else to look at.

It is also worth noting the *types* of bodies we are introduced to in our two key prisoners: the bodies of the actors playing both Gillen and Sands are archetypal visions of masculine beauty. Their bodies are athletic, lithe and naturally 'armoured' with muscle. The muscles in their arms, shoulders and chests are well developed – so much so, that even when Sands is emaciated, you can still see the outline of muscle in his upper body. If we contrast these bodies with the flabby, overweight, bodies of the prison warders that we have seen showering earlier in the opening minutes of the film, it is obvious that the prisoners are meant to embody a potent, essential masculinity for the viewer. But the visual vocabulary of *Hunger* does not just present these bodies as unproblematic emblems of masculinity, as in *Some Mother's Son*, which offers us, in Neale's words 'the spectacle of male bodies, but bodies unmarked as objects of erotic display' (2000: 262): *Hunger*'s bodies are codified for our scopophilic pleasure. When Gillen first enters his cell, the visual juxtaposition of the darkness of the walls is offset by the unblemished nature of his skin, lit with a blue light that transforms his body into something resembling a marble statue of classical, monumental masculinity and heroism.

The shot of Gillen's naked behind challenges Neale's statement that, in cinema, 'there is no trace of acknowledgement or recognition of [male] bodies as displayed solely for the gaze of the spectator' (ibid.). Granted, Neale was writing about conventional genres from Hollywood film, rather than independent cinema, and various film critics, such as Richard Dyer (2002) and Frances Pheasant-Kelly (2014), have drawn attention to the ways in which, in the thirty-odd years since Neale's article was first published, 'men in film increasingly attract a sexually objectifying gaze in their positioning as erotic spectacle' (Pheasant-Kelly 2014: 202). Pheasant-Kelly asserts that 'this revisionist viewing politics not only reflects a more generalized equality between the sexes but also corresponds to an associated ongoing crisis in masculinity' (ibid.). In a discussion about *Fight Club* (1999) and *Casino Royale* (2006), she concludes that the 'male body of contemporary cinema is … both strong and enduring but susceptible to injury and erotic contemplation' (2014: 203). There is, however, a crucial difference between the bodies of these two studio films and *Hunger*: where the viewer gains pleasure from 'the spectacle of injured/eroticized men's bodies and their capacity to endure suffering' across all three films, 'spectator pleasure' is also generated by 'viewing *conventional heroic performance*', like the self-sacrificing bravery of James Bond and the scenes of bare-knuckle fighting in *Fight Club* (ibid.; emphasis added). Furthermore, Pheasant-Kelly argues, spectators are able to 'recogniz[e] a projection of masculinity inherent in the male protagonist's *displays of violence*' (2014: 209; emphasis added) and it is through this heroism and violence that, despite being both wounded and eroticised, the male figures of *Casino Royale* and *Fight Club* retain their masculinity. This is where *Hunger* deviates. The violence of Sands and Gillen is kept carefully off-screen. Indeed, although it is easy to forget, because the film barely engages with the sectarian unrest outside the prison and never makes reference to the violent pasts of the prisoners, Sands was imprisoned on charges of possessing a firearm and was a member of the Provisional IRA. Similarly, there is no 'conventional' heroism in *Hunger*. Although some viewers will find their dirty protests and hunger striking 'heroic', it is certainly not conventional heroism, and McQueen visually feminises their bodies as an act of recuperation: through offering up their bodies as passive and victimised, McQueen negates their excessive, violent masculinity.

(Post)colonial Ireland and Troubled Masculinity

Stefanie Lehner's work on 'post-conflict masculinity' provides a particularly fruitful way of thinking about *Hunger*'s depiction of Sands' and Gillen's bodies. She writes that the 'post-conflict situation [in Northern Ireland] requires a transformation of masculinity: a switch from the formerly hegemonic retributive model of the "hard-man" to a more sensible, restorative male subjectivity – a putative "peacenik"-type' (2011: 67). Invoking the words of David Trimble, former leader of the Ulster Unionist Party, who declared that ex-paramilitaries 'would need to be "house trained" before they could enter the Northern Ireland Executive' (2011: 68), Lehner argues that numerous post-millennial texts from Northern Ireland have relocated from the political arena to the domestic one. Through this embrace of 'a feminine domestic side' she argues that Northern Irish 'post-conflict' masculinity undergoes a redemptive process, of sorts. Following on from this, then, we can read the feminisation of Sands and Gillen as an attempt to redeem their violent masculinity for contemporary audiences.

McQueen might have claimed that he 'didn't think *Hunger* is a political film, it's a human film'; but, setting aside the immediately politicised nature of his subject matter, his feminisation of these masculine Irish bodies is both political in itself and draws on a lengthy history of the discursive production of Ireland as a gendered space (see Crowdus 2009: 25). For English, and subsequently British, colonial discourse has sought to feminise Irish territory while it demonised Irish men as hyper-masculine and hyper-violent. From the early seventeenth century onwards, in line with imperial discourse in both the Old and New Worlds, Ireland was discursively constructed as a feminised territory ripe for the penetration of reinvigorated colonial powers. In a frequently quoted passage, written in 1620, Luke Gernon states that the 'Nymph of Ireland is at all parts like a young wench that hath the green sickness for want of occupying' (1966: 242). Feminised Ireland was virgin territory and yet 'the sexual promiscuity of Irish women was used as proof of the barbarity of the people' (Nash 1997: 112). In the late nineteenth century Ernest Renan declared, in *The Poetry of the Celtic Races*, that the Celtic race 'is an essentially feminine' one (1897: 8), thereby cementing the feminisation of the Irish that had begun centuries previously. Matthew Arnold, the English cultural critic also maintained that 'the sensibility of the Celtic nature, its nervous exaltation, have something feminine in them, and the Celt is peculiarly disposed to feel the spell of the feminine idiosyncrasy' (1962: 357). This discourse helped to purport the notion that these effeminate 'Celts' could not be trusted to govern themselves and so needed the firm hand of imperial paternalism to rule for them.

Conversely, writing just a few decades earlier than Gernon (quoted above), Edmund Spenser, in *A View from the Present State of Ireland* (1596), 'constructed [the Irish] as marauding males, prone to theft, torture and rape' and 'imagined [them] in terms of a supposedly resolute virility' (Jones and Stallybrass 1992: 163). Furthermore, after finding themselves at the receiving end of a discourse that attempted to construct the Irish as passive, emotional, sentimental and incompetent, anti-colonial nationalism sought to vigorously assert the strength of Irish masculinity which, as Elizabeth Butler Cullingford has noted, might be more accurately described as the 'hyper-masculinity' (1990: 6) that Ashis Nandy (1983) locates in some anti-colonial movements. It is perhaps this anti-colonial construction of hyper-masculinity that prompted Prime Minister Margaret Thatcher to ask if the Long Kesh hunger strikers were trying to 'to prove their virility' with their fasting (quoted in Beresford 1987: 212). However, what unites discursive constructions of the Irish – feminised and hyper-masculine – is the *sexualized* dimensions of both. In its 'carefully eroticised geography' (Nash 1997: 112), Ireland was either tempting virgin territory, full of licentious women, or populated by rampant, sexually irrepressible men; note how Thatcher uses the word *virility* to describe the hunger strikers, rather than courage, strength or endurance. I would posit that the legacy of both of these ideas about Irishness and gender are at work in McQueen's film. While *Hunger*'s gaze emphasises the beauty and masculinity of its bodies, it also feminises them: a move that is cemented by his decision to avoid engaging with their own violent pasts. Moreover, the hagiographic dimension to the film's subject matter, viscerally rendered by McQueen's cinematography, draws on a historiography of sexually transgressive identities. Finally, this chapter will conclude by turning to Sands' abject and famished body to argue that, in the final section of the film, McQueen's refashioning of the feminine ultimately redeems Sands.

Feminized Fasting: Transgressive Masculinity

The final third of the film charts the agonizing fast and decline of Sands' body as he starves to death. Fassbender himself lost three stone for the role – and was, at his lowest weight, 58kg: the same weight that Bobby Sands was at in the final entry in his diary. Whereas in the earlier parts of the film the camera lingers over Sands' muscles, this final section of the film turns its gaze toward his body in its abjection. An excerpt from another one of Margaret Thatcher's speeches is utilised to signal the transition into the hunger strike: 'Faced with the failure of their discredited cause, the men of violence have chosen in recent months to play what may well be their last card. They have turned their violence against themselves through the prison hunger strike to death.' This speech encapsulates the contradictory logic by which the hunger strike sought to operate; turning the body of the aggressor – the masculine, violent paramilitary soldier – into that of the victim. While it is certainly true, as Pine argues, that the film's 'stress on victimhood' works to ensure that the 'controversial politics of terrorism are abandoned' (2014: 159, 163), the film's depiction of somatic suffering foregrounds the subversive gender politics that this entails. *Hunger*'s final section affirms the primacy of the body to Sands' protest: there are protracted shots of his concave stomach, protruding hipbones, sunken ribcage and wasted muscle. Like other earlier shots of Gillen and Sands, the face is often obscured in these shots of body parts, dismembering Sands and insisting on his status as object rather than subject. Laura Mulvey's comments that the female body, which is 'stylised and fragmented by close-ups, is the content of the film and the direct recipient of the spectator's look' are equally applicable to Sands' abject male body. In one scene, Sands tenderly strokes his own ribs, truly highlighting the exhibited nature of his corporeal spectacle. There is also some argument that within an Irish context, the famished bodies of famine victims are thought of as particularly associated with the feminine. Margaret Kelleher has written about the extensive use of the starving female body as a trope for the national devastation of the Irish Famine (1845–52), noting that 'the representation of famine and its effects' is often done 'through images of women' (1997: 2).

In addition to the gaze upon Sands' shocking skeletal appearance, this section of the film maintains its previous scrutinising focus on bodily fluids. After the extended dialogue scene in the middle of the film, there is a scene within which the prisoners flood the corridor of H-Block with their urine, and it is this scene that transitions into the final section of the film: Sands' fast to death. Although we do not see the prisoners flood the floor, we do watch a warder mop up their urine in real-time; this scene takes over two and a half minutes. Prolonged, deliberate scenes such as this and an earlier scene where we watch faeces on the cell wall get washed away, force the viewer to engage with the filth within which the prisoners lived. In addition to this, the focus on the bodily fluids of the protestors works to further destabilise their gendered identities.

In Western thought, bodily fluids have been associated with the unstable, leaking nature of feminine corporeality. *Hunger* revels in its depiction of the porous, viscous nature of the prisoners' bodies, and the emphasis on this is even more pronounced in the final section of the film: we watch Sands have blood taken from him; we watch him urinate in a cup; we look at his blood and pus-stained sheets. Most troubling of all, Sands fills a toilet with blood. The vibrancy of his red blood in the toilet bowl is exacerbated by the lack of colour and the medical whiteness of the final third of the film. It is also, however, a curious paradox. In filling a toilet bowl, it is evocative of women's menstrual blood, and therefore furthering Sands' gender-neutral state, but it also underlines the exclusion of female agency. We are asked to look at Sands' blood as visceral evidence of his masculine struggle; the actual blood

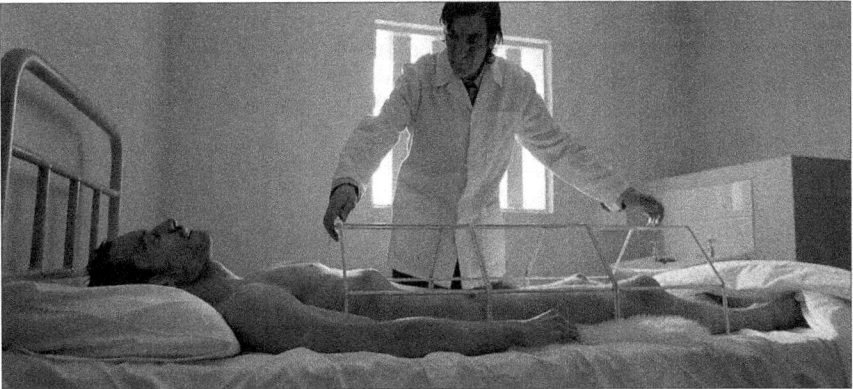

Fig. 2: Sands' emaciated body.

of menstruation from the women's bodies of the Armagh Prison dirty protest is still too abject to be screened.[7] Male blood is art; female blood is unspeakable.

Sands' most explicitly gender-transgressive moment happens during this final section. His abject, naked body is laid out on his bed in the hospital wing as he waits for his sheets to be changed. The shot is strikingly imitative of the early sixteenth-century painting 'The Body of the Dead Christ in the Tomb' by Hans Holbein the Younger (1520–22). Those familiar with the image will be reminded, again, of McQueen's desire to visually equate Sands with Christ. But the image is also highly feminised: the angle through which the shot is framed means that you cannot see his penis, instead viewers are confronted only with a mound of pubic hair.[8] Given the earlier shots of both Gillen's and Gerry Campbell's (Liam McMahon) penises – albeit brief, but entirely without self-consciousness – this seems like a calculating aesthetic choice. Retrospectively, after *Shame*, the second collaboration between McQueen and Fassbender, this decision seems even more conspicuous: it is evident that neither McQueen nor Fassbender has any qualms about full-frontal male nudity. However, this move by McQueen both feminises Sands' body *and* keeps his masculinity unscathed, for, as Peter Lehman has argued, 'dominant representations of phallic masculinity in our culture depend on keeping the male body and their genitals out of the critical spotlight' (2007: 30). This feminisation of Sands' body works to cancel the excessive, troubled reaches of his masculinity, as a violent member of the Provisional IRA, but the refusal to include his genitals in this shot ensures that he retains a solemn dignity.

Conclusion

As a hagiography of sorts, the film lingers on the beaten, vulnerable and penetrated masculine body; as a narrative about a physical protest that used bodily waste as a weapon, the focus on the fluid excesses of corporeality further complicates strictly policed cultural ideas about gendered bodies. In presenting his male leads as eroticised in the first sections of the film, and passively suffering by the conclusion of the film, McQueen feminises the bodies of these paramilitary prisoners. However, while *Hunger* can indulge in transgressive gendered identities, it is important to recognise that it is still only masculinity that is presented in a subversive manner and his appropriation of the feminine to redeem his masculine subjects is troubling. *Hunger*'s women, on the sidelines of the film, are still deeply conditioned by gender norms, as its watchful wives, sorrowful mothers and silent girlfriends testify. Furthermore, McQueen's use of Margaret Thatcher could also be read as problematic; it is noticeable that her disembodied voice is often invoked when our onscreen male subjects are at their most vulnerable (or, in the case of the urine scene mentioned above, to indicate the transition to Sands at his most vulnerable). In her essay asking 'Is the Gaze Male?', E. Ann Kaplan highlights that 'our culture is deeply committed to clearly demarcated sex differences'; therefore, 'when the man steps out of his traditional role as the one who controls the whole action', the woman 'nearly always loses her traditionally feminine characteristics on so doing – not those of attractiveness, but rather of kindness, humaneness, motherliness' (2000: 129). If the male subject deviates from the heteronormative positions and behaviours that we expect of him, the female becomes 'cold, driving, ambitious, manipulating' (ibid.). While Thatcher's hard-line response to the hunger strike and antipathy towards Republican and paramilitary violence more broadly is undeniable, the aesthetic use of her disembodied voice within the film's gender-tableaux places her in the role of aggressor. So while we might read the transgressive bodies of the prisoners as seeking to destabilise traditionally gendered-ways of seeing, *Hunger* still cannot sustain genuinely subversive gender politics and McQueen's use of the feminine seeks only to absolve his male subjects of their violent pasts.

Notes

1 I am very grateful to Dr Stefanie Lehner (Queen's University Belfast) and Dr Aaron Kelly (University of Edinburgh) for their insightful feedback on earlier drafts of this chapter.
2 The hunger strike of 1981 was the culmination of five years of protest activity aimed at securing the reinstating of 'Special Category Status' (the acknowledgement of Prisoner of War status) for Republican paramilitary prisoners and the satisfaction of five basic demands. These demands included: the right not to wear a prison uniform; the right not to do prison work; the right of free association with other prisoners, and to organise educational and recreational pursuits; the right to one visit, one letter and one parcel per week; full restoration of remission lost through the protest. Special Category Status was removed in 1976 and, in protest, prisoners first went on the blanket protest (refusal to wear prison uniform), followed, in response to increasing brutality at the hands of prison staff, by the dirty protest (refusal to 'slop out' in cell chamber pots). On 1 March 1981, Bobby Sands went on hunger strike, followed two weeks later by Francis Hughes. In all, ten men died on this hunger strike, including Raymond McCreesh, Patsy O'Hara, Joe McDonnell, Martin Hurson, Kevin Lynch, Kieran Doherty, Thomas McElwee and Michael Devine.
3 See Lehner and McGrattan (2012) and Pine (2014) for further discussion about the film's politics.
4 See Ellmann (1993) for a discussion of the silence of the hunger strikers themselves and contemplation of the parallels between the disciplining of oral space in relation to both food and speech.
5 Sedgwick writes that the 'phobic prohibition' of Catholicism is also 'famous for giving countless gay and proto-gay children the shock of the possibility of adults who don't marry, of men in dresses, of passionate theatre, of introspective investment, of lives filled with what could, ideally without diminution, be called the work of the fetish' (1990: 140).
6 *Some Mother's Son*, screenplay by Terry George and Jim Sheridan (1996: Castle Rock Entertainment, Hell's Kitchen Films). Both films, however, include moments highlighting the phallic threat of the truncheon in the hands of prison warders. I should also mention that when the two Provisional IRA prisoners, Quigley and Higgins, are welcomed onto their H-block, they are still half-naked but this is unproblematic nudity: we are to read their bodies as emblems of warrior-like, Celtic masculinity. Their walk along the corridor is accompanied by the beat of traditional Irish music; their neat patches of chest hair are

testament to their unquestionable masculinity; and they are welcomed by jubilant shouts in Gaelic from their fellow paramilitaries.
7 The dirty protest and hunger strike of Armagh Women's Prison are the subjects of Maeve Murphy's *Silent Grace* (2011).
8 Interesting parallels might be drawn here between Sands/Fassbender's body and those from medieval visual culture of 'castrated' Christ and other saints; see Mills 2001: 18–19, 31.

Bibliography

Arnold, M. (1962). *Complete Prose Works of Matthew Arnold: Lectures and Essays on Criticism*. Ann Arbor: University of Michigan Press.
Beresford, D. (1987) *Ten Men Dead: The Story of the 1981 Irish Hunger Strike*. London: Grafton.
Burns, P. (2013). 'Rethinking the Armagh Woman's Dirty Protest', in N. Giffney and M. Shildrick (eds) *Theory on the Edge: Irish Studies and the Politics of Sexual Difference*. Basingstoke: Palgrave Macmillan, 29–37.
Cox, D. (2008) '*Hunger* strikes a very sour note', *The Guardian*, 3 November.
Crowdus, G. (2009) 'The Human Body as Political Weapon: An Interview with Steve McQueen', *Cinéaste*, 34, 2, 22–5.
Cullingford, E. B. (1990) 'Thinking of Her … as … Ireland': Yeats, Pearse and Heaney', *Textual Practice*, 4, 1, 1–21.
Dyer, R. (2002) *Only Entertainment*. London: Routledge.
Ellmann, M. (1993) *The Hunger Artists: Starving, Writing, and Imprisonment*. Cambridge, MA: Harvard University Press.
Feldman, A. (1991). *Formations of Violence: the Narrative of the Body and Political Terror in Northern Ireland*. London: University of Chicago Press.
Foucault, M. (1995). *Discipline and Punish: the Birth of the Prison*. New York: Vintage Books.
Gernon, L. ([1620] 1966). 'A Discourse on Ireland', in J. P. Myers (ed.) *Elizabethan Ireland: A Selection of Writings by Elizabethan Writers on Ireland*. Hamden: Archon Books, 242–3.
Gravdal, K. (1991) *Ravishing Maidens: Writing Rape in Medieval French Literature and Law*. Philadelphia, PA: University of Pennsylvania Press.
Harris, S. C. (2002) *Gender and Modern Irish Drama*. Bloomington, IN: Indiana University Press.
Jones, A. R. and P. Stallybrass (1992) 'Dismantling Irena: The Sexualizing of Ireland in Early Modern England', in A. Parker, M. Russo, D. Sommer and P. Yeager (eds) *Nationalisms and Sexualities*. London: Routledge, 157–71.
Kaplan, E. A. (2000) 'Is the Gaze Male?', in E. A. Kaplan (ed.) *Feminism and Film*. Oxford: Oxford University Press, 119–38.
Kearney, R. (1984). *Myth and Motherland*. Derry: Field Day.
Kelleher, M. (1997) *The Feminization of Famine: Expressions of the Inexpressible?* Cork: Cork University Press.
Lehman, P. (2007) *Running Scared: Masculinity and the Representation of the Male Body*. Detroit, MI: Wayne State University Press.

Lehner, S. (2011) 'Post-Conflict Masculinities: Filiative Reconciliation in *Five Minutes of Heaven* and David Park's *The Truth Commissioner*', in C. Magennis and R. Mullen (eds) *Irish Masculinities: Reflections on Literature and Culture*. Dublin: Irish Academic Press, 65–76.

Lehner, S. and C. McGrattan (2012) 'Re/Presenting Victimhood: Nationalism, Victims and Silences in Northern Ireland', *Nordic Irish Studies*, 11, 2, 39–53.

Mills, R. (2001) '"Whatever you do is a delight to me!": Masculinity, Masochism and Queer Play in Representations of Male Martyrdom', *Exemplaria*, 13, 1, 1–37.

―― (2005) *Suspended Animation: Pain, Pleasure and Punishment in Medieval Culture*. London: Reaktion.

Mulvey, L. ([1975] 2000) 'Visual Pleasure and Narrative Cinema', in E. A Kaplan (ed.) *Feminism and Film*. Oxford: Oxford University Press, 34–47.

Nandy, A. (1983) *The Intimate Enemy: Loss and Recovery of Self Under Colonialism*. Oxford: Oxford University Press.

Nash, C. (1997) 'Embodied Irishness: Gender, Sexuality and Irish identities', in B. Graham (ed.) *In Search of Ireland: A Cultural Geography*. Abingdon: Routledge, 108–27.

Neale, S. ([1981] 2000) 'Masculinity as Spectacle: Reflections on Men and Mainstream Cinema,' in E. A Kaplan (ed.) *Feminism and Film*. Oxford: Oxford University Press, 253–64.

Pearse, P. (n.d.). *Political Writings and Speeches*. Dublin: Phoenix Publishing Company.

Pheasant-Kelly, F. (2014) 'Reframing Gender and Visual Pleasure: New Signifying Practices in Contemporary Cinema,' in G. Padva & N. Buchweitz (eds) *Sensational Pleasures in Cinema, Literature and Visual Culture: The Phallic Eye*. Basingstoke: Palgrave Macmillan, 196–212.

Pine, E. (2014) 'Body of Evidence: Performing *Hunger*', in C. Holohan and T. Tracy (eds) *Masculinity and Irish Popular Culture: Tiger's Tales*. Basingstoke: Palgrave Macmillan, 159–70.

Renan, E. (1896) *The Poetry of the Celtic Races and Other Studies*. London: Walter Scott.

Sedgwick, E. K. (1990) *Epistemology of the Closet*. London: Penguin.

Chapter 5
Male-Nutrition: Extreme Weight Loss, Socio-Cultural Transgression and the Male Body in Recent American Cinema

TOM STEWARD

In the last quarter-century of American cinema, there have been several notable instances of high-profile male film actors shedding significant weight and appearing onscreen with bodies unhealthily reduced in size, having taken on some degree of emaciation. Superficially, these actors have manipulated their bodies in preparation for shooting with diet, exercise and lifestyle changes to produce a viscerally authentic manifestation of the result (or by-product) of an illness that affects the body physically, such as insomnia, the HIV/AIDS virus, drug addiction and cancer. However, in all but the rarest cases, the underweight male body is identified with social and cultural transgression to the point of synonymy. This is in addition to any transgressive qualities associated with the specific affliction the characters possess and pertains to the audio-visual representation of the body and its configuration in the film's social and cultural contexts. In particular, these bodies challenge and disrupt traditional notions of masculinity, such as physical dominance over women and preparedness for action. The underweight male body transgresses gender boundaries, by problematising both the masculinity of the character within the diegesis of the film and conventional depictions of the male body in film and popular culture more generally. The irony is that in creating bodies which enact and epitomise disregard for socio-cultural norms, these actors have achieved far greater standing and acceptance within cultural hierarchies, such as the film and acting establishment of Hollywood and celebrity and lifestyle elites.

This chapter examines qualities of socio-cultural transgression, unstable masculinity and extra-textual cultural legitimacy accompanying the underweight male body in three recent American movies featuring performances by Hollywood star actors who have undergone extreme weight loss in preparation for their roles. While a number of performances could potentially be discussed – Matt Damon in *Courage Under Fire* (Edward Zwick, 1996), 50 Cent in *All Things Fall Apart* (Mario Van Peebles, 2011), Michael Fassbender in *Hunger* (Steve McQueen, 2008), Tom Hanks in both *Philadelphia* (Jonathan Demme, 1993) and *Cast Away* (Robert Zemeckis, 2000) – I have chosen Edward Norton and Brad Pitt's performances as (dually) Tyler Durden in *Fight Club* (David Fincher, 1999), Christian Bale's portrayal of Trevor Reznik in *The Machinist* (Brad Anderson, 2004) and Matthew McConaughey's depiction of Ron Woodruff in *Dallas Buyers Club* (Jean-Marc Vallee, 2013). While each of the comparative references above illustrate the relationship between underweight male bodies and transgression to some extent – Hanks is, after all, playing social outcasts (the latter quite literally) in both movies – my three case studies best exemplify the myriad of ways that the underweight male body resists and deviates from social and cultural conventions, laws and orthodoxies. As films which visually fetishise the body, male form and weight loss and make clear the connection between the body and society, they speak specifically to the key issues of this chapter's investigation. Each film notably addresses transgressive bodies through the prism of gender and masculinity and demonstrates how cultivating an underweight body enhances male actors' cultural status rather than marginalising them. These transgressive bodies are only attached to the stars temporarily as, once shooting is complete, they can return to their prior physiques, which are generally buff and masculine. Therefore, the actors can circumvent the social stigma of promoting unhealthy, emasculated bodies in the media and instead become icons of bodily transformation. Furthermore, the historical spread of these films suggests tropism rather than contemporaneity.

These arguments build upon, and are impossible without, an understanding based on the work of Mary Douglas that maps bodies on to society's order and relations and considers bodily representations in a 'social dimension' (1970: 70). As these are Hollywood films with stars made in and/or about late twentieth-century culture, we can relate Douglas's equivalence to specific historical and industrial contexts using Mike Featherstone, who argues that 'inner and outer body' are aligned within 'consumer culture', and sees Hollywood movies and stars promoting notions of the outer body as representation of self (1982: 118, 28). Andrew Tudor applies Douglas by attributing 'unruly bodies' in late twentieth-century horror film to 'disorder and incoherence in social life' of the time (1995: 40). In specific terms of the underweight male body (and the case studies), Sherryl Vint and Mark Bould have identified Christian Bale/Trevor Reznik's body in *The Machinist* as symptomatic of 'resistance to alienation' under late capitalism (2009: 229). Similarly, the discussion of gender in this chapter must be contextualised within critical paradigms of representing male bodies in cinema and culture. It should be noted that the underweight male body departs from the 'muscularity' and 'strength and vitality' that Richard Dyer argues 'legitimises male power and domination' (1982: 67, 69). It also challenges Peter Lehman's notion that traditionally 'ugly or misshapen' male bodies are compensated for by physical attributes of power and strength to re-instate male subjectivity and authority (2007: 12–13). Indeed, these bodies are more akin to the fragmentation and objectification that Lehman argues signifies a loss of power (2007: 19).

Scholarly precedent for parallels between 'bodily disintegration and collapse' and 'transgress[ing] cultural categories' derives from Tudor's article, 'Unruly Bodies, Unquiet Minds' (1995: 29, 31). He identifies 'bodily destruction and ... decay' in modern horror cinema as 'signifiers of transgression' and contends 'taken-for-granted boundaries of gender are problematized' (1995: 31). While the anxieties of late twentieth-century social experience are still relevant to my argument given the movies' historical contexts, I apply Tudor's observations to cinema beyond the genre of 'modern body horror' (1995: 39).[1] The duality of disintegrating bodies transgressing both gender and wider cultural conventions is also a useful paradigm. Vint and Bould's 'The Thin Men' discusses 'anorexic subjects' in both *Fight Club* and *The Machinist* (2009: 222). Interestingly, anorexia is explored as a potential protest of late capitalist alienation and consumption, and though Trevor's dissent against capitalist labour is linked to his 'emaciation' (2009: 229), neither his nor Tyler Durden's bodies are described as anorexic, and their account of *Fight Club* uses anorexia as a metaphor for a rejection of consumer culture, leaving aside the proximity of the underweight body to that of an anorexic altogether. I applaud the acute distinctions the authors make to prevent conflating underweight bodies with the disorder of anorexia and the notion of the body's socio-cultural 'resistance' (ibid.) is clearly applicable to the idea of transgression. However, this chapter will address how *Fight Club* maps social protest visually and viscerally on to the body as well as symbolically.

Fight Club

Edward Norton plays an unnamed protagonist, the Narrator, losing weight due to chronic insomnia.[2] A loss adjuster by day, at nights he does odd jobs as alter-ego Tyler Durden, a personality who starts to intrude on his regular life until his consciousness is split. Tyler is played by Brad Pitt and for the majority of the movie is assumed by Norton's character and the viewer to be a separate entity. While Norton and Pitt have muscular definition on their torsos, both actors are noticeably underweight in the roles. For the Narrator, this body is a result of both his insomnia and the physical discipline and punishment he subjects himself to, first as president of an underground boxing club and then as the leader of an urban paramilitary unit. In interviews online, Norton acknowledged he lost weight to symbolise how the character was 'falling apart' and a metaphorical 'junkie'. Though the viewer may attribute Pitt's body to the gruelling activities he shares with Norton's character, its diminished state is a clue to the eventual twist that they are one and the same person. Norton shed between around sixteen pounds for the role. Pitt embarked on a fat-burning diet and workout regime pre-production that reduced his body fat to five percent, rather than it being the product of digital manipulation, as Vint and Bould erroneously claim (2009: 232). While Pitt's chest and abdomen are considerably more sculpted and toned than Norton's, whose upper body reveals considerable emaciation, both actors appear to have abnormally reduced bodies.

It is not merely the appearances of the actors but visual contrasts within the *mise-en-scène* of *Fight Club* that highlight and exacerbate the underweight male body. Notable here is the juxtaposition of Norton's character with the corpulent body of cancer survivor Bob (Meat Loaf), as the Narrator is slammed against his engorged stomach and oversized breasts both vertically and horizontally in tight close-ups during the group therapy and fight scenes, and Tyler's beating of an obese club owner, which lacks narrative purpose except to exaggerate the disparity between the respective shapes of their bodies. Indeed, the frequency with which Norton and Pitt appear nude or semi-naked – legitimised by the proclivity for fight and sex scenes throughout the film – reinforces the difference of the actors' bodies from more socially representative male physiques that appear. There is a tension here, however, as the film wishes to normalise the underweight male body as much as it wants to fetishise it. The muscular definition of Norton and Pitt's upper bodies, complemented by warm lighting in the fight scenes which both shapes and textures the muscles, makes them look positively healthy against the other victims of bodily illness we encounter, such as the pale and gaunt terminal cancer patient Chloe (Rachel Singer). As Tyler's two bodies routinely bear the damage of disfigurements, bruises and injuries from self-harm, their unhealthy weight becomes more difficult to elicit from other physical deformities. Therein lies *Fight Club*'s ambivalence about the underweight male body as both socio-culturally conventional and yet transgressive.

The underweight male body is contradictorily positioned as simultaneously a product of late capitalist consumer society and a rejection of its excesses. As a symptom of insomnia contracted from long working hours and moonlighting, the Narrator and Tyler's underweight bodies can be related to the loss of job security and de-unionising of labour in late twentieth-century American society. Its minimal weight can be seen as an outcome of the 'single-serving' culture of processed food and commodities that the Narrator encounters in his 'tiny life' while his and Tyler's theft of body fat taken during liposuction reminds us that unnatural removal of body fat is a mainstream cultural norm. The irony of Tyler and the Narrator's balking at the masculinity of an underwear model in a public ad for Calvin Klein is that their bodies are as excessively thin as his and that they display their bodies for other men as routinely and corporately as the model in their national boxing franchise. It is this ambiguous relationship between body and society that causes Vint and Bould to use the metaphor of 'anorexia' in relation to *Fight Club* since the disorder is associated with affluent Western societies yet a rejection of its conspicuous consumption (2009: 223). The authors also note that the film's anorexic aspirations are undermined by its commodity fetishism, which accurately diagnoses its conflicting attitudes towards mainstream culture and society (2009: 227). Yet this social dialectic is not merely connected to the body by allegory but also by interactions of the underweight body with its socio-cultural contexts.

The underweight body also fights against the surplus consumption and melodramatic emotion of its society and culture. The Narrator is seen ordering a full set of Ikea furniture for his apartment from a catalogue while sitting on his bathroom toilet, the simultaneity of which sees his bingeing on commodities immediately repudiated into bodily waste and rejected by the reduced mass of his body. The Narrator and Tyler's reconstitution of liposuction by-product as department store soap uses lost body fat to curb excessive consumption by making it part of one continuous cycle, and the process even ends up further taking from the body as the 'chemical burn' of the lye used to make the soap removes the Narrator's flesh from his hand. The gross sentimentality of support group culture is represented through

Fig. 1: Tyler's (Brad Pitt) feminised clothing in *Fight Club* (1999).

Bob's obese body and excessively fatty 'bitch tits', seen in gargantuan close-up as he clutches the Narrator's body to his breast(s), and which Norton with his small frame protests. Returning to Tudor, we can see this is an instance where disruption and decay of the male body creates a loss of cultural boundaries seen in terms of sex and gender (1995: 32). As the Narrator's body disappears, it is met with Bob's challenge to traditional male physicality and behaviour as an openly affectionate man with female breasts. Similarly, it is apparent that as Tyler is removed further and further from society with his guerrilla terrorist activities, his clothing becomes more androgynous and even feminine, as it begins to resemble Marla's (Helena Bonham Carter) costuming.

The underweight male body is presented as conducive to acts of cultural terrorism and vandalism. Tyler poisons the food in a high-end restaurant when working as a waiter by urinating and defecating in containers holding the various menu items. Both the bodily functions implicit in the act and those it will compel in the diners who consume the food may produce an underweight body. In fact, one of Tyler's pranks on wealthy, conspicuous consumers is to make seagulls defecate on parked BMW cars, which consolidates the synonymy between bodily waste and cultural sabotage. The applicants for Tyler's Project Mayhem who terrorise and destroy the property of the city's financial elites are required to go without sleep or food for three days, deprivation that results in a significant loss of body weight. As all of Tyler and Project Mayhem's attacks on dominant society are made under the cover of night, it is having a body that can function without sleep that permits subversion. The interconnectedness of the dieted, disciplined body with attacks on consumption and consumer goods demonstrates that *Fight Club*'s integration of the body and society disrupts cultural ideals observed by Featherstone which associate 'body maintenance' with the sale and fetishism of commodities (1982: 19), while preserving, through Pitt, the role of Hollywood cinema and stars to promote bodily discipline (1982: 23). Outside consumer culture, such a body is also resisting the social systems and services that provide a safety net for its citizens, as demonstrated when the Narrator refuses Marla's (stolen) meals-on-wheels package.

Norton and Pitt's bodies are clearly meant as parodies of contemporaneous male body images. The bodies themselves are impossibilities; sculpted muscular physiques cancelled out by anorexic levels of weight loss and emaciation, both of which are fetishised equally by lighting and close-up. Their grooming and washing in preparation for fights is undercut by the physical abnormality they receive as a result. It seems deliberate irony that the Calvin Klein model Tyler objects to has the same body that Pitt himself famously possessed, and still possesses here in miniature form. Though there was always a danger of Pitt's stardom and pin-up status resulting in an objectification and eroticisation of Tyler's underweight male body, the actor's bodily preparations have permitted him to be a celebrity icon of male fitness and lifestyle in the media. Men's blogs, books and magazines such as *Fitness B & W*, *The Brad Pitt Diet* and *Esquire* identify Pitt's *Fight Club* body cultivation as an effective weight loss solution for men, the key to a coveted 'metrosexual' look and lifestyle (see Olesker 2015), and a sought-after celebrity physique (see Rawden 2014; Rhoades 2014). While the androgyny that the media associated with Pitt's Tyler Durden image suggests that they recognise the loss of traditional masculinity implied by the underweight body, the focus in these articles on abnormally 'low body fat percentage' as the most desired quality of his look and shape indicates that its other transgressive qualities have not been acknowledged. The reaction to Pitt's *Fight Club* body exemplifies Featherstone's argument that movie stars' health regimes promote discourses of 'body maintenance' in consumer culture (1982: 24), even if the film may actually satirise it.

The Machinist

Trevor Reznik is a factory worker who claims to not have slept for over a year, resulting in a dramatic loss of weight. Insomnia is the primary cause of Trevor's physical state, though the dénouement of the film reveals this in turn was the form his guilt and mental anguish took over killing a child in a hit-and-run accident. Trevor is played by Christian Bale, who dropped over sixty pounds in four months in preparation for the role using a combination of a strict, low-calorie diet and rigorous workouts. In the role, Bale appears with a completely gaunt face, upper body thoroughly emaciated – even 'skeletal' (Vint and Bould 2009: 222) – with visible ribs, severely contracted abdomen and an extremely narrow waist and hips. As Vint and Bould report, stories have mounted in the media about Bale's excessive dieting, unhealthy consumption of drugs and alcohol, and weight loss surplus to the demands of the role (2009: 236). These anecdotes about Bale's bodily suffering during production continue to circulate (mainly due to a recent interview with co-star Michael Ironside), with testimony to his posterior muscles collapsing and losing more weight than necessary because of body mass index miscalculations. These are in keeping with the conflation of Bale's star image with 'will-to-body transformation' (ibid.), evident in the recurrent loss and gain of weight and muscle for roles in movies such as *Batman Begins* (Christopher Nolan, 2005), *The Fighter* (David O. Russell, 2010) and *American Hustle* (David O. Russell, 2013). To wit, the majority of a 2008 BBC Wales Arts interview with Bale was spent discussing his weight and body transformations.

Though hardly necessary to do more than simply document Bale's body for the audience to conceive how drastically underweight it is, the director chooses to

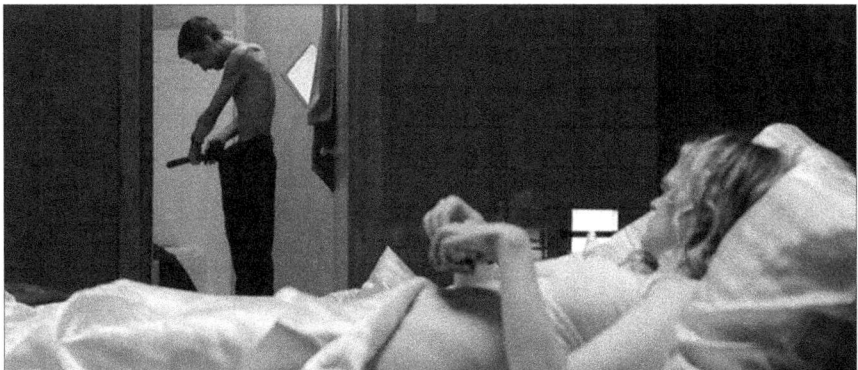

Fig. 2: Trevor's (Christian Bale) body in profile in *The Machinist* (2004).

magnify and accentuate the actor's physique to the point of spectacle. Hence the body is shot predominantly in profile and often filmed without cut-aways, including a particularly gruesome long take in which Trevor stands at a right angle in an open kitchen doorway and Bale creates the illusion of his midriff disappearing for a second. Bale is frequently directed to reclining and bending poses, such as lying in bed (despite Trevor's insomnia) and picking up clothes from the floor, allowing the audience to see bones and joints poke through the skin as they would the muscles of a circus strongman. The washed-out colour palette of the cinematography adds another element of gauntness to Bale's skin while at points he is given ill-fitting shirts and trousers to hang off his body and reveal the stark contrast between his frame and an average body. The spectral colour and shadow of the film expressively aligns Trevor's body with the supernatural, along with the association between Trevor and gothic monsters and underworlds as he descends into the sewers and compares himself to a werewolf. Some of the high-pitched radiophonic sounds on the incidental soundtrack reminiscent of classic B-movie science-fiction associate Trevor with audio filmic imagery of the extra-terrestrial. Curiosity value aside, *The Machinist* carries through the notion that Trevor represents a transgression unknown to society.

Trevor's body comes about as a result of contraventions of society's laws, conventions and routines. By refusing to sleep and continuing to work, he defies organised patterns of labour, rest and time which produce a body dually worn down by manual toil and a lack of physical recovery. Vint and Bould correctly identify 'the horror of a body reduced to mere labour power' as a critique of 'alienation' in late capitalist labour (ibid.), which conforms to the authors' impression of Trevor's condition as, like anorexia, 'a disease of affluent, industrialised societies' (2009: 225). However, Trevor/Bale's physical state more than 'materially embodies' labour orthodoxy; it is a consequence of him challenging it. Vint and Bould have it that Trevor's 'starvation' is a bodily protest against his powerlessness and slavery in industry, revealing the truth of what capitalism does to workers' bodies (2009: 231–2). These concepts are clearly present in the relationship of Trevor's body to industrial labour, but are configured differently than the authors have suggested. Trevor's co-worker Miller (Michael Ironside) is a better example of what capitalist industry does to workers' bodies, having to suffer being maimed before his bosses will pay him a salary he can live on comfortably and relying on the safety net provided to him through workers' insurance and union membership. Trevor's 'starvation' (Vint and Bould 2009: 231), on the other hand, demonstrates the dangers of being an individual that dares to live outside the ordered system of mechanised labour.

As we learn that Trevor's insomnia is a consequence of killing a young boy in a car accident and fleeing the scene, we encounter the possibility that his emaciated body is an effect of committing a violent crime against law and conventional morality that has gone unpunished. The final shot of Trevor falling asleep on the hard bed of a police cell once he has confessed confirms that this illegal, amoral act created his present body. We can add to this Trevor's flouting of sexual criminal law and traditional morality by having sex with a prostitute during his sleepless nights, which perpetuates the insomnia that forges his body. In relation to gender, we can see that the lifestyle which maintains Trevor's underweight body runs counter to his participation in heteronormative behaviour and accepted masculine practices. Trevor refuses to engage in homosocial rituals such as drinking in bars or going fishing with his male co-workers. We note from the co-workers' conversations that he once did accept invitations and later see a photograph feature a slightly overweight Trevor from previous years with co-worker Reynolds on a fishing trip.[3] The disparate body size in the photograph suggests that Trevor's skeletal physique negates his ability to partake in male culture. Trevor's body has none of the 'substitute phallic powers' that Lehman argues can re-masculinise a flawed male body (2007: 13), underscored by the impossibility of becoming a patriarch in his current condition as he merely fantasises a domestic life with single mother Marie (Aitana Sánchez-Gijón).

Vint and Bould make a compelling case that Trevor's body manifests a 'resistance to alienation' of 'labour conditions' (2009: 229, 230) and the way the action plays out against a background of worker dissent, union unrest and industrial accidents gives their assumptions credence. However, the underweight male body is not just a site of industrial malaise but of wider cultural concerns and gender problems and tensions. Trevor's emaciated body dispels late capitalist society's myth of 'body maintenance' combatting 'deterioration and decay' as well as concomitant associations in consumer culture of 'slimness', 'energy' and 'vitality' (Featherstone 1982: 18, 25). Bale's lack of muscle prevents the symbolic associations of men's bodies with the phallus and, in turn, male power that Dyer has discussed in relation to the male pin-up (1982: 66) while his anorexic-like appearance displays the absence of a strong male body that is synonymous with a loss of patriarchal power and control. Furthermore, Trevor's transgressive body challenges normalised paradigms of social protest. His socio-cultural transgressions are seen in contrast to conventional forms of deviancy, such as drinking, drugs and illicit sex, as well as means of defying social restrictions like suing employers or hedonism through bodily excess. He is dislocated from both his co-workers' conversations about drinking and illicit sexual encounters, and his own encounters with public sex, drink and drugs at the Boiler Room bar. Trevor does not seek to profit from his employers for his damaged work body as Miller did and is antithetical to the gratuitous eating, intoxications and reckless driving of his imaginary alter-ego Ivan (John Sharian).

Bale's diet and body would not, of course, become the cult object of lifestyle and fitness that Pitt's similarly gruelling exercise regimes and underweight physical form in *Fight Club* did but nor did it do what dangerous weight loss did for Matthew McConaughey in legitimating his worth as an actor. This is perhaps due to playing a character whose body suffers through vice rather than illness, or Bale's masochistic approach to visceral authenticity in performance backfiring by alienating critics rather than impressing them. Online articles accuse Bale of trivialising eating disorders (see Gonzalo 2013) while critic Roger Ebert's 2008 review of *The Machinist* expresses confusion and worry about Bale's condition rather than praise for his efforts. Nonetheless, the process of losing body mass in preparation for a role and appearing onscreen underweight in *The Machinist* helped Bale to forge a celebrity image and brand in the media as an actor who endures physical punishment to undergo bodily transformations for roles, consolidated by his 'bulking up' for *Batman Begins* and weight gain for *American Hustle*. This in turn elevated Bale to the status of the American 'Method' elite within the acting and critical community, known and praised for changing themselves physically to inhabit their characters as fully as possible. When extreme weight loss was aligned to a character with a sickness beyond his control, as with his portrayal of drug-addicted ex-boxer Dickie Eklund in *The Fighter*, Bale was endorsed by the Hollywood establishment with a Best Supporting Actor Academy Award.[4]

Dallas Buyers Club

Based on a historical person, Ron Woodruff is an electrician, small-time criminal and rodeo cowboy in Texas in the mid-1980s who contracts the HIV (and later the AIDS) virus as a result of sex with drug-using women. To portray Ron and his illness, Matthew McConaughey dropped around forty pounds using a controlled diet without exercise. McConaughey is transformed from previous appearances in film, even compared to movies made immediately prior to *Dallas Buyers Club* in which he cosmetically contaminated his clean-cut image.[5] The transformation is particularly noticeable on parts of the body which made McConaughey an object of erotic desire. His handsome face has become gaunt around the neck and cheekbones now protrude. The actor's idolised muscular torso becomes narrow and long. McConaughey looks even thinner towards the end of the movie, an effect achieved by adding minor make-up and prosthetics in earlier scenes to make the actor appear to lose weight as his condition worsens (see Miller 2014). As in *Fight Club* and *The Machinist*, the director uses compositional techniques to underline the loss of body beyond the physical change of a celebrity actor. McConaughey is costumed in oversized clothing throughout the film to emphasise the disparity between the sufferer body and both character and actor in a healthier state, particularly the large Stetson hat which hides his face and dwarfs his body. The director often poses McConaughey's body against columnar lines in frame to demonstrate his stretched torso, such as ceiling beams and the bars of bullpens in the rodeo stadium.

Unlike the other underweight bodies in this chapter where they are the impact of psychological problems, the movie associates McConaughey virus-wasted physique with imagery of promiscuity and AIDS, locating it within the inter-social and medical causes of its condition. It is first seen writhing in intercourse with two anonymous women in the bleachers of a rodeo ring and again later prior to another *ménage à trois* in Ron's trailer. His gaunt face and droopy moustache makes his body a clone of the famous newspaper photograph of Rock Hudson dying from AIDS which Ron and his friends see following the actor's death. Further connections can be made through Hudson's portrayal of a macho Texan in *Giant* (George Stevens, 1956) and parallels between Ron's character arc and Hudson's biographical journey from iconography of masculinity to that of suffering and homosexuality. As Ron comes to terms with his HIV, Kenny Rogers' version of 'Ruby Don't Take your Love to Town' plays on the soundtrack which aurally brings in popular culture signifiers of promiscuous behaviour and lifestyle. Such associations, however, are consonant with a loss of masculinity and even feminisation. We see that virility implies a loss of the strong male body that Lehman argues are compatible in normative representations of men's bodies (2007: 11). The comparison to Hudson questions the veracity of Ron's heterosexuality and alpha-male tendencies. If Rogers' song is an allegory, Ron is Ruby, a character whose permissive sexual activity has led them astray, and thus re-positioned as a female object.

Ron's underweight body signifies the undoing of archetypal modes of traditional masculine behaviour. It is telling that his bodily weakness makes him unable to fight, seen as he swings and collapses both at the hospital porter who refuses him drugs and then at his co-workers in a bar. The 'potential for action' Dyer sees as crucial in demonstrating gender power in representations of the male body is thus inhibited and further shows the underweight body at odds with masculine imagery (1982: 67). Ron's semi-legal sale of contraband drugs to HIV and AIDS victims following self-treatment immerses him in homosexual male community and culture, whether in support groups or gay clubs and bars. This is yet another reason he keeps his Stetson hat on throughout the movie, since it relates to both heterosexual and gay iconography and naturalises his passage from 'straight' mainstream culture to homosexual subculture. Ron's descent to a suffering body brings about a loss of the working-class, agrarian, South-western machismo that supports and stabilises an understanding of his own masculinity. He is ostracised by friends and

Fig. 3: Ron's body and gay subculture, in *Dallas Buyers Club* (2013).

colleagues who communalise that identity and instead surrounds himself with men who identify themselves as effeminate or transgender, such as mid-operative transsexual Rayon (Jared Leto). His business venture compels Ron to pose as social types outside of his status, regionalism and morality, such as jet-setting corporate executives and priests. As Tudor observed of horror cinema, Ron's 'bodily disintegration and collapse' equates to a loss of the fixed boundaries between the body and the social world (1995: 29).

Once again, this body type is synonymous with socio-cultural transgression. The opening scenes contort Ron's body in a litany of petty crime and illegality: gambling, con artistry, assaulting police officers, drug abuse. Given that Ron is identified with promiscuous sex from the outset, his physical suffering is seen in light of a breach of social contracts and moral standards around monogamy and abstinence. This is where *Dallas Buyers Club* differs from *The Machinist* and *Fight Club*. The (somewhat) subversive uses of underweight male bodies in *The Machinist* and *Fight Club* jar with the moral conservatism of *Dallas Buyers Club*'s representation of an unnatural physical state caused by a deviant and perverse lifestyle. Ironically, the former movies are far more sympathetic to the conditions of their protagonists even though they derive solely from their own proclivities rather than an unfortunate and unknowable disease. It's hardly surprising, then, that Ron is seen to use his body to disturb the sanctity of another morally high social institution – the Church – as he repeatedly costumes as a priest to get banned drugs over the Mexican/American border. Ron's transgressions are only forgiven when he uses his disregard for law and systems to protest federal strictures prohibiting drugs that could prolong the lives of HIV and AIDS patients. This, along with Ron's rejection of Food and Drug Administration-approved food to fulfil the mainstream-culture endorsed ideal of 'body maintenance' to promote health and prevent decay (Featherstone 1982: 18), are the terms under which his meagre body is acceptable.

The maintenance of Ron's body depends on abnegation of normative social behaviour. He refuses, unlike the majority of Americans then and now, to eat processed food, preventing his body from further health problems but maintaining his weight. His body defies casual faith citizens have in the American medical establishment, in its various corporate, federal and physician forms. Ron challenges the canon of FDA medicine approval, doctor prescription and private drug sale that conspires to give cell-killing AZT to HIV/AIDS patients. His depleted body speaks of a resistant survival over not just AIDS but also AZT. Ron's body marks his induction into the world of AIDS survival, which comes with a rejection of the widely-held (even by Ron himself) homophobia and bigotry within the heterosexual majority. While it is ambiguous as to whether Ron repudiates his prejudice (at the level of screenplay he does not), acts of the body within the movie suggest this has happened on a symbolic level. Firstly, there is Ron's physical restraint of estranged friend T.J. (Kevin Rankin) forcing the homophobe to shake Rayon's hand, and then Rayon herself, whose gaunt body and pale skin (Leto also lost over forty pounds for the role) is strikingly similar to McConaughey's as Ron.[6] In a less progressive vein, Ron's contempt for heteronormative relationships (marriage, monogamy, intercourse with one partner) is deemed responsible for his continually declining body, with his decision to pursue a tawdry sex life against a relationship with Doctor Eve (Jennifer

Garner) emphasised as his body wastes further. While Ron's return to promiscuity can be seen as him attempting to regain his former masculinity, his failures to maintain physical strength and virility in his later encounters with prostitutes suggests no traditional masculine identities are available to him in his underweight body.

The image of McConaughey as a limited, bland actor cultivated by his appearances in a succession of critically panned movies in culturally derided genres such as romantic comedy was in remission before *Dallas Buyers Club* after acclaimed performances as complex, challenging characters in sophisticated, innovative independent cinema such as *Killer Joe* (2011) and *Mud* (2012). It is clear, however, from media reports that McConaughey's thinned-down performance as Ron Woodruff 'capped' his 'critical resurgence' (Brooks 2014). He received the Best Actor Academy Award as extreme weight loss to play an AIDS victim adhered to Academy conventions for prestigious screen performance based on a glamorous star transforming themselves to the detriment of their appearance to play a 'worthy' character with disability or illness.[7] As with Bale, weight transformation allowed McConaughey to be considered a legitimate 'Method' actor but unlike the former, who has been taken seriously from early (childhood) performances, critics were clear that the weight loss signalled a career shift to more thought-provoking acting material (see Riley 2014).[8] Consistent with the reaction to Bale's weight loss, there were reservations, with some commentators calling it 'dangerous' (Lipton 2014), but McConaughey allayed these anxieties by suggesting in various interviews the worthiness of playing a character with a serious illness (see Percival 2012) and suggesting the process produced in him better citizenry and more engaged cultural membership, in finding sources of recreation and mental stimulation other than eating (see Gusmaroli 2014). McConaughey finds this to parallel Ron's increased social responsibility through weight loss (see Masters 2014). This underlines the irony of McConaughey's increased cultural status through a transgressive body in film.

Conclusion

Though each movie discussed above wields the transgressions of underweight male bodies differently, in all instances it is identified with liminal spaces outlying the mainstream of society. In *Fight Club*, the Narrator and Tyler are found in abandoned, dilapidated houses on the edge of town and fighting in the basements of nightclubs. *The Machinist* has Trevor spending his nights sitting in a diner caught in a limbo between reality and fantasy or a prostitute's apartment, and heads into the city's sewers. With *Dallas Buyers Club*, it is Ron conducting his business and life in trailer parks and motel rooms, closed rodeo rings and gay subculture bars. All bodies are identified with planes and airports. In each case, the underweight body is embedded in transgression, especially in regards to masculinity, but there are varying degrees to which these are transgressive texts. *The Machinist* uses Trevor's body to warn against going outside social boundaries but nonetheless it exposes the conventionality of other forms of cultural rebellion. *Fight Club* may be uncertain about whether underweight male bodies are products of or protests against millennial society, but that dialectic only enhances the movie's subversion of contemporary culture. *Dallas Buyers Club* is more conservative in its estimation of the possibilities for the underweight male body to transgress socio-cultural norms, only supporting the populist protests and condemning any cultural critiques outside of a Calvinistic moral code. However, it is the extra-textual responses to the actors' bodies that really jeopardise their transgressive qualities.

The preparatory weight loss and screen exploitation of an underweight body has brought Brad Pitt, Christian Bale and Matthew McConaughey to the fore of popular culture as idols of acting, art, fitness and lifestyle. This would seem to travesty the diegetic meanings of their bodies, which are to be or discuss transgressions of dominant society and culture. Through their uses of the body, culture has made them models of masculinity and professionalism when onscreen their bodies challenge gender certainty and offscreen actions irresponsibly promote health problems in the public eye. While we should not generalise about the significance of the underweight male body in recent American cinema – in *All Things Fall Apart* it really is the means to an end for playing a cancer sufferer and nothing more – we can say with some confidence that it is a commonly-used vehicle for exploring transgressive acts and ideologies. It breaks with established representations of the male body, typically transgressing gender boundaries and symbolic masculinity. What distinguishes the transgressive underweight male body from other cinematic exploitations of the body as a discourse of society is that we do not need frameworks like genre, gender stereotype, academic paradigms and allegorical reading in order to see it. The rejection of socio-cultural norms is inscribed onto the underweight male body, the way it moves and acts, and interacts with *mise-en-scène* and context, as if each instance was tattooed on.

Notes

1 Nonetheless, *The Machinist* deploys imagery and techniques from modern horror cinema to characterise the underweight male body as grotesque, monstrous and alien.
2 Since both actors are playing two versions of the same character, it would be possible to refer to both actors as Tyler Durden. However, to avoid confusion and to distinguish the performances (and bodies) of the actors, I will henceforth refer to Edward Norton as The Narrator and Brad Pitt as Tyler Durden. This assignation also befits how the actors are presented to viewers up until the revelatory final scene.
3 Surprisingly little has been said about when and how Christian Bale posed for this photograph and filmed flashback scenes in which he is considerably fuller-figured. If prior to his drastic weight loss, it suggests the process was even more rapid and excessive than reduction from an average-sized body.
4 Given the associations of Eklund's thin body with crime, deviancy, poverty and abandoned social spaces, Bale's performance in *The Fighter* could easily have been a case study for the transgressive qualities of the underweight male body in this chapter.
5 These would include *Killer Joe* (2011), *Bernie* (2011), *Mud* (2012) and *The Paperboy* (2012).
6 Though Jared Leto's performance as Rayon is a good example of a transgressive body produced out of severe weight loss, as a transgendered person undergoing a sex change she does not identify or physically manifest as male and therefore does not quite meet

the conditions for a case study in this chapter. The performance is, however, a testament to the motif of lost masculinity attached to underweight bodies in American cinema.
7 Other examples of this kind of 'uglying up' for Oscar reward include Daniel Day Lewis in *My Left Foot* (1989) and Charlize Theron in *Monster* (2003) .
8 Aside from casual homophobia and ontological snobbery, another possible cause of TV Liberace biopic *Behind the Candelabra*'s (2013) failure to win acting Academy Awards may well have been the decision to digitally remove weight from Michael Douglas representing the gay pianist in the final stages of AIDS, rather than the actor losing a great deal of weight, since this was the formula for Oscar success in Matthew McConaughey's portrayal of an AIDS victim.

Bibliography

Anon. (n.d.) 'Fight Club', edward-norton.org.; http://www.edward-norton.org/fight.html (accessed 17 December 2014).

Brooks, X. (2014) 'Matthew McConaughey wins Best Actor', *Guardian Online*, 2 March; http://www.theguardian.com/film/2014/mar/03/matthew-mcconaughey-oscars-best-actor-dallas-buyers-club (accessed 19 December 2014).

Douglas, M. (1970) *Natural Symbols: Explorations in Cosmology*. London: Barrie & Rockliff.

Dyer, R. (1982) 'Don't look now – Richard Dyer examines the instabilities of the male pin-up', *Screen*, 23, 3/4, 61–73.

Ebert, R (2008) 'Review of *The Machinist*', RogerEbert.com, 8 November; http://www.rogerebert.com/reviews/the-machinist-2004 (accessed 17 December 2014).

Featherstone, M. (1982) 'The Body in Consumer Culture', *Theory, Culture and Society*, 1, 2, 18–33.

Gonzalo, A. (2013) 'The Diet of Christian Bale for *The Machinist*', *Harlcombe Norilsk*, 13 December; http://albertogonzalo.blogspot.com/2013/09/diet-of-christian-bale-for-machinist.html (accessed 17 December 2014).

Gusmaroli, D. (2014) 'Matthew McConaughey Says Losing Three Stone for *Dallas Buyers Club* made him Smarter', *DailyMail.com*, 18 February; http://www.dailymail.co.uk/tvshowbiz/article-2561875/Matthew-McConaughey-says-losing-three-stone-Dallas-Buyers-Club-smarter.html (accessed 17 December 2014).

Lipton, J. (2014) 'Matthew McConaughey', *Inside the Actors Studio*, tx 20 February. Bravo.

Lehman, P. (2007) *Running Scared: Masculinity and the Representation of the Male Body*. Detroit, MI: Wayne State University Press.

Masters. T. (2014) 'Matthew McConaughey on *Dallas Buyers Club*', *BBC News*, 4 February; http://www.bbc.com/news/entertainment-arts-25979138 (accessed 19 December 2014).

Miller, J. (2014) 'McConaissance', *VanityFair.com*, 8 February 2014; http://www.vanityfair.com/hollywood/2014/02/matthew-mcconaughey-dallas-buyers-club-weight-loss-diary (accessed 19 December 2014).

Olesker, M. (2015) 'The Rise and Rise of the Spornosexual', *Esquire*, 12 January; http://www.esquire.co.uk/culture/features/7588/the-rise-and-rise-of-the-spornosexual/ (accessed 15 January 2015).

Percival, A. (2012) "Who's Suffering for their Art?" *The Huffington Post*, 29 November; http://www.huffingtonpost.co.uk/news/matthew-mcconaughey-weight-loss/ (accessed 19 December 2014).

Rawden, M. (2014) 'How Brad Pitt Changed Hollywood Action Movies', *CinemaBlend.com*, 1 April; http://www.cinemablend.com/new/How-Brad-Pitt-Changed-Hollywood-Action-Movies-42889.html (accessed 17 December 2014).

Rhoades, L. (2014) '54 Times Brad Pitt made me question my sexuality in *Fight Club*', *Buzzfeed*, 8 September; http://www.buzzfeed.com/mrloganrhoades/brad-pitt-made-me-question-my-sexuality (accessed 17 December 2014).

Riley, J. (2014) 'Matthew McConaughey's Independent Streak', *Variety*, 18 February; http://variety.com/2014/film/news/matthew-mcconaugheys-independent-streak-1201104820/ (accessed 19 December 2014).

Tudor, A (1995) 'Unruly Bodies, Unquiet Minds', *Body & Society*, 1, 1, 25–41.

Vint, S. and M. Bould (2009) 'The Thin Men: Anorexic Subjectivity in *Fight Club* and *The Machinist*', in M. Bould, K. Glitre and G. Tuck (eds) *Neo-Noir*. London and New York, NY: Wallflower Press, 221–40.

Chapter 6
Surgery, Blood and Patriarchal Sex: *Excision* and *American Mary*

ALICE HAYLETT BRYAN

In 2012 two North American independent films were released that featured female protagonists carrying out surgical procedures in contemporary interpretations of the mad-doctor horror sub-genre. Pauline (AnnaLynne McCord) in Richard Bates Jr.'s *Excision* (2012) and Mary (Katharine Isabelle) in Jen and Sylvia Soska's *American Mary* (2012) are two very different characters; one is a teenage outsider with an unconventional surgery and blood fetish in a sexually repressed middle-class suburban town, whilst the other is a rape victim and medical student in a world of prostitution, pole dancing and body modification. However, both Pauline and Mary's use of surgery can be read as a search for control over their lives; that through exploring and manipulating the human body, these two women seek to comprehend their position within a society that constantly alienates them. This chapter will explore the potential of these films to challenge issues of power and heteronormativity in contemporary sex and society, arguing that the depiction of women as surgeons in these films allows for a dissection of white, patriarchal, middle-class values. Using the work of the gender theorist Jack Halberstam, it will explore what happens when women pick up the surgical scalpel and begin to penetrate instead of being penetrated, asking whether this act still operates within a heteronormative structural logic, or whether it potentially allows for a queer interpretation of the penetrating female protagonist.

In April 2010 the American College of Surgeons published a report on the surgical workforce of the United States, in which it was stated that in 2008 women counted for only 21% of surgeons working in America (2010: 16). If those employed in gynaecology and obstetrics are discounted (the only sector where female surgeons nearly equal the male total at 47%), the figure drops to just 13% (2010: 16–17). Even though the number of women in surgical training outnumbers those currently practicing, in the near future men still look to outnumber women in the operating room two to one. Surgery, it appears, is very much a male domain. The same can be said for the representation of surgeons in horror cinema, where the role is almost entirely a male one. From Henry Frankenstein (*Frankenstein*, James Whale, 1931) to the Mantle twins (*Dead Ringers*, David Cronenberg, 1988) and Dr. Heiter (*The Human Centipede: First Sequence*, Tom Six, 2009), the history of the mad doctor is that of a male antagonist and his victims or creations of both sexes. Given this overt prominence of male characters in the sub-genre of the mad-doctor film – as well as in current society – the release of two horror films that portray female surgeons in 2012 is noteworthy. In a continuation of research carried out on the original male manifestations of the character on film, this chapter will look to *Excision* and *American Mary* to explore the representation of gender and sexuality in contemporary North American horror cinema, revealing how and why the deconstruction of these categories is still a necessary and insightful process.

In *American Mary*, protagonist Mary is a surgical student struggling to pay her bills. After applying for a job in a strip club she gets pulled into a world of extreme body modification surgery. In an attempt to further her career she attends a party hosted by the male surgical residents from her hospital and university, where she is drugged and brutally raped by her lecturer. With help from the strip club owner Billy, she organises the abduction of her attacker and then proceeds to torture him slowly by practicing different extreme body modification techniques on him. Forced to drop out of medical school after the rape, Mary begins to make a good living from carrying out surgical procedures, attracting clients from all over the world. However, her new life begins to unravel around her and she is eventually killed by the husband of one of her patients.

The world that surrounds Mary is one of sex, power, blood and filth. Interior locations are dark and gloomy, whilst the outside world too is often grey and cold, and indeed rarely depicted. Apart from Mary's grandmother and a police detective, all other lead characters in the film are in some way counter to the 'norm'; either they have extreme body modifications, work in the sex industry, are part of a crime outfit or abuse their positions of power. This is in stark contrast to the surroundings of Pauline in *Excision*, which is one of middle-class white American suburban life. The young social outcast Pauline wants to be a surgeon so that she can help her sister Grace (Ariel Winter) who suffers from cystic fibrosis. However, her aspirations of a medical career run a little deeper, as Pauline's fantasy life is dominated by her surgery and blood fetishes, the colourful depictions of which stand as a counter to the sterile suburbia that surrounds her. Her mother (played by Traci Lords) attempts to instil in her daughters an all-American wholesome life of school, church, cotillion classes and good manners. However, under this façade of the American dream lies an unhappy marriage, troublesome parent/child relationships and an inability to communicate with those they love.

Pauline is a teenage misfit. With her androgynous clothing and unkempt hair she goes against everything her mother is trying to enforce. Throughout the film she questions her own sanity, and makes constant requests to her parents for psychiatric help. Not taking her pleas seriously they first send her to a local minister for guidance, and by the time they agree to proper medical care it is too late. During the film the viewer is constantly questioning whether Pauline's declarations of mental illness are just an act – a cry for attention in contrast with her sister's physical disease – or a real need for care. However, the film's climax shockingly provides an answer when upon hearing that her sister needs a lung transplant, the untrained teenager kidnaps another young girl and attempts to perform the operation, killing both patients.

There are a number of key themes that feature in both *American Mary* and *Excision*, but they deal with these themes in very different ways. Both works can be seen to tackle the issue of being a woman in a patriarchal society, and the relationship between sex, power and control that comes with this position. Whereas in *American Mary* the sexual objectification of women is overt through the location of the strip club and the predatory behaviour of the surgeons, in *Excision* it is manifest in the subtle enforcement of traditional gender roles that Pauline struggles against. In her suburban world men go out to work, whilst women stay at home to raise the children, with no alternative to this lifestyle offered. These films can also be seen to comment on male and female sexuality and non-normative sexual tastes such as blood play and surgical fetishes. However, what links all these different themes together is the manner in which the idea of monstrosity is presented, and how this can be seen subvert or reinforce heteronormative gender roles in modern American society.

Mad Doctors, Sex and Violence

Rhona Berenstein (1996) has argued that traditionally the sub-genre of the mad-doctor film displays homosocial discourse – the relationships between men – behind a scant façade of heterosexual desire. Drawing on films released during the peak of the sub-genre in the 1930s, she contends that the classic mad doctor is obsessed with the masculine body, caring little about helping the sick and instead holding deistic aspirations about the creation and manipulation of the human (usually male) form. Berenstein contends that this obsession with the male body can be read as a displacement of the mad doctors' unspoken homosexual desire. She argues that although female victims and monsters do feature in these films, their role is subsumed to that of a mediator and expresser of fear – a means to symbolise horror – whilst still perpetuating a purely male-to-male discourse. Berenstein's use of the term 'homosocial' to discuss these works is twofold: 'first, as a combination of the social and erotic charges that bind rivalrous men together in narratives, and second, as a description of the manner in which patriarchy excludes women' (1996: 128). However, she argues that it would be incorrect to read these films as direct representations of a repressed homosexual voice. Instead, the homosocial exchange visible in these films comes about through the extension of patriarchal power by the attempted erasing of the need for women in the act of procreation. Being a celebration of male-to-male relationships, homosocial discourse is a fundamental part of patriarchy, yet these relationships are also always prohibited to an extent, so that patriarchal society can continue to replicate itself.

Along with Berenstein's work on the sub-genre, Barbara Creed has also referred to the mad-doctor sub-genre in both *The Monstrous-Feminine* (1993) and *Phallic Panic* (2005). Creed argues that the true source of monstrosity in these films is the idea of 'man as womb monster': the creation of life without the involvement of a woman (2005: 41–67). She contends that in these films it is the doctor who is the true monster, not his creation, by his attempts to generate life through various uncanny uterine scenarios. However, if the mad doctor is a female character, there is no need to attempt to create life, as this is achievable biologically. What, then, makes a female doctor mad? Instead of the creation of life, is it the taking of it?

Excision and *American Mary* break from the traditional mad-doctor plot in a number of ways. First there is the presence of willing patients. Apart from her rapist test-subject, those who come to Mary for their body modification surgery respect her and want her help. They are happy with the outcome, and are represented as wanting these changes for themselves, rather than to please others or fulfil any societal ideal, as is the case with most cosmetic surgeries. In her fantasies, Pauline's patients are in various states of decimation, but there is a never any suggestion of sadism in the scenes. Instead her patients worship her, their bodies willingly submitting to her advances. Critically, too, Pauline's patients are never truly dead, and even though they may be missing the top of their head, for example, they still remain mobile, entailing that her desires are not strictly necrophilic, but instead bound in the very matter of the body. Pauline's fantasies are not about creating life; indeed, in one of them she gives birth to a foetus and then destroys it in a microwave-like machine. But she does have a desire to help people and to be admired as a figure who can bring back bodies that are on the brink of abject death; treading that dangerous border and going where no others dare. Her desires are to be god-like, but they are not maternally orientated.[1]

However, the greatest contrast to the traditional mad-doctor film in these contemporary works is their critique of homosocial relationships. On the face of it, *American Mary* with its rape-revenge narrative and lack of positive male/female or familial relationships could be read as a feminist polemic against patriarchal oppression and sexual violence. The role of intercourse throughout the film aligns with Robert Jensen's definition of copulation in his radical feminist essay 'Patriarchal Sex' from 1987. Jensen argues that in patriarchal culture 'sex is fucking', and that to be a man in this culture you must be a male who fucks (1987: 533). For Jensen, fucking is about control; masculine dominance and feminine subservience; it is the eroticisation of power. As the man is the one doing the penetrating, even if he plays at being subordinate, he still holds that which produces the action, the penis. Jensen also draws links between the use of the word 'fuck' to denote sex, and its other use to express an act of violence, such as 'he fucked me over' or 'I am going to fuck him up'. Jensen argues:

> Sex in patriarchy is fucking. That we live in a world in which people continue to use the same word for sex and violence, and then resist the notion that sex is routinely violent and claim to be outraged when it becomes overtly violent, is testament to the power of patriarchy. In this society, sex and violence are fused to the point of being indistinguishable. (1987: 538)

American Mary is full of fucking in both the sexual and violent sense. Although there is only one direct scene of penetrative intercourse – Mary's brutal rape – the

Fig. 1: Mary (Katharine Isabelle) is drugged at a party whilst a group of surgeons molest an unconscious woman behind her, in *American Mary* (2012).

film depicts sex and sexual desire as something inherently misogynistic. All sexual activity in the film is linked to abuses of power, such as Billy (Antonio Cupo) using his position as an employer to get one of his employees to preform oral sex on him, or the drugging of women at the surgeons' party. Therefore, these acts could be considered as fucking due to their objectification and violation of another's body, even though they do not always involve vaginal or anal penetration. This violation is also apparent in the film's depiction of violence, where retribution and self-defence are achieved through the penetration and manipulation of the human form. Interestingly too, in a foreshadowing of his future rape of Mary, every single time that her lecturer speaks to her, he uses the words 'fuck' or 'fucking'.

The male surgery staff who dominate Mary's life are bastions of patriarchal power. They objectify the bodies that they operate on, whether male or female, by calling themselves 'cutters', removing the sense of care and empathy usually associated with medical careers. Surgery for these men is another form of fucking, the penetration and therefore control over a body, which puts them in a position of power over life and death. Assuming Mary to be a prostitute due to the money that she has recently earned from her underground surgery work, the surgeons at her teaching hospital invite her to one of their parties. Unbeknownst to Mary, at these gatherings the male doctors hire prostitutes so that they can take part in group sex, with some of the women being drugged so that the men can exploit their powerless bodies. Mary herself is drugged, and whilst the sedative begins to take hold she fails to notice that behind her a barely conscious woman has been hoisted onto a table, penetrated and masturbated over by a group of the doctors cheering each other on and filming the event. The need to drug these women (including Mary), even though they are supposedly consensual sex-workers, suggests that the men enjoy the feeling of power gained over the powerless body. Sex for them – like surgery – is not about emotion, but power. It is a homosocial experience that allows for the exhibition of competitive masculinity; fucking in the presence of other men, enjoying *their* company and rivalry more than the drugged person you have penetrated. As one doctors replies when Mary asks him if he is a surgeon: 'I'm a fucking mother fucker, no seriously babe, I cut people up for a living!' The mad doctors in *American*

Mary are not crazed loners working on secret projects, but a group of confident and successful men who have the respect of those around them.

Whereas patriarchy is represented as a depraved threat in *American Mary*, it is an emasculated obstacle in the life of Pauline, but one that ultimately pulls her under like quicksand. Her father is a pathetic figure in the shadow of her domineering mother, who constantly verbally attacks and demeans him. The other male figures in Pauline's world are the usual symbols of masculine authority; a high school jock, a maths teacher, her school principle – with portraits of Reagan and Bush on his office wall – and the Minister whom her mother sends her to, but Pauline refuses to submit to the requests of these men. She attempts to control her interactions with them, always trying to have the upper hand and the last word. Instead of commenting directly on the subjugation of women through the homosocial nature of the patriarchal project, *Excision* reveals the absurdity of Pauline's position in a male-dominated America where no one will listen to her. It is a world where beauty and conformity are encouraged in women, where – as her sister Grace informs her – boys just care about breasts. Instead of the apathetic males that surround her, it is actually her mother that really attempts to maintain this superficial society. Absurdly, when Pauline nearly drowned as a child and her father saved her by giving her mouth-to-mouth, her mother just scolded him for having a cold sore and infecting her with it. Further to this, instead of encouraging her to become a surgeon she insists that Pauline attend cotillion classes to improve her chances of getting a husband. Pauline's mother is not a monster, but the world that she perpetuates and encourages her daughters to enter into is perversely horrific.

Pauline's attempt to take control of her life can be seen in the loss of her virginity. She approaches a young track star called Adam (Jeremy Sumpter) saying that she has decided that she would like to lose her virginity with him. She purchases oral contraception, and she decides the date of their meeting so that she can be menstruating at the time and therefore bring part of her blood play fantasies to life. The young boy is so desperate to have sex with anyone, even though he has a girlfriend, that he agrees to the meeting. Like the surgeons in *American Mary*, he does not care who he fucks, he just wants to have sex. However, straight away Pauline emasculates him by inspecting his genitalia and instantly dismissing the extra-large condoms that he stole from his brother, as he is 'too small for the big kind'. She dictates the sex at first, being on top and in control. As the scene progresses it cuts between their real-life intercourse and Pauline's simultaneous sexual fantasy. In her mind, as she has sex with him the sheets become drenched in blood. Compared to the novice thrustings of their actual sex, in her fantasy the couple are locked together in pleasure, as she splashes the blood across the walls and moans in ecstasy. As this fantasy climaxes the film returns to a now silent and weeping Pauline, on her back, being slowly penetrated by an equally silent Adam. The few tears that Pauline wipes away from her eyes shows that she is not completely devoid of emotion when it comes to the loss of her virginity. However, her uncomfortable expression and the slight gestures of her hands which suggest that she wants the boy to get off her could also be read as displaying that these tears are as much to do with disappointment as anything else. If this is her example, sex in real life does not live up to her fantastical expectations. Nevertheless, after instructing him to go down on her and

Figs. 2 & 3: Pauline's (AnnaLynne McCord) sexual fantasies, in *Excision* (2012).

his bloody discovery during oral sex, Pauline appears content with the whole affair in counterpoint to the distressed Adam.

From the very beginning of the film Pauline is represented as a sexual being, with an active sexual fantasy life. These sequences are inserted throughout the film and are rich with bright lights of hospital operating rooms and the bold colour of blood. In these fantasies Pauline depicts herself as both surgeon and abject body, finding intense sexual pleasure and emotional satisfaction in both positions. The audience are introduced to her queer desires straight away as the film opens with a long-shot of Pauline sitting staring at a double of herself. Dressed identically, her fantasy doppelgänger is only differentiated by the blood that wells up out of her mouth and flows down her chest. This gory vision of herself visibly excites the watching Pauline, and as she grinds her legs together in climax her double spits out a money-shot of blood, providing a visual symbol of phallic ejaculation. This initial scene is critical in explaining Pauline's sexual tastes; she is neither sadist nor masochist, but instead a visceral fetishist with an obsession for the bloody machinery of the human body. This is in contrast to Mary, who is depicted as an object of sexual lust rather than the holder of it. *American Mary* has two sexual fantasy sequences; however, importantly they are both Billy's fantasies about Mary rather than the other way round. In the first he pictures her stripping – pouring blood all over her semi-naked body – and in the second, he imagines that she stabs him with her surgical blade. Although Billy is clearly intimidated by and infatuated with Mary she rejects his advances. It is obvious that she does have some affection for him, but this is not dominated by sexual lust, as is the case with his desire for her.

Both Pauline and Mary use surgery – the penetration of bodies – to attempt to take control of their lives. Mary is presented as being exceptionally good at what she does, and even though unqualified, gains respect from the community that she caters for. However, her use of surgery transforms throughout the film. Starting as a desire to help others, by the end of the film she uses her abilities to scare and manipulate those around her, moving from life-saver to life-taker. She threatens an innocent stripper using her surgical implements, and kills a security guard who accidentally stumbles across the now limbless lecturer. Further to this, her horrific and prolonged torture of her rapist, that eventually leads to his death, brings up the ethical question: can the revenge for rape ever go too far? In *Excision*, Pauline also views surgery as a means to take control over the events in her life that she feels powerless in confronting, namely her sister's illness. In her fantasy life her abilities as a surgeon transform her into a worshiped being, a life-saver and life giver, that animates even the decimated bodies that she comes into contact with. However, in actuality she is a deluded and emotionally unstable young woman who fails to acknowledge that surgery takes years of education and training. As the film progresses and she is faced with Grace's death, her fantasy life begins to take over, leading her to carry out her gruesome but well-intended act. Whereas the climax of *American Mary* carries with it a sense that Mary deserved her fate, Pauline's attempted surgery is both shocking and also incredibly emotional. Grace, her sister, is the one positive relationship that Pauline has, and the fear of losing her has brought on an illness to which Pauline is completely defenceless against. Yet ultimately, the blame for the death of these two young girls falls not on Pauline's shoulders, but on those of the parent entwined in the veneer of heteronormativity. This is a guilt represented so clearly in the film's closing image of Pauline and her mother finally embracing like mother and child should, but with the mother screaming out in the realisation of her involvement in what has occurred. If *American Mary* depicts the brutal patriarchal desire to fuck, *Excision* can be seen as representing the failure of heteronormativity.

Surgery and the Gendered Body

The homosocial world in which Pauline and Mary live is one that constantly omits and oppresses them: violently in the case of Mary's rape, and apathetically with its dismissal of Pauline. As Berenstein stresses, when thinking about homosociality, although the erotic subtext of homosexuality is key so too is the force of heterosexuality that sustains patriarchy. Homosocial bonds necessitate heteronormative values in order to keep men *in* control and women *under* control. Eighty years after the height of the classic mad-doctor movies, *Excision* and *American Mary* show that even though this oppression of women is now a consciously represented experience in cinema rather than an unconscious subtext, women are still being forced into performing feminine subjugated roles in the face of patriarchal society – be that society violent or farcical. In Jack Halberstam's work on the potential of the slasher and neo-splatter films to dismantle heteronormative assumptions about gender, Judith Butler's *Bodies That Matter* (1993) is drawn upon to argue that it is the way that bodies are made intelligible that binds masculinity and maleness, and femininity and femaleness. Halberstam writes: 'The masculinity of the male is secured through an understanding of his body as "impenetrable" and as capable of penetrating. Femininity, then, becomes that which can and must be penetrated but which cannot penetrate in return' (2005: 34). As Butler has discussed, these positions are integral to the structure of the heterosexual matrix; so what happens if women begin to penetrate?

Through its depiction of the exploration of the human body, the mad-doctor sub-genre has much in common with the slasher and splatter films that Halberstam discusses, and in the manner that such sub-genres shift and overlap, *Excision* and *American Mary* could equally be seen as the latest permutation of the splatter film. Halberstam argues that these films, which are focused on the borders of the body – of tearing them apart and stitching them back together again – present the potential for new understandings of gender that utilise monstrosity, power and violence. In *Skin Shows* (1995), Halberstam argues that bodies that splatter – those belonging to the characters who die – are gendered feminine as they have been penetrated. Female bodies that do not splatter, therefore, must be considered as being sutured and apart from the traditional gender construction that would equal their death. These improperly gendered women are the Final Girls of the slasher genre, Carol Clover's masculinised and non-sexualised survivors who penetrate rather than be penetrated. In *Skin Shows*, Halberstam argues that this improper gendering of the Final Girl aligns her with the monstrous as she is counter to heteronormative gender assignment, stitching gender traits together in order to defeat her attacker and take control. Therefore the Final Girl becomes a symbol of a queer female adolescent with masculine traits that has positive links to monstrosity as being something outside of the heteronormative structural logic. Halberstam argues: 'The technology of monsters when channelled through a dangerous woman with a chain saw becomes a powerful and queer strategy for enabling and activating monstrosity as opposed to stamping it out' (1995: 143). Neither Pauline nor Mary are Final Girls, however it could be contested that one of them can be considered a monster within and reinforcing heteronormativity, whilst the other follows in the footsteps of those Halberstam points towards, becoming a queer figure counter to patriarchal control.

American Mary reinforces heteronormativity through Mary's monstrosity, whilst Pauline's monstrosity can be seen to challenge it, reveal its weaknesses and expose the horror of those pushed to – and over – its boundaries. Although *American Mary* starts as a rape-revenge narrative, Mary's spiralling descent from victim to perpetrator can be seen to move her from being a positive activation of monstrosity by getting revenge on those who harmed her, to the traditional patriarchal construction of the castrating – but also fallible – monstrous-feminine. Instead of operating outside of the heteronormative structural logic, Mary's appetite for destruction once she has assumed the phallic power of penetration actually can be seen to reinforce gender roles, as the position she attempts to inhabit between them in unsustainable. Once Mary has assumed this position between genders she stops being a sympathetic character and becomes monstrous, terrorising and killing innocent people. This entails that she can never be the positive activation of the sutured figure that

Halberstam sees in the Final Girl, and is instead an unstable entity that combines a feminine body, phallic power and, critically, the will to kill in order to keep that power. At the point when she kills the security guard she becomes that which the film has previously labelled as monstrous: a person willing to violate and destroy another's body for their own gain. Her brutal attack recreates the violent fucking exhibited by the male surgeons, transforming her from being a sympathetic character reacting to monstrosity, to being a monster in her own right. Her death, therefore, is seen as just; she returns to being a splattered feminine body and patriarchal power is restored, troubling any potential feminist readings of the film.

In contrast, Pauline, who is also responsible for the death of two innocent people, offers more scope for challenging patriarchal control and heteronormativity. She constantly defies the figures of patriarchal power that surround her. However, her confrontation is still met with restriction. She is forced to go to school, to attend cotillion class and not given the access to a psychiatrist that she demands. Her unhappiness with her own lack of real power is transported into her fantasy life where she is in complete control of the proceedings. Although these fantasies are gory, they also revel in their monstrosity through playfulness and black humour. They are not sadistic, nor do they involve Pauline killing anyone. Instead, in her dream world she is both a life-saving surgeon and a dismembered body. Her fantasies are orgies of abject excess that fail to conform to heteronormative values. Pauline caresses, and is caressed by both men and women indiscriminately. It is not the gender of the body that Pauline finds attractive, but the body itself, bodies that are at the boundary of life and death, clean and unclean, pure and sullied. These bodies where gender no longer matters, are the very things that heteronormativity is trying to expel.

The full potential of the queer power of Pauline's sexual fantasies can be revealed through their relation to Halberstam's third-wave manifesto *Gaga Feminism: Sex, Gender and Age of Normal* (2012) published in the same year as the film was released. For Halberstam, Lady Gaga's willingness to be excessive, phony and unreal, and her playfulness with her own body and gender, signals a new form of feminism that is 'a monstrous outgrowth of the unstable concept of "woman"' (2012: xiii). Pauline's experimental and explorative fantasies can be read as her own form of 'going gaga': losing any sense of gender, sexuality or bodily border as she slices, stiches and sprays. Although her actual life is full of the battles of the performance of being a 'proper' young woman in middle-class America, in her fantasies being a woman does not matter, it is just *the human body* that matters. This undoing of being a woman is critical for Halberstam's gaga feminism. The category 'woman' must be undone and played with, built up, and then torn apart again. In this same manner, in her fantasies Pauline is a bejewelled queen, a latex-clad surgeon and a decapitated head. Compounding this is the fact that these fantasies are enjoyable to watch. They are original and surprising, and filmed in a colourful and bold style reminiscent of Mathew Barney's *The Cremaster Cycle* (1994–2002). As Halberstam notes, Gaga's fans call themselves 'little monsters', dressing to excess and being whatever they want to be, revelling in their own monstrosity just as Pauline loves to explore her own abject self in these beautiful but bloody sequences. It is a reclamation of the monstrous-feminine that rewrites it in a new language. Reading Pauline's desires through this lens supports Halberstam's argument that in order to break with heteronormativity we must first break with gender and deconstruct the concepts of masculinity and femininity. As Pauline demonstrates in her own sexually-driven way, this can be done by returning to the body itself and starting again. When Pauline penetrates the bodies of others she does not do so in the same manner as the objectifying surgical cutters of *American Mary*. Pauline's desire to penetrate is not fuelled by the want to fuck, but by a desire to take control in order to save lives and explore the wonders of the human body. Gender is irrelevant to Pauline. Her sexual satisfaction in her fantasy sequences is not from objectification, but from embodiment. She both penetrates and is penetrated, defying the heteronormative system that tries to tie her to just one gender performance. The totality of her position in her fantasy life is a disavowal of her feelings of powerlessness in the heteronormative world that surrounds her, a world into which she is unable to fit.

In *Gaga Feminism* Halberstam argues that in patriarchal society female desire is never given the chance to flow and develop. In North America – as well as in much of the world – girls grow up in a society that constantly bars them from expressing and exploring their sexuality. Whereas boys and men are encouraged to indulge their desires and fetishes, and be always open to more and more varied experiences, girls remain in a system of prohibition and stasis. This regulation and manipulation of sexual desire that women experience in everyday life is rooted in the homosociality of men. Women must be subservient and controllable so that they can be exchanged, whilst men are encouraged to demonstrate their masculinity through their sexual potency: the desire to fuck. However, as Halberstam notes, female sexuality is inherently more flexible in spite of these controls. To support this argument Halberstam refers to an article from the *New York Times Magazine* (2009), which discussed a study that had been carried out into male and female responses to erotic pictures. In this piece it was concluded that heterosexual and lesbian women were turned on by images of both sexes, whilst men only enjoyed the relevant gender akin to their sexual persuasion. Therefore, it can be argued that women – like Pauline – have a greater potential to look past gender and see only the body and its erotic potential. Has this willingness to assume a flexible position in their fantasy life allowed women to mentally escape the confines of their overly controlled social sex-life?

Conclusion

Halberstam argues that it is not Lady Gaga's personal political views that shape gaga feminism. Instead it is her willingness, and that of her fans, to experiment with self-representation and gender, and to tear apart the norm and rebuild it into something new that influences what she sees as a new feminism for a generation willing to embrace the queer and excessive. In the same way, this chapter has read the narratives of *Excision* and *American Mary* as an illustration of its own project rather than with reflection on the directors' intended messages. These two films show how, just as in the 1930s, the mad-doctor sub-genre can still be used to pick apart the homosocial nature of patriarchal society, albeit to uncover a potentially positive queer message rather than a repressed homosexuality that excludes women. These films perform and deconstruct the gendering of the body, and the walls of the heteronormative matrix that attempt to keep that gendering in place for patriarchal gain. The bodies in *American Mary* are gendered bodies, those that penetrate are male, whilst those that are penetrated are female. Men are represented as desiring beings who fuck, whilst women are just objects or vessels to receive them. The surgeons who are meant to teach Mary do not care about the body that they penetrate – whether sexually or medically – they only care for their own penetration, and the sharing of that penetration with other men. Pauline, on the other hand, is obsessed with the body itself; the body that transcends gender and gives pleasure though its very being. In her sexual fantasies the heteronormative matrix breaks down in her desire to penetrate and be penetrated, and in her total disregard for the gender of those she engages with. Pauline lets herself go – goes gaga – and in doing so her fantasies show how the fluidity of desire is starting to break down the dam that has been built by the homosocial relationships of patriarchy.

Note

1 One fantasy sequence does feature Pauline lying down with eight nipples and three people reverently approaching her ready to suckle. Although this obviously references breast-feeding it is more animalistic rather than maternal, and plays to her fantasies of being a worshipped deity rather than a nurturing life-giver.

Bibliography

The American College of Surgeons Health Policy Research Institute (2010) 'The Surgical Workforce in the United States: Profile and Recent Trends'.
Berenstein, R. (1996) *Attack of the Leading Ladies: Gender, Sexuality, and Spectatorship in Classic Horror Cinema*. New York, NY: Columbia University Press.
Bergner, D. (2009) 'What Do Women Want?'. *New York Times Magazine*, January 22, 2009.
Butler, J. (1993) *Bodies That Matter: On the Discursive Limits of 'Sex'*. London and New York, NY: Routledge.
Clover, C. J. (2005) *Men, Women, and Chain Saws: Gender in the Modern Horror Film*. Princeton, NJ: Princeton University Press.
Creed, B. (1993) *The Monstrous-Feminine: Film, Feminism, Psychoanalysis*. London and New York, NY: Routledge.
____ (2005) *Phallic Panic: Film, Horror and the Primal Uncanny*. Melbourne: Melbourne University Press.
Halberstam, J. (1995) *Skin Shows: Gothic Horror and the Technology of Monsters*. Durham, NC: Duke University Press.
____ (2005) 'Neosplatter: *Bride of Chucky* and the Horror of Heteronormativity', *Film International*, 3, 3, 32–41.
____ (2012) *Gaga Feminism: Sex Gender, and the End of Normal*. Boston, MA: Beacon Press.
Jensen, R. (1998) 'Patriarchal Sex', in R. Baker, K. Wininger and F. Elliston (eds) *Philosophy and Sex*, 3rd edition. Amherst, NY: Prometheus Books, 533–48.

PART II
ADOLESCENCE, AGEING AND QUEER AGENCY

Chapter 7
A Child is Being Raped! Homosexual Panic in *Mystic River*

VULCAN VOLKAN DEMIRKAN-MARTIN

At the time *Mystic River* (Clint Eastwood, 2003) was released, critics were noticing an increase in films about child abuse. For example, Amy Taubin described the 2005 Sundance Film Festival as 'a festival obsessed with childhood sexuality and underage sex' (2005: 62). Films concerning this 'obsession' can be roughly categorised according to their themes: films about adolescent sexual contact (with each other or with adults), such as *Kids* (Larry Clark, 1995), *Thirteen* (Catherine Hardwicke, 2003), *Me and You and Everyone We Know* (Miranda July, 2005), *Twelve and Holding* (Michael Cuesta, 2005) and *Palindromes* (Todd Solondz, 2005); films about adolescent rape, such as *Fat Girl* (Catherine Breillat, 2001), *Magdalene Sisters* (Peter Mullan, 2002) and *The Woodsman* (Nicole Kassell, 2004); films about false accusations of abuse, such as *Pretty Persuasion* (Marcos Siega, 2005); films about sexual contact between queer boys and adult men made by queer filmmakers, such as *Happiness* (Todd Solondz, 1998), *L.I.E.* (Michael Cuesta, 2001) and *Mysterious Skin* (Gregg Araki, 2005); and finally, films about the rape of adolescent boys by older men, including *Sleepers* (Barry Levinson, 1996), *The Reckoning* (Paul McGuigan, 2002), *The Butterfly Effect* (Eric Bress and J. Mackye Gruber, 2004) and *Mystic River*.[1]

It is worth asking why child molestation has been such a popular subject in contemporary cinema. The over-representation of abuse, rape and murder of children in films suggests the existence of more than merely concerns about violence and harm. James Kincaid claims that 'these stories are not told simply to solve a problem but also to focus and restate the problem, to keep it alive and before us' (1998: 6). He further focuses on this paradox by describing the perverse pleasure we get in retelling these stories and their details: 'We take a good, long look at what they are doing. ... We reject this monstrous activity with such automatic indignation that the indignation comes to seem almost like pleasure' (1998: 7). If, on the one hand, these films serve as a warning to parents, they also, in stark contrast, display our society's extreme curiosity about this topic.

These films also portray children as passive receivers of adult (often male) desire. The fetishisation of childhood innocence is a valuable asset of contemporary Western societies. Yet many historians suggest that childhood is a relatively new concept (see Levine 2002: xxvii) and the construction of it in eighteenth-century European societies is an unequivocal result of the diminishing need for their labour rather than the exploration of their innocence. Like other products of contemporary popular culture, films about child abuse repeatedly position children as an innocent, desireless species that 'maintain[s] its separation from the concerns of adulthood … and as somehow apart from the everyday economy of labour, meaning and value through which humans live, learn and grow' (Faulkner 2010: 107). Like Kincaid, Joanne Faulkner concludes that 'what requires scrutiny is the public's investment in the image of childhood' (2010: 108). What is presumed as part of a child's innocence is a supposed ignorance of sexual desire. Ellis Hanson maintains that 'the erotic innocence of children is founded on the presumption that they cannot possibly understand or experience sexual desire except as a trauma' (2003: 374). In actual fact, research suggests that pleasurable sexual contact can take place most often between pederasts and boys, sometimes between male children and older women, and rarely between young girls and adult men (see Waites 2005: 27).[2] However, an account of such sex is beyond visual representation in mainstream film; if filmmakers were to attempt to make such a film, they would be unlikely to secure funding. If they were to be financed, their films would be guaranteed only limited release, censorship and moral condemnation, because such films are not treated as mere representation, but an (im)moral document that endorses child abuse.[3]

In films concerning child abuse, like in real life, homosexuality and paedophilia have regularly been conflated, and moral panic, precisely homosexual panic, is an essential part of these films. Harry Benshoff proposes that gay men were represented as non-sexual sissies in film until the 1950s. As gay men started to become more visible in social life, the representation became more aggressive: they were now represented as sexual psychopaths who actively queer younger men: 'Implicit in these films and essays is the idea that "normal" young men (who engage in "normal" homosexual experimentation during adolescence) would only turn into "true" homosexuals if older "true" homosexuals continued to lead them astray' (1997: 122). It is no surprise that most gay rights advocates vehemently deny any link between (gay) sexual orientation and paedophilia. Nevertheless, 'The antihomophobic "solution" is not to insist that homosexuality has nothing to do with child abuse', suggests Kevin Ohi (2000: 195). He explains:

> The link between child molestation and homosexuality may well be … a homophobic illusion, but the effort to challenge the political ideology underlying this link – an ideology of sexual oppression in general – is better served by a thorough examination of structures uniting homophobia and abuse paranoias than by a simple debunking of this homophobic illusion as counterfactual. (Ibid.)

Ohi calls for an examination of 'structures uniting homophobia and abuse paranoias' rather than repeating that they have nothing in common. One way to examine such structures is to examine films like *Mystic River* in which the concept of child abuse lends itself into amalgamation with moral, especially queer and homosexual, panic.

The Cellar: Sexual Politics of *Mystic River*

Mystic River is based on the bestselling Dennis Lehane novel which, according to Rand Richards Cooper, is 'a piece of high-gloss crime fiction with serious literary ambitions' (2003). The film opens in the summer of 1975, Boston. A crane shot briefly studies a working-class neighborhood. Three boys – Dave, Sean and Jimmy – are playing hockey on an empty street. While they are scrawling their names in the wet cement of the pavement, a car pulls up and two men who hold police badges tell the boys they are damaging public property. They order Dave to get into their car and abuse him in a cellar until he runs away. Years later, when Jimmy's (Sean Penn) daughter is brutally murdered, there seems to be one suspect: Dave (Tim Robbins).

With its careful politics and casting, *Mystic River* is the definitive film about child rape. The film presents its didactic seriousness through spoken narrative: the characters continuously summarise what is happening in the film so that we do not miss any details, and an abundance of flash-backs keeps reminding the viewers of what happened before.[4] The film adopts a stance that demands careful viewing, functioning less as a piece of entertainment and more, in fact, as a moral lesson. It seems that not only the filmmakers but also the reviewers and award-givers have agreed that *Mystic River* makes crucial and pointed statements about key social issues.[5] In my reading, I acknowledge that the film's celebration by audiences and critics alike may be framed as indicating that the only acceptable representation of paedophilia in mainstream film is as 'abuse' or 'rape'. However, by focusing on Dave's character and interrogating the representation of the 'cellar' in the film, I argue that the film's denial of living space to Dave and his entrapment in a cellar is coterminous with an intolerance of not only paedophiles but all queer bodies.

One early, short scene is a kernel of *Mystic River*'s ideology. The scene starts with a shot of the stairs of a dark cellar. Next, we see a man descending the stairs, and a close-up of his legs. Fade out. From the man's point of view, we then see a young boy (Dave) wake up and squint disturbed by the light. From the boy's point of view, we see two men walking towards him. Then, from each man's point of view we see Dave; he looks scared and begs, 'Please, no more.' Fade out. With a sound bridge, his voice echoes and transitions into the sound of wolves. Dave is now in the forest nervously looking back. He starts to run.

The scene evokes nightmarish dreaming rather than reality, with echoing sounds and fade-outs. Although there is an overwhelming suggestion of anal rape in Dave's pleading, in actual fact, the viewer does not know what exactly happened in that cellar. Did the men rape Dave anally or did they make him penetrate them? Did they do it together, in each other's presence? Was it only oral sex that was performed on Dave (or by Dave) or was it masturbation? 'Please, no more' could refer just as

Fig. 1: The young Dave (Cameron Bowen) cowering in the cellar, in *Mystic River* (2003).

equally to any of these acts or scenarios. In this scene there is no actual representation of rape but rather an implication.

This scene only suggests what happened in the cellar not simply because depictions of child rape are unacceptable in mainstream film, but the ambiguity in the scene is also a directorial preference. Of course if it were depicted, the rape scene would be censored. As Jon Davies notes, films that deal with taboo subjects 'legally cannot show the very acts that they build their narratives around' (2007: 371). One concern of filmmakers and censors may be that some members of the audience may enjoy watching this. It has been discussed, especially by feminist critics, that rape scenes in films may unexpectedly arouse audiences or at least may be found entertaining – especially when shown out of context from the rest of the film.[6] Thus, the point of not showing these scenes may be the attempt to withhold such 'perverted' pleasures, but it may also invite some members of the audience to invest erotically in such scenes and write their own versions. Although painful sodomy is indicated, the scene's ambiguity ensures that some audiences will read the screen differently.

Since the book does not describe the scene of rape in such detail, the director reveals his storytelling preferences in the way he shoots this scene. As such, the scene can also be read as the fantasy of the director; or in other words, it displays how Eastwood fantasised that this rape took place. If there were a code for displaying anal rape without showing anal sex, Eastwood would have shot the scene using this code; since there is not one, he tries to withhold erotic investment in the rape by not showing its details, instead employing distorted sound and fade-outs that make viewers understand it is precisely painful sodomy that took place. Indeed, the cellar scene is pivotal to ensuring that the audience sees the grown-up Dave as a sexually ambiguous and dysfunctional man; in retrospect, they will not find it hard to imagine what happened in the cellar.

Filmic representations of child rape do not take place in a normal house or bedroom; these acts need to be pushed into spaces we do not associate with cleanliness. In such films rape usually takes place in a claustrophobic space, particularly a cellar. For example, in *Sleepers* four children are raped in the cellar of the reformatory. *The Butterfly Effect* has a father abuse his own and other children in the cellar of his house. In *The Reckoning*, the space of abuse is a tower but it is as dark as a cellar. In *Running Scared* (Wayne Kramer, 2006), the room in which children are raped and murdered resembles a cellar; there are no windows, just a locked door. In *Mysterious Skin*, children are not raped in a cellar but the film begins in one: an abused child locks himself in the cellar due to rape trauma. This motif is repeated so many times that the space of the cellar becomes one of the leading tropes in such films.

The cellar is located, just like the sewer, in the *underground*. Underground means out of sight, but it also connotes illegal action. We do not see a house attached to this cellar, which makes it look more like a medieval dungeon and completely removes it from the notion of a 'normal' environment. Since rape is an illegal act, it must be practiced in an abnormal environment. Yet confinement itself can be read as the *mise-en-scène* of forbidden desires, both because prisons are known to be places where illegal or 'immoral' action takes place, and because the confined space, removed from the everyday conscious world, so easily maps the Freudian topography of the unconscious.

In *Mystic River* the cellar not only lacks a house on top of it, but it is also in the middle of a forest, a place where there is no civilisation, rules or laws. Colin Flint rightly observes, 'whether it is the neighborhood or the nation-state, people adopt cognitive maps as to what should belong there and what needs to be expelled' (2004: 2). The reality of rape, which is expelled from the domesticity of the neighbourhood, is pushed away so strongly that once a child is taken from the neighbourhood, he becomes irrecoverable. David Sibley, drawing on both Mary Douglas and Julie Kristeva, adds, 'disease is a more potent danger if it is contagious. The fear of infection leads to the erection of the barricades to resist the spread of diseased, polluted others' (1995: 25). As Sibley points out, there are barricades and boundaries, and if a person falls onto to the other side he is 'damaged'. Once you cross the physical borders of the neighborhood and enter those of the cellar you become 'damaged goods'. Pointedly, the young Dave is not found after his kidnapping, as if the society left him there once the border was crossed. The audience is also informed that it took an entire 'four days' for Dave to come back from 'uncivilisation' – the geography of the forest and the cellar. 'Four days' sounds like a metaphor for the vast distance Dave has covered – as if Dave has been literally taken underground and it took four days to return to the surface. Not surprisingly, he remains dirty upon his return; once he is 'dirt', it is not possible to be clean anymore. Threatening to spread his disease of failed heterosexuality, the 'dirty Dave' is subsequently imprisoned in the family home. In the ideology that underlines *Mystic River*, there is no possibility of purification when a boy is taken into the cellar. As the adult Dave often repeats, he was murdered that day. As much as the cellar can be read as a symbolic space of exclusion it also marks a real, geographical exclusion of some members of a society.

Following Dave's kidnapping, *Mystic River* asserts that men like him will only rape particular boys. The film lays out and emphasises the differences between rapeable and non-rapeable boys. In the abduction sequence, Dave is saliently depicted as the clumsiest child in the group. When the ball he hits goes into the sewer instead of the goal, Dave attempts to claim he is so strong that he could not control the ball. His friends make fun of him; he is not strong but rather unskilled. As they finish their game and start graffitiing their names on the fresh cement, two men who claim to be policemen arrive at the scene. Since the children are damaging public property, they want to take one of them, initially Jimmy, to the police station. However, they decide he is the 'hard-case of the group', i.e. the toughest, and it is harder to convince him to go with them. The men then base their decision on whose house is the farthest, but the decision is actually made on the basis of who is the most subordinate and easiest to take away. Although later on Sean says, 'It could have been any of us', it is no accident Dave is picked.

The selection of Dave is justified, also, by a superimposition. Superimposition is a technique in which two or more shots/images are printed onto the same strip of film, thus making them simultaneously visible over each other. Ellis Hanson argues that

> superimposition is the queerest of cinematic inventions. It refuses dichotomies and delights in improbable associations. It makes strange bedfellows of disparate images, such that we can scarcely tell a juxtaposition from a caress, an accident from an intention, a person from a ghost, a reality from a fantasy, or a dreamer from a dream. (2003: 384)

With superimposition, following Hanson, it becomes nearly impossible to tell the difference between two different things, here between the victim and the molester. There are two scenes in which Dave's face is imposed on the molester's face; one as a child and another as an adult. These superimpositions serve to tie together the affinity of seemingly disparate characters. The latter superimposition is carefully positioned: it comes right after Dave is portrayed as the unsuccessful player in the group, which confirms there was something wrong with Dave already: he was meant to be picked. The superimposition allows the nuanced suggestion that the raped is as guilty as the rapist. At the beginning of the film, the adult Dave's face is initially imposed upon the molester's face; this superimposition opens up the possibility that Dave ended up like his molester (whose sexual orientation is not explained in the film). Child-abuse paranoias are often homophobic paranoias. If a male child is raped, he is expected to become homosexual at its worst or a failed heterosexual at its best. From his social conditioning, Dave should know that even if the men did not rape him, being 'taken away' by two grown-up men must grant emasculation. The film's characters agree: 'Looks like damaged goods to me,' says one of the men in the crowd gathered in front of Dave's house after the child has come back home. In its sexual ideology, *Mystic River* is utterly conservative and impotent of imagining any possibilities other than essentially homophobic ones in its script, cinematography or direction.

Dave's Monstrous Body

In classical horror films, especially those with vampires, the climactic scene often depicts the destruction of the monster. In *Monsters in the Closet* (1997), Benshoff likens monsters to gay men in the closet: 'The figure of the monster can frequently be equated (with greater or lesser degrees of ease) with that of the homosexual' (1997: 4). Fantastic genres in general can be read as geographies of queer desire (again, see Benshoff 1997). Various kinds of monsters' similarity to Otherness – other sexualities, gayness and queerness – have been discussed significantly in

Monsters in the Closet, *The Celluloid Closet* (Russo 1981) and *Hollywood from Vietnam to Reagan... and Beyond* (Wood 2003) and the film *The Celluloid Closet* (Rob Epstein and Jeffrey Friedman, 1995). Monsters have sometimes been represented as sympathetic and identifiable, and sometimes as 'a social threat which must be eradicated' (Benshoff 1997: 256). In *Mystic River*, Dave is characterised as a generic monster with influences from the ever-living zombie, full moon-obsessed werewolf and the lustful vampire.

When we first see the grown-up Dave, although he is seemingly heterosexual, there is an overtone that his heterosexuality is superficial. It is unclear whether Dave is employed; he seems to be heading back home after he walks his son to school every day. He exists, but it looks like he is not aware of his existence and hardly completes day-to-day jobs as if he is the living dead. He walks slowly, talks slowly, and most of the time looks like he is not alive but a zombie – a mindless existence. Robbins' 'successful' representation of Dave as semi-alive is most akin to a performance of failed heterosexuality, which reviewers agree is an accurate portrayal of a man abused as a child. But in a teratological sense, this dysfunctional and traumatised portrayal is conventional.

Soon the narrative requires a change in Dave's positioning as a monster. One night, Dave comes home late covered in blood; in fact, he looks as if *he is* bleeding. Taken from his wife Celeste's (Marcia Gay Harden) point of view, this shot shows Dave aimlessly looking at his hands. Celeste observes his bloody hands and torn shirt. Speaking in panic, Dave tells her that he has beaten a man who tried to rob him. She looks suspicious, as if she does not believe a word he says and questions him: 'You said you swung at him first?' From the following day, she keeps on checking the newspapers, but is unable to find anything about the incident ('There is nothing about it in the papers. I checked three time'). What is revealed the next day, however, is that Jimmy's eighteen-year-old daughter Katie has been violently murdered the night before and her body found at the bottom of an animal cage in the abandoned zoo close to the neighborhood. The adult Sean Devine (Kevin Bacon) is now a detective who takes on the case, and Jimmy starts an investigation himself. Only one person thinks she knows the murderer already: Celeste. From this turning point, Dave starts to behave oddly, almost like a mad man in contrast to his previous calm, repressed self. He watches vampire movies, says he thinks about vampires and werewolves all the time, and starts to believe he is one of them: 'Once it's in you,' Dave tells his wife, 'it stays.' What is 'it' that stays in him? Whether it is being a criminal, paedophile or homosexual, whatever he thinks has stayed in him makes him act inhuman. Not only does Dave act like a character out of a horror film, but *Mystic River*'s style plays on horror archetypes:

> Its 'realism' belongs to the nightmare. The atmosphere is deliberately grim. We don't feel the sun until the end of the movie. Tim Robbins is consistently shot to increase his menace and emphasize his six-foot-five-inch frame in cramped spaces. (Chamberlin 2004)

As Carloss James Chamberlin notes, the film becomes dark after the first hour. Most scenes are shot at night and the use of light is minimal, with Dave's face often lit from underneath, making him look dangerous and monstrous. However, it is not only the style of the film that is reminiscent of horror films. Dave becomes both *obsessed with* and *like* a character from a horror film. Not only does Dave talk about monsters, but Robbins' acting also changes completely once the formerly repressed Dave starts having emotional outbursts. The make-up adds to the monstrosity/vampiric effect; there is so much white powder on Robbins' face that we barely recognise him. His paleness now looks like a corpse who has just woken up. In this make-up and lighting, he looks more like a vampire than any other monster.

According to Nina Auerbach, the vampire genre actually owes its birth to the homoerotic relationship of the authors of the two foundational texts: Lord Byron's *Fragment of a Tale* (1816) and John Polidori's *The Vampyre* (1819) (cited in Dyer 2002: 70). From *Nosferatu* (F. W. Murnau, 1922), which depicts an effeminate vampire who has a homoerotic relationship with his male guest, to Anne Rice's *Interview With the Vampire* (1976), which was not allegedly filmed until 1994 due to its self-conscious references to homosexuality, gay men and lesbian women have frequently been portrayed as vampires – or the depiction of vampires have reminded the audience of homosexuality (see Benshoff: 271). It is in fact possible to comprehend the entire vampire genre as a discussion of homosexuality. Dyer writes:

> What has been imagined through the vampire image is of a piece with how people have thought and felt about homosexual women and men – how others have thought and felt about us, and how we have thought and felt about ourselves. (2002: 73)

Dave's fascination with vampire films is as important as his increasing similarity with the monster. As Milly Williamson points out, 'the vampire has more often fascinated us rather than terrified us' (2005: 1), and it is obvious that Dave is not terrified by watching vampire films. In another sense, fandom of vampire films is a queer pleasure in itself. In Linda Williams' article 'When the Woman Looks', she studies female audiences' relation to looking – especially to looking at a monster. One of the conclusions she reaches is that

> the female look ... shares the male fear of the monster's freakishness, but also recognizes the sense in which this freakishness is similar to her own difference. [...] In other words, in the rare instance when the cinema permits the woman's look, she not only sees a monster, she sees a monster that offers a distorted reflection of her own image. (1996: 22)

Queer audiences' fascination with vampire films, monster films and heroes with supernatural powers could be read in the same way: the appalling figure of the monster frightens the spectator, but his/her freakishness resembles the gay spectator's own. The zombie metaphor is asexual and impotent, but Dave then undergoes a monstrous transformation from the zombie toward the werewolf and vampire figures. The werewolf is sometimes, though not commonly, represented as sexual – for example, in *Underworld* (Len Wiseman, 2003). The vampire, however, is explicitly sexual – for example in *Interview With the Vampire* (Neil Jordan, 1994) and especially in *True Blood* (2008–14). Today, especially for queer audiences, 'the vampire has become an image of ... a glamorous outsider, a figure whose otherness we find versions of (sometimes ambivalently) in ourselves' (Williamson 2005: 1).[7] Therefore Dave's, like queer audiences', fascination with such films and stories symbolises a personal revelation. Dave watches each vampire movie self-consciously; to see his resemblance to the vampire, which is a frightening but also likely to be a fascinating experience. However, the story is also about the other characters' finding out the 'vampire' in Dave, which they wrongly assume to be a heterosexual vampire.

As Dyer (2001) explains, the vampire *kisses* to kill. The attack usually takes place at night in a bedroom, with the victim in a state of sexual expectation, often aroused. This sexual expression is mostly a queer but occasionally a heterosexual one in the genre; when it is a heterosexual expression it is employed as a symbol of uncivilised and violent male heterosexuality (Dyer 2002: 87). Although Kate is not raped before her murder, the way the scene is shot enhances the feeling of rape or sexual assault; a young, beautiful woman running in the forest in the middle of the night, who is then beaten to death with sticks, evidently phallic tools. Her body is found lying in an animal cage in a deserted zoo. When the camera turns to display her body in her small dress, the characters and some audiences will possibly conclude she was raped before being murdered. The use of restricted narration also limits the characters' and viewers' knowledge who assume Dave's sexual awakening comes in the form of violent male heterosexuality. Only later in the film, we find out that when he came home covered in blood, Dave had killed a pederast, a murder discussed further, below. Dyer interrogates vampirism by how it can represent queer sexuality and experience: 'In most vampire tales, the fact that a character is a vampire is only gradually discovered. [...] Much of the suspense of the story is about finding out...' (2002: 78). While the film's characters (particularly Sean, Jimmy and Celeste) are trying to find Kate's murderer, they wrongly assume that they uncovered Dave's deeply repressed and monstrous sexual self.

Zombie, werewolf and vampire figures are all parasites; zombies, like werewolves, eat humans, and vampires are bloodsuckers. Yet there is a significant difference between a zombie and a vampire: a zombie does not know how to die and is a tearful figure of pity, while a vampire wakes up from death to live glamorously as an immortal. Through Dave's murder the film encourages us to read Dave's character as a monster that has to be killed before the order can be restored. Dave can be read as a zombie who refuses to die (although he 'died' on the day of his rape), therefore Jimmy kills him. His brief encroach on the vampire territory does not challenge this reading; according to Dyer, the narrative structure of the vampire tale 'frequently consists of two parts: the first leading up to the discovery of the vampire's hidden nature, the second concerned with his/her destruction' (ibid.). As the characters expose Dave's sexual self, they also plan his eradication. In another film, this could have simply been represented as a coming out of the closet narrative; however, in *Mystic River*'s retrograde ideology about molested children, the pollution can only be eliminated by the destruction of the monster.

Deserved Murder

After a series of misleading clues that come one after another, Jimmy comes to the conclusion that Dave murdered his daughter. His ultra-masculine friends, 'the Savage brothers', put Dave into their car and take him to the Mystic River. Eastwood uses a parallel cut that links this scene to little Dave's being kidnapped by the molesters. This is also a metaphor for Dave's two deaths: the former of his psychological self, and the latter of his physical self. When they reach the banks of the Mystic River, moonlight hits Dave's face, making him look even paler than he does in the rest of the film. Although Dave continuously denies that he murdered Katie and confesses to the killing of a child molester, Jimmy makes him believe he will let Dave live only if he tells 'the truth'. Dave hesitantly accepts that he has murdered Kate; he is stabbed, shot and, finally, thrown into the river just as the police catch the real murderers. These two scenes of murder and capture are intercut with each other.

After the murder, there are three positive changes in the plot that indicate a sense of relief and the restoration of order in the community. First, the real murderers are caught. Then, in the first and only sex scene of the film, Jimmy Markum makes love to his wife, Annabeth (Laura Linney).[8] Finally, detective Sean Devine's long-missing wife suddenly, and without any reason, comes back home with their child. Thus, everyone except Dave's wife is more or less happy. The film applauds the death of the half man, the unliving and the raped. In the ideology that underlines *Mystic River*, these figures are disposable and their elimination brings relief to the neighborhood, not unlike the relief that is brought by the murder of the paedophiles and the pederast in the film. 'We bury our sins here', says Jimmy as he is murdering Dave. In this film, the molesters and the molested are both thrown into the waters of Mystic River.

At the extra-diegetic level, there is another change that shows how reluctant Eastwood is to punish Jimmy. It is implied that Jimmy has already escaped punishment for at least one murder, and although Sean pretends to shoot him with his fingers at the end of the film, it is possible that he will get away with Dave's murder as well. Eastwood thought the novel's ending was too explicit about Sean's pinpointing of Jimmy as suspect, so in the film he decided to be more vague about the ending (see Macklin 2005). In the same interview he also carefully does not comment on whether he thinks Jimmy will be captured and maintains the possibility that he will not, a silence that implicitly serves as Eastwood's wish for and affirmation of Dave's murder.

The ending of *Mystic River* delivers multiple messages. To some extent, it criticises the prejudice of society against men who were raped as children; the moral of the film is just because someone is abused, it does not mean that they will become an abuser. However, although it is emphasised that chaos cannot be overcome through violence, Dave Boyle's murder is also framed as a necessity. As the film asserts both with Dave's characterisation and with use of super-impositiosn, if he lives, Dave will always be suspect in every (sexual) crime that takes place around him. Through his murder Dave is punished not only for his misperformance of masculinity but also as a failed heterosexual. His denunciation of the sexless zombie he has been and his flourishing interest in the lustful vampire is not permitted. In Dave's characterisation, these currents can be traced: a misperformance of masculinity (being unmanly), a violent heterosexuality (the supposed rape instead of consensual sex) and failing at homosexuality (if he remained 'damaged goods' he would not be a threat to women). Hence, Dave is punished for being unreadable as a man just like he is unreadable as a monster (zombie or vampire?) – unstable, unusual and socially unuseful. Isabel Pinedo argues that 'it is only when the monster is truly dead and subject to decay that it ceases to threaten the social order' (1997: 22). In the masculine world *Mystic River* is depicting, queerness is so unacceptable that Dave's murder is portrayed as inevitable and it is represented as a horror film cliché, 'destruction of the monster'.

The Space of the Cellar: Paedophilia and Pederasty as Disease

There are common tropes associated with child abuse that we may look for in analyses of mainstream films concerning male sexual contact with children. Child abusers are typically represented as murderous villains or sadistic serial rapists, and they are reduced to two dimensional characters; for example, the merciless, boy-hungry guards of *Sleepers*, the cruel paedophile rings in *The Lost Son* (Chris Menges, 1999), the incestuous evil father who rapes his children in *Just Evil* (James Ronald Whitney, 2000), the rich local nobleman who is also a pederast and a murderer in *Reckoning*, the immoral paedophile counsellor in *The Weather Man* (Gore Verbinski, 2005) and the paedophile couple in *Running Scared*. In its most extreme, the child abuser becomes a monster, like Freddy Krueger, the protagonist of *A Nightmare on Elm Street* (Wes Craven, 1984) and its many sequels.

The two child abusers in *Mystic River* are similarly reduced to cartoon characters and they are lost in oblivion in the course of the film. One of them is said to have been killed while running from the police and the other one was arrested and 'went the noose route in his cell'. Only towards the end of the film do we learn the molesters' names were Henry and George. Were they married men? Did they have children? Were they a homosexual couple? Did they have sex with each other? Did they prefer boys to girls or did they like children of either sex? As Kevin Ohi puts it, 'an account of the paedophile's point of view is so impossible that the minimal empathy necessary even to identify a paedophile becomes a confession of errant desire' (2000: 204). Hence, it is sufficient to represent the paedophiles only in terms of their destruction, in contrast to Jimmy, who is spared such an ending.

The murdered pederast is also represented as a clichéd character. Towards the end of the film, when Dave confesses his murder of the pederast to a non-believing Jimmy, a flashback depicts the murder: the pederast is in his car, his eyes closed to indicate his enjoyment of the oral sex he is receiving. This is revealed to be Dave's point of view when he opens the car door; he then starts to punch the man and throws him out of the car. The adolescent boy is visible in a single shot before Dave tells him to run away; his blond, probably dyed hair (compared to his dark eyebrows), his childish face and absence of facial hair are visual codes that connote his homosexual identity. Gilbert Herdt argues that commercial sex between younger and older men can be read as a social event that brings older and younger men, and richer and poorer men into union (1997: 72). For example, a young boy might want to use the money to escape homophobic parents. It is not clarified whether the boy is in the car out of pleasure, for prostitution, or both; however, it is clear that the boy is running away from Dave rather than the pederast. Yet the boy's possible pleasure in such an act is unthinkable in this film's politics; where one might see psychological/sexual/financial fulfillment, Dave's characterisation means that the film is only able to imagine pain, abuse and repugnance. Although the sexual act is presented as consensual, the young boy is portrayed as a victim of the pederast, who, as we learn later, had 'three priors'. Dave asks, 'Who cares if a child molester is killed?' This is obviously a rhetorical question; nobody cares.

Mystic River blurs the lines between consensual and non-consensual sex, monstrosity and homosexuality, monstrosity and queerness, paedophilia and pederasty, paedophilia/pederasty and homosexuality; all of these pairs are conflated and reified in the film. David Sibley discusses that in stereotyping there is no interaction with the 'other'; it becomes an arrested, fixated idea about the stereotyped (1995: 18). The paedophiles and the pederast characters in *Mystic River* are in fact stereotypes, represented as perverted men hungry for boys. Like the paedophiles themselves, the space they occupy is also stereotyped in this film. It all starts with a ball gone missing in the sewer. Years later Dave tells his son, 'If we could get that manhole cover up, could be a thousand balls there'. The 'manhole' is no doubt as metaphorical as the sewer it figuratively covers. A sewer represents extreme dirt; the cellar in the film is dirty, and so is the car the molesters drive. It is full of mud and used handkerchiefs, possibly with semen on them. The film attempts to exclude not only the paedophiles/pederasts themselves, but also all of their acts, their victims and the spaces they inhabit. The dirty men are not from our neighbourhood; they are outsiders. Once they take one of us, that person is no longer one of us. This rejection is not simply about 'our neighbourhood', but on a wider scale it is also a rejection of paedophilia/pederasty in 'our civilised culture'. Such films act as a warning that pederasty/paedophilia have to be pushed strongly to somewhere outside 'us'. In the present age, the only acceptable representation of paedophilia in mainstream film seems to be as 'abuse' or 'rape'.

In this chapter I have argued that the central, if sidelined, plot in *Mystic River* is the rape scene, which can be called that only because the depiction connotes rape although there is no actual representation of rape. The characters in the film, like the audience, take for granted that painful anal rape took place in the cellar and in *Mystic River* such rape cripples the victim for life. The abusers in the film are cruel and stereotyped, and the audience is given very brief information about them so that they are not humanised. When the film depicts a pederast having sex with a teenage boy, he is treated just like the abusers by the narrative; the audience is not given any information about him and he is viciously beaten to death. In effect, in the ideology of the film there is no difference between victims, abusers, pederasts and paedophiles: all deserve to be murdered.

Notes

1. There is also a TV show that is almost entirely dedicated to child rape (*Law & Order: Special Victims Unit*; first episode aired on 1999). The same story arc is repeated episode after episode, and year after year. If the number of child rapists represented in this series were an accurate representation of the actual, physical child rapes, not a single child would have been safe in the intervening decades.
2. It is also crucial that it is not always possible to publish objective research about intergenerational sexual contact. When the American Psychological Association (APA) journal published an article based on similar research, which suggested that all adult/child sexual encounters were not detrimental to the children involved, the political pressure was so intense that APA had to release a statement repudiating the conclusions of the research (see Rindt *et al.* 1998).
3. Thus, these films are often small-budget, independent films: such as *Happiness*, *Fat Girl*, *The Woodsman*, *Palindromes* and *Mysterious Skin* (Gregg Araki, 2005).
4. Dave Heaton protests the film's self-indulgence in *Senses of Cinema*: '[this year] my least favourite film-viewing experiences were *Mystic River* and *Irreversible*, two films that were trying so hard to convince me of their importance that I just wanted to walk away, like you'd do to an obnoxious child who desperately wants attention' (2003).
5. Jonathan Rosenbaum summarises the overall approach to *Mystic River*: 'The critical community has spoken: Clint Eastwood's *Mystic River* is a masterpiece and a profound, tragic statement about who we are and the inevitability of violence in our lives – a pitiless view, in which violence begets violence and the sins of the fathers pass to later generations' (2003).
6. See Cook (1989), Clover (1992), Projansky (2001) and Horeck (2004) for a discussion of rape-revenge genre.
7. It is important to note that 'homosexual or homosexually-coded actors' have often been cast as vampires or monsters (Benshoff 1997: 175). This type of casting is might be an attempt to relate to queer audiences.
8. Annabeth's last speech may be read as the director's voice. She convinces her husband that he is not guilty because he did not know. The speech might cause some members of the audience to question her stand but also convinces us of the inevitability of Jimmy's action. The scene ends with the affirmation of her husband and we watch them making love.

Bibliography

Benshoff, H. M. (1997) *Monsters in the Closet: Homosexuality and the Horror Film*. Manchester: Manchester University Press.

Chamberlin, C. J. (2004) 'It Came from the Mystic', *Senses of Cinema*, 30; http://sensesofcinema.com/2004/feature-articles/mystic_river/ (accessed 20 December 2015).

Clover, C. (1992) *Men, Women, and Chain Saws: Gender in the Modern Horror Film*. Princeton, NJ: Princeton University Press.

Cook, P. (1989) 'The Accused', *Monthly Film Bulletin*, 56, 35–6.

Cooper, R. R. (2003) 'Eastwood's "Mystic River"', *Commonweal*, 130, 19; https://www.commonwealmagazine.org/eastwoods-%E2%80%98mystic-river-0 (accessed 20 December 2015).

Davies, J. (2007) 'Imagining Intergenerationality: Representation and Rhetoric in the Pedophile Movie', *GLQ: A Journal of Lesbian and Gay Studies*, 13, 2/3), 369–85.

Dyer, R. (2002) *The Culture of Queers*. London & New York: Routledge.

Faulkner, J. (2010) 'The Innocence Fetish: The Commodification and Sexualisation of Children in the Media and Popular Culture', *Media International Australia, Incorporating Culture & Policy*, 135, 106–17.

Flint, C. (2004) 'Introduction' in C. Flint (ed.) *Spaces of Hate: Geographies of Discrimination and Intolerance in the U.S.A*. New York, NY: Routledge, 1–21.

Hanson, E. (2003) 'Screwing with Children in Henry James', *GLQ: A Journal of Lesbian and Gay Studies*, 9, 3, 367–91.

Heaton, D. (2003) '*2003 World Poll - Part 2*', *Senses of Cinema*, 30; http://sensesofcinema.com/2004/2003-world-poll/favourites2-2/ (accessed 20 December 2015).

Herdt, G. (1997) *Same Sex, Different Cultures: Exploring Gay and Lesbian Life*. Boulder, CO: Westview Press.

Horeck, T. (2004) *Public Rape: Representing Violation in Fiction and Film*. London and New York, NY: Routledge.

Kincaid, J. R. (1998) *Erotic Innocence: The Culture of Child Molesting*. Durham, NC: Duke University Press.

Levine, J. (2002) *Harmful to Minors: The Perils of Protecting Children from Sex*. Minneapolis, MN: University of Minnesota Press.

Macklin, T. (2005) 'Plant Your Feet and Tell the Truth', *Bright Lights Film Journal*; http://brightlightsfilm.com/plant-your-feet-and-tell-the-truth-an-interview-with-clint-eastwood/#.VnbdlhV97IU (accessed 20 December 2015).

Ohi, K. (2000) 'Molestation 101: Child Abuse, Homophobia, and the Boys of St. Vincent', *GLQ: A Journal of Lesbian and Gay Studies*, 6, 2, 195–248.

Pinedo, I. C. (1997) *Recreational Terror: Women and the Pleasures of Horror Film Viewing*. Albany, NY: State University of New York Press.

Projansky, S. (2001) *Watching Rape: Film and Television in Postfeminist Culture*. New York, NY: New York University Press.

Rindt, B. *et al*. (1998) 'A Meta-Analytic Examination of Assumed Properties of Child Sexual Abuse Using College Samples', *Psychological Bulletin*, 124,1, 22–53.

Rosenbaum, J. (2003) 'Vengeance Is Theirs', *Chicago Reader*; http://www.chicagoreader.com/chicago/vengeance-is-theirs/Content?oid=913590 (accessed 20 December 2015).

Russo, V. (1981) *The Celluloid Closet: Homosexuality in the Movies*. New York, NY: Harper & Row.

Sibley, D. (1995) *Geographies of Exclusion*. London and New York, NY: Routledge.

Taubin, A. (2005) 'Ostriches in the Snow', *Film Comment*, 41, 2, 62.

Waites, M. (2005) *The Age of Consent: Young People, Sexuality and Citizenship*. New York, NY: Palgrave Macmillan.

Williams, L. (1984) 'When the Woman Looks', in B. K. Grant (ed.) *The Dread of Difference: Gender and the Horror Film*. Austin, TX: University of Texas Press, 15–35.

Williamson, M. (2005) *The Lure of the Vampire: Gender, Fiction and Fandom from Bram Stoker to Buffy*. London and New York, NY: Wallflower Press.

Wood, R. (1986) *Hollywood from Vietnam to Reagan*. New York, NY: Columbia University Press.

Wood, R. (2003) *Hollywood from Vietnam to Reagan ... and Beyond*. New York, NY: Columbia University Press.

Chapter 8
Crash-and-Burn Girls and Culpable Parenthood: Negotiating Sexualisation Discourses in Independent Cinema

JOEL GWYNNE

Over the last two decades contemporary cultural production has testified to an increasing fascination with both girls' bodies and girlhood as a social category. Scholars such as Marnina Gonick have understood this pronounced interest as an expression of the 'uncertainties elicited by the rapid social, economic, and political changes taking places due to neoliberal policies' (2006: 5), asserting that neoliberalism's emphasis on personal responsibility has advanced scrutiny upon young women as consumers and citizens; the new generation on whom the future depends. This scrutiny has led to considerable claims upon contemporary girls, with competing narratives in academic discourse and popular culture positioning them in markedly antithetical ways, either as standard bearers of neoliberal success and post-feminist agency, or as abject figures who are in-crisis or at-risk. This oscillation between understanding girls as agentic and understanding them as disempowered has been theorised as a 'can-do/at-risk dichotomy' (Harris 2004: 18), yet it is the at-risk girl who has, unsurprisingly, attracted greater critical investigation. Indeed, academic research and social commentary has been particularly interested in exploring the vulnerability of the at-risk girl exposed to multiple threats under patriarchy and capitalism. Some of these have secured notable commercial success, not least Mary Pipher's *Reviving Ophelia: Saving the Selves of Adolescent Girls* (1994) and Rosalind Wiseman's *Queen Bees and Wannabees* (2002). Many of the 'crisis' issues addressed by these texts – from relational aggression to eating disorders to concerns regarding sexual behaviour – have also become central to depictions of girlhood in popular culture in coming-of-age films such as *Thirteen* (Catherine Hardwicke, 2003), *Mean Girls* (Mark Waters, 2004), *The Sisterhood of the Travelling*

Pants (Ken Kwapis, 2005), *Pretty Persuasion* (Marcos Siega, 2005) and *The Babysitters* (David Ross, 2007) – to name only a few – all of which centre on the complex negotiations and exchanges of adolescent female friendships.

Given that the female body – and the young female body in particular – is subjected to intense public enquiry in popular and post-feminist media culture, it is not surprising that anxieties surrounding girls' sexual behaviour remain a central trope of adolescent cinema, often focusing on young women attempting to navigate the nebulous terrain of desirable and punishable sexual mores. If, as Sara McClelland and Michelle Fine assert, female sexuality has been historically linked with 'excess and fears of what lurks over the border of what is required, necessary and sufficient' (2008: 86) then female adolescents are required to remain especially vigilant in their sexual conduct. The line that divides girls' normative and deviant sexual behaviour has become precariously narrow and difficult to discern in recent times, especially in Anglo-American contexts where a sexualised appearance is a highly prized form of erotic capital and yet sexual activity remains primarily, if not exclusively, condemned. Sarah Hentges has noted the manner in which adolescent cinema often confronts female sexuality in complex ways, asserting that the 'terrain of teen films offers a variety of representations of sex education (from school and parents) as well as its own form of sex education' (2006: 35), yet she maintains that when 'plot lines do include sex, it is most often the boy actively pursuing sex' (2006: 13). Mainstream adolescent cinema can be perceived, then, as an inscription and reflection of other forms of popular culture where the female adolescent as a sexual subject or sexual citizen remains fundamentally invisible (see Egan 2013). To account for the absence of girls' sexual agency within cinema it is important to understand the ways in which contemporary culture disempowers girls even as it attempts to protect them from disempowerment, particularly in the wake of moral panics surrounding the sexualisation of youth and the mainstreaming of pornography.

Danielle Egan and others have noted that the current discourse on sexualisation narrows its range of concern to a particular demographic – the white, middle-class and heterosexual t(w)eenage girl (see Renold and Ringrose 2008; Egan 2013). Unlike other socially divisive topics, sexualisation has accumulated currency as discourse where both politicians and policymakers (conservatives and liberals alike) are able to find common ground in their attempts to safeguard the 'innocence' of the vulnerable, middle-class girl against the alleged pervasiveness of the sex industry. It is a discourse that has produced provocative, protectionist narratives which inspire strong reactions in their invocation of anxieties surrounding sexual corruption and defiled innocence. According to commentators, the media sexualisation of children is responsible for the ascent of 'the promiscuous and emotionally deficient teenager' (Papadopolous 2010: n.p.), resulting in young women's inability to form healthy intimate relationships and their descent into destructive behaviour such as binge eating, intercourse with older men, under-age pregnancy, prostitution and suicide (see Durham 2008). Protection narratives seek to resist the degeneration of the young by asserting that young girls require immunity from multiple risks which primarily fall into the categories of: i) consuming sexually salacious materials; ii) moving beyond the protective gaze of the parents; and iii) interacting with individuals deemed socially marginable or transgressive. Taking protectionist narratives as a cultural context for exploring issues surrounding girls' sexual agency, this chapter is concerned with exploring two films, *Thirteen* and *Trust* (David Schwimmer, 2010), which engage with all three of the aforementioned risks. Produced almost a decade apart, *Thirteen* and *Trust* are useful texts for examining how all three risks can be understood within the milieu of cultural anxieties concerning social transformations such as the emergence of children as active consumers and the rise of social networking. More significantly, the chapter will discuss how contemporary independent film positions parents as crucial mediators of girls at risk in ways which disempower them.

Crash-and-Burn Transformations

As films focusing on adolescent experience, *Thirteen* and *Trust* pursue a number of generic themes such as identity transformation, peer pressure, rebellion and parental conflict. In *Trust*, a suburban family are forced to negotiate the aftershock of their daughter's loss of virginity to a sexual predator whom she meets at a hotel after communicating via online chat and phone. In *Thirteen*, the audience witnesses a teenage daughter's descent into drug abuse, underage sex and self-harm after forging a close friendship with a socially delinquent peer in lieu of a strong and positive parental role model. As two films with female teenage protagonists, *Trust* and *Thirteen* share similar narratalogical and thematic concerns despite focusing on families of differing socio-economic circumstances. In *Trust*, fourteen-year-old Annie Cameron (Liana Liberato) is the daughter of affluent parents, residing in suburban middle-class Chicago, while *Thirteen* focuses on working-class teenagers Tracy Freeland (Evan Rachel Wood) and Evie Zamora (Nikki Reed). Tracy's mother Melanie (Holly Hunter) is a divorced hairdresser struggling to financially and emotionally support her once studious but increasingly rebellious daughter, whose new best friend, Evie, has established herself as a destructive presence in Tracey's life. Like Tracy, Annie in *Trust* is also positioned as a well-behaved teen seeking affirmation from more popular and rebellious peers, yet one whose loneliness contributes to her decision to explore cyberspace in her search for a soul mate. *Thirteen* reflects anxieties concerning the consequences of peer pressure on girls at a vulnerable stage in life, and is thus primarily interested in identifying adolescent transgression as a consequence of negative, external social forces. *Trust* is in this respect similar, for Annie's transgression of underage sex occurs through contact with a negative external influence in the form of 'Charlie', a middle-aged Physics teacher who masquerades online as an older teenager. As films dealing with adolescents, it is perhaps not surprising that both narratives focus on transformation. Both *Thirteen* and *Trust* demonstrate acute anxieties in their rendering of young female characters on the verge of adulthood, at a life stage of visible and invisible becoming where the biological changes of puberty, emergent sexuality and the formation of significant peer relationships all intersect.

Even though adolescence has for more than a century been pathologised by adults as a developmental period of difficulties and disturbances – requiring a variety of interventions and reforms – the films discussed in this chapter are more interested in documenting difficulties and disturbances rather than exploring the social circumstances which create them. Both *Thirteen* and *Trust* can be usefully understood as texts which are symptomatic of the contemporary fascination with troubled white teens, or what Sarah Projanksy has termed 'the crash-and-burn' girl. Citing high-profile girl celebrities such as Britney Spears and Lindsey Lohan, Projanksy has persuasively argued that the intense media preoccupation with their various 'transgressions' demonstrates the imbrication of can-do and at-risk discourses which showcase 'the can-do girl who has it all, but who – through weakness and/or the inability to live with the pressure of celebrity during the process of growing up – makes a mistake and therefore faces a spectacular descent into at-risk status' (2014: 4). While teen stars such as Spears and Lohan ostensibly 'have it all', the cultural fascination with their descent into drug abuse functions 'as a warning to all young women that failure is an ever-lurking possibility that must be staved off through sustained application' (Gonick 2006: 23). Simply put, the successful, neoliberal can-do girl must remain vigilant, lest she become at-risk.

The opening scene of *Thirteen* highlights the fragile status of girlhood and renders the abject transformation of Tracy acute through the use of flashback. The audience sees Evie and Tracy sniffing solvents in a bedroom, and the hysterical laughter accompanying this act marks them as 'unruly women' (see Karlyn 1995). Their transgression is accentuated by a soundtrack of hard rock music and close-up shots of the girls' heavily made-up faces. More significantly, a close-up shot of Evie's mouth reveals her tongue stud; a signifier of the sex industry and an early indication that the film is concerned with the hypersexualisation of young women. This dramatic opening is juxtaposed with a flashback of Tracy four months earlier. In marked contrast, Tracy is now seen walking her dog, wearing age-appropriate, if not immature, clothes; a pair of jeans with patchwork designs on the thighs. She is without make-up, and her hair is styled in bunches; read by the audience as a consummate image of fetishised girl-next-door innocence. Tracy's rapid transformation from ideal daughter to social deviant occurs as a consequence of her contact with Evie, and commensurate with the cultural construction of girls' sexual expres-

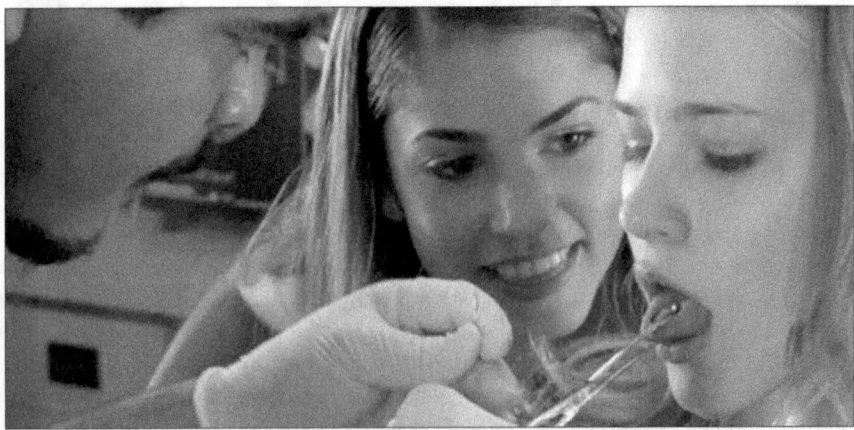

Fig. 1: Tracey's (Evan Rachel Wood) descent into abjection in *Thirteen* (2003).

sion as taboo, the narrative makes apparent that Evie's open sexual expression is the primary reason why Tracy descends into deviancy.

Our first introduction to Evie occurs vicariously. Prior to her onscreen arrival she is sighted from distance by a boy in school, who states to the camera: 'Looks like Evie grew up this summer.' The camera pans to the left, rests on Evie flicking her hair, and then tracks the movement of her lower body as she walks, specifically her exposed waist. Even prior to speaking, Evie is understood to be a highly sexual presence, and her clothing marks her out as working-class and subcultural. Valerie Walkerdine has noted that, in historical terms, 'dangerous, licentious sexuality has been constructed as the purview of working-class women that may potentially contaminate an idealised, sexually innocent, or at least "coy", purer guise of, middle-class feminine sexual subjectivity' (1997: 78). The film affirms such a statement at various junctures by continually emphasising how Evie destroys the lives of those with whom she associates. Her abundant sexuality attracts not only the boys in the school, but normative girls such as Tracy who admire her confident sexual performance in an institutional culture where female corporeality is subject to public scrutiny, evaluation and condemnation. In this regard, the film's representational strategies suggest that the uncontainable sexuality of minority working-class girls such as Evie arouses acute anxieties as a contamination of the middle-class heteronormative ideal of childhood innocence. Indeed, it remains significant that Evie's transgressive sexuality accords with her status as a minority, for while her ethnicity is never defined in the narrative she has dark skin and dark features; the actress who plays her is of Cherokee and Italian descent. Evie's ethnicity is in marked contrast to Tracy who as blonde-haired, blue-eyed and pale-faced, corresponds with contemporary culture's vision of childhood innocence and heteronormativity (see Projansky 2014). Tracy's descent into drug abuse, theft and underage sex serves as a reminder to the audience of what can happen to 'ordinary' girls who mix with working-class, minority girls.

Consuming Sexualized Tweens

In counterpoint to Tracy, Annie in *Trust* remains law-abiding throughout the film. As a middle-class girl with affluent parents she is safely removed from the contaminating influence of working-class peers. In the narrative, her crash-and-burn transformation occurs as a consequence of navigating the unsafe space of the Internet; a location beyond parental supervision. The threat to Annie comes not in the form of a girl, but a male sexual predator; more specifically, a middle-aged teacher masquerading online as a high school Junior. Yet, despite this key difference, both films share the position that even though outsiders such as a deviant peers and sexual predators undoubtedly pose an imminent threat to vulnerable young girls, the real danger lies in children's susceptibility to the twinned influences of the mass media and consumer culture. In this way both films speak to moral panics which have emerged in recent years concerning girls 'growing up too soon' and engaging in risky behaviour. Mary Celeste Kearney has argued that radical transformations in the physical and social experiences of teenage girls 'have made the differences between female childhood, adolescence and adulthood increasingly difficult to discern' (2002: 129), and *Trust* begins with a discussion concerning age-appropriate behaviour. On Annie's fourteenth birthday her brother presents her with a dress 'like the one you saw on *The Hills*'; her parents interject and ruminate on whether such role models are acceptable for young girls. Even early on in the narrative the audience is therefore led to conclude that Annie's decision to go to a hotel with a middle-aged man later in the film may be a consequence of mass media influence; she is not an agent, but a victim.

The reinvention of youth citizenship as consumer power has been largely enacted through young women. As standard bearers of consumer citizenship, young women are emblematic of the 'problematic knitting together of feminist and neoliberal ideology about power and opportunities' (Harris 2004: 165). Like *Trust*, *Thirteen* is also concerned with the complex imbrication of consumerism, empowerment and disempowerment in the form of sexualisation, depicting teens as voracious consumers who are inappropriately heterosexualised by capitalism and the media. At an early point in the film the audience sees Tracy heading out to meet Evie, and as she travels on the bus we see her eyes meeting several billboards advertising Armani and other global brands. In order to stress the force of these advertisements, we are presented with a fast-paced montage of close-up shots of the billboards. After meeting Evie at a clothes store, Tracy observes her friend steal several items, and after leaving the store Tracy opportunistically steals a wallet from a woman's handbag. The film constructs the teenagers as both deviants and victims who are guilty of criminal offences, but only due to their inability to resist the pressures of consumer culture. More significantly, the film demonstrates a commitment to underscoring the imbrication of consumer culture and the sexualisation of young women. At one point in the film Melanie enters Tracy's room and finds a thong, on the front of which is printed a cartoon picture of a dog and the text 'Wanna bone?' The cartoon design integrating both sexual suggestion and the cultural signifiers of childhood implicates consumer culture as central to the eroticisation of innocence. The scene implies that Tracy's consumption of erotic products positions her as a victim of discourses which reinforce the post-feminist and neoliberal notion that success and power for young people are increasingly linked to sexualised consumption practices. By constructing her in this way, Tracy is conceptualised as an embodiment of a new cohort of bad girls 'indulging in disordered consumption' and enacting 'the gains of feminism in problematic ways' (Harris 2004: 29). While Tracy clearly sees buying such products as empowering, culture produces such girls as problematic, posing a threat to both themselves and to the sanctified status of childhood. Sexualised by capitalism, we are encouraged to read Tracy as embodying the ethos of a pornified culture where consuming sexualising materials catalyses unsavoury desires and subjectivities.

Both *Trust* and *Thirteen* can therefore be read as anti-sexualisation films. They are texts which underscore the power of the mass media, capitalism, commercial culture and, in counterpoint to these forces, reinstate the complete passivity of girls. The films support the contention that sexualisation is pandemic in its reach and impact, permeating all aspects of the landscape of girls' lived experience. Sexualisation discourses are, of course, difficult to resist and critique. As Danielle Egan has asserted:

the twining of defiled innocence, precocious sexual promiscuity with a clearly defined antagonist – popular culture – makes this discourse deeply seductive and its rhetoric self-evidently true. Its omnipresence and the consequences involved make critique almost impossible and often politically suspect – after all, who can be for the sexualization of young girls? (2013: 19).

Like Egan, I remain attentive to the destructive effects of the media, yet what interests me in this chapter is how films such as *Trust* and *Thirteen* propagate disempowering messages about girls' lack of agency when faced with potentially damaging external influences. The films affirm female adolescents as the most powerless individuals in our culture; their bodies are viewed, consumed, eroticised and fetishised, and yet they ultimately have no control over their lives. Their power as consuming subjects is negated and nullified by the insistence that they make abject choices, and yet they are held up as objects of consumption. Irrespective of the severity of the commercial exploitation of young women's bodies, *Trust* and *Thirteen* refuse to recognise that the body is not always a source of anxiety. In *Thirteen* in particular, even though Evie and Tracy demonstrate corporeal confidence, a conception of their bodies as sites of positive self-expression, identity creation and pleasure is entirely overlooked. This is most clear in a scene in which both girls dress up in pink feather boas to perform a skit, and are inexplicably admonished by Tracy's mother.

The most aggressive assertion of teen girls' powerlessness comes in *Trust*. As in *Thirteen*, the film draws peer pressure to the fore in ways which illustrate the pervasiveness of sexualisation. When Annie is invited to a house party hosted by a popular girl in school, she finds her peers topless riding plastic horses and teaching each other how to perform oral sex on inanimate objects. Annie excuses herself and leaves the room, and in doing so renders herself childlike and vulnerable in comparison. The conflict between Annie's desire to be perceived as a mature young woman, and yet her inability to deal with the emotional, psychological and physiological complexities of sexual relations, is a key narrative concern. Indeed, when Annie meets her online boyfriend Charlie for the first time, she discovers that he is not a high school junior but rather a middle-aged man. When she shows her disappointment, Charlie persuades her that age is not important, stating: 'I thought you were old enough to understand that.' By exploiting Annie's anxieties surrounding her perceived immaturity – anxieties generated by her aggressively sexual peers such as Serena – Charlie is able to persuade Annie into following him to a hotel, where they have sex.

While figures such as Charlie are clearly external threats to childhood innocence, the fact that Annie succumbs to the desires of a sexual predator is in no small part attributed to the sexualisation of girls by the mass media. Her father, Will (Clive Owen), is an advertising executive currently involved in a marketing campaign for a new line of clothes. He is complimented for his 'work in the tween market' at several points in the film, and the campaign for his new line of clothes features several young models in various stages of undress. Upon seeing, for the first time, the adverts that his team have developed, he flippantly remarks: 'These are definitely for a clothing company, right? Then why isn't anyone wearing a shirt?' Later on in the film after he learns of his daughter's sexual activity, he revisits the adverts once again and begins to hallucinate; the images transform and morph into the image of his daughter in sexually suggestive poses. The association is heavily indicative of Will's guilt; it implies that the advertising industry he works for – and its sexualisation of young women – is directly responsible for what happens to girls like his daughter. In this regard, *Trust* reifies public discourses which lament the commodification of childhood at the hands of manipulative marketing strategies, and in doing so denies agency to teens by refusing to acknowledge their capacity to act as discriminating and active consumers/sexual citizens who are able to resist external demands.

Culpable Parenthood

Transgressive girls in *Thirteen* and *Trust* are thus disempowered in a number of ways. They are positioned as impressionable youth exposed and vulnerable to external threats both personal and political, such as deviant individuals and mass media institutions. Understood in this way, Annie, Tracy and Evie can only be perceived as young women making heinous decisions or, at the very best, compromised choices. Yet, just as both films under discussion negate the agency of young women, they also absolve young women of responsibility for their actions. Indeed, even though both films make it abundantly clear that external threats are factors in the sexualisation of young women, it is parents who are rendered ultimately responsible for their children's wayward behaviour. In *Thirteen*, Tracey's mother Melanie is constructed as loving but non-conformist. She is perpetually clad in denim, and styled as an old-school rocker. At the start of the film her daughter's attire is the epitome of youthful innocence, and this contrast between mother and daughter implicitly suggests that the former's descent into deviancy is, one some level, attributable to the latter's own deviance from the normative scripts of motherhood. The dominant cultural understanding of motherhood idealises mothers as guardians of children's welfare, responsible for the preservation, growth and social acceptability of their children (see Ruddick 1982). This is a primarily white, middle-class construction of motherhood which has been professionalised by medical and childcare manuals, producing limited definitions of appropriate ways that children should be reared. Single working-class mothers, in particular, experience difficulties in attempting to adhere to idealised images of motherhood and constructions of 'normality' and 'commonsense' parenting; access to childcare, safe access to outdoor space and a safe living environment is, after all, a class privilege (see Katz 1994).

In lieu of exploring the complexities of her circumstances, *Thirteen* instead seeks to render Melanie as an abject mother. The film focuses on parental irresponsibility, demonstrating how she does not invest enough time into nurturing her daughter. This is evoked in one scene in particular in which Tracy attempts to read poetry to her mother; in a hurry to leave the house, Melanie is dismissive. In failing to support her daughter's creative and academic pursuits, the film implies that Tracy's decent into deviancy is an apt punishment for mothers who abdicate from the maternal role. Furthermore, Melanie is unable to maintain a stable relationship with an 'appropriate' life partner. Melanie's estranged husband has no time for his daughter due to work commitments, and her new boyfriend is neither a consistent nor a positive influence. He drifts in and out of family life, spends most of his time residing in a halfway house, and even uses drugs. Melanie is thus constructed as a character who makes poor decisions for herself and for her daughter, despite being cognisant of the importance of good parenting models. At an early point in the narrative arc Melanie confesses that she was herself without a mother when she was young. Such a confession works to intensify her status as an abject mother by suggesting that absent mothers produce abject daughters; abjection becomes generational, rendering mothers as perpetually responsible for their daughter's abjection.

Like *Thirteen*, *Trust* similarly disempowers girls by shifting the narrative away from teen sexual agency towards the territory of parental culpability. After learning of Annie's sexual encounter with Charlie, her father Will takes a prurient interest in uncovering the salacious details of their rendezvous. He acquires the transcripts of her sexually explicit IM (Instant Messaging) conversations, and declares, 'She's 14. Where the hell did she learn this? Our daughter sounds like a fucking porn star!' In doing so, the film once again summons moral panics surrounding childhood sexualisation, but also works to express the view that despite negative external influences the solution to sexualisation lies much closer to home. After Will begins searching the National Sex Offenders Registry database in a bid to find the man who took away his daughter's virginity, his wife questions his response: 'She's in pain and she needs you and you're sitting there doing nothing.' The film implicitly critiques both moral panics surrounding sexualisation and hegemonic masculinity; the former by depicting Will joining a group hyperbolically named PervertTrackers, and the latter by showing how his obsession with retribution and violence occurs at the expense of his daughter's welfare.

While this emphasis on the responsibility of parents in protecting their children may appear to be commendable, such a narrative thrust functions to elide the voices of teens while gatekeeping the idyll of childhood innocence. Significantly, in *Trust* Annie's subjective response to her sexual encounter with Charlie is obscured amidst both the moral indignation of her parents and the medical pathologisation of the encounter. In the film, the sexual encounter itself is depicted in ambivalent terms; the deep focus shots of various parts of Annie's anatomy conveys a sense of objectification, disorientation and a lack of control, and yet after the implied rape Annie remains committed to Charlie. In an attempt to placate her parents, Annie matter-of-factly declares: 'It's not that big a deal. We met up on Saturday. We had sex. We're in love' – and yet while these words appear to be agentic the audience is instead encouraged to believe they are nothing more than a coping mechanism in response to the atrocity. Annie is, it is implied, attempting to make the rape intelligible by forcing the events within a romantic script rather than one which positions her as the victim. Such attempts to empower herself are consistently denied. When Annie meets a counsellor and describes intercourse with Charlie as 'like I was watching it from above', the counsellor informs Annie that she 'found a way to remove or distance [herself] psychologically'. The film makes it progressively clear that Annie is deluded about both her feelings for Charlie and his for her; we learn that he has attacked multiple girls using the same tactics of online seduction, and that his IP address can be tracked to the Czech Republic. Despite Annie's conviction that he is 'sweet and nice and very funny', the audience knows better; Charlie is a sophis-

Fig. 2: Annie (Liana Liberato) in *Trust* (2010) finally accepts her victim status.

ticated sexual predator, and Annie is a deluded young girl. By placing knowledge in the hands of adults within the film narrative, Annie is further disempowered, and a complete submission to adults occurs at the close of the film when her victimhood is brought brutally to the fore. After an FBI agent shows Annie photos of three other girls who Charlie raped, she finally declares: 'He raped me. How could I have been so stupid?' Annie's devastation at the close of *Trust* makes a significant statement about the objectification of teens in culture. Annie is a victim of external influences, which occur in the form of peer pressure, sexualisation by the media and consumer culture and sexual predators. She is also a victim of parental neglect. While the film's commitment to illustrating the potential dangers that teens face is politically well-intentioned, the agency and subjectivity of the teen is lost; the dénouement implicitly celebrates the position of parents as moral custodians and adolescent agency is nullified.

Conclusion

Adolescents are culturally recognised as 'awkwardly placed between childhood and adulthood: sometimes constructed and represented as "innocent" "children" in need of protection from adult sexuality, violence and commercial exploitation: at other times represented as articulating adult vices of drink, drugs and violence' (Valentine 2004: 6). The movement between representing teen experience as wholesome and representing it as deviant often materialises as a pronounced tension in cinematic depictions of adolescence. While key creative forces such as directors and screenwriters may be keen to articulate the divergent lives of adolescents across the spectrum of innocence and experience, they are also forced to remain attentive to consumer demands and the expectations of markets and culture. In a cultural climate where the reverence of childhood innocence holds sway, the depiction of transgressive childhoods via the cinema screen remains restricted in mainstream cinematic production. In light of these restrictions one can expect taboo content to hold a certain degree of ambivalence in mainstream cinema, and despite being independent productions the films discussed in this chapter also demonstrate their ambiguity by sensationalising adolescent resistance and ultimately containing such resistance. Childhood is seen as threatened by pressures towards early maturity, highlighting a fundamental contradiction in discourses around children and adolescents: childhood is regarded as a natural state and yet one that is also at risk, requiring vigilance in order to protect, preserve and manage it. *Thirteen* and *Trust* perpetuate totalising discourses concerning teen sexuality; they function as moralising cautionary tales that fetishise working-class sexuality and dramatise the contamination of middle-class suburbia. These films could be read as especially disappointing since, as Sarah Hentges notes, girls often 'take more control of their sexuality in independent films' (2006: 15). While ostensibly offering 'edgy' representations of girlhood, the films' narrative emphasis on the role of parents in protecting children from harm renders these films conventional. Furthermore, in attempting to understand the causes of teen transgression, complex cultural and interpersonal determinants such as poverty, familial conditions, curiosity and, perhaps most importantly, desire, give way to a simplistic commitment to the all-encompassing power of the mass media and commodities.

Bibliography

Durham, M. G. (2008) *The Lolita Effect: The Media Sexualization of Girls and What We Can Do About It*. Woodstock, NY: Overlook Press.

Egan, R. D. (2013) *Becoming Sexual: A Critical Appraisal of the Sexualization of Girls*. Cambridge: Polity Press.

Gonick, M. (2006) 'Between "Girl Power" and "Reviving Ophelia"', *NWSA Journal*, 18, 2, 1–23.

Harris, A. (2004) *Future Girl: Young Women in the Twenty-First Century*. New York: Routledge.

Hentges, S. (2006) *Pictures of Girlhood: Modern Female Adolescence on Film*. Jefferson, NC: McFarland.

Karlyn, K. R. (1995) *The Unruly Woman: Gender and Genres of Laughter*. Austin, TX: University of Texas Press.

Katz, C. (1994) 'Textures of Global Change: Eroding Ecologies of Childhood in New York and Sudan', *Childhood*, 2, 103–10.

Kearney, M. C. (2002) 'Girlfriends and Girl Power: Female Adolescence in Contemporary U.S. Cinema', in F. Gateward and M. Pomerance (eds) *Sugar, Spice and Everything Nice: Cinemas of Girlhood*. Detroit, MI: Wayne State University Press, 125–42.

McClelland, S. I. and M. Fine (2008) 'Rescuing a Theory of Adolescent Sexual Excess: Young Women and Wanting', in A. Harris (ed.) *Next Wave Cultures: Feminism, Subcultures, Activism*. New York, NY: Routledge, 83–102.

Papadopoulos, L. (2010). *Sexualization of Young People Review*. London: Home Office.

Pipher, M. (1994) *Reviving Ophelia: Saving the Selves of Adolescent Girls*. New York, NY: Ballantine Books.

Projansky, S. (2014) *Spectacular Girls: Media Fascination and Celebrity Culture.* New York, NY: New York University Press.

Renold, E. and J. Ringrose (2008) 'Regulation and Rupture: Mapping Tween and Teenage Girls' Resistance to the Heterosexual Matrix', *Feminist Theory*, 9, 3, 313–38.

Ruddick, S. (1982) 'Maternal Thinking' in B. Thorne and M. Yalom (eds) *Rethinking the Family: Some Feminist Questions.* London: Longman, 34–52.

Valentine, G. (2004) *Public Space and the Culture of Childhood.* Farnham: Ashgate.

Walkerdine, V. (1997) *Daddy's Girl: Young Girls and Popular Culture.* Basingstoke: Palgrave Macmillan.

Wiseman, R. (2002) *Queen Bees and Wannabes: Helping Your Daughter Survive Cliques, Gossip, Boyfriends, and the New Realities of Girl World.* New York, NY: Harmony Books.

Chapter 9
'Please be a good boy': Challenging Perceptions of Paedophilia in Contemporary US Cinema

AMY C. CHAMBERS

Mysterious Skin (Greg Araki, 2004), *Hard Candy* (David Slade, 2005) and *Little Children* (Todd Field, 2006) are emblematic of a cycle of films released in the early twenty-first century that engage with the issues surrounding child abuse. These films, alongside other examples including *L.I.E.* (Michael Cuesta, 2001), *Birth* (Jonathan Glazer, 2004), *The Woodsman* (Nicole Kassell, 2004) and *Notes on a Scandal* (Richard Eyre 2006), offer a balanced and therefore controversial representation of the paedophile by giving both paedophiles and their victims a voice. Paedophiles are presented as sympathetic, caring, broken and, in some instances, victims themselves. Children are reframed as active figures with an often-burgeoning sexuality that further complicates the relationship between the abuser and the abused. Rather than aligning with the Western media's 'stranger danger' moral panics of the 1980s and 1990s, these films attempt to offer a complex response to a taboo subject.[1] Their developed characters contrast with the 'characters' circulated in news media of the demonised paedophile and the damaged victim by providing a nuanced response to the crime, and its impact upon the lives of both victim *and* perpetrator.

Mysterious Skin tells the divergent tales of two boys, Neil (Joseph Gordon-Levitt) and Brian (Brady Corbett), who experience sexual abuse at the hand of their Little League coach (Bill Sage). Whereas Neil grows up to be a male prostitute, his counterpart Brian is practically asexual. Neil rejects the idea that he was a victim and the film narrative explores the notion of victimhood by placing the character in role of both victim and perpetrator. Coach is framed as a fantasy figure who appears in dream sequences when Neil fellates his clients in later-life as a teenage prostitute. The seemingly cocksure Neil is compared to his clearly damaged counterpart Brian who develops a pervasive fantasy that explains his blackouts: alien abduction. *Hard Candy* subverts the role of the victim; Hayley (Ellen Paige) the juvenile anti-hero essentially grooms the paedophile, Jeff (Patrick Wilson), through an online chat room. She defines herself as an avenger seeking justice for molested girls by abusing Jeff on their behalf. *Little Children* explores some of the difficulties experienced by a sex offender and their family when rejoining a community after his release from prison. In this final film the victims of abuse are not necessarily just little children. Each film approaches the figure and the role of the paedophile in individual and public discourses and uses them to explore often socially unacceptable forms of sex and desire, whilst also transgressing traditional boundaries concerning conceptions of children and adults, and abusers and victims.

The child abuse panics in the US during the 1980s and 1990s were underpinned by an apparent upsurge and increased reportage of sophisticated paedophile rings and child abuse by the clergy and other authority figures. These issues were reflected in TV-movies like *Do You Know the Muffin Man* (Gilbert Cates, 1989), that features a neighbourhood day-care centre where children are being systematically abused, *Judgment* (Tom Topor, 1990) and *The Boys of St. Vincent* (John N. Smith, 1992), that revolve around the abuse of boys at the hands of the clergy, and the horror of organised paedophile rings in *Bump in the Night* (Karen Arthur, 1991). These movies presented the paedophile as unremarkable and 'camouflaged by ordinariness' (Rafter 2007: 225), which made him more dangerous because he could blend into a neighbourhood unnoticed. The monstrous paedophile can also be found as a horror figure; for example, Freddy Krueger (Robert Englund) from *A Nightmare on Elm Street* (Wes Craven, 1984) is 'coded as a child molester' (Heba 1995: 110); this actual monster is an embodiment of the nightmare and consequences of abuse.[2] These earlier images of the paedophile align with media images that frame them as 'monsters', 'beasts' and 'fiends' (Thomas 2005: 21).

This chapter analyses the different representations of desire, victims and abuse in a cinematic turn that subverted images of the monstrous in cinematic child abuse narratives. This cycle was made possible by the independent sector of the American filmmaking industry that exists both in parallel to the traditional Hollywood system, and in isolation from it. The early 2000s were one of independent cinema's 'most commercial periods' with a boom in globally successful films made with limited budgets and limited studio interference (see King *et al.* 2013: 3). *Mysterious Skin*, *Hard Candy* and *Little Children* were all made on low budgets with smaller independent production companies rather than mini-majors or the indie wings of major studios. Gregg Araki, director and screenwriter of *Mysterious Skin*, agreed to a lower than planned budget for the film because he 'never, never wanted the movie to be too big, because it was fairly controversial material and [he] didn't want to have to water it down to make it palatable for a mini-major-type company' (2005: n.p.). In order to explore the controversial issues of abuse and desire at play in the child abuse narratives central to *Mysterious Skin*, *Hard Candy* and *Little Children*, independent production was essential.

Independent cinema permits a more nuanced representation of abuser/abused narratives that neither demonises the abuser nor strips the abused of agency.

Films such as *Mysterious Skin*, *Hard Candy* and *Little Children* sit outside of the constraints of the Hollywood industry's control; American independent cinema has a wider scope for experimentation and transgression. These films represent both the perpetrator and child as fluid characters that do not neatly fit into traditional definitions, allowing for the development of a more involved narrative beyond the genre confines of horror, thriller and melodrama. This film cycle contrasts heavily with the mass media's moral panics about child molestation that retain a binaristic definition and focus upon 'stranger danger' rather than the more likely threat from within the home or family community. The mass media controls how certain 'folk devils' are presented by offering a restricted reporting of the 'facts', as Stanley Cohen notes: '[the] media have long operated as agents of moral indignation in their own right: even if they are not self-consciously engaged in crusading or muck-raking, their very reporting of certain "facts" can be sufficient to generate concern, anxiety, indignation or panic' (1972: 9–10). In *Mysterious Skin* the abuser is a baseball coach, a trusted member of the community; in *Hard Candy* the paedophile really does not look like, as Hayley remarks, the 'kind of guy who needs to meet girls on the Internet'; and in *Little Children*, even though Ronnie (Jackie Earle Haley) fits into the visual stereotype of the paedophile (weak and pathetic), his childlike persona and loving mother, May (Phyllis Somerville), subvert the perceived characteristics of the paedophile that might include a past of physical or sexual abuse, neglect, a broken home or a definable, possibly untreated, mental illness.

This independent cinema cycle in the early 2000s provides images of the paedophile in a manner that transgresses traditional binary definitions of victims and victimisers, and considers complex questions concerning the social construction of sexuality, desire and innocence. This cycle constitutes a form of trauma cinema that offers not only a cathartic space for the victim but also the perpetrator.[3] This is most clearly seen in *Little Children*, where chapters of the film are told from the perspective of the paedophile, Ronnie. The film opens with Ronnie under the glazed gaze of his mother's collection of little porcelain children (Hummel figurines) as he watches a newscast reporting his release from prison. He is pictured alone and isolated, but as Ronnie is in suburbia he is constantly surrounded by temptation. Yet it is not so much a confession from the perpetrator that this cycle of cinema allows for, but an opportunity to give dimensions to the traditionally monstrous paedophile and de-sexualised innocent child. The experience of trauma is not homogeneous and the films under discussion here do not resort to prototypical representations of victims and villains, and neat ethical resolutions.

Trauma cinema stylistically promotes 'vivid bodily and visual sensations' (Walker 2001: 214) over 'verbal narrative and context' (Herman 1992: 8). The trauma of the past, or, in the case of *Hard Candy,* the present, is characterised 'through an unusual admixture of emotional affect, metonmyic [sic] symbolism and cinematic flashbacks' (Walker 2001: 214). *Mysterious Skin* opens on a delighted child being showered with candy-coloured cereal in washed-out slow-motion shots that gives the film a dream-like texture. Memories of abuse are presented as dream sequences; they are both fantasies and nightmares as Neil and Brian attempt to come to terms with their fractured memories and traumatic pasts. The opening act of *Hard Candy* uses tight framing to give the film a simultaneously innocent and intimate sensation, and as a

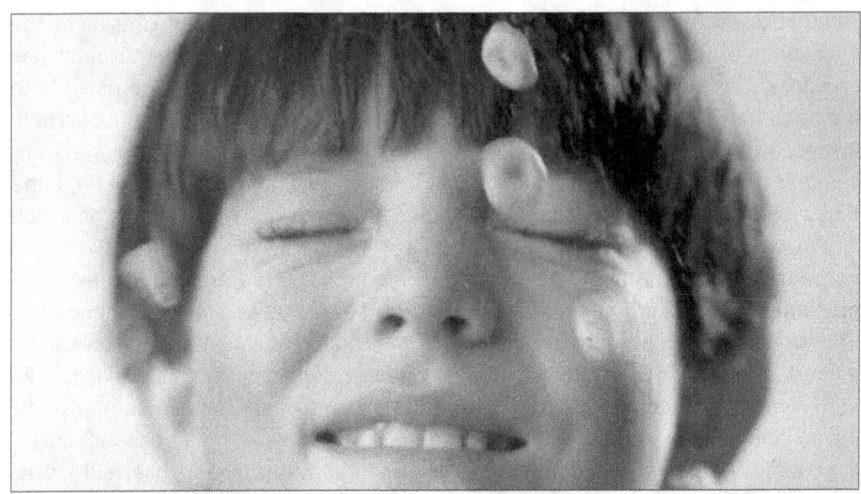
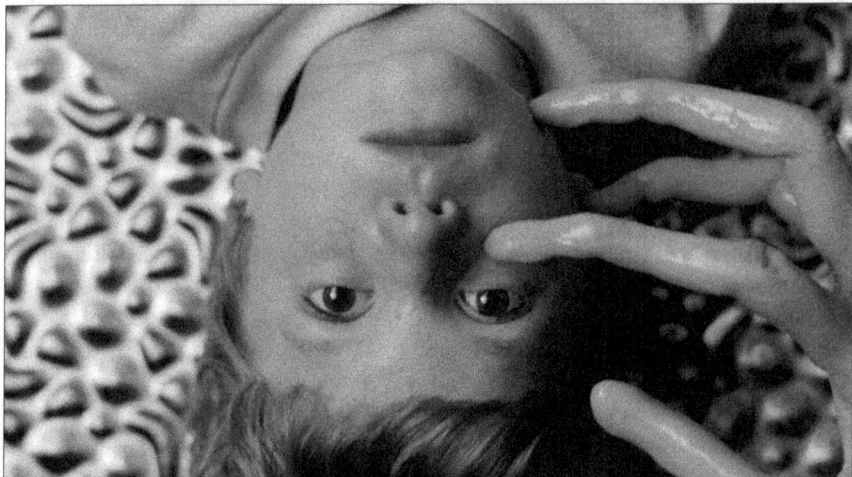

Figs 1 & 2: Fantasies and nightmares: A younger Neil's (Chase Ellison) candy-coloured dream-like experiences of paedophilia contrast with Brian's (George Webster) clinical alien nightmares in *Mysterious Skin* (2004).

seemingly naïve Hayley is driven to Jeff's home the sparse dialogue is overcome by visuals: pastel-coloured dreamy images of the drive are enhanced with artistic lens flares and slow-motion shots of the couple as they laugh, talk and flirt. It is a form of visual storytelling that allows for discussion of memory and personal experience in a way that does not necessarily require verbalisation.

This chapter is split into three sections that discuss the transgressive nature of this cycle of paedophilia-related cinema. The first section of this chapter explores the construction of the paedophile in traditional narratives and how the image of the paedophile begins to be deconstructed by films released in the early 2000s. For example, in *Mysterious Skin* the paedophile is a simplistic secondary character given no history or motivation allowing for the focus to be upon the two abused boys, and although his essentially off-screen actions (child abuse) are undeniably deplorable, the paedophilic Little League coach is not a monstrous figure. It contradicts the social construction of the paedophile theorised by James R. Kincaid and Michel Foucault. The second section analyses the different ways in which *Hard Candy*, *Little Children* and *Mysterious Skin* contravene traditional ideas about victims. In *Hard Candy*, Hayley actively takes on the role of the victim and justifies her role as an abuser by presenting her actions as a form of revenge and community cleansing. *Little Children*'s paedophile, Ronnie, is a broken subject who fails to understand the consequences of his actions. When his mother dies, Ronnie takes extreme measures in attempts to follow her deathbed instructions: 'Please be a good boy.' The abused characters in *Mysterious Skin* struggle to accept their position as victims and they construct excuses and elaborate fantasies to avoid accepting what has happened to them. The final section of this chapter considers different forms of abuse by looking at the child as abuser and subversion of the idea that children are unknowing participants in abuse. *Little Children* explores the previously unknown family of the abuser, and further complicates the construction of the paedophile by providing a back-story of a loving home and a happy childhood. This is then contrasted in *Mysterious Skin* when the ineffectual parent is presented as a possible cause for child abuse as they inadvertently provide the opportunity for the paedophile to manipulate and violate a child.

Monsters and Innocents

In *Mysterious Skin*, *Hard Candy* and *Little Children* the paedophiles are not simply monsters lurking in the shadows, and the children they desire are not necessarily de-sexualised innocents cared for by dutiful parents and concerned communities. As noted by Karen Lury in *The Child in Film*, the child figure can be a 'complex and powerful agent' (2010: 4) that allows filmmakers to play upon audience expectations for the definition of childhood and how children should act. Both 'child' and 'childhood' have become almost mythic concepts that are embedded and entangled within contemporary Western culture. By reframing the child as an active and perhaps erotic figure filmmakers can transgress 'conventional modes of identification and expressions of sexuality' (ibid.). While *Mysterious Skin*, *Hard Candy* and *Little Children* are all distinct films, they do come together to argue for a more fluid understanding of child sexuality, and also a more complex reading of the paedophile by moving beyond simplistic caricature.

Paedophiles are often utilised in both fictional and factual discourses as figures that society can project its most sinister fears and anxieties upon. In order for the paedophile to function in this fashion they must be, as James R. Kincaid (1992; 1998) argues, kept at a distance – an evil person defined only by their actions as child abusers. By keeping the paedophile at the edges of society both literally and figuratively in reports and stories, the paedophile is culturally marked as 'other', and thus 'a complex image of projection and denial' (1992: 5). Societal constructions of sexuality, which have resulted in positioning children as complete innocents, 'creates a space' for the paedophile, a space that 'we can bet will not go unoccupied' (1992: 3). Kincaid argues that the demonised paedophile is a necessary element within a society – a locus of cultural fears that acceptably explains the eroticisation of children in contemporary society. The 'myth of child molestation' (1998: 5) has become an intrinsic part of US culture, and the stories that surround the abusers and the abused are given clear boundaries and resolutions. Kincaid notes that in cinema children are often 'scoured free from eroticism' (1998: 124) but when filmmakers do eroticise child actors and transgress the image of the chaste child they must 'invent quite extraordinary sleights of hand, be satisfied with a marginal movie, or bear up under a storm of outrage'.

Despite their controversial approach to paedophiles and child victims the independent films released in the early 2000s did not cause a 'storm of outrage'. They rejected the construction of victims, and indeed perpetrators of child abuse, as being without individual agency both on- and off-screen. Traditionally children are framed as innocents and victims, and this section looks at the construction of childhood innocence as a Western concept that is not internationally universal. Michel Foucault theorised that 'childhood' gradually emerged as a concept in the seventeenth century as the young were increasingly perceived as something innocent to be protected, disciplined and educated. The development of the idea of childhood also changed concepts of the family and home as 'a dense, saturated, permanent, continuous physical environment which envelops, maintains, and develops the child's body' (1984a: 280). Philippe Ariès also argued that childhood was not recognised as a distinct phase of human life until relatively late in human history and that the sentimental idea of the child as an innocent resulted in the 'attitude and behaviour towards childhood' that required 'safeguarding it against pollution by life' (1962: 119). Children should be pure and under the protection of their parents, in some senses stripped of their own sexual identity. Foucault argues, and Kincaid agrees, that the de-sexualisation of children has had 'the consequence of sexually exciting the bodies of children while at the same time fixing the parental gaze and vigilance on the peril of infantile sexuality' (1984b: 62). It became a sexual taboo for a child to be considered sexually attractive and/or the subject of sexual pleasure, and those that did see the young as erotic figures, and worse those who acted upon these desires, become the monstrous 'other'.

Emma Wilson explores an approach to childhood that analyses the representation of the child's 'own experiences and sensations' (2005: 330). She considers this a 'deconstructive process' that moves beyond examining the figure of the child in terms of its meaning to adults, which has been the focus of much of the cultural studies scholarship prior to 2005 and the release of the cycle of films under discussion here. Wilson instead focuses upon the construction of childhood outside of the restrictive idea of innocence. As she remarks: 'innocence emerges as the dominant fantasy in whose terms children have been variously represented, protected and desired. This fantasy in itself has been seen as in part responsible for the very disempowerment of the child' (2005: 331). This aligns with Kincaid's and Foucault's argument that by failing to give children agency and retaining a classification of innocence the child becomes a fetishised fantasy object. The distinction between child and adult is widened by the adhesion to childhood innocence; children are there to be protected, revealing child vulnerability and the '[confirmation of] adult power' (Holland 2004: 144).

Mysterious Skin actively subverts the image of the innocent child as the children are granted agency and complex post-abuse narratives. It shows how traumatic events in childhood are integral to understanding Neil and Brian as young-adults. *Mysterious Skin* attempts to close the gap between child and adult by indicating that both can be powerful and vulnerable. Coach, the paedophile, is neither monstrous nor fully realised as he is essentially a mechanism for exploring traumatic childhood experiences. The film is not about Coach and instead challenges the presentation and construction of the victim with Brian and Neil driving the narrative forward. *Little Children*'s Ronnie and *Hard Candy*'s Jeff are well-developed characters offering a progressive representation of the paedophile as human in comparison to the sketchy, unnamed Coach who is a narrative device rather than a character. *Mysterious Skin* garnered some negative press upon release because it did not demonise the paedophile and, according to protesters, it provided a 'how-to manual that could instruct potentially paedophilic viewers in the mechanisms of successful "grooming" behaviour' (Green and Goode 2008: 77). The director, Gregg Araki, chose to challenge the perceptions of child abuse by showing the effect abuse can have upon a child and most controversially gives an eight-year-old, Neil (Chase Ellison), sexual agency as he openly explores his newfound sexuality by spying on his mother having sex and masturbating over men in his mother's issues of *Playgirl*. *Mysterious Skin* does not give the paedophile much room to grow as a character; he is a catalyst for the story about the boys rather than a character in his own right. Alongside the other key adult figures, including the boys' parents, Coach is not given a name. Adults are not the focus of the film and their individual stories lack details or resolution. It appears that Coach receives no punishment for his actions; he only lives on in the present-day narratives as a ghostly figure haunting Neil and Brian.

In *Little Children* the paedophile, Ronnie, is more than a ghostly apparition or a nightmare. He takes a central role in the narrative and his transgressions are part of the film's wider discussion of culturally rejected forms of love, desire and sex. His attraction to children is wrong, and *Little Children* does not justify this behaviour but purposefully, as director Todd Fields explains, 'never comments on him' (2005: n.p.) or his crimes. Ronnie takes a childish approach to his interactions with other people and attempts to please his mother who, despite his offences, still sees Ronnie as her 'miracle'. In one scene, he goes to a swimming pool full of children during a heat-wave, fails to fully appreciate how his actions have caused panic and is removed by the police – as he is pulled away he shouts 'I was just trying to cool off!' Ronnie goes out on an ill-fated date with a woman from a lonely-hearts column called Shelia (Jane Adams) 'as a sort of expression of love' for his mother (ibid.). The awkward date ends with Ronnie asking Shelia to drive to a secluded playground so that he can masturbate. Ronnie is an 'inadequate adult' (Green and Goode 2008: 74) who cannot manage his desires or look after himself; he needs to be cared for by his mother, and once she dies he is lost without her moral and emotional guidance. *Little Children* acknowledges Ronnie's struggles and invites a compassionate response from its audience as the paedophile himself is child-like.

The children and adults presented in *Mysterious Skin* and *Little Children* do not fit into the binary constructions of the child and adult, nor child and child abuser. These films as part of a broader cycle test the moral boundaries of acceptable representation of child abuse narratives. Paedophiles are presented as victims of their own desire, or of a threatening other. Paedophile narratives are shown to be multi-faceted in ways that do not comfortably sit within expected child abuse narratives. The abuser is shown as a flawed human, and the children are given their own stories and motivations separate from the narratives that are so often constructed for them. The victim is not always easy to identify and in each of the films discussed it may shift between adults and children.

Accepting and Rejecting Victimhood

The cycle of paedophile-based films released in the 2000s focuses upon victim-hood. But they do not provide a neat means of understanding the definition of the 'victim' or its apparent opposite in the 'abuser'. The distinction is blurred as the characters and stories develop, and adults and children are ambiguously marked and represented. What are the implications of making the audience empathise with the paedophile, if only temporarily? This is particularly noticeable in *Hard Candy*, *Little Children* and *The Woodsman*, where the paedophile protagonist, Walter (Kevin Bacon), is presented as a traumatised victim of his own taboo desire. Walter does not define himself as a victim, but the filmmakers do and it is only when he attacks another paedophile – and his face appears momentarily in place of the man he's hitting – that the audience and indeed Walter are offered a sense of resolution. *Mysterious Skin* does not punish its paedophile and, unlike the other films discussed in this chapter, the abuser is a secondary sketchy character. The victims struggle with their experiences and neither Neil nor Brian fully accept (or reject) their victim-hood. This liminality is important to this cycle of films as it purposely forces the audience to 'make up their own minds' (Fields 2005: n.p.). The distinctions between

Fig. 3: Alluringly innocent: Hayley (Ellen Page) presents a carefully constructed androgynous child-like image in *Hard Candy* (2005).

victims and perpetrators are purposely murky and viewers are forced to question the actions and motivations of not only the adult but also the child characters.

The fourteen-year-old Hayley Stark actively takes on the role of the victim; she is a meta-victim. At the beginning of *Hard Candy*, the paedophilic Jeff and the audience who view the story-world through his experiences in this opening sequence are drawn in by Hayley's carefully managed innocence. She is first introduced as a fresh-faced girl with a smear of chocolate frosting on her lip. She sways between maturity and innocence as her coquettish and intelligent conversation contrasts with her apparent shyness and youth. Jeff appears to be in charge of the situation when Hayley joins him for a dreamy ride to his home expressed through the pastel sun-bleached hues and slow-motion cinematography. Both Jeff and the viewer are tricked by Hayley's child-like representation until her true intentions are revealed – the camera's 'persistent gaze at her innocent young face' (Henry 2014: 71) makes the audience anxious as they fear what the sexual predator will do to the teenager. Yet, as the alcohol and tranquilisers flow, Jeff quickly loses control of his body and his mind, as his virtual fantasy girl becomes his literal nightmare. In a reversal of the tightly-framed shots of the seemingly innocent Hayley, later close-ups of a traumatised Jeff become the camera's focus, shifting audience sympathies uncomfortably towards the paedophile (if only temporarily). Jeff asks who the 'hell' she is when it is clear that she is not the innocent girl she created on the Internet, and Hayley responds: 'I am every little girl you ever watched, touched, hurt, screwed, killed.' She sees herself as giving molested and perhaps murdered girls the opportunity for revenge.

Hard Candy disrupts the distinction between abuser and abused. Hayley is a liminal character on the verge of adulthood and she rationalises her own abusive actions by victimising a paedophile. It is unclear if she has been molested, or whether she is using the devastating, traumatic experiences of other girls as justification for acting out her own violent fantasies. Jeff is not Hayley's first victim; she is a repeat offender and audiences are challenged by the idea that Hayley might gain pleasure from traumatising the paedophiles she has entrapped. It is also unclear if her manipulation of Jeff and his eventual suicide should be considered morally acceptable because the victim is a paedophile. Hayley transgresses the notion of the innocent child. She is not asexual and innocent; she uses her pubescent sexuality and fabricated naïve personality to manipulate her intended target. Jeff is the subject of Hayley's vigilante justice but it is difficult to see Jeff as a true victim: even the final act of his suicide is performed to protect his reputation rather than to atone for his paedophilic sins.

In *Little Children*, Ronnie is a demonised source of anxiety for his local community but he is permitted to develop as a multi-dimensional flawed character with a family and future that deserves representation. In contrast to *Hard Candy*'s Jeff, Ronnie's final act is self-mutilation; he castrates himself in order to 'be a good boy' following the death of his mother. He would rather hurt himself than break a promise he has made to his mother to be good. He is a victim of his own desires that he cannot control and his self-castration is not necessarily an attempt to punish himself but a drastic and naïve way of preventing himself from re-offending. A campaign is mounted to force Ronnie out of the neighbourhood, but the warning posters featuring a picture of his face and the extensive graffiti on his mother's house do not seem to affect him. He is detached from his actions and how he is perceived in the local community. Instead it is his mother who is the victim of the vigilante crusades as she washes 'EVIL' off her front path, and confronts the *de facto* vigilante leader Larry (Noah Emmerich) on her doorstep. She is worried about how it impacts her son as she tries to build his confidence and reassure him with phrases like, 'You did a bad thing, but that doesn't mean you're a bad person'. Her death is presented as a consequence of the abuse she has sustained.

Both *Little Children* and *Hard Candy* give their paedophile characters names and a sense of identity. *Mysterious Skin* does not. *Mysterious Skin* is told almost exclusively from a child's, and later a young adult's, perspective through voice-over and uncomfortable point-of-view shots of abuse. But the children's experiences differ: Neil sees pastel colours, slow motion and intimacy, and Brian sees blurry ominous figures and blackouts. Both boys in some senses reject their role as abused children and thus victims. Brian suffers from dissociative amnesia and has repressed the traumatic childhood memories of rape and searches for explanations of the time he is missing by exploring the possibility of alien abduction. He has recurring nightmares that reveal fragments of truth amongst disturbing images of aliens and probes. Dream sequences are used in Neil and Brian's parallel stories and where Brian sees trauma and alien abduction, Neil creates dreamy memories of his experience with Coach that are frequently cross-cut into moments when Neil is being fellated by clients. Neil fantasises about Coach during sex and throughout the film the audience are confronted with the idea that his abuse was a positive experience. Sexual fantasising is something that an individual does rather than being something that is forced upon them (see Dwyer 2009). Whereas Brian is apparently sexually repressed – a possible reaction to his early exposure to sex – Neil is quite the opposite. He actively rejects his role as the victim and fondly recalls his time with Coach. Coach is never given a name and has little screen time, but his actions are a catalyst for the development of the main characters. He is compared to the swimsuit models Neil sees in his mother's *Playgirl* magazines, a surface image and a dream. Society gives little sexual agency to pre-pubescent children and by viewing his abuse as sexual enlightenment, and Coach as his 'first love', Neil contravenes this restrictive image of the child. Whereas Brian's experience validates the monstrous child molestation discourse, Neil rejects it.

Neil is an affront to the traditional understanding of what a child should be as his purity has been tainted by abuse. He repeats the abusive acts committed against him by bullying and coercing other children into engaging in indecent acts. Neil is not only given agency and presented as having a developing queer sexual identity, he is also revealed as an accomplice. In one of the most disturbing sequences in *Mysterious Skin*, Neil acts out the role of the abuser. Eleven-year-old Neil and his best friend Wendy (Riley McGuire) are out unsupervised for Halloween and they lure a mentally challenged child away from his friends. Once alone Neil puts firecrackers in the child's mouth and sets them alight despite Wendy's protestations. Inevitably the child is hurt and Neil attempts to resolve the situation with oral sex. Neil uses sex to distract and placate his victim using the phrases and tone utilised by Coach to calm and coerce Neil into sex acts. In the later stages of the film, when Neil and Brian's stories begin to merge, it is revealed that Neil was present when Brian was abused – he was used to coax unwilling or nervous boys, including Brian, into engaging in sex with Neil and Coach. As a fifteen-year-old prostitute he actively invites older men to use his body to act out their inappropriate and essentially paedophilic fantasies. This disregard for himself is seen to stem from his abusive past – he is a victim, and in the final shots of the film as Brian weeps at the full realisation that he was abused, Neil comprehends the magnitude of aiding Coach in his paedophilia. The film resolves in a far more conventional fashion than the majority of its run-time predicts; *Mysterious Skin*'s ambiguous ending can be interpreted as a moment of realisation for Neil who had so actively rejected his own victimhood. These children were violated against their will, and Neil helped; the final scene shows Neil finally accepting himself as both a victim and an abuser and experiencing feelings of both acceptance and guilt.

Hard Candy, *Little Children* and *Mysterious Skin* do not conform to traditional definitions of childhood. *Hard Candy* and *Mysterious Skin* present child characters with sexual confidence and agency who are aware of their actions although not necessarily of their consequences. *Little Children* presents the paedophile as a complex character; Ronnie might be perceived as mentally ill rather than fully aware of his actions. The film still holds him accountable for his sexual offences (he has been punished with imprisonment) but he is offered redemption and hope for the future by the filmmakers as he attempts to 'cure' himself and be 'a good boy'. In contrast, the paedophile-as-victim presented in *Hard Candy* neither seeks nor deserves forgiveness. All three films manipulate and explore the apparently oppositional concepts of victim and perpetrator; characters exhibit traits of both often simultaneously and by transgressing the notion of the child as a desexualised figure. They question the absolute demonisation of sex offenders and the restricted agency afforded to children. These independent productions transgress the image of the child and the paedophile. By deconstructing these binaries the films also raise questions about abuse and its definition. It can take many forms, and each of the films question its construction and impact upon the narratives of both victims and abusers themselves.

Shades of Abuse

By presenting complex child characters who are damaged by their experiences and situations, and paedophiles who are also victims of desire and perceptions potentially out of their control, this cycle of paedophile- and child-abuse themed films allows for the questioning of the boundaries. *Hard Candy*'s Hayley and *Mysterious Skin*'s Neil are minors, aged fourteen and fifteen respectively. They each take on the role of the abuser with Hayley acting as a vengeful meta-victim, and Neil as a child who is complicit in the abuse of other children. The distinction between seemingly opposite positions, emotions and moral stances are shown to be fluid and unstable. In both *Hard Candy* and *Little Children* characters die as a result of sustained mental abuse, questioning whether there is an appropriate punishment for a paedophile and if they can or should be allowed redemption. *Mysterious Skin* also explores different forms of child abuse beyond the sexual by looking towards parental negligence and asking if poor parenting is another form of abuse even when it is unintentional.

Mysterious Skin, in its presentation of Neil, conforms to the idea that children who are abused go on to perpetuate that abuse upon others. Neil kidnaps and rapes another child. He goes far beyond bullying or pranking. Neil uses the boy's disability (read innocence) to manipulate the situation as Coach has taught him; he takes on the role of the abuser. As Vicky Lebeau remarks, Brian 'can be seen as the very image of the abused child, his face erased by the experience of sexual abuse at the hands of Coach and, indeed, his prop, Neil. But Neil's sexuality does not fit the more or less conventionalised narratives of child sex abuse' (2008: 130). Brian acts as a counterbalance to Neil throughout the film; his responses are more acceptable and expected. Neil and Brian's childhood experiences influence each of them differently, but their shared history does not equate to a shared future.

Neil and Hayley are 'symbol[s] of a childhood lost' (Lebeau 2008: 108); they are damaged by their early exposure to sex and detailed knowledge of abuse. Hayley is not given a back-story and thus no excuse for her behaviour. She indicates that she has a sister, but as she taunts Jeff it is revealed that most, if not all, of the personal details she has disclosed to him are false. Like her online identity 'Thonggrrrl', 'Hayley' is an unstable character – she is difficult to trust and empathise with. Everything she does in the film is a manipulation. Hayley tortures Jeff as she 'performs' a castration but, like her personality on- and offline, the castration scene is fiction. Jeff watches in horror as Hayley, armed with surgical equipment, a medical textbook and a video camera, apparently gelds him. But after the procedure is complete Jeff discovers that he is still complete and that the video feed of the castration was an instructional medical video. Hayley does not physically harm Jeff; he perpetrates the only physically abusive actions after he escapes from Hayley's impromptu operating table. Hayley uses props to aid her mental torture: videos, medical equipment and drugs. Jeff hits Hayley and chases her with a knife, but it is she who ultimately prevails as she convinces Jeff to hang himself. She is alarmingly aware of her own sexual agency and it forces the audience to consider, and more disturbingly imagine, what has led her to this abusive point.

Little Children places the paedophile within a family context and argues that abusive adults are not always a consequence of abused or abusive children; it is difficult to interpret Ronnie's paedophilic actions as a response to a neglectful childhood. His attraction to children is controversially envisioned as a compulsion. There is opportunity to compare his mother May to Mrs. Bates, the overbearing mother figure in *Psycho* (Alfred Hitchcock, 1960), but whereas the off-screen 'Mother' is a little more than a 'grotesque' figure of Norman Bates' (Anthony Perkins) and, indeed, the audience's imagination (see Dick 2000: 240), May's compassionate on-screen mothering shows a woman who has accepted if not forgiven her son's compulsive crimes. May still sees her son as a child who needs her guidance and she believes he can be rehabilitated with her support. When May dies Ronnie is left alone, and the 'only child who is critically wounded in *Little Children* is Ronnie' (McAlister 2008: 18) because without his mother to guide him he tries his best to resolve his sexual problems by hurting himself. May is a victim of the community response to her son, people who are only able to see him as the dangerous sex offender confirmed in playground gossip and news headlines. She represents the families who suffer alongside the abusers, the unseen victims of the cycle of abuse. May is a tragic character whose every action is inspired by an unlimited love for her child.

Even though Ronnie has a protective and devoted mother he still acts upon his paedophilic desires – his offences are not the result of poor parenting or an abusive childhood. Negligence becomes part of the cycle of abuse; inactivity and failure to protect the child from other predatory adults is seen as a form of child abuse. In *Mysterious Skin* absent and ineffectual parents are portioned some of the blame as both of the abused children are made vulnerable to the paedophile by a lack of parental care. Neil's mother, Mrs. McCormick (Elisabeth Shue), although loving towards her son, is shown as a perpetual teenager with a string of inappropriate boyfriends. Neil learns from his abuser as other children might learn behaviours from their parents. Coach is a fantasy father as well as a sexual fantasy for Neil – they go to movies, play video games and play with their food. Coach, from Neil's perspective, takes on the role of his father; similarly, in *L.I.E.*, Howie (Paul Dano) is looked after by a paedophile, Big John (Brian Cox). Big John makes advances on Howie, but when he is rejected Big John backs off but chooses to keep Howie safe until his own father is able to take care of him. The paedophile is shown as a father figure who gives the children the intimacy and emotional support they crave. As Joel Dossi remarks, 'the horror of being abused by a trusted adult looms. This duality elicits contradictory emotional responses from both his victims and the audience' (2005: 65). Adults are flawed characters who are in their own way abusive. In *Mysterious Skin* Brian's ineffectual father is partially to blame for his abuse; Mr. Lackey (Chris Mulkey) sees his bespectacled little boy as a failure – he cannot play sports, and he wets the bed, faints and has chronic nosebleeds. Mr. Lackey has little time for his son and it is when he forgets to collect Brian from a Little League game that Coach is offered the opportunity to molest the abandoned child. Questions of responsibility, neglect and abuse underpin *Mysterious Skin* and use of the child's point of view further contravenes the traditional understanding of paedophile and child victims by placing paedophilia within the broader spectrum of abusive and neglectful relationships.

Abuse is a fluid concept in this early twenty-first century cycle of child abuse films. The expected characterisation of the abuser is transgressed as the notion of abuse is deconstructed. Alongside physical sexual abuses these films present other forms of abuse including negligence, mental abuse and self-mutilation. *Hard Candy*'s shifting sympathies question how a lack of physical evidence should be understood, whether Hayley deserves punishment, and if her vigilante justice constitutes a victimless crime. *Little Children* also considers mental abuse, as neither Ronnie nor his mother are physically abused by Larry or other members of the concerned community. Like Jeff, Ronnie and his mother are harmed by mental abuse – the abuse exacerbates May's heart condition and she dies, and Ronnie mutilates himself in order to be a 'good boy' for his mother and to appease, however naïvely, the neighbourhood who call for his castration. Abuse takes another form in *Mysterious Skin* as a child commits child abuse; Neil as abuser is seen to repeat the rhetoric and rationalisation of his abuser and thus this becomes an extension of the original abuse. Whereas the film's neglectful parents become part of the abuse rather than being innocent bystanders, they are partly responsible for the crimes committed against their children. The primary case studies all interpret abuse as a fractured concept that vilifies and identifies not only paedophiles but also children as active figures alongside their families and local communities as contributors to the cycle and interpretation of child abuse. *Little Children*, *Hard Candy* and *Mysterious Skin* attempt to broaden the understanding and representation of child abuse in twenty-first century US cinema by destabilising accepted caricatures and expected power relations.

Conclusion

Mysterious Skin, *Hard Candy* and *Little Children* are 'cultural artefacts of the intense anxiety attached to emerging conceptions of the child in the early twenty-first century' (Lennard 2014: 161). They promote, if not entirely reflect, a need to reassess the societal construction of childhood and children. By moving the paedophile out of the narrative shadows and actively crafting a more multi-dimensional characterisation, filmmakers can raise questions about the dangers of stereotyping both abusers and their victims. The films under discussion here were all made for an adult audience and attempt, if only momentarily, to give adult viewers 'an awareness of helplessness' and 'sensitise [them] to the experience (and suffering) of children and so engage [them] more voluntarily, changing [their] perspective on childhood' (Wilson 2005: 330). By telling these stories from the perspective of the child and, in the case of *Little Children*, the paedophile, the filmmakers endeavour to alter audience understanding of victims and perpetrators by provoking 'involuntary emotions' and placing the viewer in the seemingly helpless position of the victim (ibid.). *Mysterious Skin* actively subverts the image of the innocent child and firmly positions the film in the light of child rather than adult experience. *Hard Candy* defines and redefines audience perceptions of who is the victim and who is the abuser, forcing the audience into the perspective of both. *Little Children* represents the paedophile as a complex character who can be a victim not only of his own desires but also the pressures of family and the public.

These films give previously under- or entirely un-represented figures representation through cinematic form and style. The child's perspective is given priority through camerawork and visual imagery that mirrors their subjective experiences. The viewer 'experiences' Neil and Brian's abuse in *Mysterious Skin* through closely framed shots with Coach filling the screen and obscuring the view of the child. The dream-like sequences in both *Mysterious Skin* and *Hard Candy* offer a childish image of an adult experience – sex and grooming in *Mysterious Skin*, and a car ride for a teenage girl on the way to an exciting stranger's home – although the latter's use of this visual tone and style essentially serves to confuse the viewer in the understanding of relationship between child and abuser. In *Little Children,* the camera explores the world from the perspective of the paedophile eliciting empathy if not sympathy from the audience. All three films provide their previously under-represented figures, both child and adult, with a voice that allows for an exploration of the complexities of their character that extends beyond monstrosity and innocence.

Complex meditations upon child sexuality and agency, and adult culpability are found in films that are ghettoised and only available to smaller, more active audiences due to their independent mode of production and limited release. The three case-study films – *Mysterious Skin*, *Hard Candy* and *Little Children* – frame the act and consequences of abuse in a morally indecisive fashion with constructions of desire, innocence, victimhood and agency being treated in a way that provides no clear answers or judgements for the audience. As Vicky Lebeau states in her monograph *Childhood and Cinema*, 'it is a mark of the achievement of contemporary cinema that it continues to engage the sexuality and sexual dissidents of children and adolescents' (2005: 128); these films engage with these issues in a rebellious fashion not only in terms of representation but also narrative construction. They refuse to tell a single story about abuse, and the relationship between children and adults. Child abuse and its media construction is challenged and reframed, and adult audience members are invited to make up their own minds about with whom their sympathies should lie.

Notes

1 The term 'moral panic' was coined by Stanley Cohen in *Folk Devils and Moral Panics: The Creation of Mods and Rockers* (New York, NY: St. Martin's, 1972), a study of public reactions to the deviant behaviour of the 'mods' and 'rockers' youth of Great Britain in the 1960s and 1970s.
2 Jackie Earle Haley, who played the paedophile Ronnie in *Little Children* was himself later cast as the child molesting Freddy Kruger in Samuel Bayer's 2010 remake of the *A Nightmare on Elm Street*.
3 Raya Morag proposes the trauma of the perpetrator in her 2013 monograph *Waltzing with Bashir: Perpetrator Trauma and Cinema*. She frames the perpetrator within the twenty-first century's new wars and the clash between civilians and soldiers in unconventional battlefields.

Bibliography

Araki, G. (2005) 'The Wonder Years', interview by P. Bowen, *Filmmaker*, http://filmmakermagazine.com/archives/issues/spring2005/features/wonder_years.php#.VRHkDpOsWYI (accessed 24 March 2015).

Ariès, P. (1962) *Centuries of Childhood: A Social History of Family Life*, trans. R. Baldick. New York, NY: Vintage Books.

Cohen, S. (1972) *Folk Devils and Moral Panics: The Creation of Mods and Rockers*. New York, NY: St. Martin's.

Dick, B. F. (2000) 'Hitchcock's Terrible Mothers', *Literature/Film Quarterly*, 28, 4, 238–49.

Dossi, J. (2005) '*Mysterious Skin*', *Cinéaste*, 30, 3, 65–6.

Dwyer, S. (2009) 'Pornography', in P. Livingston and C. Plantinga (eds) *The Routledge Companion to Philosophy and Film*. New York: Routledge, 521–2.

Fields, T. (2006) 'Playground Rules', interview by S. Macauley, *Filmmaker*, http://filmmakermagazine.com/archives/issues/fall2006/features/playground_rules.php#.VQL1vCusWig (accessed 13 March 2015).

Foucault, M. (1984a) 'Truth and Power', interview by A. Fontana and P. Pasquino, in P. Rabinow (ed. and trans.) *The Foucault Reader*. New York, NY: Pantheon Books, 51–75.

Foucault, M. (1984b) 'The Politics of Health in the Eighteenth Century', in P. Rabinow (ed. and trans.) *The Foucault Reader*. New York, NY: Pantheon Books, 273–89.

Green, L. and S. Goode (2008) 'The "Hollywood" Treatment of Paedophilia: Comparing Some Cinematic and Australian Press Constructions Between 2003 and 2006', *Australian Journal of Communication*, 35, 2, 71–85.

Heba, G. (1995) 'Everyday Nightmares: The Rhetoric of Social Horror in the *Nightmare on Elm Street* Series', *Journal of Popular Film and Television*, 23, 3, 106–15.

Henry, C. (2014) *Revisionist Rape-Revenge: Redefining a Film Genre*. New York, NY: Palgrave Macmillan.

Herman, J. L. (1992) *Trauma and Memory*. New York, NY: Basic Books.

Holland, P. (2004) *Picturing Childhood: The Myth of the Child in Popular Imagery*. London: I.B. Tauris.

Kincaid, J. R. (1992) *Child-Loving: The Erotic Child and Victorian Culture*. New York, NY: Routledge.

____ (1998) *Erotic Innocence: The Culture of Child Molesting*. Durham, NC: Duke University Press.

King G., C. Molloy and Y. Tzioumakis (2013) 'Introduction', in G. King, C. Molloy, and Y. Tzioumakis (eds) *American Independent Cinema: Indie, Indiewood and Beyond*. New York, NY: Routledge, 1–8.

Lebeau, V. (2008) *Childhood and Cinema*. London: Reaktion.

Lennard, D. (2014) *Holy Terrors: The Child Villains of Horror Film*. Albany, NY: State University of New York Press.

Lury, K. (2010) *The Child in Film: Tears, Fears and Fairytales*. London: I.B. Tauris.

McAlister, J. F. (2008) 'Unsafe Houses: The Narrative Inversion of Suburban Morality in Popular Film', *Liminalities: A Journal of Performance Studies*, 4, 1, 1–25.

Morag, R. (2013) *Waltzing with Bashir: Perpetrator Trauma and Cinema*. London: I.B. Tauris.

Rafter, N. (2007) 'Crime, Film and Criminology: Recent Sex-Crime Movies', *Theoretical Criminology*, 11, 3, 403–20.

Thomas, T. (2005) *Sex Crime: Sex Offending and Society*. Portland, OR: Willan.

Walker, J. (2001) 'Cinema: False Memories and True Experience', *Screen*, 42, 2), 211–16.

Wilson, E. (2005) 'Children, Emotion and Viewing in Contemporary European Film Viewing', *Screen*, 46, 3, 329–40.

Chapter 10
Nowhere Teens: Following Gregg Araki's Queer Adolescents through the End of a Century

ARNAU ROIG-MORA

The body of the teen has historically been represented as a site of struggle for identity/ies as it embodies the crossroads in the human transit from child to adult. The list of American movies dealing with the process of reaching maturity is long, since it represents a pivotal moment in our life for the definition of the self, and thus an interesting starting point to explore the personal growth of a character. Who we were and who we become are linked in teenagehood and, as such, it remains one of the most crucial periods of our existence. The numerous examples of the period under analysis here, like John Hughes' filmography of the late 1980s, or the variety of successful and popular takes on the teen movie of the 1990s – *Clueless* (Amy Heckerling, 1995), *Kids* (Larry Clark, 1995), *The Craft* (Andrewe Fleming, 1996), *Romeo+Juliet* (Baz Luhrmann, 1996) or *Cruel Intentions* (Roger Kumble, 1999) amongst many others – speak to the importance of the genre and its mass appeal.

In order to analyse the figure of the queer teenager as a site of struggle, and, more precisely, the teenage body as the space in which it takes place, this chapter explores the cinema of Gregg Araki. Araki is a Californian filmmaker who has been creating different narratives of coming-of-age since the late 1980s. His guerrilla-style early films granted him a critical recognition and an underground cult filmmaker status. His breakthrough work was to come in 1992 with *The Living End*: Jon (Craig Gilmore), a movie critic, is diagnosed HIV+ and simultaneously meets Luke (Mike Dytri), a sort of queer 'midnight cowboy'. Together they take a liberating road trip *à la Bonnie and Clyde* (Arthur Penn, 1967) or *Thelma & Louise* (Ridley Scott, 1991), confronting the world and enjoying their path to an unavoidable death. Right after *The Living End,* and still enjoying its critical acclaim, Araki moved on to what will become his most known period: the 'Teen Apocalypse Trilogy'. Composed by *Totally Fucked Up* (1993), *The Doom Generation* (1995) and *Nowhere* (1997), the trilogy focuses on teen characters alienated by society, disenfranchised as queers or outcasts and confused about becoming adults. Araki's teens embody the concerns and anxieties of the decade of the 1990s, which saw – in the flesh of their teens – the decaying effects of AIDS and the violence of homophobia, the pressures of gendered beauty standards and the enormous impact of disenfranchisement of the newer generations resulting in a rise in the number of teen suicides.

If we want to situate these three cinematic productions in the history of American cinema, it is essential to talk about New Queer Cinema, despite the various problems in defining this wave after B. Ruby Rich (2000) declared its death. The label 'New Queer Cinema' (NQC) was coined by Rich in 1992, and gives cohesion to the many queer independent films that were released in the early 1990s by directors such as Todd Haynes, Gus Van Sant, Jennie Livingston or Gregg Araki. Rich saw in all of them the usage of what she calls the 'Homo Pomo' style: 'appropriation and pastiche, irony, as well as reworking of history with social constructionism very much in mind' (1992: 32). The permeability of queer theory and politics into NQC is obvious, from the appropriation of meaning and its reworking into the queer discourse, to the presence of constructionist theories.

In her introduction to *New Queer Cinema: A Critical Reader* (2004) Michele Aaron, acknowledging NQC as a contested category, manages to set characteristics that somehow give a certain cohesion to the wave: giving voice to the marginalised, eschewing positive imagery, and defying tradition and 'the past', cinematic conventions and, ultimately, death. These characteristics were also galvanised by a phenomenon largely explored by many authors in relation to queerness: the AIDS pandemic. The presence of a common enemy, AIDS, made the LGBT community very visible, which in turn heightened social fear and homophobia and triggered a rise in gay bashing. There was something 'new' about NQC: an intention to fight for a better situation in the community, escaping gay normativity and the wishful thinking derived from the huge accomplishments in previous years for LGBT people. AIDS also frames the event in a precise temporality – the end of the 1980s until the end of the 1990s – which is the central timeframe and context to understanding the NQC label.

The three Araki movies, then, participate in this postmodern pastiche, giving voice to marginalised teens and blatantly eschewing a positive cleaned-up homonormative imagery: the queer misfits that populate Araki's trilogy steal, kill, doubt and suffer in ways that the characters of mainstream gay cinema of the 1990s did not – some examples are: *Threesome* (Andrew Fleming, 1994); *In&Out* (Frank Oz, 1997); *The Object of My Affection* (Nicholas Hytner, 1998); *Philadelphia* (Jonathan Demme, 1993); *Jeffrey* (Christopher Ashley, 1995) or *I Think I Do* (Bryan Sloan, 1997). The filmmaker's style reappropriates genres (like the road movie, teen movie or documentary film), providing a queer alternative to classic cinema. It does also play with intertextuality, like in the use of James Duval as the main character for all three movies, or in its constant references to pop culture through its aesthetics and cameos.

A sense of defiance against the status quo and political correctness is, as well, a key idea in describing the attitude and tone of the movies and the characters of the trilogy. The explicit defiance of cinematic conventions, especially the linear narrative of classic cinema, is very much present in both *Totally Fucked Up* and *Nowhere*. The spectator is never sure about the 'reality' of what is being shown, or the different levels of mediation, blurring the borders of the unreal. Drug-induced perceptions, dreams, fantasies and surreal sequences force us to navigate the text without fully knowing where we are at any given moment. Defiance of the past and tradition come in both form and substance: Araki dismantles classic narrativity while his teens defy society, adults and their institutions. Finally the ultimate defiance of death is explicitly given in *The Doom Generation* – protagonists try to escape numerous murderers and psychos – but also in *Nowhere* in the shape of teen suicide and in *Totally Fucked Up* represented by AIDS.

This defiance of the status quo, conventions and stereotypes proves vastly important in Araki's work, and for his queer viewers. Stereotypes and/or lack of representation are particularly important for teenagers, as Michael Warner explains: 'Heterosexual ideology, in combination with a potent ideology about gender and identity in maturation ... bears down in the heaviest and often deadliest way on those with least resources to combat it: queer children and teens' (1993: xvi). Queer teens, then, lack an inherent proximity with similar identities/subjects to model themselves after. This might lead to alienation, loneliness and feeling of despair since none of the main institutions surrounding or available to us – school, church, family – provide locations for connecting with comparable identities. Media, then, has a decisive role in the construction and (self-)acceptance of LGBT identities, since the media are the main available source of acknowledgement of non-normative sexualities. Araki is aware of that and by placing his queer stories, characters and plotlines onscreen he is making a political statement on what needs to be visibilised, and claims a public space for his (queer) teens and their problems.

Suicide and Homophobia: *Totally Fucked Up*

After an intertitle that reads 'It's my party and I'll inseminate if I want to', we see a home party where six teenagers are spread on the floor surrounded by decorations made of inflated condoms. The gay couple, Deric (Lance May) and Steven (Gilbert Luna), and their gay friends Andy (James Duval) and Tommy (Roko Belic), are there together at the request of lesbian couple Patricia (Jenee Gill) and Michele (Susan Behshid), who in exchange for drinks and snacks ask each of them to ejaculate for a homemade artificial insemination. This scene is one of the most memorable of the film, and narrates one of the strategies that these six teenagers resort to, that of queer solidarity, in order to resist social homophobia and overcome the limitations imposed onto them (for example the difficulty of parenthood for a same-sex couple in the 1990s). Araki constantly fluctuates from showing and highlighting the problems the teens encounter, to offering ways of resisting such problems.

Totally Fucked Up is the choral story of a group of six queer teenagers and their lives in a lonely and sometimes terrifying Los Angeles. We follow their experiences thanks to the camcorder of one of the male characters, Steven, who is preparing a documentary about their lives to 'show how things really are, 'cause nobody is gonna show it on TV', which is precisely what Araki does in his movies. However, the film is more of a collage of very small audiovisual pieces, combining the film clips with handheld camera shots, intertitles and television images. The four gays and the lesbian couple form a dysfunctional family of their own that will help them navigate the doubts and concerns of teenagehood and their alienation from a desolated city in which nobody seems to care about anyone.

Centred on the topic of suicide, *Totally Fucked Up* starts with a very revealing image, that of a news report titled 'Suicide Rate High Among Gay Teens', which discusses the percentage of gay teens that have committed suicide according to the National Institute of Mental Health. This explicit reference will be continuously revisited during the whole film. Barely minutes later, the characters are having a conversation under a highway bridge, framed by an 'END' traffic sign and an adult couple of master and slave wandering around like mistress and dog, chain included. This conversation retakes the suicide theme from the opening article, this time discussed out loud by the six characters. It will appear again in the telling of a double suicide by gay teens in love during Andy and Ian's (Alan Boyce) conversation in an empty gas station. Andy deems this suicidal pact romantic, while Ian just thinks it is sad. The theme of suicide is highlighted formally by the constant use of a post-punk soundtrack including dark-mood songs by the Jesus and Mary Chain, references to Joy Division (whose singer Ian Curtis committed suicide in 1980 and shares the name with Andy's boyfriend), or the song 'Teenage Suicide' by Unrest. The film's intertitles also help convey this idea, with texts like 'gave up' or 'the young and the

Fig. 1: Opening shot in *Totally Fucked Up* (1993).

hopeless'. Steven, the filmmaker, will also confide to his camera that he wishes he were dead, after he and Deric break up.

Finally, there is the tragic ending of its main character, Andy. After realising he's been cheated on by his boyfriend, and having had unprotected anonymous sex, Andy calls in despair each of his friends to find no answer and decides to kill himself by drinking a cocktail of cleaning products, emphasising how loneliness and isolation can lead to suicide. Suicide is a continuous reference throughout the movie and calls attention to the rising number of teen deaths in the 1990s. But despite its centrality, suicide is not an isolated theme. The opening article explains that the teens committed suicide for their 'failure to succeed as heterosexuals while betraying their feelings of homosexuality because of society's prejudice'. Also, when Andy and Ian comment on the double suicide, they add a final note about the father of one of the teens saying 'he's better off dead than queer'. In a scene where Andy is in his swimming pool, a T-shirt saying 'It's Society's Fault' will be prominently displayed. Suicide, then, is related directly to society's homophobia, which becomes another conducting theme of the movie and a central point in Araki's critique.

Totally Fucked Up is very explicit about homophobia. The promiscuous character, Tommy, is thrown out of home after his parents discover his stack of gay porn. We can only see him being pushed out of the door and then thrown his shoes. However, the scene becomes clearer later when, with a bruised eye, he explains what happened to his friends in Deric's room, and tells how his parents 'freaked out' after he said 'Yes, I'm a homo'. In another scene, Andy nonchalantly tells Ian on the phone about a psychopath in Hollywood who kills hustlers and severs their heads after putting their penises in their mouths. Most importantly, Deric gets gay-bashed in the street by a band of dressed-up and faceless individuals. Deric's attack is preluded by images of South Carolina's senator Strom Thurmond's homophobic rant, in which he compares queers to 'vermin coming out of the closet marching down the street', and declares that God has them on the way of 'marching down the street to the graveyard' before clapping his hands and smiling.

With this way of presenting homophobia, putting together Thurmond's speech and Deric's bashing, Araki makes a political statement and connects social prejudices with anti-gay violence. However, *Totally Fucked Up* not only denounces the social climate in which these teenagers live but offers as well points of resistance for the characters to face this situation. For example, Tommy's expulsion highlights queer solidarity when Deric proposes that he stay at his place as long as he needs too. At some point, even Tommy is happy that he has been forced to grow and find a place for himself, explaining it to Deric as a positive development in his life. In a similar manner, Deric's bashing brings together all his friends and paves the way for Deric and Steve's reconciliation.

Another prominent way of resisting homophobia is the referencing of pop culture. The intertitles 'Tom Cruise: the Rock Hudson of the 1990s' and 'Mel Gibson: homophobic a-hole' serve as a background for the conversation that the guys are having about the celebrities they find sexually attractive. The characters turn the tables on the well-known homophobic ideology of Gibson and Cruise's negation of his suspected queerness to position them as the teens' objects of desire. In a similar manner, they adapt the heterosexual romance game 'Heartthrob' and add some campy information queering the whole game and finding a space for self-representation, while Michele says how boring heterosexuality is. Other subversions of popular culture are the ironical use of television fragments, porn movies and public announcements juxtaposed to the film's 'reality'. By playing with format and intertitles, Araki resists being just a passive recipient of social homophobia and violence, and creates a critique of such circumstances through the use of form and content. The appropriation of the public space and media for denouncing purposes that the ACT UP group famously used in the 1990s is also echoed through the teens' T-shirts, where we can read the previously mentioned 'It's Society's Fault' or ACT UP's 'Read My Lips' slogan over a gay couple kissing.[1] Moreover, ACT UP's reference links perfectly with the subjacent topic that, according to José Arroyo, is pivotal for NQC: 'AIDS is why there is NQC and what it is about' (1993: 71).

To sum up, *Totally Fucked Up* is constructed by Araki as a reclaiming of the public/media space to show the lives of queer teenagers, the ways they confront social homophobia and the effects of such environment on the teens, especially through teen suicide. AIDS is also present – and branded as 'government sponsored genocide' and 'biological warfare' by the lesbian couple – amongst the main concerns that the teens explain to the camera, but, unlike in *The Living End*, it does not occupy the centre of the narration. This tendency towards displacing AIDS from the centre will continue to grow in Araki's following movies, while the range of problems that the teens face expands.

Violence and Sex: *The Doom Generation*

In a grocery store owned by a Korean family, a boy and a girl buy some snacks and cigarettes for a total amount of $6.66. The clerk threatens to shoot them for throwing a cigarette butt on the floor, while a giant sign over the two teens' heads reads: 'Shoplifters will be executed.' When they reach into their pockets and find no money, the Korean clerk gets really angry, and is about to use his shotgun on them. A third character enters the scene and facilitates the couple's escape wrestling with the clerk and his wife, which results in blowing the clerk's head off with his own shotgun. This killing is difficult to take seriously, represented in an over-the-top manner, with the head of the clerk flying some feet away, mustering some incomprehensible sentence and vomiting a green-yellow liquid. The exaggeration of violence to the point of humour, the constant threats from society to the teens and the continuous escape from their crimes is, from that point on, the conducting theme of this road trip to nowhere that the three main characters will embark on. It also allows Araki to ironically connect with his audience, as well as connecting to his larger critique of society's obliviousness to anti-gay violence.

In *The Doom Generation*, teen lovers Jordan White (James Duval) and Amy Blue (Rose McGowan) save young Xavier Red (Johnathon Schaech) from a fight, and set out to escape on a journey in which they will defy death and violence while experimenting with their sexualities in an unexpected 'throuple'. Their family names, like the palette of white/blue/red colors used in *Totally Fucked Up*, symbolically locate the action in the United States, contextualising the homophobic atmosphere of the film. In this queer road-movie, the spectator follows the sex/love story of the teenagers trying to escape death and the apocalypse in a threatening landscape in which adults around them are the main danger they constantly face. *The Doom Generation* continues the theme of violence exerted on the teens' bodies that we saw in *Totally Fucked Up*, and links this to the unconventional sexualities of the characters.

Jordan and Amy are a young couple discovering together the secrets of a new relationship. In the opening scene, at a bar called Hellhole, Amy looks bored and Jordan offers to go together to 'heaven'. The movie cuts to their car in a parking lot where the couple try to have sex. However, Jordan is too self-conscious and afraid of AIDS, so they never consummate. While they are kissing after this interruption, Xavier enters the scene by being pushed against the car by a group of young men who call him a 'cocksucker' and try to beat him. This incidental encounter sets off the trip that the three of them will take, and in which both Amy and Jordan will discover the pleasures of sexuality through the tempting suggestions of Xavier.

From the very beginning, Xavier exploits the fascination that Jordan feels for him, and navigates the verbal attacks of Amy until he finally seduces her. There are scenes of voyeurism: Xavier watching the couple have sex in the bathroom from behind a half-shut door, masturbating and finally licking his own sperm, and Jordan watching Xavier and Amy have noisy sex from the window of the hotel and also masturbating. Xavier also teaches Amy to use her finger to stimulate his anus while having sex, and though she finds it repulsive at first, she later convinces Jordan to let her do it to him. Xavier also gets closer and closer to Jordan during the film, although Jordan seems oblivious to his sexual advances at first, and confesses in the car that he has had sex with a dog his family owned. In the final scene, after tossing a coin to decide who will have sex with Amy first, Xavier wins and Jordan waits patiently in the car. When it is Jordan's turn, Xavier decides to join the two of them and this time he and Jordan share caresses and kisses for the first time.

Fig. 2: Xavier (Jonathon Schaech) spies Amy (Rose McGowan) and Jordan (James Duval) having sex in *The Doom Generation* (1995).

Similar to the way in which *Totally Fucked Up* dealt with homosexuality, *The Doom Generation* focuses on polyamory and bisexuality.

Sexuality is pervasive throughout, and the audience soon discovers the irony behind the subtitle 'A heterosexual movie by Gregg Araki' that we see at the beginning, since the three of them engage in less and less normative monogamous heterosexual sex acts as the film progresses. It is also the unrestrained sexuality of the adults surrounding them what will cause constant problems to the trio. Under the impression that Amy is their former lover, totally random people in each of the places they stop begin to harass the teens, and even attack them after Amy doesn't recognise any of those allegedly 'former lovers'. We can see how the theme of violence against the teenagers is again present in this film, although this time they are not as innocent as the characters in *Totally Fucked Up*. Amy, Jordan and Xavier kill, beat, cut and/or dismember several of the attackers they encounter, starting with the severed head of the Korean clerk to the worker of the drive-in who follows them to the hotel, to, finally, the lady that thinks Amy is her 'kitten' in a bar. The teens are both criminals and victims, a twist that Araki employs to ambiguously address the topic of structural violence as he did in *The Living End*, showing the characters in a complex and ambivalent way, avoiding a linear and positive representation and offering the opportunity to fight oppression.

However, it is the last scene which brings together the tone of *Totally Fucked Up* and *The Doom Generation*: after Amy interrupts the threesome because she needs to pee, Jordan and Xavier stay on the mattress they have found in an abandoned warehouse. In that moment, someone extinguishes the fire that illuminates them and starts to sing a homophobic song ('Two little fags, sitting on a fence, one eating ass the other giving head…'). Through a flickering light – that we already saw during Deric's bashing in *Totally Fucked Up* – the spectator receives glimpses of the action that follows. A band of naked neo-Nazis with red swastikas on their chest torture and beat the three of them while singing the Star Spangled Banner, and rape Amy on an American flag they lay on the floor. They finally castrate Jordan (who has already been threatened with having his member cut 'like a chicken head' in the bar scene) with gardening scissors, and put his penis in his mouth – similar to the story of the psychopath killing Hollywood hustlers in *Totally Fucked Up*. Amy takes revenge killing one of the neo-Nazis with the same gardening scissors they used and Xavier helps her finish the other two.

Despite the random acts of violence that we see throughout the film, this is the only one taken seriously. This one is not treated like the previous killings, and through the death of Jordan, Araki places at the forefront the effects of homophobic violence over the teens' bodies. Although the other acts of violence in the film are treated with disregard by the protagonists – much like the moving of corpses, crazy people yelling or masters walking their slaves like dogs in *Totally Fucked Up* are received with a total lack of attention by the characters – this final scene is akin to Deric's bashing or Andy's suicide, and brings to the movie the seriousness of the problems for US queer teenagers in the 1990s. Nevertheless, *The Doom Generation* seems to be more preoccupied with stylistic features – a concern that will increase in *Nowhere* – than in making a political statement and, although the critique to the situation that the teens live in is present, the heavy-handed final scene leaves us

Fig. 3: Space conveys the characters' mood in *Nowhere* (1997).

with little solace and Jordan's death seems to be in vain. Araki moves away from explicit politics and realism into a more metaphoric take on the matter, connecting humorously with his audience.

Of course, there are also references to suicide – Amy expresses her desire to slit her wrists in the first scene; Jordan responds in the car that 'there is no place for us in this world'; and Xavier explains how his mother killed his father and then herself. The influence of society in the violence around them appears through the news anchor on TV that puts together 'homosexuals, Satanists and other dangerous groups' or the montage of the sword fight they have in a bar with images of *Mortal Kombat* – a videogame that caused moral panic for its violence and possible effects on teenagers (see Crossley 2014). However, it is much more residual than in *Totally Fucked Up*, and the criminal/victim position of the protagonists is less successful in its critique than that of *The Living End*. *The Doom Generation* appears to be a transition from Araki's early political films denouncing AIDS and homophobia to his next phase in which he perfects his auteuristic style and aesthetics to the detriment of the social commentary of his movies.

The Apocalypse of White Privileged Teenagers: *Nowhere*

The closing title of the trilogy, *Nowhere* retakes and amplifies the choral structure of *Totally Fucked Up* (from 6 to 19 characters) and, thanks to a much higher budget, makes it into a queer hallucinogenic version of teen shows like *Beverly Hills 90210*. The title, as Dark Smith (James Duval), the main character explains, refers to Los Angeles, a non-space through which these privileged but alienated adolescents navigate aimlessly. *Nowhere* completes the transition that *The Doom Generation* started towards auteur aesthetics, and retakes many of its features: the Godardian colour palettes; the expression of the characters' mood through the space they are in; and the constant references to pop culture in form of celebrity cameos, including Chiara Mastroianni, Traci Lords, Shannon Doherty, the Brewer twins and Jaason Simmons from *Baywatch*. However, this focus on form rather than content has earned the movie some criticism, like Kylo-Patrick Hart's claim that Araki is 'losing focus' and 'taming queerness' (2010: 51, 52).

Indeed, it is true that the explicit political critique of *The Living End* and *Totally Fucked Up* seems absent in this piece, but due to its approach to sexuality, suicide and society's pressures, *Nowhere* cannot be labeled as completely apolitical. With this film, Araki wanted to create a mainstream text and use mainstream language (see Chang 1994: 53) and as in any process of mainstreamisation, the radicalism moves to a secondary role. *Nowhere* shifts the focus from the gay sexuality of *Totally Fucked Up* to revisit other dissident ways of experiencing sex, like bisexuality and polyamory (already present in *The Doom Generation*), incest, BDSM and role-playing through its various characters: the presence of the twins (played by Jordan Ladd and Ryan Philippe) and their connection when they experience sexuality that leads them to having simultaneous orgasms; the trio formed by Dark, his girlfriend Mel (Rachel True) and her lesbian lover Lucifer (Kathleen Robertson); the dominatrix couple Kriss and Kozy (Chiara Mastroianni and Debi Mazar) and the S&M roleplaying of Alyssa (Jordan Ladd) and her boyfriend Elvis (Thyme Lewis); all of these relations show the variety of sexualities present in this supposedly 'mainstream' movie, and all of them are again representing the deviant sexualities that Araki uses in his films.

On top of that, the movie expands the causes of alienation and violence over the teens' bodies, leaving behind the specificity of queer teenagers and using privileged youth from Los Angeles as its victims. Alienation from society takes the form of an impending apocalypse that was already present in *Totally Fucked Up* through different signs: in the street we read 'The Rapture is Coming' and in the clothes store 'Prepare for the Apocalypse'; Jordan and Amy's premonitions ('I have the feeling that something is going to happen tonight'); and the constant reference to the diabolic number 666 in the price of everything the teens buy. The apocalypse serves as a background for the spiral of destruction that *Nowhere*'s characters are about to suffer, while the movie explores problems that are common amongst teenagers, such as the pressure of beauty standards or the use of drugs in order to escape from reality.

The pressure of beauty standards – that we implicitly see in *The Doom Generation* through Amy's diet based on cigarettes and Coke – takes a central place in *Nowhere* via the scene in the teens' local hangout cafe, The Hole. We can see three of the girls – Alyssa, Dingbat (Christina Applegate) and Polly, also known as 'Egg' (Sarah Lassez) – sharing a chocolate dessert. They look at it for a moment before plunging into a three-way binge, accompanied by upbeat electronic music. Once the dessert is over, Dingbat exclaims 'glug' and they check each other to see if anyone's going to vomit. Dingbat says she promised her mother not to, Alyssa responds that she is just going to do 'a bunch of speed' and burn the calories, and Polly, having no answer, suddenly runs to the toilet to purge.

The use of drugs is an overarching theme in the film as well, present during a game of 'kick the can' where each of the participants take some acid, or more importantly through the character of Bart (Jeremy Jordan) and his addiction to heroine. His addiction and relationship with boyfriend Cowboy (Guillermo Díaz) is in fact one of the main plotlines. Actually, it is not coincidental that both Polly and Bart suffer more prominently the effects of alienation and impending doom, since it is these two characters that will end up committing suicide.

Suicide in *Nowhere* is framed by the lack of communication with the teens' families. This same topic is somewhat highlighted in *Totally Fucked Up* through the framing of Deric's mother's legs – a way of defacing her representation and highlighting her absence – and the inability of Andy to call her as the last option before suicide, even though he has her on his speed-dial list. In *The Doom Generation*, Jordan tries to reach his parents to justify his absence and only finds an answering machine that 'hangs up on him', and Amy postpones the call during the whole film, pointing towards the carelessness of their parents about their children's disappearance. In *Nowhere* this lack of communication is articulated through the constant barriers between parents and children – closed doors between Dark and his mother or Polly and her father, telephone lines between Polly's brother and the parents or even a different language between Bart and the Sighvatsson family. Both Polly and Bart will end up killing themselves at home, found by their families, constituting the ending scenes of the film before the final scene.

In the final scene, Dark welcomes Montgomery (Nathan Bexton) into his room after he disappeared during the 'kick the can' game. They finally lie in bed together and confess their love. What seems like a happy ending for at least one of the characters is truncated by Montgomery's sudden explosion and transformation in a giant cockroach. It is not the first time something bizarre happens in the movie, since Dark has seen a giant lizard beaming three girls away with a laser gun, and later Mongomery during the 'kick the can' game. Extraterrestrial presence – 'aliens'– functions in *Nowhere* as a metaphor for alienation and also a reminder of the coming of the apocalypse. It also gives the film a more humorous tone that, as in *The Doom Generation*, helps the viewer better digest the random acts of violence, while giving more seriousness to the death of Polly and Bart. It seems that Araki does not want us to take his representation of social violence and the exaggerated characters and situations in the movies too seriously, while giving a different tone to the suicides and homophobic murders by contrast.

In *Nowhere* we can see the culmination of Araki's aesthetics, and a cleaner style and narrative. However, we also note the distancing of the director from queer politics and a will to explore teenagehood as a whole rather than centre on queer teenagers. For this reason, *Nowhere* disappoints queer audiences looking for the political and in-your-face early Araki. However, under its mainstream appearance and ostensible superficiality, we can still find Araki highlighting the problems the teens face, as well as a critique of social alienation, albeit presented in a more metaphorical way. Araki displaces the crudeness of *The Living End* and the intertwining with reality of *Totally Fucked Up* to offer a movie that much more subtly and ironically addresses similar topics.

Epilogue: *Kaboom*

We have seen how Araki moves from very political critiques of social homophobia, starting with *The Living End* and *Totally Fucked Up*, to more metaphorical and open-ended representations of teenagehood in films such as *The Doom Generation* and *Nowhere*. We also note how queer sexuality diminishes its presence in his films – from gays and lesbians, to potential bisexuals, to mostly heterosexuals – while the violence on the teenagers remains or even increases: one suicide and one bashing in *Totally Fucked Up*, one serious murder and various sexual harassments and exaggerated murders in *The Doom Generation*, and two suicides and a murder in *Nowhere*. Many years later *Kaboom* (2010) follows the trilogy with a fourth part that follows this tendency towards apolitisation.

Araki's teens are harbingers of the moment and witnesses in their own bodies of the social events and transformations of the time, so much so that Araki's depiction of late teenagehood in *Kaboom* – allegedly the closing piece of a tetralogy – radically transforms its teenagers despite the enormous connections they still share with those in the trilogy. In an interview for *Cahiers du cinéma*, Florence Maillard asks him about the changes between the trilogy and *Kaboom*, highlighting the more than ten years gap between them. Araki answers: 'young people are not so worried about limitations, while twenty years ago, this generated a lot of questioning [...] Youth has nowadays this attitude of "it doesn't really matter" that I find very healthy. Youth is a period for experimenting, without anxiety' (2010: 38). It is as if the new century has brought peace to the anxiety of Generation X teenagers in the eyes of Araki – or perhaps this could also be attributed to his own distancing from teenagehood. Whatever the reason, this issue is clearly reflected in the tone of *Kaboom* and the lives of its characters. In age terms, whereas the movies from the 1990s showcase teenagers as protagonists – providing interesting explorations of intra-familiar relationships and the formation of identity – in *Kaboom* the teenagers are already young adults, discursively increasing their agency as individuals and acquiring a (privileged) voice of their own as members of society.

Kaboom continues the progression towards a more aesthetical and open-ended discourse, losing the radicalism of Araki's first texts, employing sexuality as something that 'happens' instead as an opportunity to comment on heteronormativity. The threat of AIDS is seen as something from the past: the only time it is implicitly mentioned is when Smith (Thomas Dekker) is having unprotected sex with Hunter (Jason Olive). They stop for a second, and Smith asks Hunter if this is something he does frequently, only to continue the act after Hunter's negation. This trivialisation of AIDS corresponds to the current climate among gays, where the shift from a death sentence to a chronic disease has rendered AIDS as increasingly innocuous to the eyes of the community. Homophobia is almost completely erased from the movie, except by the fact that the endangered characters are queer. There is no homophobic violence or public denigration in the film, not even by the 'super-straight' characters like Thor (Chris Zylka). The only comment, albeit very metaphorical, about society's pressures over the teens is on religion, through Smith's father sect, which will cause the end of the world. If religion started to appear in *Nowhere* as one of the causes of suicide through the TV preacher that seems to encourage Polly and

Bart to end their lives, in *Kaboom* it takes the form of a sect that wants to end the world and makes it explode at the end (thus the title of the movie). Araki has lost interest in radical texts that allow a public space for queer teens onscreen, and in the political commentary of society's pitfalls.

Araki's teens of the 1990s are not impervious to the social turmoil of the period. The economic and ideological problems of the decade, such as the remnants of the Reagan and Bush administrations, are imprinted in their bodies, sometimes violently, and hinder their possibility of a future and their full transformation into adults. If the body of the teen is normally a difficult space to inhabit, uncertain of the steps to take towards maturity, Araki's teens are configured as a desperate clarion call on the eradication of our children, our future society. Araki not only denounces this situation and calls attention to the way in which society participates in the violence exerted against queer youth, but also succeeds in giving a space to minority sexualities that often are underrepresented or completely absent from the media. Araki's works, and other NQC movies, were very successful and necessary in the early 1990s because they offered a contrast to other films dealing with homosexuality that tried to sanitise public perception of homosexuals. Araki's unapologetic representations show that queer youth is neither perfect nor flat or univocal. They are wrong, they make mistakes and they fight back.

These teens are disenfranchised both from an outside threatening world, in which queer teens are not welcome, as well as from the inside, uncertain of their own core values and sense of purpose. But in Araki's work, this does not stop them from looking for solutions or using their survival instincts. These teens are abject bodies that need to become productive in order to find their meaning in a capitalist Mecca like Los Angeles, in order to become subjects, but somehow, between their parties and sex, they find a way to exist and carry on. Facing the hardships of economic recession, absent parenting and the overwhelming threat of AIDS, Araki's teens decide to escape this logic of reproduction and defy society and death on their own. In order to do so, they create alliances and surrogate families and use their hurt and oppressed bodies for pleasure and for the discovery of their sexualities. In a similar manner, queer activism tried to revert the normative view over homosexuality as expendable – and AIDS as a 'gay pandemic' – through the creation of alternative support networks and bonds transcending blood-related family. Trying to enjoy their abject positionality by exploring intimacy with other outcasts, Araki's teens show, without sweetening the situation or the use of clichés, how love and desire are the only tools that will build our own future: a future that might never come, or not come on time. But a future in any case.

Note

1 ACT UP or 'AIDS Coalition To Unleash Power' was an activist group that became famous in the US during the AIDS crisis for their use of the public space and media to call attention to the situation of the pandemic, countering the institutional silence about the topic.

Bibliography

Aaron, M. (2004) *New Queer Cinema: A Critical Reader*. New Brunswick, NJ: Rutgers University Press.

Arroyo, J. (1993) 'Death, Desire and Identity: The Political Unconscious of "New Queer Cinema"', in J. Bristow and A. Wilson (eds) *Activating Theory: Lesbian, Gay and Bisexual Politics*. London: Lawrence and Wishart, 70–97.

Crossley, R. (2014) 'Mortal Kombat: Violent game that changed video games industry'; http://www.bbc.com/news/technology-27620071 (accessed February 2015).

Chang, C. (1994) 'Absorbing Alternative', *Film Comment*, Sept/Oct, 47–53.

Hart, K.-P. (2010) *Images for a Generation Doomed: The Films and Career of Gregg Araki*. Lanham, MD: Lexington Books.

Maillard, F. (2010) 'Boom Generation: Entretien avec Gregg Araki', *Cahiers du cinéma*, 660, 38–9.

Rich, B. R. (1992) 'New Queer Cinema', *Sight and Sound*, 2, 5, 32.

____ (2000) 'Queer and Present Danger', *Sight and Sound*, 10, 3, 24.

Warner, M. (1993) *Fear of a Queer Planet*. Minneapolis, MN: University of Minnesota Press.

Chapter 11
Unsettling Heteronormativity: Abject Age and Transgressive Desire in *Notes on a Scandal*

EVA KRAINITZKI

The Academy Award-nominated *Notes on a Scandal* (Richard Eyre, 2006) presents one of the most visible portrayals of an ageing female protagonist in recent mainstream film. A complex and intriguing character, Barbara Covett (Judi Dench), has been described in popular discourse as a 'flesh-creeping menace' and 'Hannibal Lecter in drip-dry knitwear' (Richards 2006: n.p.). This chapter suggests that despite Barbara's characterisation as the monstrous, abject villain (so vividly described above), her figure can be appropriated as *queer*.

Focusing on Barbara's age-inappropriate behaviour as transgressive of socially prescriptive 'graceful ageing', this chapter intersects the category of ageing with *queer* in the 'radical sense, the upsetting sense, the invocation of which connotes the dirty, the abject, and the irredeemable' (Hartman 2013: n.p.). It adopts a feminist approach to the concept of monstrous abjection (see Kristeva 1982; Creed 1993; Shildrick 2002) to explore it in relation to the categories of old and queer, at the centre of Barbara's ability to unsettle structures of heteronormativity (and to an extent homonormative identity politics). She transgresses categories as a woman who simultaneously embodies same-sex desire yet resists a lesbian identity. With an ageing studies lens, this chapter explores the act of 'ageing disgracefully' in relation to anachronism (see Russo 1999) and queer failure (see Halberstam 2011), and claims Barbara as a transgressive figure in the tradition of feminist, lesbian and queer theory. It thus invites viewers to adopt resistant or oppositional viewing positions in order to reclaim other stereotypical characters produced by popular culture.

Mainstream Anglo-American cinema has not been kind to older women. Extensive research illustrates how they are represented less favourably (see Markson

2003), with fewer and less complex roles available to actresses of a 'certain age' (compared to their male counterparts) in what seems to suggest the endurance of Susan Sontag's (1972) double standard of ageing. Furthermore, roles available for older actresses, including 'mother, grandmother, domestic servant, spinster, infirm person' are, as Imelda Whelehan posits, 'narrative function more often than narrative fulcrum' (2010: 170). Elizabeth Markson remarks that available types include the 'good' old woman or the 'bad' old woman, and that the latter is 'more likely to be shown as grotesque, even asexually "unfeminine", than her good counterpart would' (2003: 89).

As the trope of invisibility is slowly being substituted by new images of older female bodies, new stereotypes and possibilities emerge, including the 'graceful ager' or the 'sexy oldie' (see Vares 2009) in the 'older bird chick flicks' that now portray older women as sexually desiring and desirable, without being 'punished for expressing their sexuality' (Tally 2008: 129). This new mode of visibility does nonetheless present certain limitations, as it is mostly restricted to 'gracefully aged' older women and their age-appropriate love interest, framed by the norms of heterosexual romance.[1] Despite a growing interest in representations of ageing, few academic accounts explore ageing beyond the heterosexual ageing body in cinema, something this chapter seeks to address. Barbara is an interesting character who seems to challenge simultaneously two paradigmatic modes of representing female ageing on screen; namely, the image of the asexual older woman, and the emergent image of the gracefully aged, 'sexy oldie'.

Outside of the frame of heteronormativity, there are even fewer images, as a result of a 'triple jeopardy – as a woman, as an older person, and as a lesbian' (Poor 1982: 171). Recent representations of older lesbian, bisexual or queer women can generally be subsumed under two main representational paradigms – they appear as grotesque and predatory, or as de-sexualised apparitional figures (see Castle 1993), as I have argued elsewhere (see Krainitzki 2012). Under the guise of old age, earlier stereotypical modes of lesbian representation in film seem to have gained new levels of cultural acceptability. Following an identity politics approach, *Notes on a Scandal* can be recognised as a return to former tropes of representation, resembling pre-gay-rights and women's liberation movements of the 1960s, which in itself raises questions about the pervasiveness and continuation of certain cultural images of ageing, gender and sexuality. Its protagonist, Barbara Covett, is an amalgam of lesbian stereotypes, reminiscent of the 'creepy' spinster figure – for instance, Mrs Danvers in Hitchcock's *Rebecca* (1940), the predatory vampires of the 1970s Hammer films or the butch lesbian in *The Killing of Sister George* (Robert Aldrich, 1968). One reviewer traces this parallel when describing Barbara, in line with George, as a vindictive 'older, unfulfilled lesbian' who 'preys' on younger women (see Torrance 2007).

Most reactionary elements contained within *Notes on a Scandal* derive from the adaptation process that follows former representational paradigms inherent in mainstream production's inability to create alternative screen images of non-normative sexuality and old age. Focusing on the intersections of gender, age and sexual identity, the following section seeks to understand how *Notes on a Scandal* combines former modes of representing predatory lesbians in film with the conventional portrayal of the ageing female body as abject other. A brief consideration of the adaptation process highlights the ideological framework in which Barbara is conceived.

Adapting Barbara: An Identity Politics Approach

From a positive images perspective, which derives from debates in early feminist film criticism (see Waldman 1990) and has informed gay and lesbian identity politics – similarly concerned with the absence of 'positive' representation (see Weiss 1992) – Barbara does indeed stir up former stereotypical representations of the pathological lesbian, from a pre gay-liberation society. *Notes on a Scandal* is based on Zoë Heller's homonymous 2004 novel (or *What Was She Thinking? Notes On A Scandal* in the United States), adapted for the screen by playwright Patrick Marber and directed by Richard Eyre. Some reviewers note that Barbara's character, who is more sympathetic in Heller's source novel, underwent a radical transformation in the Marber/Eyre adaptation (see Shakespeare 2007; Torrance 2007). The film portrays the friendship between Barbara, a History teacher at a comprehensive school in London, and new Art teacher Sheba Hart (Cate Blanchett). When Barbara discovers that Sheba is having an affair with one of their students, Steven Connolly (Andrew Simpson), she decides to use this knowledge to her advantage, manipulating Sheba into unconditional friendship. When Sheba fails to commit entirely to their friendship, Barbara discloses Sheba's secret to a fellow teacher. Banned from her family home, Sheba moves into Barbara's flat while awaiting the court hearing. Eventually she discovers Barbara's diary and reads about Barbara's true feelings, and that it was Barbara herself who revealed the affair. A violent confrontation follows. Sheba eventually returns to her husband, while Barbara resumes her search for companionship.

Voice-over narrative establishes the link between Heller's literary first-person participant narrator and Eyre's screen adaptation, but the novel's essence is lost. With Barbara's transformation from an unreliable first-person participant-narrator to on-screen co-protagonist, the intimacy and complete immersion into Barbara's worldview enabled in Heller's novel does not translate onto the screen. Barbara's interaction with other characters results in a change of focalisation, despite the voice-over monologues, which for the most part recreate her diary's words. The cinematic rendition of Barbara's diary entries code her as psychotic rather than as the unreliable narrator presented in Heller's novel. The intensity of Barbara's feelings is revealed in expressions such as 'spiritual recognition', 'companions' or the admission that 'She [Sheba] is the one I've been waiting for' and 'the pressure is intense when two women share their lives'. Evocative of the proto-lesbian notion of romantic friendship, this type of language clashes with the screen images of contemporary twenty-first-century London, confirming Barbara's delusion.

Adam Sonstegard, who provides a detailed analysis of the major differences between Heller's novel and Eyre's film, suggests that the film 'disappointingly collapses many of the book's possibilities', translating 'the intimacy of Barbara's diary into an unsettling voice-over narration' (2013: 151), and favours Sheba over Barbara (2013: 249). While 'we are potentially on Barbara's side as readers, we are encouraged to be against the mean old lesbian we see on screen' (2013: 151). Heller admits that some of the alterations made to her novel change the core message (see Thorpe 2006; Shakespeare 2007). In the film adaptation, Barbara is 'more overtly lesbian and more monstrous than in her original novel' (Shakespeare 2007: n.p.). In one interview Heller revealed:

> The book is partly a kind of defense of the post-menopausal woman, particularly women who reach a certain age without being married and acquiring property [...]. If I've succeeded in the book at all, you should have some sympathy for this character, even though she's a bit nutty. (In Cohen 2007)

Genre and characterisation turn an older female character with latent homosexual tendencies into a psychopathic villain. Malinda Lo regrets the return of the 'evil lesbian', adding that 'all of the stereotypical qualities of the psychotic lesbian stalker are laid upon the character of Barbara Covett' (2006: n.p.). A complex and multifaceted literary character in terms of her intentions, motivations and, ultimately, her sexuality, is thus reduced to a series of stereotypes. This illustrates the difficulty of representing an intersection of ageing femininity and homoerotic affect on screen.

Barbara is ambiguous enough to keep the viewer wondering about her sexual identity. Whether her obsession with Sheba stems from a (possibly repressed) same-sex desire or mere loneliness is debatable. Barbara can be read both as a very lonely, heterosexual single woman, who is desperate for friendship, or as a 'closeted' or even 'repressed' lesbian woman, who (inadvertently) crosses socially established boundaries of female friendship. This ambiguity is reflected in some of the film's reviews, in which the word 'lesbian' is carefully avoided. Barbara is defined as a 'treacherously lonely spinster' (Jones 2007: n.p.) or 'lonely desperate teacher' (Richards 2006: n.p.). These reviews match the official tone adopted by the cast interviews. Judi Dench describes Barbara as 'a very, very lonely person who craves affection and to have any friend of some kind' and adds, 'I think there are a lot of people out there just like that who have been lonely all their lives and dream of friendship' (in Tapley 2006: n.p.). Cate Blanchett rejects one interviewer's suggestion that the film emphasised the source novel's '"lesbian" undercurrent' (Porton 2007: n.p.) with the following remark: 'I don't think Barbara would use any label to define her sexuality. I find it genuinely ambiguous. There's an overwhelming, intense need for connection, though, that Sheba simply can't reciprocate' (in ibid,). It is precisely this ambiguity and indecision regarding the character's identity that allows the queer approach taken in this chapter. Barbara unsettles heteronormative categories of the asexual older woman, while simultaneously resisting homosexual identity. Regardless of this ambiguity, there are scenes that evidence Barbara's attraction to Sheba, the standard alignment between camera and Barbara's longing gaze upon Sheba's body as she dances; or as she stretches to hang up Christmas decorations at school and a naked stretch of skin catches Barbara's attention. One scene in particular, explored later, is particularly relevant in illustrating Barbara's desire for Sheba.

For a lesbian- or bisexual-identified viewer (including this author), or those familiar with the representational tropes of homosexuality in film, Barbara's characterisa-

Fig. 1: *Notes on a Scandal* (2006) codes Barbara (Judi Dench) as a voyeur.

tion does evoke familiar 'negative' stereotypes of lesbians on screen, in particular the neurotic, sadistic and repressed lesbian (see Weiss 1992: 1). The atmosphere of secrecy, gossip and shame surrounding Barbara's sexual identity resemble *The Children's Hour* (William Wyler, 1961), where another teacher's 'unnatural' feelings come under scrutiny with rather more dramatic effects.

One way Barbara is textually coded as a lesbian is through the voyeur motif, as illustrated by the opening scene, when she looks out from the top of her classroom window and sees Sheba cycling through the school gates. Her desire is constructed as abject through the stalker motif, as evidenced in the scene where Barbara picks up one of Sheba's lose hairs and plays with it. The stalker/voyeur imagery recurs at other crucial moments in the film, for instance, when Barbara peeks through the art studio's door and observes Sheba and Steven in a moment of intimacy. The director admits that a 'stalker motif' was chosen to represent Barbara and describes her feelings as 'adoration bordering on obsession' (Richard Eyre's commentary on the DVD edition).

The complex intersection of hetero(sexism) and ageing in this film leaves us to wonder if her character would have been constructed otherwise if the homoerotic undertones were absent. The flood of insults directed at Barbara exemplifies how age enhances any insinuations of singlehood or non-normative desire – 'crone', 'dyke', 'vampire', 'bitter old virgin', 'friggin' freak'. As Barbara Macdonald and Cynthia Rich argue, ageism needs be understood as 'a point of convergence for many other repressive forces' (1984: 61), that nonetheless often goes unchallenged. Comparing Raymond Berger's description of the stereotype of the old lesbian in the 1980s to Barbara's characterisation two decades later illustrates the enduring presence of the stereotype of the 'heartless and unemotional' lesbian, who is 'lonely because younger lesbians find her unattractive' (1982: 237), who despite this 'attempts unsuccessfully to seduce them, but soon finds herself without family and friends, bitter until death' (ibid.). The construction of same-sex desire and affection as shameful, and the correlation between pathological loneliness and predatory possessiveness implied by this film, means Barbara matches former modes of representing homosexuality on screen.

As has been recognised in recent scholarship, there are limitations to an identity politics approach; indeed 'positive' images, just as 'negative' images, tend to remain static and suppress complexity and contradiction (Becker *et al.* 1995: 27). As Clare Whatling suggests, when demanding positive images we need to ask 'positive for whom', and consider 'whose lesbian life represents reality?' (1997: 83). Having identified the intricate stereotypical elements of Barbara's characterisation, the next section of this chapter claims her as a queer figure.

Appropriating Barbara: Queer Transgressions

Moving away from an identity politics perspective and adopting a more subversive stance, one that claims 'negative' portrayals as empowering, this section considers Barbara in the light of the transgressions of New Queer Cinema characters (see Aaron 2004; Rich 2013).[2] If, as Michele Aaron suggests, queer is at 'its most expansive and utopian' when it 'contests (hetero- and homo-) normality' (2004: 5), challenging age-appropriate norms can certainly be seen as contesting normativity. Acting one's age demands a 'behavior that conforms to norms' (Laz 1998: 86). As will be explored, Barbara's refusal to age 'gracefully' can certainly be understood as transgressive of or 'untethered' from '"conventional" codes of behaviour' (Aaron 2004: 5). As Judith Butler has argued, 'for heterosexuality to remain intact as a distinct social form, it *requires* an intelligible conception of homosexuality and also requires the prohibition of that conception in rendering it culturally unintelligible' (1999: 98). Although Barbara is intelligible according to former representational modes of prohibited homosexuality, she is rendered unintelligible within a twenty-first-century context with its 'new' lesbian visibility and the gracefully aged 'sexy oldie' of mainstream cinema. Barbara's portrayal places her beyond culturally intelligible notions of a youthful desirable and desiring body (as has been the norm for both the heterosexual and the lesbian cinematic body). Her failure to age 'successfully' can nonetheless be interpreted though the lens of Jack Halberstam's 'queer failure', which recognises 'failure as a way of refusing to acquiesce to dominant logics of power and discipline and as a form of critique' (2011: 88). Queer failure opens up alternative understandings of 'unsuccessful' ageing (the failure to comply with the prescriptive notions of 'positive' or 'successful' ageing), casting it as purposefully disgraceful, and queer, and thus transgressive of normative structures.

Appropriation of monstrous figures as empowering is well established in feminist, lesbian and queer film studies (see Whatling 1997; Dyer 2002; Smelik 2004). Deborah Jermyn (1996) suggests a feminist appropriation of the female psychopath sub-genre in order to open up visual pleasures for spectators even when all that these reactionary texts seem to offer is female masochism. Richard Dyer identifies the 'malignant lesbian power' of stealth as one of the attributes of the lesbian vampire figures, who seduce women 'not by direct assault or honest seduction but by stealth' (2002: 32). The vividness of these representations might be appropriated as a radically lesbian feminist image (ibid.). Anneke Smelik (2004) finds value in the 'murderous lesbians' of *Heavenly Creatures* (Peter Jackson, 1994) and *Butterfly Kiss*

(Michael Winterbottom, 1995), reading them as disruptive of the hetero-patriarchal establishment in the tradition of New Queer Cinema. Whatling identifies a sense of 'nostalgia for abjection in lesbian cinema spectatorship' (1997: 79). She claims that a 'knowing and invested audience' (1997: 80) might find certain 'extra-filmic pleasures' in infamous texts, such as *The Children's Hour*, *The Killing of Sister George*. and *The Vampire Lovers* (Roy Ward Baker, 1970). Kyle Buchanan's review adopts this perspective, as he welcomes *Notes on a Scandal* as 'a bracing alternative' (2006: n.p.). As this chapter suggests, Barbara is indeed a bracing alternative, although not to 'the saintly, buttoned-up gay lawyers of *Philadelphia* and *Will & Grace*' Buchanan refers to (he cites homonormative representations of gay male characters rather than lesbians), but rather an alternative to the youthful and (hetero)sexualised lesbian characters populating our screens.[3]

Following Whatling's 'nostalgia for abjection', Barbara could thus be approached from a perspective where the 'tragedy of being the lesbian outside representation is recuperated to the dark glamour of the margins' (1997: 92). As an older woman who refuses to behave according to gender and age-appropriate norms, Barbara remains at the margins of cinematic representation. Barbara ages 'disgracefully' by chosen age- and gender-inappropriate objects of desire. She does so queerly by unsettling hetero- as well as homo-normative identity categories.

Before I explore Barbara's otherness in terms of a 'queer failure' (Halberstam 2011) to age gracefully, I contextualise her ability to unsettle heteronormativity through the notions of abjection (Kristeva 1982), the monstrous-feminine (Creed 1993) and Shildrick's monstrous encounters with the vulnerable self (2002).

The Ageing Monstrous-Feminine

Jeffrey Cohen notes that one can understand a culture by the monsters it engenders, arguing that the 'monster's body quite literally incorporates fear, desire, anxiety, and fantasy' (1996: 4). The possible relationship between cinematic monsters and queer viewers has also been addressed elsewhere (see Benshoff 1997) and the horror genre in particular is densely populated by female figures construed as abject monsters, such as the witch, the vampire, the lesbian. Although *Notes on a Scandal* is not a horror film/thriller, nor Barbara a monster/psychopath, she embodies the monstrous, produced at the border between 'normal and abnormal sexual desire' (Creed 1993: 11), and is positioned as the abject of patriarchal society, as well as the abject of youthful, heteronormative femininity. The film also resembles what Jermyn describes as the 'invasion-of-the-home' sub-genre, thrillers where 'a malign invader threatens the sanctity of the home' (1996: 253). This is evident in the scene culminating in the melodramatic outburst of Sheba's husband, Richard's (Bill Nighy): 'Why is she *always* here? What kind of fucking spell has she cast on you?'

According to Julia Kristeva, abjection can be understood as 'what disturbs identity, system, order. What does not respect borders, positions, rules' (1982: 4). The normative and normalised body disturbed by the abject is in this context an idealised youthful heterosexual body. According to Kristeva, the abject is part of the subject, while simultaneously constituting that what has to be rejected: 'Not me. Not that' (1982: 2). The abject causes discomfort, it unsettles the sense of self, of identity, it has to be expelled for order to be restored (1982: 4). The older lesbian combines, hereby, three types of abjection – femininity (always already 'other'), lesbianism (outside heteronormativity) and old age (the not-young as non-normative body) – excluded from a norm that is not only heterosexual, but youth-centred.

Barbara's ageing body carries the mark of the villainous monster as illustrated by the bathroom scene analysed in the next section of this chapter. Barbara is prosthetically aged through a combination of a bald patch and a wig, as Dench mentions in an interview (see Goodridge 2006). In what follows I analyse one particular scene where Barbara's body is portrayed as abject other and consider whether it can be read as disruptive of heteronormativity.

Transgressive Bodies

The naked body of an older woman not 'morphed by cosmetic surgery' (Markson 2003: 99) is rarely seen on screen. Margaret Cruikshank notes that the absence of naked older bodies perpetuates the 'shame of aging' and 'deprives women of all ages from knowing what old bodies look like' (2009: 152). Given 'the western obsession with the body of youth' (Woodward 1991: 62), and mainstream cinema's perpetuation of 'the youthful structure of the look' (Woodward 2006: 163), it is understandable that the ageing female body is still seen as taboo, usually constructed as *unwatchable* (see Coupland 2013). As more daring representations of female ageing appear on screen, normativity is challenged and the boundaries of what is represent*able* and watch*able* are expanded (see Vares 2009).

In *Notes on a Scandal*, the ageing female body is constructed as abject (of the youthful, heteronormative body). The old-fashioned pink bathroom tiles in the background set the scene as the camera pans slowly from left to the right, from Barbara's white knees to her upper body. One hand raised, clasping a cigarette, the other shielding her naked breast, ensuring this scene's *watchability*. The lighting is harsh, and the bath water looks tepid, whitish, stagnant. Her face and hair appear

Fig. 2: Barbara's (Judi Dench) body bears the 'stigmata' of abject old age.

sweaty rather than freshly washed. The ageing female body is here portrayed as grotesque and abject, 'the very quintessence of the abject' (Sandberg 2008: 128). This scene follows Barbara's revelation of Sheba's affair to a fellow teacher. Barbara looks anxious, remorseful as she smokes and stares up onto the ceiling. Barbara is the grotesque malign older woman (see Markson 2003: 89).

The camera gives the viewer a high angle of her wrinkled face and the greying roots of her hair, 'the "stigmata" of abject old age' (Gilleard and Higgs 2010: 4). In this scene, attention is drawn to Barbara's hands, a motif reiterated throughout the film, as illustrated through the intertitles in one of the film's trailers: 'One Woman's Life / Is In Another Woman's Hands'.[4] The camerawork transmits this obsession with Barbara's hands, through a succession of close-ups: from the opening scenes, when she is writing her diary, to the crucial moment when Sheba and Barbara formally introduce each other. Camera movement confers a sense of unease whenever Barbara's and Sheba's hands touch; the camera tilts down and closes up on their first handshake; each subsequent 'touch' confirmation of a looming threat. When Barbara picks up one of Sheba's long blonde hairs, the close-up emphasises Barbara's fetish. Then, from the moment Barbara encloses Sheba's hand, with a promise not to reveal her secret, Sheba's fate is in 'another woman's hands'. The female hand bears the undisguised 'stigmata' of age, and the focus on both women's hands enhances their age difference and Barbara's monstrous otherness. It implies, as I explore next, the taboo of the old/er female flesh touching young/er female skin. And yet, against the film's construction of Barbara as other, the concept of the abject allows us to recast Barbara's non-normative body and this body's embodiment of queer desire as sites of positive transgression. As Chris Gilleard and Paul Higgs emphasise, abjection is 'not a position that is devoid of power' (2010: 2). Barbara's is constructed as abject, yet her desire for an age-inappropriate and same-sex body is transgressive of intelligible forms of desire.

The Monstrous Encounter

In line with Julia Kristeva (1982) and Barbara Creed (1993), Margrit Shildrick argues that women, defined in opposition to masculine ideals of reason and civilisation, have always been branded as 'out of control, uncontained, unpredictable, leaky ... in short, monstrous' (2002: 31). For Shildrick, the transgressive potential of the abject 'other' lies in its ability to unsettle the norm, the normal self. The encounter with the 'other' disrupts our own sense of being; we are made to recognise the monster as both 'other' and part of our self:

> The encounter with the others who define our own boundaries of normality must inevitably disturb for they are irreducibly strange and disconcertingly familiar, both opaque and reflective. They enable us to recognise ourselves; they are our own abject. (2002: 69)

The film constructs Barbara and Sheba as opposites in terms of class, age and attractiveness. Sheba 'and her like' are the affluent, upper-class, attractive, younger women who constitute the norm/alised category against which Barbara emerges as

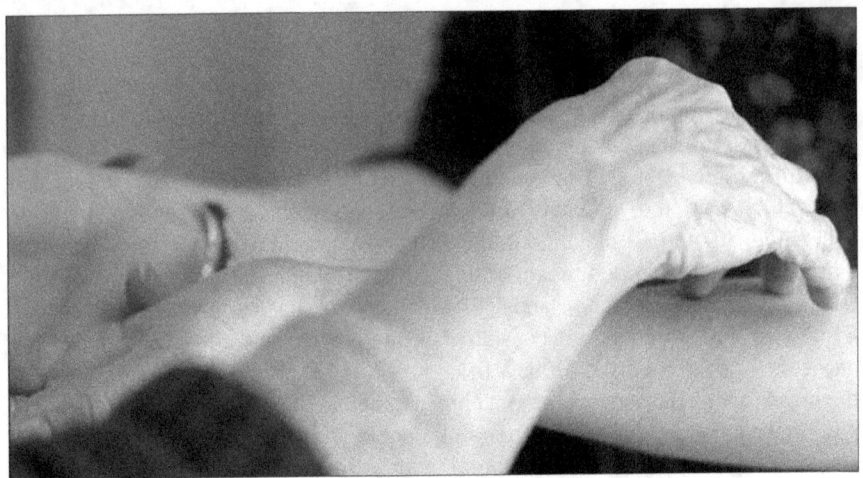

Fig. 3: Touching Sheba – innocent tickling or metonymic sexual encounter?

the abject 'other' (despite Shaba's own age-inappropriate sexual relationship with an underage pupil). A close textual analysis of a scene where Barbara touches Sheba's arms illustrates Shildrick's notion of the vulnerability of normality, 'it is through touch that we may come face to face with our other selves' (2002: 107). Both are sitting at Sheba's kitchen table, Barbara seeking her friend's support after her cat's death. Sheba, who is obviously dressed for a romantic encounter with Steven, seems impatient. Barbara lingers, then offers a compliment: 'I like that top. It suits you.' This innocent compliment, usual among friends, gains a different meaning as the scene unfolds, and in retrospect, can be read as a clumsy pick-up line. It is risky and transgressive both in terms of age- and sexual norms.

Barbara reminisces in an attempt to be comforted: 'When I was at school, if one of us had had some bad news or was a bit down, we used to stroke each other. You know, someone would do one arm and someone else the other. It was a wonderful sensation. Did you do that at your school?' 'No', Sheba retorts. 'It's incredibly relaxing – for the giver and the receiver', Barbara continues. Coinciding with the final part of this line, the camera aligns with Barbara's gaze, and tilts down from Sheba's face to a close-up of Sheba's cleavage; followed by a close-up of Barbara's hands as she encloses Sheba's. She invites Sheba to close her eyes – 'It doesn't work if you don't' – and begins to stroke Sheba's arms, slowly and sensuously running her fingertips along Sheba's open palm, then along her bare forearm and back, up and down.

Sheba's reaction is ambiguous; are Barbara's fingertips tickling her, or is she embarrassed or enjoying the sensation? According to Shildrick, our vulnerability to the monstrous encounter has 'the potential to confound normative identity' (2002: 5). If Sheba is experiencing pleasure, however fleetingly, this means her boundaries have been disturbed (fingertips, as opposed to hands are relatively gender- and age-*less*). Realising the erotic potential of this gesture, or merely uncomfortable, Sheba asks Barbara to stop. This remark establishes Barbara's desire as inappropriate. Barbara's attempt to seek human contact, whether or not fuelled by homoerotic desire, is cast as abject. The speech act of reminiscence ('when I was at school') fails to frame her gesture as innocent child play. When Sheba opens her eyes and asserts the boundaries with a stern 'That's enough', Barbara's gesture is suddenly redefined as inappropriate in terms of heteronormative scripts and the unwritten rules of female friendship.

Barbara's awkward attempt to fulfil her need for human touch falls short of the usual gender- and sexually-transgressive behaviour celebrated by New Queer Cinema, yet as far as non-normative ageing subjectivities are concerned, this scene enables an exploration of 'queer failure' as queer success. The director's comments on the DVD describes this scene as a performance of a 'freaky sexuality', as 'really quite disturbing'. This reveals the film's underlying misogynistic and gerontophobic structure, which renders Barbara as excessively grotesque and abject and makes it difficult for the viewer to rejoice in Barbara's unruly behaviour.

Contrary to this normative interpretation, Barbara's attempt can be read as a success by drawing on the significance of hands within lesbian theory. As discussed, several close-ups draw attention to Barbara's hands, seemingly to culminate in this symbolically charged scene. From a lesbian studies perspective, the importance of the 'lesbian hand' cannot go unnoticed. Lisa Henderson remarks: 'We do, after all, wear some of our sexual equipment naked, in public, at the end of our sleeves' (1999: 43). Combining our knowledge of Barbara's solitary, untouched existence, with the symbolism of the hand in lesbian film, the act of Barbara's fingertips touching Sheba's arms emerges as metonymic of a sexual encounter. From Barbara's perspective, this kind of intimacy is exceptional, out of the ordinary for someone 'so chronically untouched' (as she confesses in voice-over). The sexual undertone of the phrase 'the giver and the receiver' is further emphasised by the close-up of Sheba's cleavage. Barbara's pleasure is evident as a joyful smile appears on her face; she has accomplished her 'conquest', not by 'honest seduction but by stealth' (Dyer 2002: 32).

If Halberstam concedes that 'from the perspective of feminism, failure has often been a better bet than success' (2011: 4), Barbara's failure allows her to 'escape the punishing norms that discipline behavior' (2011: 3); to resist 'dominant logics of power' (2011: 88) by breaking the taboo of the ageing flesh, as well as heteronormative definition of the sex act as penetration. Whereas Barbara's ageing hands are seen as abject in a youth-oriented society, in this scene they embody her transgressive desire. From an oppositional, age-positive, lesbian stance, her 'textured hands' are 'erotic emblems' symbolising a 'middle-aged sexual wisdom' that Joan Nestle recognises in herself and seeks out in other women (1991: 182). Barbara's daring overture can be seen as an example of queer 'disgraceful ageing as, under the pretence of 'childhood play' an erotically charged moment occurs.

The Scandal of Ageing Disgracefully

As has been mentioned, a negotiated reading position would allow the viewer to approach Barbara as an empowering transgressive figure. Whereas the film's heteronormative structure invites identification with Sheba, the resistant viewer engages with Barbara who, like Smelik's 'murderous lesbians', expresses a 'complex psychic life' (2004: 70). Barbara is similarly 'bordering on the insane' (ibid.), yet offers what Jermyn describes as 'progressive or oppositional possibilities for female spectators', enabling them to exercise 'a behaviour in which they are not usually allowed to indulge' (1996: 252).

Barbara's disgraceful ageing contains the 'power to disrupt the social order' (Gilleard and Higgs 2010: 3). Against social norms that dictate women should age gracefully (see Fairhurst 1998), ageing *dis*gracefully subverts prescribed age-roles. Behaving in a non-age-appropriate way, or age-role bending, is often considered a libratory anti-ageist act (see Swinnen 2012). This type of behaviour is not without its risk, as suggested by Mary Russo (1999). According to her, 'anachronism is a mistake in a normative systemization of time' (1999: 21) and thus involves the risk of 'not acting one's age', which is 'not only inappropriate but dangerous, exposing the female subject, especially, to ridicule, contempt, pity, and scorn – the scandal of anachronism' (ibid.).

From an ageing studies perspective, the unspoken scandal in *Notes on a Scandal* is precisely the 'scandal of anachronism'. Barbara is punished for not acting her age within a film that constructs her desire as 'scandalous'. Interrogating the impossibility of a relationship between Sheba and Barbara – when at the end of Heller's novel, they are living in the same house and Barbara assures the reader that Sheba 'knows, by now, not to go too far without me' (2004: 244) – uncovers the film's heteronormative ideology. As opposed to the source novel, the film negates the queer uncertainty we find in the novel's ending and reinforces heteronormativity through narrative closure. At the end of the film, Sheba returns to her family home, welcomed by husband Richard, and heteronormality is thus restored. The last scenes return to Barbara as she approaches a young woman on a park bench. As they shake hands, the film insinuates Barbara is destined to relive the same tragic plot over and over again in an endless pursuit of companionship, only to be rebuked by one friend after the other; first Jennifer, her former colleague, then Sheba and, as can be expected, her new acquaintance Annabelle (Anne-Marie Duff).

Reading the final scene through a combination of ageing disgracefully and queer failure opens up another meaning. Barbara approaches an unsuspecting Annabelle and, with 'stealth', moves from small talk, to a formal introduction (sealed by their handshake), to an invitation to the opera. Those familiar with Heller's novel can dismiss the film's heteronormative happy-ending, and take an oppositional stance to rejoice in Barbara's queer, transgressive behaviour as she approaches her next *victim*. Aligned with Barbara, we can believe as she does that Annabelle is the one she has been waiting for.

Conclusion

Barbara's characterisation is an unusual example of the conflation of gyno-, geronto- and homo-phobia in one cinematic figure, illustrating the pervasiveness of normativity in today's cultural texts. Embodying our culture's fears and anxieties, she is construed as psychotic villain and abject other, a threat to heteronormative femininity including the youthful imperative. Drawing on feminist, lesbian and queer theories of appropriation, Barbara can be read 'against the grain' and thus be perceived as transgressive of heterosexist and ageist modes of representability. Barbara, who is ageing disgracefully, taking the risk of anachronism and failing spectacularly, combines more than one level of abjection and monstrous otherness.

Imogen Tyler (2009) questions the potential of abjections, especially individuals who inhabit an abject subjectivity on a daily basis, rather than a temporary, textual spectator position. While understanding the limits of queer theory and abjection, not the least for older lesbian women, this chapter combines a tradition of resistant or oppositional readings with age-critical theories. Taking an ageing studies approach to queer transgression, it opens up alternative understandings of abject-ageing characters like Barbara, inviting viewers to identify moments of resistance where normativity is unsettled by characters refusing to 'act their age' and/or desiring *queerly*.

Notes

1 See, for instance, Nancy Meyers' romantic comedies *Something's Gotta Give* (2004) and *It's Complicated* (2009).
2 Queer theory provides the foundations for the type of queer defiance characteristic of New Queer Cinema (see Stacey and Street 2007). The conventions and images that emerged from this 'moment' in queer cinema history have also been located in other films, beyond the decade of 1990s (see Smelik 2004).
3 For instance, *The L-Word* (2004–2009), to use a television text that better illustrates the contemporary landscape of lesbian visibility than the examples referred to by Buchanan.
4 See Fox Searchlight's video; https://youtube/AruRpjQquQQ.

Bibliography

Aaron, M. (2004) 'New Queer Cinema: An Introduction', in M. Aaron (ed.) *New Queer Cinema: A Critical Reader*. Edinburgh: Edinburgh University Press, 3–14.
Becker, E., M. Citron, J. Lesage and B. R. Rich (1995) 'Lesbians and Film', in C. K. Creekmur and A. Doty (eds) *Out in Culture: Gay, Lesbian, and Queer Essays on Popular Culture*. London: Cassell, 25–43.
Benshoff, H. (1997) *Monsters in the Closet: Homosexuality and the Horror Film*. Manchester: Manchester University Press.
Berger, R. (1982) 'The Unseen Minority: Older Gays and Lesbians', *Social Work*, 27, 3, 236–42.
Buchanan, K. (2006) 'The Evil Lesbian: Judi Dench Breathes New Life into a Stereotype We Used to Hate', *The Advocate*, 18 December.
Butler, J. (1999) *Gender Trouble: Feminism and the Subversion of Identity*. New York, NY: Routledge.
Castle, T. (1993) *The Apparitional Lesbian: Female Homosexuality and Modern Culture*. New York, NY: Columbia University Press.
Chang, J. (2006) 'Notes on a Scandal – Film Review', *Variety*, 11 December.
Cohen, D. S. (2007) 'Novelists Second-Guess 2006 Scripts', *Variety*, 7 January.
Cohen, J. J. (ed.) (1996) *Monster Theory: Reading Culture*. Minneapolis, MN: University of Minnesota Press.

Coupland, J. (2013) 'Dance, Ageing and the Mirror: Negotiating Watchability', *Discourse & Communication*, 7, 1, 3–24.

Creed, B. (1993) *The Monstrous-Feminine. Film, Feminism, Psychoanalysis*. London and New York, NY: Routledge.

Cruikshank, M. (2009) *Learning to Be Old. Gender, Culture, and Aging*. 2nd ed. Lanham, MD: Rowman & Littlefield.

Dyer, R. (2002) *The Matter of Images: Essays on Representations*. 2nd ed. London and New York, NY: Routledge.

Fairhurst, E. (1998) '"Growing Old Gracefully" as Opposed to "Mutton Dressed as Lamb": The Social Construction of Recognising Older Women', in S. Nettleton and J. Watson (eds) *The Body in Everyday Life*. London: Routledge, 258–75.

Gilleard, C. and P. Higgs (2010) 'Ageing Abjection and Embodiment in the Fourth Age', *Journal of Aging Studies*, 25, 2, 135–42.

Goodridge, M. (2006) 'A Bitch of a Job for Dame Judi', *The Evening Standard*, 5 October.

Halberstam, J. (2011) *The Queer Art of Failure*. Durham, NC: Duke University Press.

Hartman, A. (2013) 'Structural/Sexual Transgression: Todd Haynes' *Poison* as a Critique of Homonormativity', *Bright Lights Film Journal*, 31 October; http://brightlightsfilm.com/structural-sexual-transgression-todd-haynes-poison-as-a-critique-of-homonormativity/#.VSEdNdyjOSo (accessed 5 March 2015).

Heller, Z. (2004) *Notes on a Scandal*. London: Penguin.

Henderson, L. (1999) 'Simple Pleasures: Lesbian Community and *Go Fish*', *Signs: Journal of Women in Culture and Society*, 25, 1, 37–64.

Jermyn, D. (1996) 'Rereading the Bitches from Hell: A Feminist Appropriation of the Female Psychopath', *Screen*, 37, 3, 251–67.

Jones, A. (2007) 'Just Judi, the Super Trouper', *Birmingham Post*, 24 February.

Krainitzki, E. (2012) 'Exploring the Hypervisibility Paradox: Older Lesbians in Contemporary Mainstream Cinema (1995–2009)'. Unpublished Doctoral Thesis, University of Gloucestershire, UK.

Kristeva, J. (1982) *Powers of Horror: An Essay on Abjection*. New York, NY: Columbia University Press.

Laz, C. (1998) 'Act Your Age', *Sociological Forum*, 13, 1, 85–113.

Lo, M. (2006) 'Review of *Notes on a Scandal*.' *After Ellen*; http://www.afterellen.com/Movies/2006/12/notes.html?page=0%2C (accessed 10 April 2008).

Macdonald, B. and C. Rich (1984) *Look Me in the Eye: Old Women, Aging and Ageism*. London: The Women's Press.

Markson, E. W. (2003) 'The Female Aging Body through Film' in C. A. Faircloth (ed.) *Aging Bodies: Images and Everyday Experience*. Walnut Creek, CA: AltaMira Press, 77–102.

Nestle, J. (1991) 'Desire Perfected: Sex after Forty', in B. Sang, J. Warshow and A. J. Smith (eds) *Lesbians at Midlife: The Creative Transition*. San Francisco: spinsters book company, 180–3.

Poor, M. (1982) 'Older Lesbians', in M. Cruikshank (ed.) *Lesbian Studies: Present and Future*. New York: The Feminist Press, 165–73.

Porton, R. (2007) 'Trusting the Text: An Interview with Cate Blanchette', *Cineaste*, 32, 2, 16–19.

Rich, B. R. (2013) *New Queer Cinema: The Director's Cut*. Durham, NC: Duke University Press.

Richards, O. (2006) 'Notes on a Scandal' *Empire Online*; http://www.empireonline.com/reviews/reviewcomplete.asp?FID=11137 (accessed 31 August 2010).

Russo, M. (1999) 'Aging and the Scandal of Anachronism' in K. Woodward (ed.) *Figuring Age: Women, Bodies, Generations*. Bloomington, IN: Indiana University Press, 20–33.

Sandberg, L. (2008) 'The Old, the Ugly and the Queer: Thinking Old Age in Relation to Queer Theory', *Graduate Journal of Social Science*, 5, 2, 117–38.

Shakespeare, S. (2007) 'Filming in Progress – Authors Keep Out', *The Evening Standard*, 23 January.

Shildrick, M. (2002) *Embodying the Monster: Encounters with the Vulnerable Self*. London: Sage.

Smelik, A. (2004) 'Art Cinema and Murderous Lesbians', in M. Aaron (ed.) *New Queer Cinema: A Critical Reader*. Edinburgh: Edinburgh University Press, 68–79.

Sonstegard, A. (2013) '*Notes on a Scandal*, Teacher's Edition', in P. Demory and C. Pullen (eds) *Queer Love in Film and Television: Critical Essays*. Basingstoke: Palgrave Macmillan, 245–55.

Sontag, S. (1972) 'The Double Standard of Aging', *Saturday Review*, 23 September, 29–38.

Stacey, J. and S. Street (2007) 'Introduction: Queering *Screen*', in J. Stacey and S. Street (eds) *Queer Screen*. London & New York: Routledge, 1–18.

Swinnen, A. (2012) 'Introduction: *Benidorm Bastards*, or the Do's and Don'ts of Aging', in A. Swinnen and J. Stotesbury (eds) *Aging, Performance, and Stardom: Doing Age on the Stage of Consumerist Culture*. Münster: LIT Verlag, 7–14.

Tally, M. (2008) 'Hollywood, Female Sexuality, and the "Older Bird" Chick Flick', in S. Ferriss and M. Young (eds) *Chick Flicks: Contemporary Women at the Movies*. New York, NY: Routledge, 119–31.

Tapley, K. (2006) 'Judi Dench, *Notes on a Scandal* – Lead Actress Contender', *Variety*, 13 December.

Thorpe, V. (2006) 'Illicit Passions and a Walk on the Red Carpet', *The Observer*, 17 December.

Torrance, K. J. (2007) '*Scandal* Gets a Free Pass: Lesbian Stereotype Sneaks by P.C. Watchdogs', *The Washington Times*, 5 January.

Tyler, I. (2009) 'Against Abjection', *Feminist Theory*, 10, 1, 77–98.

Vares, T. (2009) 'Reading the "Sexy Oldie": Gender, Age(Ing) and Embodiment', *Sexualities*, 12, 4, 503–24.

Waldman, D. (1990) 'There's More to Positive Images Than Meets the Eye', in P. Erens (ed.) *Issues in Feminist Film Criticism*. Bloomington, IN: Indiana University Press, 13–18.

Weiss, A. (1992) *Vampires and Violets: Lesbians in Film*. London: Penguin.

Whatling, C. (1997) *Screen Dreams: Fantasising Lesbians in Film*. Manchester: Manchester University Press.

Whelehan, I. (2010) 'Not to Be Looked At: Older Women in Recent British Cinema', in M. Bell and M. Williams (eds) *British Women's Cinema*. London and New York, NY: Routledge, 170–83.

Woodward, K. (1991) *Aging and Its Discontents: Freud and Other Fictions*. Bloomington, IN: Indiana University Press.

―― (2006) 'Performing Age, Performing Gender', *NWSA Journal*, 18, 1, 162–89.

Index

abuse/abuser 3, 5, 27, 46, 48–51, 90, 93, 103–7, 109, 112–14, 131–44 ; mental abuse 141, 143; *see also* child abuse
Academy Award 81, 84, 86n.8, 161
ACT UP 152, 159n.1
Addicted 22
adulthood 104, 121, 123, 128, 139
ageing 161–73; disgracefully 161, 171–2; female body 2, 163, 168–9; femininity 2, 164; womanhood 6; graceful ageing 161, 171–2; heterosexual ageing body 162; naked older bodies 168; old and queer 161; older women 2, 104, 161–2; post-menopausal woman 164; sexy oldie 162, 166; unsuccessful ageing 6, 166; *see also* body
AIDS 73, 81–4, 86n.8, 148–9, 152–3, 155, 158–9, 159n.1
Aldrich, Robert 162
All Things Fall Apart 74, 85
American College of Surgeons 89
American Hustle 78, 81
American independent cinema 133
American Mary 4, 89–100
American Psycho 26
Anderson, Brad 3, 74
androgynous 77, 78, 90, 138
Anglo-American culture 3

A Nightmare on Elm Street 113, 132, 145n.2
anorexia 75, 76, 79
Antichrist 27, 31
Apatow, Judd 14
Araki, Gregg 2, 3, 6, 103, 115n.3, 131–2, 137, 147–59
audience: art-house audiences 9; audience expectations 2, 9, 135; audience of homosexuality 110; contemporary audiences 65; female audiences 100; mainstream audience 2; *see also* queer audiences
avant-garde 2

Babysitters, The 120
Bale, Christian 4, 74, 78–81, 84–5, 85n.n.3,4
Bates Jr., Richard 89
Batman Begins 78, 81
Bear (video installation) 57
Birth 3, 131
bisexuality 154, 156
blood fetishes 90
Blumberg, Stuart 2, 9, 14
body: body modification surgery 90, 92; crucified body 60; as a cultural artefact 2; as death 39; emasculated bodies 74; eroticised body 2; of extreme weight 2,

177

body *cont.*
    73–85; famished bodies 66–7; hyper-sexualised 3, 26; Irish bodies 65; Lacan's torn body 38; modern body horror 75; non-normative body 3, 168–9; in pain 58; of prisoners 61, 64, 67, 69; queer bodies 6, 105; sexual body-horror 36; starving female body 67; transgressive body 2, 4, 27, 45, 80, 84, 86–87n.6; violence against the 58; *see also* female body and male body
Boys of St. Vincent, The 132
Bump in the Night 132
Butterfly Effect, The 103, 106
Butterfly Kiss 166

Cahiers du cinéma 158
cancer 73, 75, 76, 85
Cannes 57
cannibalism 45–6, 48–50
capitalism 3, 74–6, 79–80, 119, 120, 124, 159; neo-liberal capitalism 34
carnal/carnality 25, 26, 36; neo-liberal carnal culture 26
carnographic 3, 4, 25
carnotopia 25, 40
Casino Royale 64
Cast Away 74
Catholicism 53, 59, 60, 69n.5
censorship 1, 104
Chambers, Cedric 1, 3
child abuse/child abusers 3, 5, 103–5, 108, 113, 131–2, 135–8, 141–5
childhood 5–6, 59, 84, 104, 123–9, 135–7, 141–5, 171; memory 30; sexual agency 3; sexuality 103, 127; female childhood 123; fetishisation of childhood 104; queering of childhood 5; traumatic childhood 13, 17, 137, 140; *see also* innocence
child molester *see* paedophilia
Children's Hour, The 165, 167
child sexuality 6, 135, 144; de-sexualisation of children 136

Choke 3, 9, 13–14, 16, 18–21
citizenship 124
Clanagan, Jeff 22
Clark, Larry 103, 147
Clueless 147
corporeal decay 26, 27, 39
Courage Under Fire 74
Craft, The 147
Cronenberg, David 27, 38, 90
Cruel Intentions 147
Cuesta, Michael 103, 131

Dallas Buyers Club 3, 4, 74, 81–5
Deadpan (video installation) 57
Dead Ringers 90
Deleuze, Gilles 27, 29–31, 33, 35
Demme, Jonathan 74, 148
Depardieu, Gérard 14
diegetic 85; extra-diegetic 13, 112; non-diegetic 14, 49
disability 84, 142
Don Jon 3, 9, 12, 14, 16, 18–20, 25
Don Jon's Addiction see Don Jon
Doom Generation, The 6, 148–9, 152–5, 156–8
Douglas, Mary 74, 107
Do You Know the Muffin Man? (tv movie) 132
drug abuse 83, 121–3
Dyer, Richard 43, 47, 64, 74, 80, 82, 110–11, 166, 171
dystopia 25–8, 36, 39, 40n.1

Eastwood, Clint 5, 103, 106, 112, 115n.5
emasculation 74, 94, 108
enfreakment 52
erectile dysfunction 17
eroticism 2, 4, 10–11, 22, 40, 43–4, 48, 51, 58, 60–4, 66, 68, 78, 81, 91–2, 96, 99, 104, 106, 120, 124–5, 135, 136, 170, 171; eroticisation of children 104–6, 136, 124; *see also* feederism
Excision 4, 89–99
Eyre, Richard 2, 131, 161, 163, 165

Falardeau, Eric 3, 25–7, 36–7
Fassbender, Michael 16, 26, 58, 63, 66, 68, 70n.8, 74
Fat Girl 103, 115n.3
fat-phobia 4, 45, 50
fatsploitation 43–54
Feed 4
feederism 4, 43–54
female agency 67
female body 2, 4, 45, 58, 60–1, 67, 120, 163, 168–9; young female body 120; *see also* ageing
female psychopath 166
female surgeons 89–90
female victims 53, 91
feminine idiosyncrasy 65
feminisation 4, 65, 68, 82
feminism 53, 124; post-feminist agency 119; post-feminist media culture 120; pre-feminism 53–4
Ferrara, Abel 3, 9, 14, 15, 19
fetishism 17, 45, 69n.5, 74, 76–8, 89–91, 95, 99, 104, 122, 125, 129, 136, 169; *see also* childhood
Field, Todd 6, 131, 137, 138
Fight Club 3, 4, 64, 74–8, 81, 83–4
Fighter, The 78, 81, 85n.4
Final Girls 97
Fincher, David 3, 45, 74
Fly, The 27
Foucault, Michel 135–6
Frankenstein 90
Freudian law 31–2
Freud, Sigmund 4, 26, 27–9, 35, 37, 107
Friends 52

gaga feminism *see* Lady Gaga
Gainsbourg, Charlotte 3, 21, 28, 32
gay: anti-gay violence 151–2; cinema 148; clubs 82; culture 52; iconography 82; literature 22; men 104, 108, 110, 167; pandemic 159; porn 151; proto-gay 69n.5; rights 104, 162; sex 16, 35; sexuality 3, 156; spectator 110; subculture 84; teens 150

Giant 82
Gillen, Davey 58, 62–6, 68
girlhood 5, 119, 122, 129; girls' sexual agency 120–1; *see also* innocence
Glazer, Jonathan 3, 131
Gordon-Levitt, Joseph 9, 13, 14, 16, 18, 20, 25, 131
Gregg, Clark 3, 9, 13–15
Guardian, The (newspaper) 9, 11, 58
Guattari, Félix 27, 29–31, 33

hagiography 58–61, 68
Halberstam, Jack 5, 6, 89, 96–100, 161, 166–7, 171
Happiness 103, 115n.3
Hard Candy 3, 6, 131–45
hard-core 3, 27, 35, 39
Hardwicke, Catherine 5, 103, 119
Harron, Mary 26
Haynes, Todd 2, 148
Hays Code 43; *see also* Hollywood
Heavenly Creatures 166
hedonism 80
Heller, Zoë 163–4, 172
hero/heroine/heroism 12–13, 16, 18, 20, 21, 31, 48, 49, 58, 59, 61, 64–5, 110; anti-hero 132; superheroes 39
heteronormativity 6, 11, 44, 60, 68, 89, 96–100, 123, 164, 168, 171–2; behaviour 80; desire 2–3; domesticity 54; femininity 167, 172; male gaze 59; relationships 83; roles 91
heterosexuality 1, 82, 107, 109, 111, 152, 166; heterosexual desire 91; heterosexual ideology 149; patriarchal heterosexual system 5, 96; queer heterosexuality 1, 3; violent heterosexuality 111, 113
Hitchcock, Alfred 61, 142, 162
HIV *see* AIDS
Hollywood 2, 4, 9, 43, 45, 52, 61, 64, 73, 74, 77, 81, 132, 133, 151, 154
homoeroticism 63, 110, 164, 165, 170
homonormative 148, 161; representations of gay male 167

homophobia 83, 86n.8, 104–5, 108, 114, 148, 149–52, 154–5, 157–8
Homo Pomo 148
homosexuality 5, 10, 82, 96, 104, 110, 113–14, 151, 154, 159, 164, 166; gay iconography 82; homosexual identity 113, 164; homosexual panic 103–14; homosexual subculture 82; homosexual women 110; representing homosexuality on screen 166; repressed homosexual voice 91, 99; homosocial 80, 91–4, 96, 99–100
hook-up culture 10
horror 2, 13, 25–7, 31, 33–6, 45–54, 89, 90, 91, 97, 109, 132, 142, 143, 167; body horror 4, 36, 75, 79; cinema/film 4, 48, 49, 74, 75, 83, 85n.1, 90, 108–10, 113, 133; of fat 51; of psycho-sexual-corporeal decay 36; see also mad-doctor and fatsploitation
Hudson, Rock 82, 151
Hughes, John 147
Human Centipede: First Sequence, The 90
Hunger 3, 4, 57–69, 69n.2, 74
hunger strike 69n.4, 70n.8
hyper-sexual 3, 11, 25–8, 37–8; see also sex

I Am a Sex Addict 3, 9, 12–13, 17, 20–1
illness 73, 76, 81, 84, 91, 96, 133
In&Out 148
incest 113, 156; emotional incest 18
indie-auteur 3, 9, 10
innocence 3, 5, 6, 104, 120, 122–8, 133, 136, 139, 142, 144–5; see also childhood
insomnia 73, 75, 76, 78–80
intercourse 26, 32, 37, 82, 83, 92, 94, 120, 127
Interview With the Vampire 110
intimacy 17, 18, 21, 22, 36, 140, 143, 159, 163, 65, 171; intimacy disorder 16; phobia of 35
I Think I Do 148

I Want Your Love 22

Jawbreaker 43
Jeffrey 148
Jensen, Robert 92
Judgment 132
Juno 14
Just Evil 113

Kaboom 6, 158–9
Kafka, Franz 27, 36–9
Kant, Immanuel 38–9
Kassell, Nicole 3, 103, 131
Kids 103, 147
Killer Joe 84, 85n.5
Killing of Sister George, The 162, 167
Kincaid, James R. 103, 104, 135–6
Knocked Up 14
Kramer, Wayne 106

Lacan, Jacques 35, 38–9
Lady Gaga 98–100
Last Temptation of Christ, The 57
Lawnmower Man 46
Lehane, Dennis 105
Leonard, Brett 45–6
lesbianism 99, 110, 149, 150, 152, 156, 158, 161, 162, 164–8, 171, 172, 173n.3; evil lesbian 165; lesbian identity 161, 163; lesbian stereotypes 162, 165; lesbian vampire 166; murderous lesbians 166, 171; new lesbian 166; older lesbian 162, 164, 165, 173; older predatory lesbian 6, 162; proto-lesbian 163; see also ageing
LGBT 46, 148, 149
L.I.E. 3, 103, 131, 143
Little Children 6, 131–45, 145n.2
Living End, The 147–8, 152–7
Livingston, Jennie 2, 148
Lost Son, The 113
L-Word, The (tv series) 173n.3

Machinist, The 3, 4, 74, 75, 78–81, 83, 84, 85n.1

machismo 82
mad-doctor 4, 89, 90–2, 96–7, 99; see also male body
Magdalene Sisters 103
male body 2–4, 45, 57–8, 61–4, 67–8, 73–85, 85n.n.1,4, 91; full-frontal male nudity 68; male body parts 4, 58; male physique 57, 76; naked bodies of men 2;
male sexual predator 123
Mapplethorpe, Robert 1
martyrdom 57, 58–61
masculinity: alpha-male 82; Celtic masculinity 69–70n.6; hegemonic masculinity 3, 127; iconography of masculinity 82; Irish masculinity 66; hyper-masculinity 3, 60, 66; loss of masculinity 82, 85–86n.6; male fantasy 33–4; masculinity and heroism 64; misperformance of masculinity 112–13; New Masculinity 53; post-conflict masculinity 61, 65; pre-feminist masculinity 53; queer masculinity 58; transgressive masculinity 57–69; ultra-masculine 112; ultra-virile masculinity 61; unstable masculinity 73; violent masculinity 58, 65
mass media 5, 123–6, 129, 133
masturbation 16, 50, 105
McConaughey, Matthew 4, 74, 81–5, 86n.8
McNair, Brian 10–12
McQueen, Steve 2, 3, 4, 9, 25–6, 34–6, 57–69, 74
Me and You and Everyone We Know 103
Mean Girls 119
Melancholia 27
ménage à trois 28, 40, 82
menstruation 67, 68, 94
mental illness see illness
Metamorphosis, The 27, 39
metaphor 43, 75, 107, 110, 112, 114, 155, 157, 158; anorexia as a metaphor 75, 76; eating as a metaphor 43; metaphor for alienation 157; zombie metaphor 110

Method actor 81, 84
metrosexual 78
middle-class 5, 46, 53, 89, 90, 98, 120, 121, 123, 126, 129
mise-en-scène 75, 85, 107
misogyny 44, 54, 93, 171
monogamy 27, 40n.1, 47, 83, 154
monstrosity 5, 6, 27, 39, 85n.1, 91, 95, 97, 98, 103, 108–11, 114, 133, 135–7, 144, 161, 164, 166, 169, 170, 173; monstrous-feminine 91, 97, 98, 167–9; monstrous paedophiles 6, 132, 133; monstrosity/vampiric effect 110; villain/monster 48
motherhood 126; absent mothers 127
Mud 85
Muriel's Wedding 52
Murray, Samantha 44, 45
muscularity 74
mutilation 50; self-mutilation 139, 143
My Big Fat Greek Wedding 14
Mysterious Skin 3, 6, 103, 106, 115n.3, 131–45
Mystic River 5, 103–14, 115n.n.4,5

narrative: child abuse narratives 138, 142; cinematic/film narratives 2, 52, 128–9, 131; competing narratives 119; conventional narrative 62; linear narrative 2, 149; narrative-driven drama 57; narrative structure of the vampire 111; narrative suspense 48; Paedophile narratives 138, 144; post-abuse narratives 137; present-day narratives 137; protectionist narratives 120–1 rape-revenge narrative 92, 97; traditional narratives 134; voice-over narrative 163
National Sex Offenders Registry 127
Neale, Steve 61–2, 64
neoliberalism 4, 10, 26, 33, 36, 38, 119, 122, 124; neo-liberal capitalism 34; neo-liberal carnal culture 26; neo-liberal carnotopia 39, 40; neo-liberal culture 26, 27;

neoliberalism cont.
  neoliberal ideology 114; neoliberal policies 119; neo-liberal sex life 35; neo-liberal sexual utopia 39

new feminism 99
New Man 56
New Queer Cinema 2, 148, 166–7, 171, 173n.2
New York Times Magazine 99
nihilism 26
9½ Weeks 43
Northern Ireland 57, 65
Norton, Edward 4, 74, 75–8, 85n.2
Notes on a Scandal 2, 6, 131, 161–73
Nowhere 6, 147–9, 152, 154, 155–8
NQC *see* New Queer Cinema
nymphomania 28–32,
Nymphomaniac 2, 3, 9, 13, 14, 21, 25–40
Nymphomaniac (second volume) 14, 27, 30, 39

Object of My Affection, The 148
Oedipus complex 29
other 136
Otherness 108, 111, 167, 169, 173
orgasm 18, 30, 31, 34–5, 39, 43, 47, 156; loss of 27, 30

paedophile 5, 6, 31, 105, 109, 112–14, 114, 131–45, 145n.2; as a father figure 143; representation of the paedophile 131, 137
paedophilia 5, 6, 104, 105, 113–14, 131–45; *see also* child abuse and pederasty
Palahniuk, Chuck 14
Palindromes 103, 115n.3
Parenthood 119, 126–9, 149
Passion of the Christ, The 57
patriarchy 11, 29, 30, 80, 89–100, 119, 167; hetero-patriarchal establishment 167; repressive patriarchal codes 28; patriarchal control 97–8; patriarchal heterosexual system 5; patriarchal utopia 39

pederasty 104, 111–14; *see also* paedophilia
penetration 45, 65, 93, 96–7, 100, 171
perpetrator 97, 131, 133, 136, 139, 141, 144, 145n.3
phallus 29, 80; phallic power 29, 80, 97–8
Pheasant-Kelly, Frances 64
Philadelphia 74, 148, 167
Pitt, Brad 4, 74, 75–8, 81, 85, 85n.2
pornographication 3, 10, 22
pornography 2, 10–12, 19–20, 25, 35, 120, 124, 127, 152; cyber-porn 11; gay porn 151; hardcore porn 3, 27, 39; Internet/online porn 11, 16, 19; pornosphere 10; *see also* sexual addiction
post-World War II 10
POV 62
Pretty Persuasion 103, 120
prisoner 4, 58, 61–4, 67–9, 69n2, 69–70n.6
promiscuity/promiscuous 12, 27, 40n.1, 54, 65, 81–4, 120, 125, 151
Prophet, The 1
prostitution 3, 14, 16, 17, 20, 35, 80, 84, 89, 93, 114, 120, 131, 141
Provisional IRA 65, 68, 69n.6
Provisional Irish Republican Army *see* Provisional IRA
Psycho 26

queer 1–6, 103–15; audiences 110–11, 115n.7, 157; bodies 6, 105; desire 6, 95, 108, 169; discourse 148; failure 6, 161, 166, 167, 171, 172; female adolescent 97; heterosexuality 1, 3; power 98; solidarity 149, 151; teenager 6, 147–59; transgressions 166–7; visions 60; women 162; *see also* New Queer Cinema

rape 5, 14, 17, 45, 65, 89, 90, 92, 93, 96, 103–14, 127, 128, 140, 154; adolescent rape 103; child rape

rape *cont.*
    105–6, 115n.1, 142; rapeable and non-rapeable boys 107; rape-revenge 92, 97, 115n.6; rape trauma 107; representation of rape 106, 114; *see also* child abuse/child abuser
Rebecca 162
Reckoning, The 103, 106, 113
Romeo+Juliet 147
Running Scared 106, 113

Sadean 36–40; Kantian-Sadean 38; sexual utopia 36; Thanatos 36; torture 38
sadism 25–40, 92
sadomasochism 13
Sands, Bobby 58–60, 63–9, 69n.2, 70n.8
Schwimmer, David 5, 121
scopophilia 61–5
self-affirmation 31
self-mutilation 139, 143
self-realisation 26
sex: anal sex 106; anti-sexualisation 124; childhood sexual agency 3; consensual and non-consensual sex 47, 48, 113, 114; de-sexualised 133, 135, 162; illicit sex 17, 80; impersonal sex 20; meaningless sex 32, 33, 35, 36; mechanical sex 29, 39; oral sex 38, 93, 95, 105, 113, 125, 140; as a political tool 30; promiscuous sex 27, 83; sex industry 90, 120, 122; sex object 53; sex offender 127, 132, 141, 142; sex/sexual identity 2, 136, 140, 162, 164, 165; sexual criminal law 80; sexual culture 10, 28, 40; sexual dystopia 27; sexual expression 54, 110, 123; sexual fantasy 94, 95, 143; sexual gratification 10; sexual ideology 108; sexual liberation 33; sexual predator 121, 123, 125, 128, 139; sexual revolution 3, 10–12, 29, 33, 37; sexual taboos 2; sexualisation of young women 124, 126; sexually repressed middle-class 89; underage sex 103, 121, 123; violent sex 37; Western sexual culture 28; *see also* sex addiction films
sex addiction films 3, 9–22; comedy-drama 13; cyber-porn addiction 11; recovering sex addicts 20
sexaholism 17
Sex and the City 34
sex, lies, and videotape 9
sexploitation movies 22
sexuality: compulsive sexuality 3; female sexuality 6, 91, 99, 120; feminine sexuality 29; freaky sexuality 171; healthy sexuality 12; polymorphous sexuality 29
Seven 45–7
shadow-self 15
Shallow Hal 52
Shame 2, 3, 9, 13, 16, 21, 25–8, 33–9, 57, 68
Shone, Tom 9
Siega, Marcos 103, 120
Sisterhood of the Travelling Pants, The 120
skeletal 67, 78, 80; *see also* body
Skow, Jon 25
Slade, David 3, 131
Sleepers 103, 106, 113
social transgression 1, 4
Soderbergh, Steven 9
sodomy 106
Some Mother's Son 62, 64, 69–70n.6
Sontag, Susan 162
Soska, Jen and Sylvia 5, 89
Spartacus 57
starvation 60, 79, 80
suicide 13, 35, 59, 120, 139, 148–9, 149–59; *see also* gay teens
Sundance Festival 14
superimposition 108
synonymy 73, 77

taboo 1–3, 106, 123, 128–9, 131, 136, 138, 168–9, 171
teenagehood 147, 150, 157–8

teen girls 3, 125
Thanatomorphose 3, 4, 25–8, 36–7, 39
Thanks for Sharing 2, 3, 9, 14–17, 20–1
Thatcher, Margaret 66, 68–9
Thirteen 5, 103, 119, 121–9
threesome 16, 28, 35, 36, 39, 156; *see also ménage à trois*
Threesome 148
Time 25
Totally Fucked Up 6, 148–58
trauma 3, 13, 17, 27, 36, 45, 48, 104, 107, 109, 133, 137–40, 145n.3; *see also* child abused/child abuser and childhood and rape
True Blood 111
Trust 5, 121–9
Turner Prize 57
Twelve and Holding 103
12 Years a Slave 57

underweight male body 3, 73–7, 80, 85, 85n.n.1,4; *see also* male body
Underworld 110
utopia 1, 5, 25–7, 33, 34, 36, 40n.1, 166; sexual utopia 33, 34, 36, 39; utopian-dystopian 25, 28; utopian imperatives 1

Vallee, Jean-Marc 3, 74
vampire 43, 108, 109, 110–11, 113, 115n.7, 165, 167; effeminate vampire 110; as a heterosexual expression 111; predatory vampires 162
Vampire Lovers, The 167
Van Sant, Gus 2, 148
victimhood 66, 128, 131, 138–41, 145
victims 3, 5, 6, 16, 53, 76, 90, 114, 124, 132, 133, 135, 136, 138–39, 141, 143, 144; of abuse 132, 144; AIDS victims 82; child victims 6, 136, 140, 143; construction of 136; famine victims 67; female victims 53, 91; paedophiles/pederasts victims 114, 131, 143; teens 154, 156
villains 113, 133
virgin/virginity 29, 127, 165; loss of 94, 121
virility 57–69
Virtuosity 46
von Sternberg, Josef 61
von Trier, Lars 2, 9, 14, 27–30, 37
voyeurism 62, 153, 165; double-voyeurism 62; voyeuristic looking 61

watchability 168
Weather Man, The 113
weight loss 2, 4, 73–85, 85n.3, 85–86n.6
Welcome to New York 3, 9, 14, 15, 19, 21
werewolf 79, 109–11
Will & Grace 167
Williams, Linda 10–12, 27, 110
Woman on Top 43
Woodruff, Bille 22
Woodruff, Ron 74, 81, 84
Woodsman, The 3, 103, 115n.3, 131, 138
working-class 82, 105, 123; girls 123; mother 126; teenagers 121; women 123; sexuality 129

Zahedi, Caveh 3, 9, 13, 16, 17
Zimbardo, Philip 11
zombie 109–10; sexless zombie 112, 113; *see also* metaphor

GPSR Authorized Representative: Easy Access System Europe, Mustamäe tee 50, 10621 Tallinn, Estonia, gpsr.requests@easproject.com

TABLE OF CONTENTS

GRATITUDE	v
FOREWORD	xi
INTRODUCTION	xiii

Goals and Paradigms — 1

Journey towards your goal	1
...nding desire	13
	29

— 33

	36
	40
	43
	45

— 49

	49
	51
	54
	55
	60
	62

85
87
88
91
94

97
97
99
101
102
104

You Receive More When You Give — 65

Giving and its impact on receiving — 65
The Law of Attraction and its relationship to giving — 68
Embodiment of both these theories — 69
Journal page — 70

Age Is No Barrier — 73

Is it too late? — 73
The key to changing our thinking — 74
Is it possible for you? — 75
You're in good company — 77
Sometimes impact takes time — 78
Life lessons and their use when older — 79
Journal page — 82

Belief

What it means to me
The most important ingredient
How do we create it?
The power of belief
Journal page

Guidance

My decision to get help
Bob Proctor's journey
Finding your own mentor
Masterminding
Journal page

Abundance   107

A lack of money isn't the problem	107
Your money patterns	111
Get clear on why you want more	111
Millionaire traits	112
"I can't afford it"	114
Other common blocks and pitfalls	117
Creating a new self-image	120
Money management	126
Journal page	129

Self-Care   133

"I'm so busy"	133
What I do to relax	136
Why is time out important?	137
Some self-care ideas	137
Journal page	139

Freedom   143

This is what I've learned so far	143
"The cave you fear to enter holds the treasure you seek"	145
Ideas of how to free yourself	147
What's next?	148
Journal page	150

AFTERWORD	153
ABOUT THE AUTHOR	155

FOREWORD

Dear Reader,

Thank you for joining us here! Investing in yourself is the best decision you can make, so well done for making it this far. Big things are coming, I assure you.

While I'm excited for Brett to have his latest bestselling book out into the world, I'm even more excited about how your life will change as a result of what you learn, implement, and reinforce.

Throughout these pages, you'll get a front-row seat to Brett's journey, including some brutally candid and raw accounts that led to heartache, misery, and near-bankruptcy. It's daunting to confront our past misdeeds – especially those that have created the rut we might feel trapped in today – but I know Brett was only too willing to reveal his darkest times because his mission is to inspire you to transcend your own pain, embarrassment, and fear.

Ultimately, he wants you to find meaning, happiness, and prosperity in your life before it's too late.

With each page you turn, my wish is that you're equally honest with your own introspection, as Brett has been. Shame builds on us gradually but being upfront about it is not only the best way to create empathy with others – it's the best way to find (and build) your tribe, too.

I'm grateful to have spoken on stages all over the world, but despite how many people are in attendance, only a minor percentage actually want to change. As my friend John Assaraf (who also starred in 2006 film *The Secret*) says, "Help the people who want the help, not the people who need the help." And the best way to do that is to find out whether the people you want to serve are interested or *committed*.

Brett is committed to your success. What follows this foreword is an easy-to-read blueprint for living life on your own terms, creating financial freedom, and establishing enriching relationships with people who can transform your life.

There's just one thing missing, and that's YOUR commitment.

I'm sure you're excited to dive in, so I won't hold you up any longer. I just want you to remember one thing, and it's my favourite Napoleon Hill quote: "Action is the real measure of intelligence." What you do from now – as a result of reading this book – will determine your success.

If you're tired of the same old routine, it's time to shake things up. And my friend Brett D. Scott is here to help.

Onwards and upwards always,

James Whittaker

[Author of *Think & Grow Rich: The Legacy* & *Andrew Carnegie's Mental Dynamite*]

INTRODUCTION

Richard Branson dropped out of school at 16 to start his first magazine and record store. His mother bailed him out financially, and he was bankrupt more than once. Yet Branson has become one of the most successful British entrepreneurs in history, worth an estimated $5.5 billion. He travels the world, participates in crazy stunts, takes big risks, and inspires millions with his approach to business. How does a nice, self-effacing, "average" guy get to this level of prosperity? What did he do differently to thousands of others trying to advance their business? Is he just lucky, or is there a missing ingredient you just need to grasp?

The great news is that all of these are completely accessible to you, too.

Financial success and fulfilment may not come overnight, but there are many changes you can make to the way you think, feel, and live, that will make a world of difference. You may not be flying a hot air balloon to the Arctic Circle anytime soon, but you could be driving that car, having that relationship, or building that business you've previously only dreamed of.

Right now, though, it feels like you're never quite going to get there – like there's something stopping you, but you don't know how to break through that invisible barrier and launch into the life you truly desire.

Are you making sales and earning a good income, but you seem to have hit a ceiling in your earnings, and can't work out how to break through?

Is your relationship stale and unfulfilling, or even on the brink of collapse, but you can't be honest about your feelings and also can't work out what's going wrong or how to fix it?

Do you set yourself goals, and often achieve them, but nothing is really lighting you up? Do you sometimes miss out on opportunities, but can't work out how to change it?

Does it feel like you can have, do, or be *more*?

You're not alone.

A 2012 HILDA (Household, Income and Labour Dynamics in Australia) survey states the lowest life satisfaction at age 45. An Australian Bureau of Statistics survey reports the 45–54 age bracket as being similarly dissatisfied.

But does it have to be like this?

Heck, no.

There is absolutely light at the end of the misery tunnel. While a goal to move forwards provides motivation and inspiration, that end result we are looking for is not attainment of the goal itself. You've heard that glib expression, "It's not the destination, it's the journey", for good reason. The real goal is the man you become along the way. Once you have addressed the inner demons that have been holding you back, and kept you 'safe', even fearful, the opportunities that open up to you will be boundless. Aiming for one specific, financial or life goal is just a very small starting point in a gargantuan field of promise and opportunity.

This can happen for you, even if you don't know where to start, feel overwhelmed, or don't have the money for coaching or personal development programs.

The secret is in learning how to manifest what you want, how to create more productive personality traits, and how to feel more confident, deserving, and worthy. The process and tools you'll learn in this book will help you create success and confidence in any area of your life, and by using them, you'll no longer feel like you're guessing or fumbling in the dark. Ultimately, my hope is that with the tools I will teach you, you will achieve more out of every area of your life.

By the time you've finished this book, you'll feel empowered to improve your circumstances, motivated to take action, and have a proven blueprint to follow.

Through the stories, lessons, and takeaways in this book, you will be inspired to take practical action in your life.

Success for most of us isn't about winning the lottery or having your fantasy football team come out victorious at the end of the season. The dreams of most dissatisfied men over 40 are related to the goals you probably had in your twenties and thirties, when you watched your mates buy multiple properties and businesses, take more than one holiday a year, and catch all the breaks in life that you seemed to miss.

This is your opportunity to discover the real secret to having it all. Whatever your mind can conceive, I promise you, it can achieve.

This book is overflowing with my learnings and understandings of how absolutely anyone can achieve more in life. If you believe that all your longings are possible, take the action consistently and apply what I'm suggesting, and you will be able to achieve results far beyond where you ever thought possible. How do I know? Because I'll be teaching you some of the Universal Laws that have been taught to me.

In my own life, when it came to my health, wealth, and relationships, I was getting a passing grade in one out of three. I might have been earning well at different times in my career, but the money seemed to slip through my fingers with ever increasing speed.

Wealth: Within a few months of using the Universal Laws in my life, everything has changed. I view money differently and enjoy the energy flow of both giving and receiving. I believe in abundance, never feel short of money, and I'm well on my way to financial freedom. I've achieved this through providing a service that shows people how to create the life they desire, so it's truly the most rewarding way of living and earning.

Health: My only passing grade. A personal trainer in the fitness industry, this was the one area I succeeded in without much effort or resistance.

Relationships: Each time I attempted a "love" relationship, the list of pros and cons I constructed about my mate would prompt me to end the relationship within only a few months. That is, if they didn't beat me to it. When I did commit, I damaged my marriage beyond repair. My personal relationships with family and friends were 'okay', but many of them were strained by my poor habits, such as the inability to stick with basic social arrangements. My relationships have improved substantially, and I enjoy rich friendships with quality people.

People in my sphere of influence, who have been living this way for years longer than I have, have seen incredible success as well.

Example 1: Megan Kamei, an incredible woman from my mastermind group, she's originally from Canada, but currently living the digital nomad lifestyle with her husband Aramei and two beautiful children. During 2019, after a few years of learning and applying everything you will read in this book, Megan finally cracked the $100,000 per month turnover and is now living the dream of helping thousands of others live theirs.

Example 2: Tom Bilyeu, not (yet) in my circle of influence, but I am inspired daily by his content. I see myself in his "before" story. A self-made billion-dollar business owner (Quest Nutrition) and 9-figure multimillionaire, Tom tells a story about when he was unemployed and getting up at midday – he asked his girlfriend's dad for her hand in marriage, and was promptly declined. Tom promised him that he would soon change his mind, as he was determined to change the current situation and prove that he was a worthwhile son-in-law. In 2016, when the father-in-law visited the multi-million-dollar Quest Nutrition factory, and Tom asked him again if he would grant him the honour, the man broke down crying with gratitude that his future son-in-law honoured his promise.

Tom now has a business called "Impact Theory", a media company which helps influencers become game changers by developing three stages of their business: community building, incubation and then building and selling. Impact Theory has over 1.5 million followers and the podcast show has interviewed many of the most successful influencers including Gary Vaynerchuk, Tai Lopez, and Tim Ferriss.

Example 3: Kim Calvert is one of Proctor Gallagher Institute's top consultants; the first person to earn the Diamond pin, which is awarded for the person who manages to activate 300 clients in a 12-month period. It was created in 2019, especially for her and now others are following. But what's so special about Kim is that she was a shy, quiet nurse who, only three years earlier, was earning a maximum of $35,000 per annum. This example should prove to anyone that no matter what your personality and financial position is – if you want something, or to be someone, strongly enough – you will achieve those goals and reap the rewards if you are prepared to learn and apply what I outline in this book.

Example 4: Joel Bushby, this legend has a business called "TNT" or "The Natural Transformer" and his business was one of the first influential social media "online" personal trainer businesses. He is armed with an award-winning physique and a lovable larrikin attitude. Joel has since gone on to include his girlfriend Steph in their thriving business, where they have an amazing community, excellent 100% natural products and science-backed programming.

Joel has always followed Law of Attraction principles and been his own unique shining light, that so many others have loved and adored (including me). He gives more than he receives, and you'll definitely be hard pushed to find someone with a heart as big as this guy.

This book will awaken the sleeping success story inside of you and help you build the life you've dreamed of, but not thought possible; The life that myself and thousands of others are currently living.

A life where you have freedom – SUPERCHARGED FREEDOM!

Let's get started.

Goals and Paradigms

The journey towards your goal

"Hi Brett, this is Lyn."

My admin manager never calls so early in the morning.

"We've just done an audit on our accounts, and we have a problem."

This doesn't sound good.

"Over the last 18 months, you've managed to overcharge us by over $50,000."

Silence.

"What?" I didn't really get it. Overcharge? How the fuck did this happen?

"Yes. We are going to have to get to the bottom of this, you've invoiced us for roughly $50,000 more than you should have since you started with us." Lyn sounded calm but I could feel the tension in her voice.

Fuck.

"You're going to have to pay it back."

I felt my heart stop. Or maybe I just wished for a moment that it would, and I wouldn't have to deal with the inevitable pain of what would come next.

How was I going to pay back such a large sum, when I was already struggling?

I had been working as a sales manager at a company called Trainer HQ, which helps personal trainers grow a business through specialised fitness industry business coaching. My strengths were in people skills and responding to the needs of others, not in computers or admin. It was a thriving, busy business, and I'd excitedly sent invoices to accounts when clients signed up, not keeping track of those who ended up pulling out and not following through on their commitment.

Over time, this added up, and while I had unknowingly over-charged (albeit aware of my poor habit of miscalculation with money in general), I was fortunate to work with a group of incredible individuals, who even though shocked, annoyed and pissed-off this happened, allowed me to work off the debt.

I kept working for them in a sales capacity and was able to pay back the debt fairly quickly, in less than a year in fact.

But the moment I found out that I had this debt was like the metaphorical straw which broke the camel's back.

I had been repeating this pattern my entire adult life. Make a little bit of money, gain confidence, make a bit more money, feel the tingle of success, do something which fucks it up and have to start all over again. I'd overspent, under-prepared, won awards, then hide back in my box.

Time after time, I'd done the same things. I'd never 'quite' reached the pinnacles of success I inherently knew I was capable of.

In 2018, I was opening a new gym while continuing my work at Trainer HQ part-time. I loved my work with Trainer HQ. The guys I worked with are outstanding people, I loved the clients we worked with – personal trainers who were growing businesses, and the challenge of helping them grow a successful business in a saturated market. So, the day-to-day work was great.

But I wasn't happy.

There was something missing, but I couldn't put my finger on it.

I would get up in the morning, do my morning affirmations, go to the gym, have my healthy smoothie and jump in my Subaru to drive the 30 minutes to work. I'd crank up an audiobook in the car and easily strike up conversations that turned strangers into friends.

But something wasn't adding up.

Why aren't I enjoying this as much as I should be? There's nothing actually wrong but I still don't feel like I'm happy or thriving.

It was a frustrating feeling. I didn't want to be trivial or superficial or focus on the material, so it wasn't that necessarily – it was a deep-seated yearning for something more which wasn't being fulfilled.

Over a decade earlier, my mate Hunter had shown me the film The Secret, which is about the Law of Attraction and manifesting the life you desire.

Bob Proctor was one of the experts in The Secret and stood out to me as someone whose message I really liked. For 13 years I had been liking his social media posts and receiving his email newsletter ... and one day I received an email from the Proctor Gallagher Institute, which would ultimately change my life.

SUBJECT: Are you ready for a change?
Have you been stuck?

It was an invitation to his world-famous Paradigm Shift event, live-streamed from Los Angeles.

I sat down with a coffee to watch the event online. As soon as Bob walked on stage, I could feel the energy of those present at the live event.

"If you can see it in your mind, you can hold it in your hand," Bob said.

"A paradigm is a multitude of habits stored in the subconscious mind," he continued. "Once we change the paradigms that are controlling the outcomes in life we don't desire, we can start attracting the life we truly do," he said.

I really can change, I thought.

I reached up to wipe away a tear which had sneakily dripped out of the corner of my eye. *Why on earth are you crying?*

As I watched Bob speak, lightning bolts of revelation kept hitting me.

You can do this.

Your old life doesn't define you.

Anything is possible.

Oh my God, you're going to be successful this time.

I felt around down the side of the lounge for a tissue box as the tears started flowing. It was like my heart, my soul, my energy, my whole being, had been broken down over time, until I didn't even know who I was anymore ... and now I had finally been broken open.

I was ready.

I vowed that I was NEVER going to be the man I had been, living a life of failure, broken dreams, and numb emotions. I was going to change and make a big impact in the world.

I knew I was ready to change, and contacted Bob Proctor's organisation, but everything hadn't come together yet.

I was still waiting for clarity on the best way forward, so that I could implement all their teachings into my life.

I don't want to get all woo-woo on you, but I do believe that the universe is always working in our favour. When we are not getting the message, it just speaks louder.

In my case, this was in the form of a message from an Instagram follower. I had been posting motivational material for a while and sharing some of the wisdom I'd seen from Bob Proctor; and one day, a guy named Marcus messaged me, seemingly out of the blue.

> *Marcus: Hey mate, how long have you been following Bob Proctor?*
>
> *Me: About 12 years, after seeing him in The Secret.*
>
> *Marcus: What's your favourite quote of Bob's?*
>
> *Me: If you can see it in your mind, you can hold it in your hand.*

Marcus: Classic. Love that one too.

The conversation went on for a couple of days. I really enjoyed the conversation, and could see that he was switched on, interested, and asking great questions ... but there was no information on his profile about what he was selling.

Me: So, what are you actually selling?

Marcus: Oh no, I'm not selling anything. In fact, the reason that I contacted you was that I wasn't sure if you had a coach or mentor you were working with.

Me: How does that work? Are you working with one yourself?

Marcus: Yeah, actually, I'm working with one of Bob Proctor's Inner Circle Consultants and her name is Mariko. Would you be interested in having a chat with her?

It felt freaky. I had only just been thinking about how I could go further with the things I had been listening to.

That's how it began.

I signed up to work with Mariko, my first mentor and coach. And she took me through the program, which would ultimately change the trajectory of my life.

The work Mariko would take me through was part of *Thinking Into Results*, the signature program of the Proctor Gallagher Institute.

Settled in front of my computer for Lesson One, I was excited about the new life I was about to create.

Bob explained the different types of goals – the type of goal you've already achieved, the goals you are confident you can achieve, and the big, scary goals which represent your wildest dreams, but have no idea how you'll achieve.

I loved the theory, but my longstanding habits and fears – which had momentarily faded away when I handed over my money – kicked back into gear.

Right, what do I really want?

I want to figure out how to fix my life and then help other men do the same. I want to write a book which reaches millions of men, and I can travel around the world doing it.

Great. That's exactly what I want.

Okay, but how am I going to do that? You're not the type of person who can do that stuff.

But Bob's already explained that you don't have to know the 'how'. You just have to want it enough.

I do want it ... But that doesn't mean I'll get it.

This is a classic example of paradigms in action.

Have you ever had a thought or thoughts like this? When you've considered a positive, life-altering decision and then, as quick as you consider the idea, another stronger reinforced 'knowing' hits you and destroys that beautiful image you were building?

This is because of your paradigm.

Throughout this book, you'll hear me discuss the word paradigm. A paradigm is buried in your subconscious mind; a mental program that has almost total control over your habitual behaviour.

> *"Our subconscious mind runs 24 hours a day, seven days a week." Brian Tracy*

It doesn't have holidays, it doesn't get time off for good behaviour; it simply operates all the time, exactly like a computer. Even when we sleep, our subconscious mind creates our dreams.

When you want to make a change in your life, you may start to entertain an idea such as "I want to set up a business", "Create more time freedom", or "Earn more money than I've ever earned". You think, "Yeah, that's a great idea, I want that". While it's in your conscious mind, it might feel scary, but achievable.

It's only when you make the committed decision to reach your goal, take actions towards them, and get emotionally involved in the outcome, does the paradigm decide to kick in and have its say. You'll counter your ambitious dreams with thoughts like "I'll never make that much money", "I don't know to set up a business", or "Relationships never work out for me".

A paradigm is a multitude of beliefs stored in your mind. You don't need to consciously think about them. They are just there. They're a little like a computer program which is running automatically – and you operate based on the program contents. If you introduce a thought or idea which is totally different from the program you've been running, it simply does not compute. New ideas and taking new actions can be scary, so while the paradigm is trying to keep you safe, you'll feel uncomfortable, you'll have doubt and worry, and most people simply give up on the idea once they encounter this.

Maxwell Maltz, MD, in his book, *Psycho-Cybernetics*, explains that, "It is no exaggeration to say that every human being is hypnotised to some extent either by ideas he has uncritically accepted from others or ideas he has repeated to himself or convinced himself are true. These negative ideas have exactly the same effect on our behaviour, as the negative ideas implanted into the mind of a hypnotised subject by a professional hypnotist."

The paradigms I was running were almost the entire reason I was never able to achieve true success in my twenties and thirties, no matter how hard I tried or said I wanted it.

Whether it was being a Les Clefs d'Or Concierge, a more successful magazine publisher, a real estate business owner, or a fitness business owner – every time I had an opportunity to step up and reach the next level in my career or business, I would self-sabotage or attract an external condition for why it would not manifest properly. Instead of reaching for elite status in my concierge career, I quit and went into a car rental role; instead of getting a mentor to help with the magazine expansion when I hit challenges, I gave it away; instead of leveraging my real estate award to achieve long-term status in the industry, I took on another role with shorter term benefits. You get the idea ...

I was on track to reach higher levels of success with multiple careers and businesses, but my paradigms simply didn't agree with me having more. I threw away opportunities, I gave up too soon, I sabotaged myself time and time again.

Closely associated with your paradigms are your "self-image" and "self-worth". If your paradigms are operating to give you results you don't necessarily want, your self-image will be impacted over time, because you start believing you're not good enough to have what you want.

> *"The self-image is the key to human personality and human behaviour. Change the self-image and you change the personality and the behaviour."*
> *Maxwell Maltz, MD*

Your paradigms, self-image, and self-worth are closely linked. In this book, we'll explore how to address all of them, where the opportunity to be most successful is in addressing only a couple of areas at a time. This means you can't address everything at once. It takes time and persistence. I'll teach you how to address one or two things at a time, until they become second nature and firmly embedded in your subconscious, before you move onto the next area for improvement.

Over time, it's entirely possible to up-level every area of your subconscious mind, and therefore, your life.

Working out what you want

So, what do you want?

For me, it was living on purpose, feeling like my life had meaning, living in the house of my dreams, earning the money I wanted to earn, travelling the world, and sharing what I was learning through a book.

If you could dream up your ideal life, what would it look like?

- Would you have a certain career or your own business?
- Where would you live? What would your house be like?
- What would your relationship be like? Your romantic one as well as the relationship with your family and friends.
- What would your health and fitness level be like? What kind of body would you want? What would your energy levels be like?
- How much money would you earn?
- How often would you go on vacation? And where?

This is just a starting point, but you get the gist. Take a few moments to write down what your life would be like if nothing was off limits.

It doesn't matter if you think the goal is an impossible dream. In fact, the bigger the goal, the more room there is for growth.

Success is not the end result or the outcome, it's the journey. Growth is the ultimate goal.

"I'll be happy when I've made a million dollars ..."

"I'll be happy when I get a six-pack ..."

"I'll be happy when I'm having sex four times a week ..."

Do you say these type of things to yourself?

I know I said these type of things to myself for years. What I didn't realise is that while I was striving for goals, I wasn't enjoying or learning from the journey to get there.

When we rush through to reach our goals, we're missing out on the growth, the lessons, the enjoyment of what we're doing, and the learning along the way. And that is actually part of what makes up success.

Real success is earned in little increments. In small peaks and troughs that add up over time to ultimately get closer to that one defined "goal".

> *"Success is the progressive realisation of a worthy ideal." Earl Nightingale*

Besides, have you ever reached a goal and immediately felt underwhelmed?

My book coach Cat Mora, who is helping me bring this book to life, shared her experience.

"When I published my first book, I knew that most self-published authors sell less than 100 copies ... so I declared that I would be happy if I sold 100 copies. As soon as my pre-sales hit 100, I changed my mind. 'I'll be happy when I sell 500 copies,' I said. When the sales counter reached 500, I immediately decided I'd need to sell 1,000 copies to feel like I'd really made it."

Does this sound familiar? The moment you reach a goal, you straight away move the goalposts? The goal is no longer enough. Perhaps a voice deep inside says, "Well, if you reached it that easily, it can't be worth much." Or, "If I reached that goal so easily, maybe I could do more. Maybe my goal isn't big enough."

You may struggle to enjoy your goals once you reach them, especially if they are within easy reach. Cat might have been better off reaching an initial goal of 1,000 books. Then she could have celebrated each 100-book milestone, rather than feeling a sense of emptiness each time she reached it and it was a massive anti-climax.

This illustrates why we need to set massive goals, and how important it is to enjoy the experiences along the way.

You need to create a big goal and then plan the steps to get there. You won't know exactly how to get there, but you can put small steps in place – keep moving forward (or even sideways sometimes) and stay on the path.

They say that when flying from Los Angeles to New York, it's never done in a straight line. The aeroplane's path appears on a map to fly away from the final destination, but then curve back in an arc. Therefore, if you took off from LA, you need not fear the apparent direction of the aircraft; ultimately, there is a higher plan in place, and you will reach your destination by putting your trust in the hands of skilled pilots. Along the way, you may encounter turbulence, bad airline food, and a stinky fellow passenger whose elbows keep ramming you in the ribs – but if you just have your complimentary snacks and beverages, you'll get there eventually. You may even (metaphorically) kiss the ground when you disembark at arrivals.

Don't be fooled into thinking you must know every detail or every step in your goal-attaining journey. With your desired outcomes clearly in mind, unexpected events will fall into your path, which will test you, help you grow, and eventually propel you towards your goals.

Understanding desire

When you have thought about what you want in your life, the next step is to think about why you want it.

It was March 2014, and for a few years my wife and I had imagined living in Noosa, a beautiful seaside town in Australia. We took most of our vacations there and always hoped we could make this dream a reality. I created a vision board to see ourselves living there, complete with pictures of the beach, a stunning house, fit people running on the beach, and the beautiful car we wanted parked in our driveway.

The vision board was crammed with all the great things I wanted in my life – watches, successful businesses, and overseas trips.

What I didn't know then was how important it was for me to really hone-in on my biggest desire. We would glance at the vision board before we went to sleep, smile at it knowingly when we woke up, and occasionally talk about how much we wanted the things which were on it. We were basically waiting for the vision board, and our enthusiasm for it, to do the work.

The missing link was that we weren't getting laser-focused on one big part of the vision board and affirming and feeling it every single day, and taking small action steps to lead us in the direction of that big goal.

Napoleon Hill says in *Think and Grow Rich*, "Desire is the starting point of all achievement."

There is a difference between a goal and the desire to reach it, and both are important. We want to reach goals because of how we think we will feel when we reach them. We want a nice car because of how we think we'll feel when we drive it. We want to earn a certain amount of money because of how we believe we'll feel when it lands in our bank account, or when we spend it. The "thing" itself is not really the goal – it's the impact that we believe reaching the goal will have on our life – our desire for having that thing.

But this is part of the journey I mentioned before – it's important to learn how to "feel" that way now, and feeling that way will not only bring you closer to your goal, it will help you enjoy the ride.

> *"You must be working towards a definite purpose, backed by a burning desire to have it achieved." Napoleon Hill*

So why do we need desire? What is the importance of it, and how does it affect your outcome in life?

The dictionary describes desire as *a strong feeling of wanting to have something*. The "feeling" is what's required to help you achieve your desired goal.

Desire is the connection to whatever we want to attract in our life. This is why it's important to focus on achieving something we truly desire, which gets us excited, so that we can really get into that feeling ... and this is the foundation of attracting more of those good feelings into our life.

You may have heard of the "Law of Attraction", and maybe you've even disregarded it as some hippy-dippy-shit. There are actually twelve Universal Laws, and while I'd grown up in a spiritual household, I didn't encounter them until much later in life – when I saw *The Secret*.

This opened me up to a whole new world of possibility.

In essence, the Law of Attraction says that in order to get the things you want in life, you must identify how you think having them will make you *feel*, and then feel that way on a daily basis. The law says that feeling this way more often will put you on the same frequency, or vibration, as the things that you want, and you will come closer to them because you will attract more of those good things into your life.

As an example, have you ever had one of those days where you wake up in a bad mood? Not for any particular reason, but you just feel like shit. You kick your toe on the bed as you get up to go to the bathroom, you sigh when you notice that the toilet roll hasn't been refilled, you're frustrated because there's no milk in the fridge for your coffee ... and when you leave for work, there's more traffic than usual and some d@#khead cuts you off and makes you miss the green light. The more you feel angry and focus on your anger, the more crappy things happen, increasing your feelings of anger.

This is the Law of Attraction at work.

Conversely, when your day starts off great, you whistle in the shower, notice the aroma of your coffee, and smile as you glide into light traffic, making all the green lights on your way to the office.

Also, the Law of Attraction.

The more you feel a certain way and focus on that feeling, the more events seem to happen – good and bad –

which create more of that feeling. You will also take action based on how you feel, and the more action you take in that direction, the closer you get to sustaining that feeling all day long.

If you are angry and frustrated, you drive faster, slam your foot on the brake, and yell obscenities at the slow person in front. If you are happy and relaxed, nothing bothers you, and you take the opportunity of a red light to turn up your favourite song on the radio.

This is the power of feelings. And feelings are the basis of desire. It's this desire which propels us forward to live the life we end up living.

If you want a life full of great things – where you achieve your goals and have everything you've dreamed of, then find the desire which is fuelling you, and work towards feeling that way every day.

Having the goal, maybe expressed on a vision board, is great, but the feeling is king. When you decide to start affirming your goal on a daily basis, which I'll explain shortly, you need to make sure you get emotionally connected every time you program it.

First, let's delve more into goals.

Why are goals important?

Napoleon Hill spent over 25 years studying and interviewing more than 500 of the world's most successful individuals of that period to discover and catalogue the aspects which made these people successful, and the one common denominator was they all made quick decisions and they all set goals.

Have you ever jumped in a car and just taken off without a plan, and hoped you'd end up somewhere awesome? Have you ever thrown a wad of cash across the travel agent's desk and said, "Hello, please book me a holiday to anywhere", and hoped the lovely person would choose Fiji or Hawaii and not Afghanistan or Syria?

I think not.

Without a goal you're moving towards, you'll be like the majority of people who either don't have a goal, or if they do, don't have it written down and are not consistently programming and moving towards attaining it.

A 1979 Harvard Business study found that in a graduating MBA class, 84% of the class had no set goals at all, 13% of the class has set written goals but no concrete plans to reach them, and 3% of the class had both written goals and concrete plans.

Ten years later, the 13% of the class who had set goals but not created plans were making twice as much money as the 84% of the class who had no goals at all. And more impressively, the 3% of the class who had both written goals and a plan to achieve them, were making ten times as much as the rest of the 97% of the class.

So, what would consist of a good goal? Start with something you can visualise. If you can picture it in your mind, it has a greater ability to be achieved because we think in pictures. Your goal should be something that drives you, excites you, and will motivate you to build a burning desire for its attainment.

The clincher is ensuring it's big enough. Even if you think you've come up with something really big, it's very likely your conscious mind will automatically put a limit on it, because you've never achieved it before. It will seem unattainable, and so your conscious mind will fight to make it more "realistic" in order to feel comfortable.

This is where many people go wrong. The problem with goals that are too "realistic" is that they don't elicit a burning desire to reach. They can feel a bit "meh".

For example, you might set a goal of earning $80,000 a year. Great. But what if that's how much you earned last year? Or you might want to buy a GT Mustang, and you already own a Mustang. You already know how to achieve these goals. They're safe. They don't fill you with dread ... or excitement.

But perhaps you currently earn $80,000 and you set a goal of earning $150,000. You think, *Well, if I hire an assistant to do this, and I run some ads in that, and I raise my hourly rate by $20, I'll just be able to make it.* Again, it's quite a nice goal, because you'll be earning nearly double, and if you think about the tweaks and changes you can make to what you're already doing, you're pretty sure you'll get there.

What would happen if you currently earn $80,000 in your own business but you want to dream big, really big? Things have been growing and ticking along nicely. You've got some big ideas and have had some great wins ... and you decide you want to bring in $1,000,000 in revenue within a few years. What? Ridiculous. Or is it?

It's a big goal like this that motivates and excites us. The mere idea of getting even close to that figure fills us with spine tingling exhilaration. It also scares the shit out of us, but that is part of the fun.

I'm being glib, but when you think about a big goal like this, fear will definitely come up. All of your self-doubt and limiting beliefs will come into force. You will think of all the reasons you can't achieve it.

We've all been there.

But when you think about it, if someone, anyone, has achieved it, then why can't you?

"If you can see it in your mind, you can hold it in your hand." Bob Proctor

Bob Proctor, and many other successful people who inspire me, talk about the importance of these big, lofty goals. If you think about your goal and it really excites you, but then you immediately get scared and think of all the reasons it's way beyond what you think you can achieve, then you know you're on the right track.

That's the kind of goal worth working towards.

Then you need to use this "fear" to drive you forward. Turn your fear into excitement and drive. If you think of a goal and then immediately think – *Who am I to achieve such a thing?* – that's where the real magic happens.

Rather than standing in our way, this fear can be the catalyst to greatness. Fear can be useful, because it indicates that we're moving towards something worthy. It's a little like the 'fight or flight' mechanism we are naturally born with. You can feel the fear and run towards it anyway, or you can back off and run in the other direction.

Do you remember back to when you were a kid, and thought about what you wanted to be when you grew up? Chances are your goal has gone through a lot of iterations. When I was ten, I wanted to be an astronomer. Not an astrologer or an astronaut – an astronomer. The guy who looks through a big telescope and maps out the sky. They are extremely important people who watch what's happening outside of earth, and can be instrumental in advances in energy, defence, aerospace and medicine.

I had this dream from the age of 10-13 and was super excited to visit the Perth Observatory with my mum. She knew I had a love of stars and arranged for me to meet the resident astronomer.

"What grades do you get in maths?" he asked, peering over the top of his glasses.

"Mostly As and Bs," I said, puffing my chest out.

He nodded. "How about physics?" he said.

"I haven't done it," I said, nervously drawing a circle on the carpet with my shiny brown brogues.

"And what about calculus or algebra?" he asked.

Again, I replied, "No, haven't done those either." *I'm only 13, you know.*

He looked at me with an expressionless face, scratched at his facial hair and said, "If you aren't an A student in all of these, then I'd suggest this career is not for you."

And poof, just like that, my dream was turned to dust. All the nights I'd spent gazing up at the sky, wondering what mysteries were beyond what my eye could see; the expensive telescope my mum bought me for Christmas that I dragged outside to explore stars and planets; the dreams I'd had of working for NASA or the government, impressing them with my knowledge of the sky – all of it came crashing down.

My dream was too large to be real. There was no way I could achieve it – at least not according to the bearded guy wearing cords I'd met at the observatory.

It didn't cross my mind that I could learn all those skills I needed. I could take steps towards my dream by reading and studying and practising. I could take the long journey to reach my goal, fuelled by the excitement of reaching my objective and meanwhile enjoy the learning along the way. I just gave up.

Have you ever thought about something you wanted to achieve, and then either your own sensibilities, or the voice of reason from someone else, convinced you it wasn't possible?

Just know that it IS possible to achieve those big goals. Instead of, like me, giving up on them the moment there is resistance – whether it be from an internal or external force – find the excitement in the challenge and go for it.

Taking action

While I loved *The Secret*, and it was a major turning point in my life, I also recognise there was one major thing missing.

The need to take action to achieve your goals.

The understanding of your paradigms and how they get in the way is essential for you to master. This knowledge allows you to take action and reprogram these paradigms by replacing the non-productive habitual behaviours you have created with more positive and useful ones. Actions which lead you closer to the outcomes you desire.

I've desired many things in life and not quite achieved them. Why? Because my paradigm controlled my behaviour, and the behaviour was to continually retract from taking the required action which would fulfil the destiny of achievement.

In 2007, I won an award for my achievement in real estate. In the industry for less than three years, I was recognised by the Real Estate Institute of Victoria as Residential Salesperson of the Year. I loved real estate, I loved working with clients to sell their homes and achieve top dollar, and I had a passion for creating a great experience for both the seller and the buyer.

The principals of my agency asked me to buy into a partnership with them at one of their other locations. Cruising along happily on a retainer plus commission role, I was honoured to be asked, but scared to death of the big commitment and the move from comfort into uncertainty.

At the same time, a competitor agent had seen my award and offered me a sales manager role at their agency. It was a prestigious, seaside location, where people flocked to buy homes in the summer, and they were offering me a fat paycheque as a base salary, that was about the equivalent of what I'd worked hard to achieve, including commission, in my current position.

I weighed up the options. *Do I stick with these guys and invest money in a new direction which might fail? I don't even know how to run an agency. What if they realise I have no idea what I'm doing? It would be a lot of work, too. It would take years to see any return. It might not work out anyway. Or do I take this new job with the easy money and finally buy that shiny grey BMW I've been eyeing at the dealership on Nepean Highway?*

I took the sales manager position.

A few months later, everything fell apart. The beautiful location I was working in turned out to be completely devoid of buyers in the autumn and winter months, and my wife was driving a four-hour return journey to work every day. I wasn't enjoying the work because of the lack of action, and the whole situation was completely unsustainable.

It was what I'd always done. Looking back now, I can see my years of doing the same. Embracing opportunities and rushing towards shiny new objects, but once I'd established a certain level of comfort with what I was doing, I'd avoid stepping into unknown territory and taking risks.

What might have happened if I had taken the action of investing in the new agency? The guys from my original agency are thriving today, and at the time of writing, have over 200 properties listed at up to $4,000,000 apiece. The agency I went to as sales manager is now closed.

Envision your goal and feel deeply into how you will feel when you reach it. Be excited by the unknown.

And take action, even when it scares you.

But what if you really don't believe you can achieve the lofty goal that just crossed your mind?

Subconscious acceptance

You've probably heard the saying, "I'll believe it when I see it"?

In fact, it's the other way around. You will see it, when you believe it. When you believe strongly that something is possible, you are more likely to work towards it. But believing something new, big, or scary doesn't just happen. "Belief" is only attained once our subconscious mind accepts the idea that we are consciously thinking about.

We have two minds: our conscious and subconscious. The difference is quite significant. The conscious mind is our "thinking" mind; it's where we imagine ideas, it's our creative faculty, and it's where you can entertain any idea whatsoever, and you have the ability to accept or reject as being true or possible, based on your experience.

The subconscious mind is totally deductive, it can only accept an idea that's been accepted as a belief. This means that trying to achieve something which, deep down in your subconscious, you don't believe is possible for you, is futile.

Imagine you've decided you want to earn $100,000+ a year, yet the most you've ever earned is $50,000. You may make a plan of how to achieve the extra $50,000, yet simply making a conscious decision to achieve that will likely not enable you to "make it happen". You see, the subconscious is accustomed to making $50,000, so just like an autopilot correction in an aeroplane, your internal GPS will find a way to fix your variation to the program and return to its original destination of only $50,000. It doesn't know how to operate at the $100,000 level ... unless you practise daily the habit of affirmation of the goal, mixed with feeling those "end goal" emotions.

Let me side-step for a moment to talk about your current personality traits and habitual behaviours. You may be surprised to learn that most of these programs/paradigms we are running were installed prior to the age of about five (depending on whose research you listen to). In our earliest years, we are only operating using our subconscious mind. Our conscious mind starts to build once we get to those formative childhood years of somewhere between three and seven years-old.

Research[1] shows that we are absorbing an incredible amount of information and turning it into beliefs and behaviours, right from infancy, and possibly even before that. Many researchers believe that some traits are handed down through generations, via our gene pool.

So, if they are so ingrained, how do we change them?

According to leading science-based researchers, Dr Bruce Lipton and Dr Joe Dispenza, there are only three known ways to influence your subconscious mind, which will result in changing your behaviours permanently.

---

1   https://drjoedispenza.net/blog/the-waves-of-the-future/

Affirmations

The first, and the only one you have total control over, is affirmations via spaced repetition, which we also call autosuggestion. According to Dr Dispenza, affirmations are "new, positive thoughts repeated again and again in order to build them into the structure of our brain." Spaced repetition in this context is most easily described as repeating these affirmations, writing them down, and feeling them on a daily basis over an extended period. This is also called autosuggestion, because you are suggesting new ideas to your subconscious mind so that they become automatic and programmed.

For example, some popular affirmations are:

- "I am so happy and grateful now that money comes to me in increasing quantities from multiple sources on a continuous basis."
- "I am the architect of my life; I build its foundation and choose its contents."
- "My marriage is becoming stronger, deeper, and more stable each day."
- "I love feeling fit and strong. It is easy for me to eat well and exercise regularly."

Affirmations are said with positive language and as though you already "have" the "thing" in your life, rather than you just aspire to have it. So, you wouldn't say, "I am no longer overweight and unhappy," or "I am looking forward to being fit and strong ..." By wording in the positive/present and *feeling* it to be true, you will attract your desire into your life more easily. This takes us back to how the Law of Attraction works. Feeling how you want to feel and focusing on what you want your life to be like in order to bring about more of those good feelings and situations.

For more information about affirmations or help with creating yours, please visit my website superchargedfreedom.com.

Emotional impact

A second way of changing our behaviours permanently is through an emotional impact, which is often delivered via a negative situation such as a death in the family. No matter the specifics, it's a deeply profound and impactful situation which is out of your control.

Imagine something really devastating has just occurred – in my case, a $50,000 debt out of nowhere. And your immediate reaction is to fall to the floor, curl up in a ball and cry. (If you're not a man who cries, then there may be some other physical release.) At that moment, your brain will kick into survival or fight/flight mode, and automatically try to problem solve. *I'm going to be bankrupt again, was my first thought. I never want to be in this situation again. When I figure out how to fix myself, I'll write a book and teach others how to do the same*, was my next. My brain was already moving me through the devastation and creating a plan for thriving, not just surviving, on the other side.

Another example is from my childhood. As a 12-year-old boy in high school, I recall the moment I started to rebel against my life with dishonesty. My three best friends, with whom I'd been close since primary school, approached me at lunchtime.

"Oi, Brett, I heard you told Lara that Graham had the hots for her," said Julian, squinting at me with disdain.

"Well, he does, doesn't he?" I said, tucking into my cheese and salami sandwich.

"Well, yeah, but she didn't need to know that," Graham said. "Why are you such a goody-two shoes all the time?"

Before I could defend myself and spout the lessons about being truthful I had heard from my mother over the years, Andrew jumped in. "Yeah, we've decided we don't want to be friends with you anymore."

They sauntered off, talking loudly, elbowing each other in the ribs and barely threw a backwards glance in my direction.

Sitting there in my tearful state, I decided being "good" was clearly not a great thing.

From that point on, I tried my hardest to be anything but. I started skateboarding with my new mates from the skate park, listening to Run DMC, and throwing around attitude. Nobody would be able to criticise me for being an angel ever again.

I didn't realise it at the time, but that event, and subsequent behaviours, would impact me for years to come. This is what happens with emotional impact.

Essentially, your survival thought will tend to be positive, and because you're in a deeply emotional state, feeling all the feelings, your subconscious accepts it immediately. This removes the need for creating affirmations and using repetition to embed them into your subconscious – it happens instantly and automatically.

Hypnosis

The final method of creating permanent behaviour change is hypnosis[2]. In 2003, Harvard Professor Emeritus Gerald Zaltman revealed in his study of Neuroscience that at least 95% of our thoughts and decisions originate from the subconscious level of the mind. Which means there's

---

2 https://psych-k.com/wp-content/uploads/2013/10/FanninWilliams.CQ-copy.pdf

only a very small percentage left for the conscious mind to assert its decision-making ability.

Another study by Tor Norrentranders in his book *The User Illusion, Cutting Consciousness Down to Size*, explains that, remarkably, the conscious mind processes at an approximate rate of 40 bits of information per second, while the subconscious mind processes at approximately 40 million bits per second. This stands as proof of why it's important to reprogram the subconscious, and if we can only consciously process at a minimal rate, hypnosis seems a logical step.

Hypnosis is usually administered by a psychologist, psychotherapist or trained hypnotherapist. Simply put, hypnosis is a state of highly focused attention or concentration, often associated with relaxation and heightened suggestibility. Not everyone can be hypnotised, usually those who are trusting, and more intuitive, which is around two-thirds of adults. A person's attention will be so focused, often called a "trance-like" state, that anything going on around the person will be temporarily blocked out or ignored.

Dr. Bruce Lipton PhD, recommends a type of hypnosis called Psych-K which was created by Rob Williams over 27 years ago. This technique has been proven to get to the root cause of certain beliefs in the subconscious mind and change them. (psych-k.com)

Journal page

> *"Setting goals is the first step in turning the invisible into the visible."* Tony Robbins

- How is your goal journey going? What is something big that both excites you and scares you, that you could choose to go after?
- Have you got your goal written down?
- What action steps will you take to get to your goal? Create a plan. Remember, the plan can change as much as required, the goal stays the same!
- What subconscious beliefs are controlling your current results?
- Which non-serving habits are you going to change? What part of your paradigm really needs cleaning up?
- If there truly was no limitation to your abilities, what would you LOVE to do?
- Write out a list of beliefs which then become behaviours i.e. habits you emit that you know are getting you the outcomes/results you do not want. With that list, write the opposite on another sheet of paper, burn the negative (1st list) and then number the positive in order of most important and work on each one for 30 days or until they're a new belief/behaviour and of course, result!

Super-Charged Freedom

Goals and Paradigms

Super-Charged Freedom

Your Truth

It's 3am. I open the front door and close it softly behind me. I creep into the kitchen and open the fridge. The light from the fridge serves as my guide so that I can sneak around and do what I need to, without disturbing Elissa.

If I drink a bottle of water and take some ibuprofen, I won't be hungover tomorrow.

Images from my night are running through my mind. Loud, pulsating music, strobing lights, party pills and plenty of drinks to wash them down with. I had been out with my mate, who was always the life of the party, and we'd strutted our way through a handful of clubs before tumbling into a taxi when we'd finally run out of cash.

"I'm heading over to Doug's place to have a few drinks and play pool. If I drink too much I'll stay over," I'd said to my wife after dinner the night before. "We might go to the pub, but I doubt it."

Doug and I had already planned a big night, just like the ones we usually had, but as usual, I didn't want to tell my wife. I knew she wouldn't approve, so it was easier to avoid an argument by playing down my plans for the night. Of course, I didn't actually give her the opportunity to react differently, because I never gave her the full story.

A few hours later, I'm sitting at the counter, drinking juice and no doubt looking shady as hell.

"Hey, babe, how was your night?" Elissa says as she breezes into the kitchen for her breakfast.

"Oh, pretty uneventful," I say, looking down. "I had a bit too much to drink, so I slept on Doug's couch for a bit."

She comes over to give me a kiss and then disappears to get ready for work.

What she doesn't know won't hurt her, and I haven't cheated or done anything wrong, so it's fine.

I'm just having fun.

***

This pretty much describes every weekend at that stage of my life. I wasn't living my truth. I wasn't honest with my wife about the kind of fun I liked to have, because I knew she wouldn't accept it. I loved her more than words, and I didn't want to put myself in a position where she might leave, because she didn't approve of my behaviour.

Rather than changing the behaviour or being honest with her – to give her the opportunity to talk it through – I just continued doing what I wanted to do, and kept her in the dark.

I wasn't being honest with myself about how I wanted to live, and I wasn't being honest with her. In that situation, nobody wins.

Does this sound familiar? You may not be partying with your mates, but maybe you're watching porn, spending too much money, gambling, or staying in touch with ex-girlfriends.

You can't be honest with your partner, your family, or your colleagues, because you are too afraid of the ramifications.

Why is this a problem? Lots of people live this way, right?

Think about drug addiction. For many people, taking drugs habitually is something which only affects the drug-taker. However, there are other, far-reaching impacts. That person might commit crimes to get the money to buy the drugs, their family may be in disarray, they may come home and be violent with their partner, spend their family's money on drugs instead of bills and necessities, and there is a larger cost to society of catering for drug addicts in hospitals, addiction centres, and far, far more.

So, personal drug addiction, at surface-level, may not appear to directly harm others, but its impact is far-reaching.

I use this as an example, because we often judge our own behaviours, our small decisions, our day-to-day habits, as not impacting our lives, much less other people. We think that they're just little vices that don't affect others, and besides, if we were perfect, everybody would be so intimidated, we'd have no friends. We don't think there's a need to change or get help. We don't want to admit our flaws to our loved ones. We just continue the behaviours and get on with our life.

What we don't realise is that when we're being dishonest with ourselves in this way, we're not in alignment with our core values. We're not in harmony with the universe; and we won't bring more of the good things we desire into our life.

The universe doesn't judge you about whether something is "good" or "bad", but it will judge whether you're being honest with yourself. It does respond to your vibration. Everything has its own frequency and operates at a certain vibration. If you're not operating at your highest frequency and vibration, it will be very difficult for you to attract and keep what you desire in your life.

> *"I fully realise no wealth or position can long endure unless built upon truth and justice." Napoleon Hill, Self-Confidence Formula*

Why are truth and honesty important in your quest for success?

Because truth and honesty are both habitual behaviours. Being truthful is simply delivering what you believe is true. Being honest is not offering anything to anyone that is dishonest. Why? Because you allow yourself internally to expand. When you do the opposite, it's like placing a roadblock on momentum. Think about a time when you let go of being angry at someone and offered forgiveness, you immediately felt like you could move forward, right? It's very similar and has amazing positive responses in life.

What is truth?

Historically, people with power and money tend to have the most followers. Truth, humility, and sacrifice are often not valued.

That was until Gandhi.

In May 1893, a steam train was shuffling towards Pretoria, South Africa. Mahatma Gandhi was on his way there from Mumbai, about to start his career as a lawyer. "Get out of this seat, you filthy Indian," grumbled a white passenger. Gandhi refused and hence was forcibly removed at Maritzburg station.

According to this account, while contemplating what had just taken place over his skin colour, and while brooding and freezing, Mohandas "Mahatma" Gandhi started his pursuit of truth and firmness, or passive resistance. Working as a lawyer and lobbying government, Gandhi led India to economic independence in the 1930s, however Britain wouldn't let go until 1947, where it split the country into Muslims and Hindus; a move Gandhi only agreed to in the hope they would finally resolve their differences and have peace. In 1948, an extremist Hindu shot Gandhi dead and almost one million people showed up the next day, following the procession to Gandhi's cremation on the banks of the Holy Jumna River.

Gandhi's passionate pursuit of peace and truth gained him a massive following, and he was the most famous and well-respected non-powerful and non-wealthy person in the world. I believe people were drawn to Gandhi because of his pure approach to having an influence. Maybe in him, they saw themselves as they would like to be.

Truth certainly has its value.

In my own life, particularly in my pre-rebellious years, there were plenty of opportunities to be truthful. Sitting in class in grade seven English, my teacher was writing on the blackboard. "Sir, that's not true," I said to his spelling of "organisation". "My mum said it's 'organization' with a 'z'." Growing up with a single mum, she was my source of truth. The wise woman who had brought me up to question, grow, and flourish. In reality, I'm unsure whether she told me "z" or whether it was simply something I watched on Sesame Street years earlier, but the fact remains, I believed this was true.

He glared at me, cheeks turning red. "This is in the curriculum, Brett. Don't argue with things you don't understand."

Do you have memories like that? Where you've been taught an idea and a teacher or someone of authority tells you that you're wrong?

In this situation, which is the truth? How do you know?

Is truth the same as "honesty"? Some would argue they're different. I believe they're related, but there is a subtle difference. "Being honest" is not telling lies and "being truthful" is speaking what is true to you, which could include lies you are unknowingly telling yourself.

Imagine you're an actor, and winning an Oscar is your goal. You're a good actor, you've been in a few good shows, and you've got some talent, so it's still a huge goal, but it's plausible at least. Now, add into this picture the fact that your actor friends, agent, and family all tell you that you're a good actor, but it seems a little unrealistic to reach for this goal, as you've never been in any notable film projects and you seem to get cast in the same type of roles.

This is honest feedback, right? Is it the truth? It's true in their minds, but you've heard the stories of people like Jim Carrey who worked as a janitor and a security guard and was a struggling comedian before finally getting a break in the hit show *In Living Color*. Or how *Sex and the City* star, Sarah Jessica Parker, was born and raised in a coal mining town in Ohio, the youngest of four children, until her mother remarried a truck driver and another four children followed. She managed to find success at a young age, but it was definitely against the odds. Comedian Eric Bana appeared to come out of nowhere when he made his transition from Australian comedy TV shows and the funny film, *The Castle*, to be cast as the hero character Bruce Banner, who turns green when he gets mad in *The Hulk*.

Let's break down your current situation, related to your Oscar dreams.

- **Honest account of your situation:** You do not have the experience, exposure, or opportunity to win an Oscar.
- **Lies you are unknowingly telling yourself:** *I'm not good enough to win. I'm not talented enough. I can't get Oscar-worthy roles here in Australia. I'm too old to start a professional acting career.*
- **Truth:** You have a desire to win an Oscar. You have the dedication, commitment, and hunger to improve your acting, get more film experience, perhaps relocate to Hollywood (or get an artist's visa), and you can imagine yourself onstage accepting it.

Although your current situation might be perceived to lead to a certain outcome – e.g. as a relatively unknown actor, you are unlikely to win an Oscar – and the people who give you "honest" feedback are looking at this as truth or reality, what is the truth?

The truth of your ability to succeed is completely up to you.

My truth may not be the same as yours.

But the same principles apply to us both. The more you embody the truth of what you want to *be* or *have* in your life, the faster you will attract those desires into your life. If someone, anyone, can win an Oscar, why can't you? It *is* possible. Once you are not blocking yourself from the full extent of your potential, you've removed the shackles and enabled yourself to move forward. Limiting yourself by some dim perception of "honesty" or "reality" is like having wings which are weighed down with water. Once the wings are dry and you embrace your full potential, you can fly.

Make a decision to discover what your truth is. Are you being truthful with what you really want? Are you telling yourself lies about your potential and possibilities? Are you being derailed by what is currently "honest"?

One of the ways you can uncover your truth is by journaling. I've included journal pages in this book to help.

"Truth" in this context is primarily about your goals and dreams, and the courage to believe that they are real and possible.

Truth in a related context is about being truthful with where you're at, what you're doing, how you feel, and why you do the things you do. In line with this, it's also related to what you say to other people, and if you are truthful with others in the pursuit of living your life and getting what you want.

If you're not being truthful with yourself, or others, are you being dishonest?

Dishonesty

"No Liss, I don't have any outstanding parking fines," I declared, knowing full well that I did. Elissa had seen the discarded Council envelope in the bin and wondered what had been in there. She knew my recklessness with parking, and I'd racked up my fair share of fines over the years.

I reasoned with myself that I'd pay them off without her knowing and I didn't want her worrying. It was a load of BS, but I simply didn't want to get into an argument. I hated listening to a lecture and defending myself, so it was easier to say what I needed to get through. And I was an expert at justifying my behaviour, especially to myself.

Isn't dishonesty the opposite of truth? No. I know what you're thinking; we just went through all of this in the last section, didn't we? Yes and no.

If you truly want to break free of your past and have a successful future, I really want you to start to comprehend what "dishonesty" means for you. Do you find yourself telling "white lies"? Do you hear yourself telling someone something you feel they want to hear, rather than giving them your honest opinion? Do you choose what you say – "lies" – to avoid getting into an argument?

This might not be relevant for you, and dishonesty may not be one of your habits. If, however, you can relate to one or all of these, or can think up more appropriate scenarios, then I want you to start considering each of your own past examples of dishonesty.

Create a list of times when you were deliberately dishonest and then write down the outcomes from doing/saying what you did. Next to it, in a second column, what are the possibilities if you had chosen to be honest instead?

Here are some examples:

Dishonest thing
- Spent joint account money without talking to partner.
- Called in sick when you weren't because you wanted to attend a party.
- Added skills to resumé that weren't true.

Outcome(s)

- Argument to ensue, trust broken, short-term satisfaction.
- Get caught out, someone mentions they saw you at the party.
- Landed the role, tested on fake skill and lose job.

Possible outcome if I was honest

- Partner saying, "Yes, happy you asked," or offering more funds to get something even better than you intended.
- Offered the day off because you were upfront or even given a free day as a thank you for your extra effort given lately.
- Still got the job because they liked how you presented or you didn't land that job, but they had another role that suited your skillset.

When we choose not to tell the truth in every situation, we are generally making an assumption on the potential outcome based on our past experiences and habitual behaviour. The crazy thing is, you might upset people by being honest, but they are more likely to forgive you than how they would react if they found out later that you'd lied. Most people hate being lied to and will hold a grudge longer, or form harsher judgements against you, than if you initially told an unpleasant truth they had to deal with. And this way, you will both know that you did the right thing.

I spent 39 years trying to control outcomes via my dishonesty, with other people for sure, but mostly with myself. Sounds crazy to say out loud, but I actually felt in those moments that it was better for me and the other person to not create drama by being truthful.

Then, in August 2014, with one phone call from my manager about my $50,000 debt, it all came to an abrupt halt. The debt may not have been directly as a result of dishonesty because it was a genuine mistake due to my poor accounting habits, but it helped me to realise that I alone was the reason my life was such a ridiculous roller coaster. It was my own fault that the downward descent of the coaster came off the rails and crashed into a fiery ball.

I'll be forever grateful I caused that crash, as I would not be here telling you the story and helping you "break-free" if I hadn't.

Embracing truth and honesty

When you take hold of your use of truth and honesty, you are actually in full control of your life and destiny. You are in control, not only of what happens in your life, but also how you feel. You will feel happier in general, because you will know your actions are always coming from a place of integrity.

Whenever you are making decisions about your actions, you are always thinking about what the outcome might be. *What will she do/say if I say that? What will he do if I show him the problem?* You can easily spend your life worrying about what ifs and maybes.

On the other hand, when you choose honesty and truthfulness, you can focus instead on how it makes you feel. The choice to be honest and truthful just feels good. And when you feel good, you bring more situations and events into your life, which also makes you feel good.

***

In my quest for enlightenment, I have done a lot of reading. One group of authors captured my interest with their five agreements (Ruiz et al, 2012). The five agreements are:

- Be impeccable with your words.
- Don't take things personally.
- Don't make assumptions.
- Always do your best.
- Be sceptical, but learn to listen.

I love them all – and they are so simple – but the first one has stood out to me in my time of growth. **Be impeccable with your words.** To me, this means having integrity with how you speak to others, making a commitment and sticking to it, and ensuring truth in everything you say and do.

I was working as a concierge at a five-star hotel in Melbourne in the 90s, where a well-known Australian TV commercial celebrity with his own line of products stayed with us on a regular basis.

This one fateful night, a poor unsuspecting room service attendant received a call from the star asking for them to attend his room, as he wanted to show them something. That something was to be a whole cooked chicken being booted down the hall at the attendant in a rage. "Tell the bloody chef to cook this thing properly, for fuck's sake!" he yelled, followed by a tirade of even more colourful language.

As a man, as a celebrity, as a human – he was not impeccable with his words.

Let's do better.

Journal page

> *"Truth will always be truth, regardless of lack of understanding, disbelief, or ignorance." W. Clement Stone*

- How truthful are you with yourself?
- What untruths have you been telling yourself?
- Growing up, we are told all sorts of untruths. What are some that you remember, which you feel don't serve you? Example – money doesn't grow on trees (which teaches us that money is limited.)
- Have you ever told a lie? If so, what are some that you know are not healthy?
- How does being truthful help you with your goal?
- Do the exercise outlined in this chapter. Choose a decision that you could lie about or tell the truth and what the outcome would be in either column.
- I've found that by stating aloud positive attributes I'd like to have, even physical ones, that by stating them consistently and daily, with feeling, I started to see and feel myself differently externally. What are some new parts of you that would help you become stronger within yourself? Example: more caring, more focused, physically look better?

Your Truth

The Hero

Superman and discovering it's me

Can you recall your favourite character growing up? Some kids at my school liked GI-Joe, Barbie, Wonder Woman or Batman (like my son) and I personally loved He-Man and Star Wars characters like Luke Skywalker. But Superman was always my number one.

When I was around 10 years-old, living in Perth, Western Australia, I used to have amazing dreams of flying with Superman. In one dream, I was at Disneyland and he flew down and said, "Take my hand," and we soared up into the air. It was truly as if it had happened, and I still remember it like it was yesterday.

The feeling of flying was incredibly liberating. Feeling free and having a birds'-eye view of the world gave me a rush, even in the moments I first woke up and was still partially in my theta state.

My mum sometimes talks about a time when I was 3 to 4 years of age and I begged her for a Superman costume, but because I was so adventurous, she feared I would jump off the roof. She bought me a Batman costume instead. I had seen the cartoon where Batman glides everywhere, so I thought, *close enough* and much to my mum's horror, took myself to the roof of our low-set house and jumped. Luckily, a rose bush broke my fall, and my Batman costume mysteriously disappeared the next day.

On my 21st birthday, I finally got the courage to get a tattoo. I had planned a large Celtic symbol and a North American Indian armband design but decided to first get a smaller one placed somewhere not visible, in case I couldn't handle the pain and abandoned it part-way through. That tattoo was the Superman symbol.

There are a few other Superman stories I could share, like the 500-strong comic collection I used to own, however the essence of all this is the fact it was focused on a character created outside of myself.

Experts in child psychology believe that one of the reasons children love pretending to be superheroes is that it allows them to have a sense of power and freedom that they don't have in their day-to-day life with parents and teachers.

But adults do this too. Many successful business people and entertainers adopt alter-egos and characters outside themselves to step into new and unfamiliar territory in a safe way. For example, church-going Beyoncé Knowles created Sasha Fierce to allow herself to strut on stage with the sexy dance moves and risqué costumes that went against her religious upbringing. It took several years before she was able to "retire" Sasha and be comfortable with being herself in those situations.

During the intense period of personal growth I've had over the past year, it dawned on me that the reason Superman remains an important part of me is that it's a mirror. I recognise the strength, compassion, and freedom Superman represents. It was also no surprise to learn that dream interpreters say that dreaming about flying represents freedom, and that adult men are the most common group to dream about this.

As a child, I don't know if I wanted freedom, but I believe adopting Superman's persona was a "crutch" for me to be more than I believed was possible on my own.

It's also interesting to note that Superman hides his identity and, therefore, the "truth". This is something I spent most of my adult life doing.

Now I have learned to merge my love for Superman with my own traits and see this former obsession as a positive rather than a crutch. I may not have x-ray vision or an ability to fly, but I do have the noticeable qualities he has, such as courage, compassion, kindness, and the pursuit of justice.

In this unexpected way, I have learned how to help other people achieve their superpowers or "discover" their inner superhero. We always have them, they're just lying dormant.

We all have a superhero inside us

Why is finding your superhero important?

Are you in a job you hate or where the boss is always on your back? Being like a superhero will allow you to confidently cope with the day-to-day and push through challenges, or it can also give you the courage to leave.

Perhaps you're in an unsatisfying relationship, but you are too afraid to leave. Being a superhero will give you the strength to make the tough decisions which need to be made to honour your worth – which could be leading change in the relationship or moving away from it altogether. Either way, you'll find the power to have the relationship, and the life, that you deserve.

For several of my clients, the challenges they're facing are related to starting a business. They may have left a day job, or be on the verge of doing so, to open their own business, but they're afraid of failure. They feel that the safest option is to open a franchise or copy another person's exact business model. Becoming a superhero gives them the confidence and power to go out on a limb and do something which lights them up and truly resonates with their greater life purpose.

How do you discover your superhero? Does everyone have one? How long will it take to find it?

First, identify where you want to have more strength, power, and confidence, then make a committed decision that you are ready and willing to do what it takes to become your own superhero.

It's important to note that, for most people, finding an external source can help you unlock your inner hero. This is because we can't see our own blind spots, limitations, and mental programs that stop us from achieving our goals. We let ourselves off the hook too easily. Having an experienced and trained person alongside us to guide us and keep us accountable is often the difference between achieving your goals and staying stuck where you are.

Therefore, the next step is to gather people around you who will support and guide your new quest. Research coaches and mentors online who have either achieved what you want to achieve or have the knowledge you believe will help you. Ask other successful friends, acquaintances, or peers who they have worked with or recommend. Search on social media and follow potential coaches for a while, to see if their posts and videos resonate; and/or go to reputable sources, such as the International Coaching Federation (ICF) to find someone you feel an affinity with. Coaching can be done in-person or just as effectively online using video calls.

I trained with the Proctor Gallagher Institute, who have a heavy focus on how to work with your mind holistically, to change your life. At the in-person meetings, I am surrounded by inspirational and awe-inspiring individuals whose levels of success motivate me daily.

Find the one which feels right for you, and then take action to commit. Even making this first move to commit feels like magic. People and opportunities which were not there previously will feel like they "magically" appear.

The third step is to think about the qualities your superhero has that you want to adopt in your life. Is it courage you seek? Or is it strength, resilience, or persistence? Put on your metaphorical superhero costume and act as though you have those traits already. How would the superhero version of you think, feel and act in challenging situations? Feel into that. Get emotionally connected to those qualities and the idea of feeling that way. Feel the freedom of having those attributes.

When you do this, your whole body and spiritual vibration and frequency will shift, and it will slowly become your new normal. Once you start operating on this new, elevated level, you will be able to meet your internal superhero.

As your own superhero, you will be able to face challenges head-on. You will have the courage to overcome those obstacles which previously felt insurmountable.

You can face that difficult boss, open that new business, change or end that unfulfilling relationship. Whatever you want in your life, you can achieve.

Embracing your superhero

For years, I operated under the same principle – always have a new job lined up before I leave the old one. I was so afraid of not having a safety net, even when my day-to-day had become unbearable or unsustainable.

In my previous role, before starting my current coaching business, I was working with a great bunch of guys, who I also learned a lot from and was grateful to, but I knew I wanted to branch out and do my own thing. Despite the financial stress I'd caused us all, I'd settled into a comfortable existence with their company. I enjoyed the work, and both liked and respected the team. Yet, once I had my heart set on creating my own business and helping others, my days felt longer, and small hiccups that occurred were frustrating and more difficult than they'd been previously.

My future was calling, and I wasn't answering.

Once I embraced my own inner superhero, I had the confidence to do things differently.

I had a couple of clients and the vision of what I could achieve, but I didn't have the income to support myself from the business alone. I thought, *What would Superman do? Would he stay in a job he knew he had reached his limit with? Or would he leap into the unknown and fend for himself?*

I leaped.

And I've never regretted it. Not for even one day.

Self-image

Think about the wicked queen in *Snow White*. She stands in front of the mirror every day, asking for validation about being the fairest beauty in the land. The mirror always replies that she is indeed the most beautiful.

Do you ever stand in front of your mirror at home and say loving things about the person looking back at you?

Now, of course, the queen was the epitome of vanity, but only accepted compliments from an external source. Once Snow White took over her position as the fairest in the land, her faux confidence crumbled. If, on the other hand, the queen had truly believed in her own beauty and other positive attributes, she may never have ordered the huntsman to kill Snow White.

Which of your traits is the huntsman in your life story? When do you let your insecurities get in the way of celebrating another person's success? Have you ever spread lies or perpetuated gossip, aimed at somebody you are jealous of? Or instead of helping someone else to achieve their dream, have you served your own needs and sabotaged them in the process?

This is by far one of the most important lessons any one of us will encounter on this journey towards "Super-Charged Freedom", because there's a direct correlation between the internal image of yourself and your results in life.

We often aren't aware how damaged our own self-image is. It's highly important, even critical, that you understand that once you focus on establishing or restoring positive beliefs about yourself, you will need to go through a process of programming these more positive attributes into your subconscious mind. Just deciding that you are smart, capable, creative, or a good problem-solver, isn't enough to change your life. You need to take action to embed these ideas into your subconscious by reprogramming how you think and feel about yourself on a daily basis.

"I'm so average, and so bland. I have no idea why anyone would want me and I'm sure that my husband is going to cheat on me or leave me," a client of mine said when we first started working together. I looked at the smart, funny, attractive woman in front of me and if I hadn't seen this so many times from other clients, I would have been surprised and in complete disbelief she could hold such ridiculous beliefs about herself.

Judy's relationship with her husband had started out strong, but over the years, they had fallen into a pattern of arguing about her absolute confidence that he would find someone better. She watched his every move, accused him of flirting, and checked his phone as often as possible, just to catch him in the act.

"Deep down, I know he wouldn't cheat, but I can't stop myself from worrying about it," she said. "If I can catch him, then I can just end it and put myself out of this misery."

The truth was that her partner adored her and, to our knowledge, was completely faithful. But Judy's own insecurities wouldn't allow herself to believe that anybody would want her and love her enough to be loyal. "I just don't feel like I'm enough," she said.

Their relationship had reached breaking point. Her husband wasn't able to convince her of his fidelity, and he was getting tired of trying.

Through our work together, Judy finally realised that her negative feelings about herself were the thing getting in the way of having a thriving relationship, and it had nothing to do with the words, thoughts, or actions of her husband.

Judy isn't the only client I've worked with, or person I've spoken to at one of my speaking events, who feels this way. So many amazing souls I've encountered have a poor or damaged self-image, self-worth, or critical self-belief, which gets in the way of their relationship, their business, their career, their health, or their general happiness.

Years ago, I was also my own biggest critic. Whenever something didn't work out, or I'd made a decision that didn't result in the outcome I wanted, I would think, *Why am I so stupid? What is wrong with me?* I regularly backed myself into a corner, feeling down and becoming physically sick from being so run down. I felt an overwhelming compulsion to party, drink, and date a string of women who would make me feel better in the short-term.

In direct contrast to the way I felt about myself, others saw the outside mask I was wearing. "You're always so positive and happy," they would say. And while my personality was predominantly optimistic, and positivity certainly saved me from a complete downwards spiral when I faced major challenges such as divorce and bankruptcy, it was purely a mask that was covering up all the damage that was there internally.

On the outside, I was the guy at the bar buying drinks and partying to trance music, but on the inside, I was doubting myself, questioning my every move, and admonishing myself for any small mistake or perceived failure.

Have you ever caught yourself saying these things?

- I'll be right. I don't need help. I can sort this out.
- If I tell her this, she will react like this, so I better do that.

- I'm equipped to handle this. I don't want to burden them.
- I can't be successful because I'm (insert your belief).

Do you make excuses to cover up really dealing with the root cause?

Many of us don't deal with the root cause of an issue at hand. Sometimes we do this on purpose, and sometimes we are truly unaware that something deeper is at play. We treat the effect or behaviour we are displaying, thinking that's the issue, when in fact, our behaviour is due to a whole set of other underlying beliefs or traits.

Another client of mine wasn't getting the results he wanted in business. He created affirmations about earning millions of dollars, but it wasn't happening in reality. He wasn't even moving closer to that goal. In working together for a short time, we made the connection between his beliefs, stemming from childhood, and his current results. Growing up in a working-class family, he had always been told that significant money was out of reach for "people like them".

Although he was going through the motions for making a change in his economic status, his deep-held beliefs weren't allowing him to get there.

Once we cleared these beliefs by creating affirmations to replace the negative self-talk, he was on a completely new trajectory. Within weeks, things in his life began to change. He landed 5-figure contracts, made more money in less time, and started spending more enjoyable time with his young family.

Why do we focus on the surface-level behaviours or results in our life, rather than addressing the hidden ones? Because they are visible, tangible, and while sometimes those things need to be changed, that won't correct the "cause" of our real problem. It's like placing a band-aid over a broken bone!

How can we fix this? How can we repair our self-image? First, create a list of behaviours you consider negative or undesirable on one sheet of paper and on another sheet write out all the "polar opposite" or more positive desired ones you would prefer.

Then it's time to start programming these positive behaviours into your subconscious mind, after we burn or shred the negative.

- From the positive list you created, pick the top one or two you'd like to focus on first.
- Write out an affirmation for each one, focusing on what you'd like to achieve. For example, "I am honest with everyone." And "I exercise every day."

  Keep it in present tense: i.e. .Don't write, "I will be honest with everyone," or "I will exercise every day."

  Make it positive language: i.e. Don't write, "I'm not dishonest anymore," or "I'm no longer lazy and inactive."

- Write them out every day, morning and night, 100 times each. Most people find it easiest to do this first thing in the morning, before they look at emails or social media, and last thing at night, before they sleep, when their brains are most primed to accept subconscious messages.
- Read them out loud as you write them. *Feel* into the statements, don't just write and say them without feeling. The feeling is important.
- Literally shred and/or burn the negative list. It's a symbolic way of removing these from your subconscious mind.

The process of writing these out will trick your brain into believing and accepting them as truth. This will help with creating new neural pathways and new behaviours to go with these new beliefs.

Like any new habit, it will take 21-28 days to really lock-in and have your mind accept the new program/paradigm.

Courage

The yellow brick road was by far one of the biggest tests any of the characters along with Dorothy would ever face. The Tin Man finally found his heart, the Scarecrow received a brain, and the Lion got his courage. The interesting symbology I read from this is that each character, including Dorothy, all had to go through their own trials to get what they truly wanted. They practised embodying their deepest desires, and therefore did the work of uncovering them, even though it was without realising it. When they met the Wizard to ask for what they wanted, it turned out they had achieved their desired traits on their own. The path they took had actually allowed them to discover their gifts for themselves.

We have all done this in our own lives. Waiting for someone else to give us validation or permission to achieve our goals. Giving the power to others to make us feel a certain way. Allowing someone else's opinion to decide if we're worthy to achieve something.

The reality is that if we know what we want, and go after it with courage, we can achieve it.

Courage seems to build with your self-image, too. The stronger you feel inside as a person, the braver you become when you know you've got to step outside of yourself to truly make magic happen.

Having a purpose also gives you the necessary courage to do certain things you would normally consider a roadblock or a difficulty you'd rather not face. Why? Because your purpose is bigger than you; it's usually driven by a passion or a skill you have, and you have an easier time putting your ego aside in its pursuit.

In the Wizard of Oz, the Cowardly Lion is afraid of everything. To the point he can't even sleep. He agrees to go on the journey with Dorothy to meet the Wizard of Oz to see if he could be helped with some courage.

The Wizard does help the Lion; he gives him a dish of unknown liquid to help him remove the fear. The Lion argues that the liquid courage is only temporary, however the Lion's ability to face fear in times of danger certainly doesn't match his sentiment.

I personally feel like many of us, when we are lacking something, it's never receiving something outside that fixes us, it's what we do inside and the repetition of the practice of doing that which we fear or feel we lack that builds our confidence.

Are you ready to be brave?

Journal page

> *"A hero is someone who has given his or her life to something bigger than oneself."* Joseph Campbell

- Which superhero do you relate to? Or if you're not into superheros, what characteristics would you choose as superpowers?

- Additionally, what's one superpower you would love to have and how would you use it for good?

- Can you see some holes in your internal self-image? If so, what are they? Example: I lack belief in everything I do. I feel unworthy of success. I am not as confident as I would like to be.

- What are some of the positive aspects of your self-image you already know you have? Examples: kindness, positive energy, growth mindset.

- Do you have the courage to change your life? How will you start? List three things to help you focus on getting started.

- What impact do you think focusing on a superhero or superpowers will do to help your inner 'self-image'?

- To obtain new aspects of your internal self-image, we need to go through a repetition process of affirmations. What is the number 1 new belief/behaviour you're going to implement?

The Hero

Super-Charged Freedom

You Receive More When You Give

Giving and its impact on receiving

At the age of 12, I could have written the following about Christmas:

Christmas Eve is here, and I've been told to go to bed at 8pm. I know that Santa's not real, but I still love Christmas Day. I spent the past week finding small gifts for my mum and my grandmother. I love waking up early and racing out to see what Santa (Mum) has packed into my Santa bag, but I also love seeing their faces when they finally open up the gifts I chose.

As an adult, my anticipation of Christmas is quite different. It's no longer the same excitement for me personally, even though I still get gifts from my mum, but there's still an incredible sense of joy watching the anticipation of my son, who wants to get up early and unwrap what Santa brought.

The Bible quote and often quoted saying, "It's better to give than to receive," is not just a cliché. Giving and receiving are different aspects of the flow of energy in the universe, and you will receive more when you give. Most of my life I've been a giver, always happy to help and make people feel welcome. I even made a career of it as a concierge in hotels for nearly a decade. I also worked as a waiter, a bartender, a landscaper, a personal trainer, and a coach. All were service-oriented roles, and I got enjoyment out of giving. I wanted to be liked, and I knew that people would be grateful and responsive to my gifts of service.

I can remember picking flowers for my mum as a young boy, because I knew it made her happy. Or offering to help older people cross the road or carry their shopping. If a friend was moving house, I'd offer to help them move ...

But we don't give in a vacuum. When we give, we also receive. Sometimes, we have a bias towards what we will receive when we give, and sometimes, the receiving is a bonus by-product. When I helped people move house, for example, I did anticipate they would offer pizza and beers at the end of the day. But when I gave flowers to my mum, it was genuinely because I wanted to see her happy and bring a little bit of joy into her day.

Therefore, you could view your giving as a positive, a negative, or neutral, based upon your motivation to give.

While I explained that giving and receiving are on the same energy wavelength, an important distinction is that there is an order to it. The order is first to give, and then to receive.

Many of us are pushing to receive. "Give it to me now," or "I gave you that, so you have to give me something in return."

When you are fuelled by receiving, it's no longer giving, it's trading.

The greater impact you can make on your fellow man in a positive way, the greater impact you'll have in your own life, and it won't always – in fact most times – WILL NOT come from the place you gave it.

Stop focusing on the short-term impact of your giving – i.e. thinking about what you'll immediately receive back. Trust that the universe will flow gifts back to you, in time, and for your greater good.

Do you give with the spirit of true and honest service, without expecting anything in return? Do you give to genuinely help, including helping others without them even knowing it was you? Would you give even if the recipient didn't find out who gave?

W. Clement Stone, who worked with Napoleon Hill in the 1950s, said that one of his keys to success was doing something every day for another person, usually without them knowing who had done them the favour. "Your most precious valued possessions and your greatest powers are invisible and intangible. No-one can take them. You, and you alone, can give them. You will receive abundance for your giving," he said.

Today, "how" I like to give has changed. It has to be honest. I have a no BS approach to helping people as a coach and mentor. It's not about being liked or how the giving is received. It's not about winning brownie points or influencing how others see me. My giving is about how I can truly help and serve. I give in true service, even if it's confronting and they get pissed-off at me. At least they'll know where they stand and that I'm always saying it with the right intentions.

Isn't that the best service one can give?

Giving with a higher purpose in mind will raise your frequency to a higher vibration, and that's when you attract more goodness into your life.

How can you think selflessly on a daily basis? How can you go out of your way to help someone or leave a person feeling better as a result of being near or with you?

True freedom is found in giving without hoping or waiting for something to come back to you. Ironically, you are more in control of receiving and having happiness in your life when you're not actually trying to control outcomes from your giving.

The Law of Attraction and its relationship to giving

- The LOA is about focusing on the feelings you want to feel when you achieve your goal.
- One aspect of this is giving with joy, focused purely on feeling great about giving. Ultimately, you will attract and receive more great things into your life which brings about feelings of joy.
- Most people want happiness. It's not about focusing on "things", but about how you believe you'll feel when you have these things in your life.
- The LOA can also be used to bring other emotions and feelings into your existence.

Embodiment of both these theories

- Rhonda Byrne created The Secret without years of experience and was not fully knowledgeable about the Law of Attraction.

- She was focusing on giving and sharing the knowledge she had, and on learning as she went. This was evidenced by multiple things being left out of the movie, such as the need to take action towards your desires.

- She has received more than a hundred-fold what she put in. She was broke when she made the film, and is worth $100 million today.

- At the same time, she has inspired many others to live a life at a higher vibration, in service to others. She inspired me to change my life and also introduced me to other people I admire.

- I am writing this book without having reached my full potential. I'm in service to those reading and bringing you on the journey of abundance with me. I don't know everything yet.

Journal page

> *We make a living by what we get, but we make a life by what we give."* Sir Winston Churchill

- What does it look like for you when you "give"? What happens?
- Giving and receiving are one and the same, you cannot have one without the other. However, do you expect to receive something in return from someone when you give? If yes, what and why? And if no, what makes you think that?
- You may have heard the expression, "It's better to give than receive." Do you agree with this and why?
- It has been said that the path to your desired level of wealth and abundance is factored in by your level of giving. What does this mean to you? How can you apply it?
- What is something you could do today for the next 30 days that allows you to give consistently, without expecting anything in return?
- The Law of Attraction is dictated by the Law of Vibration. And if everything you truly desire (positive) is on a higher vibration than you're currently on, what things could you decide to do daily to get into the right vibration to attract? Examples: Gratitude practice, journaling, meditation, yoga, exercise ...
- What are some aspects in your life that you'd truly love to attract and why?

You Receive More When You Give

Super-Charged Freedom

Age Is No Barrier

Is it too late?

In working with clients and speaking at events, I've had the privilege of holding space for many different men and women, particularly those facing and overcoming challenges past the age of 40.

I've heard multiple stories of adversity, regretted decision-making, struggle, frustration, and sometimes hope about what the future might bring. Often, however, the stories of hope are tinged with defeatist paradigms about the person's ability to make the changes, do the work, or achieve their goals.

"I've tried so many things to change my life and nothing seems to work ..."

"As soon as I start to see some growth, I fall back into my old ways ..."

"I'm too old to start again ..."

"If I was younger, I would ..."

Do any of these sound familiar?

If so, you're not alone. It's easy to feel this way when you have essentially been living day-to-day, just facing the road ahead in the same way you always did. Going through the motions, doing what needs to be done, putting out the fires, putting one foot in front of the other. It is a rare human who stops to evaluate where they actually are and makes a decision to really shake things up.

Why is it then, that even when somebody makes a decision to change, that results can seem rare and hard to come by? One of the reasons is that until you go out of your way to reprogram your paradigms (and I talked about affirmations as a way of reprogramming your beliefs in an earlier chapter), you will keep operating under your old paradigms. This means that you will keep acting based on the same beliefs, thoughts, and actions as you did before. When you do this, you will keep getting the same results as before.

"We cannot solve our problems with the same thinking we used when we created them," Albert Einstein is quoted as saying. Another favourite is, "Insanity is doing the same thing, over and over again, expecting a different result!"

But when we are inside our own unique situation, it can be impossible to see that we are, in fact, doing the same thing as before.

The key to changing our thinking

If you really want to make changes and unlock the power and freedom in your life, don't do it alone. A significant barrier to achieving change is not getting help. If we want to stereotype what it's like to be a man, it would be fair to say that many men feel like they don't need help. Even if they recognise that help would be beneficial, they may struggle to ask for it.

In my coaching practice, and in conversations with coaches and mentors in my peer community and mastermind groups, I have heard this referenced numerous times. Clients who struggled for years until they worked with a coach or mentor, and then finally exploded on the trajectory they had previously only been dreaming about.

When you work with somebody who is trained in recognising and disrupting unhelpful ways of thinking and behaving, you can accomplish much more than you ever thought possible before, or indeed attained on your own.

Is it possible for you?

Let's look at some stories of inspirational people who have achieved great success well into the double digits.

In 2003, at the age of 70, Yūichirō Miura reached the freezing cold summit of Mt Everest. It was an incredible feat for anybody, let alone a little grey-haired man from Tokyo. Miura returned to his home successful and an inspiration to people of all ages, holding the Guinness World Record for being the oldest person to conquer Everest.

Over the ensuing five years, three more men in their seventies did the same. Not to be outdone, Miura returned to Everest twice more, and successfully scaled the summit, taking back his record on two separate occasions. Not only did he prove that age is no barrier to reaching dizzying heights, he underwent two heart surgeries for cardiac arrhythmia in the interim.

In the celebrity world, despite Hollywood's tendency to worship youth, stories of success over 40 are plentiful.

While on our honeymoon, my wife and I were doing some shopping and popped into a cinema to see a comedy called *The 40-Year-Old Virgin*, starring Steve Carell. Beyond the movie magic of the chest waxing scene and many other embarrassing moments I hoped never to experience, the best part was discovering that this actor had only gotten his first big break at the age of 43. A big year for Carell, he was in the TV show *The Office* at the same time, becoming one of comedy's leading men.

More well-known names who earned their big breaks later in life are:

- **Samuel L. Jackson:** What many don't know is he struggled with drug addiction for two years before getting a break at age 43, in Spike Lee's 1991 movie, *Jungle Fever*. Then, he went on to perform his stand-out role in the 1994 film, *Pulp Fiction*, alongside John Travolta, who was 46 years-old.

- **Martha Stewart:** Martha was well into her 40s before she landed the role of "America's housewife". Prior to that, she worked in catering and fashion modelling.

- **Henry Ford:** Not many people know that Mr Ford was an engineer working for Thomas A. Edison before he founded the Ford Motor company when he was 40. Five years later, he produced the famous "Model T" Ford car.

- **Reid Hoffman:** As we know, many social media businesses were founded by young tech geniuses. Not Mr Hoffman, he was 35 when he founded LinkedIn in 2002. Eight years later, he took it public and became a billionaire.

- **Julia Child:** Ms Child hadn't even eaten French food until the age of 36, then because she was absolutely stunned by this cuisine while living in France after World War II, she studied it until she had enough knowledge to host the TV show, *The French Chef*, at 51 years of age.

- **Alan Rickman:** This actor got his big break as Hans Gruber in *Die Hard* alongside Bruce Willis when he was 41 years of age. He gave up his graphic design career in his mid-20s to get into acting, spent years working in theatre, and it took more than 15 years to reach international film stardom.
- **Ray Kroc and "Colonel" Harland Sanders:** Ray was 52 when he met the McDonalds brothers, and the Colonel didn't become a chef till the age of 40 and used his social security cheques to begin franchising KFC at 65. He didn't become an icon until he sold the company at 75.

You're getting inspired, aren't you?

You're in good company

Napoleon Hill interviewed 500 successful people for his book *Think and Grow Rich* in the 1930s.

One story told of an accountant who applied to get into university and study law after the age of 40. Friends and family warned him that he had a wife, kids, and bills to pay, but he knew that he'd be much happier, and ultimately successful, by pursuing his passion. He completed his four-year degree in only three years and his new career was a roaring success.

"Most of the truly successful people I've interviewed didn't have their big wins till after the age of 40," Hill is quoted as saying. He states from an analysis of over 25,000 people that most who succeed in an outstanding way, are generally over the age of 40, and sometimes well beyond 50.

At the same time as I watched Bob Proctor's *Paradigm Shift* event, I was working as a manager at a gym in Maroochydore, Queensland, Australia. Driving an hour each way gave me the perfect opportunity to put my newfound inspiration and beliefs into practice.

Inspired by Bob Proctor, I had started reading *Think and Grow Rich* daily, like others may read the Bible. I then discovered it as a recording on Audible, and utilised my driving time to listen to that, as well as other motivational books and podcasts. At the time of writing, I have listened to and read the book almost 20 times. Whenever I hear the soothing tones of Earl Nightingale narrating Napoleon's words, I feel a fresh sense of empowerment.

My dreams are truly within reach, and so are yours.

Sometimes impact takes time

There are times, though, where what you have "decided" does not impact on your beliefs, thoughts, or actions, until much later. It's a process.

When I saw the movie *The Secret*, I finally woke up to the unsatisfactory way I'd been living my life and how it could be different. I finally understood my plethora of possibilities and felt confident there was a way I could attract the things I wanted in my life. But I didn't change things overnight. I started attracting good things into my life, but what the movie didn't teach was the entire "order" required by following the Universal Laws, and that by applying these, we have a greater ability to restore or reprogram our internal self-image. This is not a quick fix, and it takes work, but by moving with the Law, you will find it easier to adopt, apply, and discover your power.

It took me 13 years to truly understand why I wasn't achieving what I really wanted, and in fact, I was going backwards. I was in a repetitive cycle of two steps forward, three steps back. Can you relate?

Looking back, this extended journey to success was a positive. It meant that I could fully understand the frustrations and barriers to effectively changing paradigms and achieving new goals. In my coaching and mentoring business, I use this knowledge and experience daily with my clients.

I will ask you the same question I ask them:

Do you feel or have you felt like you are on a hamster wheel? Does it seem as though you adopt a new practice or work towards forming a new habit, but the actions don't last more than a few days?

You are not alone.

Be assured that once you make a decision to change your life, you have taken a major and crucial first step towards reaching your goals. Beyond that, daily action must be taken to reprogram your old paradigms, but help is available. This book, along with other books I reference, and the support and guidance of a coach or mentor, may make all the difference between you either celebrating your successes or beating yourself up that you failed once again.

Life lessons and their use when older

In 1935, at the ripe young age of 45, Harland David Sanders was awarded the title of Kentucky Colonel by the Kentucky Governor for his service to the community – which was not a war service award. By 1939, the USA guide "Adventures in Good Eating" put Colonel Sanders gas (Shell) station eatery on the map, and by 1952, the first KFC opened in South Salt Lake in Utah. In 1955, at 65 years-old, he sold his first restaurant outside of Kentucky and with only a $105 social security cheque to support him, he started to set up franchising across the country. By 1964, at age 73, Colonel Sanders sold the franchise business for $2 million. He kept the rights for Canada and also became the face and brand ambassador – and to this day, his image is still being used.

One thing I've noticed since being 40+, and starting to reach new levels of success, is that I'm less encumbered. What I mean by this is that I'm not driven by nightlife or distractions, which can easily derail us. In my 20s and 30s, my head was turned by every shiny, fun-looking object, good looking woman, or opportunity to party. Even though I was presented with information and teachings that I knew at surface-level, I wasn't able to properly understand or use them because of my over-arching and non-productive paradigms, poor habitual behaviour, and self-sabotaging cycles.

In my real estate years, I was surrounded by savvy investors and clever business people who were setting up their financial futures in an impressive way. When I won my real estate award, my immediate thought was along the lines of, "Now I can command a higher salary." More money meant more fun, more "things", more of the lifestyle I enjoyed. At the same time, the exceptional men who were principals of the agency I worked for offered me an opportunity to buy into and expand the business. In line with my values at the time, I thought, "But that would mean spending my money to invest and taking home a lesser salary." It felt like a move that would take me further away from my goals at the time.

I knew that I wanted a home, investment properties, and a stable financial future, but the pull towards the party lifestyle and short-term gains was stronger. I did have the awareness that I needed to move away from some local friends who supported my less-healthy habits, and that played a part in not sticking around to join the ownership team; but for the most part, it was not an attractive offer, because I was in the fast lane, and taking responsibility for growing a business would slow me down.

Looking back now, part of me regrets it, but at the same time, I recognise that it was an important part of my learning and growth. I simply didn't have the insight into why I was doing the things I did, and how a different path would serve me better. The only choice I could see that would help me slowdown, was physically moving to another location.

I had seen the movie, *The Secret*, and loved it, but at that time, I interpreted it more as a "magic pill" which would change my life … some day. The concept of putting in the work was a completely foreign idea, and I unconsciously waited for my new, more grown-up life to drop into my lap, at some stage in the future, when I was ready for it.

Maybe that's the point of those decades in our development.

With a bit less hair and a few more wrinkles, our perspective changes. You can truly focus, get locked-in, and enjoy incredible growth that may not have been feasible for you when you were younger.

Whether you're 20-something, or over 70, I truly believe there's still time to make it happen. The foundation to change is to for you to get locked-into what drives you, discover your passion and what you're good at, and start to build a "worthy ideal" that you can strive to. When you go through the process of replacing non-productive paradigms with positive ones, you can truly have the life you've always imagined!

Are you ready to go?

Journal page

> *"You are never too old to set another goal or to dream a new dream."* C S Lewis

- Have you felt as though you missed the boat of success? If yes, what was it that made you feel that way?
- What are some of the limitations that have slowed you down or stopped you in the past?
- What lessons have you learned years ago that will help now?
- Now that you know it's possible for you to have true success, what are some of the actions you feel that could help? What changes will ensure your success?
- Have you used a mentor/coach before? If yes, how did it go? If no, my advice is to find one. What areas of your life and business do you think a great mentor could help you with?
- Many highly successful people have found it at an older age. If you're older than you imagined you would be when you reached your desired level of 'success', (like me), what does success look like for you? How important is it?
- What can you do today to get the wheels in motion?

Age Is No Barrier

Super-Charged Freedom

Belief

What it means to me

A gentleman was walking through an elephant camp, and he spotted that the elephants weren't being kept in cages or held by the use of chains. All that was holding them back was a small piece of rope tied to one of their legs.

As the man gazed upon the elephants, he was completely confused as to why the elephants didn't just use their strength to break the rope and escape the camp. They could easily have done so, yet they didn't even try.

Curious and wanting to know the answer, he asked a trainer nearby why the elephants were just standing there and never tried to escape.

"When they are very young and much smaller, we use the same size rope to tie them, and at that age it's enough to hold them. As they grow up, they are conditioned to believe they cannot break away. They believe the rope can still hold them, so they never try to break free."

The only reason that the elephants weren't breaking free and escaping from the camp was that, over time, they adopted the belief that it just wasn't possible.

The word 'belief' means everything to me. Beliefs form the foundation of our world. Without belief in what you're working towards, you simply will not manifest it into your life. "I'll believe it when I see it," is the age-old phrase we're conditioned to say. I've since learned a different way.

You'll see it, when you believe it.

Our subconscious mind is the mental storehouse of our beliefs. In fact, paradigms are beliefs. That's why we repeatedly attract things into our life that we don't actually want. Sometimes they're false beliefs that we accepted as children, and other times they're beliefs we've created along the way.

One example is related to sleep. We've all heard the expression, "The early bird catches the worm." But how early is early? What time are you getting up? I have gotten out of bed at 5 or 6am for years, to go to the gym. A few months ago, I read Hal Elrod's book, *The Miracle Morning*. An eye-opener in many regards, one of the points Hal makes is that when we go to bed, we set the intention for how we'll wake up. If we believe we'll wake up tired, cranky, and will need 12 coffees to function, that is indeed what will happen. We may decide to create a new habit and set our alarm for a certain time – in my case I decided on 3.33am – but we're thinking, "Oh man, I'll need a massive coffee tomorrow." In that moment, we are creating the belief that we will wake up tired, and your mind will deliver the exact situation you created.

When I switched that belief and decided that I would wake up refreshed and energetic, ready to go through my new morning routine of feeling gratitude, sending love, writing and journaling, and meditating; everything changed. I do wake up feeling full of life and energy. I jump out of bed without a backwards glance, ready to dominate the day.

It all comes down to what we believe. And what we believe dictates our actions, and our actions create our results.

So yes, BELIEF is my favourite word.

The most important ingredient

I poured in the milk and started whisking away with my fork. The two eggs I cracked into the bowl were completely mixed in, making a nice orangey-white colour. I added some chilli flakes and keep stirring. I like a little spice in my scrambled eggs.

Now this is a very simple thing to create, yet there's an order to it. Most recipes require order; "do this, add that, make sure you've done that before this, etc."

My point is that *belief* is an important ingredient in your recipe, but it's not the only ingredient. Without all the things done in a certain way, it will simply be a wish or a hope, not a success plan. You need desire, awareness of your productive and non-productive behaviours, belief that what you want is possible, the ability to make quick decisions to respond to opportunities, and flexibility to change direction in the pursuit of your goal.

In Chapter 1, you made a list of what you want. I asked you to get really specific and also to dream big. The beauty of this is that you're really using that magical part of your mind, imagination.

This word "belief" is going to truly allow you to work like a magician and pull you towards what you truly desire. Sounds easy, right? Yes, sometimes it can be. What you're seeking, is also seeking you. However, when those tricky paradigms are at play, the ones you've got programmed that have you feeling less than worthy or not quite as good as Daryl Bloggs down the road, you'll find that getting your mind to BELIEVE is a bit harder. That's where you'll need to reprogram it.

Bob (Proctor) recommends that when you decide the new paradigm or program you want to run, write it out 100 times in the morning and 100 times at night and watch what happens. It won't be long until you're starting to feel how you need to feel to get into a "belief state".

Start writing down some of your "non-productive actions/behaviours" and decide on one or two that you want to change, so you can start to build more belief in your dream.

It's a recipe you can design. Go on, start now!

How do we create it?

The Power of Awareness by Neville Goddard truly nails the ideas behind belief. He teaches how to go beyond your imagination, and truly conjure the *feeling* of already having what you desire. Not how it will feel when you get there. But how it feels right now to already be there.

Can you get yourself into this state? The more you can do it and really visualise and "feel" how it feels, smell the scents, almost touch certain parts, you will create that belief, and in turn, you will manifest what you desire super-fast. You will experience the quantum leap that people talk about.

After years of personal development and believing in the Law of Attraction and manifestation, I still suffered through many bouts of doubt and questioning. *Will I ever really make this happen? Is this just a pipe dream? Am I setting myself up for disappointment?*

When I read Goddard's take on attracting your desires, it flipped a switch for me. I went from dabbling in this practice to taking it on as my natural state. I used my imagination to feel into desired situations on a regular basis; to the point that I intentionally blurred the lines between current events and imagined ones.

At the time I first read this book, I was working with a couple of clients who were not putting in the work required to achieve the transformation they had come to me for. Both wanted to quit the program, deciding it was "too hard" to get what they desired.

"I can't see how this is going to work for me," Dan had said, looking at the floor during our video call. "It obviously works for others, but I guess a loser like me is never going to get what I want."

My conversation with Jacob was similar.

I knew it wasn't the case for either man, and despite using my coaching skills and tools to support them, they both appeared to be falling into a deeper, darker hole in every call.

As a committed coach, I didn't take it upon myself to be attached to or responsible for their outcomes, but I equally did not want to let them off the hook. I wanted to see these men achieve their greatest dreams. After all, that was my role as their mentor.

Having just read Goddard's book, I was inspired to change my own approach. Throughout the day, when that familiar threat of overwhelm would creep into my conscious thought, I would immediately interrupt that program and replace it with my new, desired state. I imagined the way I wanted the calls to go. I pictured my clients smiling, happy, and eager to move forward. I thanked the universe for giving me this opportunity for contrast.

"While I don't want to continue to coach this type of client, I am grateful for the experience, and this is how I see Dan and Jacob feeling about themselves moving forward – doing the work, getting into the right mindset, and accomplishing insane results," I would say, while closing my eyes and feeling the immense glow of satisfaction I knew I would feel when it happened as I had pictured it.

At that time, although I had experienced the Law of Attraction in other areas of my life, where I was the person who was directly impacted on, or had to make changes, the idea of being able to influence the outcome for others felt beyond my grasp. A small part of me held an element of doubt beneath the surface of my confidence.

But I knew it was possible. I'd seen it for myself, and I'd seen it many times in others, especially within the mentoring group I was a part of. So, I trusted, and I believed. I really, really believed.

Within days, the scenario with both men changed dramatically. The conversations I had with them so closely resembled the ones I had imagined that it was almost scary. Some of the details I had envisaged, such as the wording they would use when they decided to stick with my program, manifested with uncanny accuracy.

"Brett, you were right," Jacob said, grinning at me from across the pond. "I'm so glad you didn't give up on me. I know this is going to work and I'm already feeling the change."

That's the power of belief.

The power of belief

You've decided what you want. You've set a goal. You know you're going to achieve it.

Or perhaps you're like I was, currently stuck on that last one.

Why? Because you don't truly believe yet, and are saying to yourself, "I'll believe it when I see it."

Despite this being a saying we've heard by everyone from our granddad to our colleagues, it's completely backwards.

You must *believe* first, in order to see it.

We MUST reprogram our minds to get into the state of belief. If you're disconnected from what you consciously think you want, it's almost guaranteed to be due to non-belief.

That's why I put so much value into this word, and so should you.

Just recently I found new meaning in the famous quote by Denis Waitley. I had spent around two years hearing this quote and never quite understood how it applied to me.

"It's not who you are that holds you back, it's who you think you're not!"

I had been invited to be part of an amazing Men's Summit and was working closely with an inspirational group of successful men. Every speaker was asked to share a story that would be relatable to the audience and had a theme of what it meant to be a man.

While I was preparing for the event, I happened to read this quote again. But this time, I saw it differently. I felt a strong need to dig deeper into this quote and find its meaning in my life.

I suddenly saw it very differently. It's crazy to think you can hear something over and over again and then finally, when you dig for the answer by asking questions, it simply "unfolds".

People always looked at me as a non-typical male, and subsequently I looked at myself that way. I had grown up with predominately all-female influences – my mother, grandmother, two aunties, and I had no father figure or male role model in my life. I felt deeply connected to my feminine and particularly with my wardrobe of bright colours and flowery shirts, I appeared as far from a beer-swilling Aussie bloke as you can get. I didn't get into fights, and I found it easy to talk to women.

However, on closer inspection of my years of self-sabotage and not living or speaking my truth, I had an epiphany.

Holy shit, I realised. *I am just about as "typical male" as they come.*

- I didn't show my feelings at all (I hadn't cried as an adult until the financial incident I mentioned at the start of the book).
- I was only fully honest when it suited me.
- I always thought I could fix situations myself because I was a "strong" man.
- I never asked for help. Looking back, I had many opportunities to change my situation by doing this, but was blinded by my own ego.

Despite appearances to the contrary, internally (where it matters) I was definitely using all the personality traits/behaviour that were attached to some poor self-beliefs. It wasn't conscious – these behaviours and habits were simply effects of the root cause, which was my belief. I had a damaged self-belief and lack of self-worth, and I didn't acknowledge that until I shone a light on it in 2018, when I started truly doing the work on myself.

Once you get the awareness of what's wrong or not working, decide to take action and find a way to reprogram it without quitting, you're guaranteed to start seeing dramatic changes in your life, just as I did.

Journal page

> *"Success is often achieved by those who don't know that failure is inevitable."*
> Coco Chanel

- This was the most important change I needed to make. What beliefs or behaviours do you recognise that are not serving you?

- What are 1 or 2 scenarios in your life that you feel you failed in and what could you have done differently to change the outcome?

- Which beliefs do you possess that you instinctively know are holding you back, and why?

- To manually change a belief/behaviour, we need to write out a positive (opposite) of the current belief/program running and start affirming it with feeling, as if we've already achieved it. Write on one sheet of paper the way you currently operate (negative or non-productive) and on another sheet, the positive/preferred. Focus on doing one of these (starting with the most important) for 30 days or until you see the change in your results.

- I mentioned that in order for affirmations to be effective, we have to get into the feeling "as if we already possess", however I know some people have trouble imagining something they've never done. So, ask yourself some deep questions. What could one or two of them be?

- There is a quote "it's not who you think you are that holds you back, it's who you think you're not that does." How does this relate to you?

- If you could wave a magic wand and fix any belief/behaviour, which ones do you believe would have the most significance in your transformation?

Belief

Super-Charged Freedom

Guidance

My decision to get help

In the movie *The Matrix*, Neo finally realises that he's living in a simulated reality and Morpheus trains him to become "The One", harnessing his special skills to bring peace to the Matrix.

As someone who didn't ask for help for most of my life, the message in this movie has a lot of significance for me.

I went through years thinking that I could sort things out on my own. I didn't need anyone's advice or guidance. I was certainly keen on being successful and making money, but I didn't truly invest. I didn't go to the next level of implementing and mastering, and of making the lessons I was presented with part of my life. Not surprisingly, when I did read a book or listen to a podcast, I didn't take the required actions and didn't move the needle much in my life as a result.

In November 2018, when I finally had my epiphany that I was going to be successful in my own way, I knew it was time to truly plant, water, and nurture my seed of success. I knew I had to stop trying to figure it out alone and stop thinking that I had the knowledge I needed. After all, my financial dire straits and general life situation was evidence that I hadn't mastered all that I learned and read about.

Once I made the decision to get help, I just had to find the right person to guide me. This is exactly the time I was contacted on Instagram by Marcus, the young guy I mentioned in an earlier chapter. He then introduced me to Mariko, who became my coach and was the catalyst to my first tastes of genuine success.

At this stage, I didn't even have savings to get started, but Mariko gave me a few tips to manifest the deposit I required to get started, and two days later it was green lights. When you're truly, subconsciously, connected to the reality you want, magic starts to happen.

From that point on, it wasn't all smooth sailing and, the truth is, when you decide to engage help and learn and apply the necessary skills to succeed, it's confronting. You often need to stop some bad behaviours and paradigms, and when I say stop, I mean swap. Because if you simply stop a negative paradigm without replacing its polar opposite, often a new negative will take its place.

In the few years since, my life has changed dramatically. With the help of numerous mentors and coaches, I'm now thriving in most areas of my life.

Bob Proctor is my ultimate guide and mentor for changing my paradigms and beliefs; James Whittaker (author of *Think and Grow Rich: The Legacy* and co-producer of the movie with the same name) is my performance coach; Cathryn Mora (director of Change Empire Books) is my book coach; David Meltzer is my business coach; as well as other coaches for my health, fitness, and general wellbeing.

In each one of those areas, I've had unprecedented progress and growth, and I know unequivocally that I wouldn't have reached these outcomes alone.

Ultimately, when you need help because things aren't working the way you'd like, stop and decide if you would benefit from a guide in the area you're struggling. It will be the ticket to the fast train, overriding your unicycle.

Bob Proctor's journey

Bob tells the story of when he decided to start his journey, he was earning $4,000 per year and owed $6,000. *That's not a big deal*, I thought at the time, then immediately concluded that it was much like saying you earn $40,000 per year and owe $60,000. The fact he could come out of that and reach such a prosperous place within a relatively short amount of time is incredibly impressive. But this wasn't the part of the story that sold me on Bob.

The part that truly resonated with me was the action he took and the results he got after his first mentor, Ray Stanford, had suggested that Bob read *Think and Grow Rich* by Napoleon Hill. He said, "Bob, if you read and follow the instructions in this book, you'll get rich," and Bob's response was, "I can't read." It wasn't quite true – Bob could read – but he hadn't read much since school.

Bob asked Ray why this book was so important and how he knew it could work for him. Ray replied by asking Bob these questions, "Have you ever seen me without money?" and Bob replied, "No." He then asked, "Have you ever seen me sick?" and again Bob replied, "No." Finally, he said, "Do you ever see me unhappy?" and, of course, Bob had never seen Ray unhappy at all. Then Ray went on to say, "Bob, whenever I see you, you're asking someone for a couple of bucks. You never have money. You often have a cold or look unwell, and many times I've seen you quite depressed," and Bob agreed with these statements, as confronting as they were.

Ray said, "This book will find you happy, healthy, and wealthy, just like me. However, there's one important key to ensuring this will work for you."

Bob asked, "What's that?"

"You MUST have discipline."

Bob read *Think and Grow Rich* religiously. He wrote down on a card that he wanted to earn $25,000 for the year, which in 1961, with his previous track record this was a ludicrous idea. He kept working on his affirmation of the goal and when that year ended, he actually earned over $100,000. In the following few years, he earned over $1,000,000.

So how did he make the money? He came up with an idea. *Why don't I start a cleaning business? I'll clean floors; I'm not proud,* he thought. He started the business in Toronto and grew it into a multi-national company with offices in Canada, the United States, and England.

Bob recalls that at one point, he wondered how on earth he had really achieved those heights. He had virtually no schooling and no business experience, but was eager to learn more. He'd been listening to Earl Nightingale's record, *The Strangest Secret* for a while, and wondered if he could work with him? Earl and his business partner, Lloyd Conant, were pioneers in teaching people personal development, and their business was very successful. He approached them for a low-paying job so that he could observe their practice, and Lloyd introduced Bob to a little green book called *The Science of Getting Rich* by Wallace D. Wattles. This was Bob's next "all-in" program, and after five years of working with Earl and Lloyd, Bob decided to start his own business.

That "little green book" was also the inspiration for Rhonda Byrne in creating the hit movie *The Secret*.

Finding your own mentor

"I don't want to pay someone to help me ... I don't have the money ... What if I don't get anything out of it?"

These are the things I said to myself multiple times over the years. I worried that investing in a coach or mentor was out of my reach. It felt like a risk, and I decided that doing it myself was the best option.

Looking back, this was a key factor to me not fully reaching my goals and achieving my dreams. I would achieve a certain level of success and then back away from them or not go all the way. Something was often getting in my way, but it wasn't obvious what that was.

Once I invested in coaches, everything changed. I realised that my aversion to getting and paying for support was a barrier to my success.

If you're like I was, or most people who come to me for coaching, you know what you want and you have goals, but at some point along the way, worry, doubt, and fear kick in and override your ability to move in that direction.

Make the decision now to invest in a coach or mentor for an area which is important to you. If you want to reach new heights in your life, relationship, and business or career, find someone you resonate with, someone who inspires you. Their words and energy need to really make you feel something special.

Getting referrals is valuable, but go beyond this and do your own research. Talk to prospective coaches or mentors and see if you are a good fit for each other. This is important, because when you trust in someone to help you, you need to know that you like them and also that they've got the necessary experience to help you.

A great coach WILL NOT give up on you. Even if you piss them off. A great coach or mentor does what's required to help you grow, and growth isn't always "sunshine and rainbows", otherwise everyone would be winning.

Search online, make a shortlist, go to some seminars, workshops, watch their videos on YouTube or organise a Discovery session. Take some time to work out who feels right for you. But then GO! Take ACTION as soon as you can. Why? Because making a quick decision is one of the common denominators of success. Some of the most successful people make quick (calculated) decisions and rarely change their mind, if ever. The opposite to this (which I was) is taking loads of time to decide and changing your mind frequently.

Do your research and then DECIDE!

Masterminding

If you already have the support of a coach/mentor, a mastermind adds another important realm to the manifestation of your dreams and desires. Masterminding with people with the right intention and order will help you dramatically. As an individual we "know what we know", and only have our own experiences to search through when making decisions.

In addition to having the influence of experienced people, being in a mastermind offers great accountability. If you say you're going to do something and you return the following week, you want to be able to say you did it.

Who you mastermind *with* is crucial. Make sure everyone is fully committed to positive change and growth. If you choose a few people (no more than 8-10) and one of them is out of harmony, it will totally disrupt the power of the mastermind.

Choose carefully. Try to find people who are quite different from you, or who have more success. If you truly want to grow, you need the right people. As the saying goes, "If you're the smartest person in the room, you're in the wrong room."

Napoleon Hill mentions in *The Power of the Mastermind* that even Andrew Carnegie (richest man in the world in the early 1900s) owed much of his triumph to masterminding with other successful people. Henry Ford and Thomas A. Edison did it too. In fact, many of the current world's thought leaders, including Bob Proctor and Tony Robbins, owe some of their achievements to masterminding.

Can you think of some people you could do this with starting next week? Even start with one or two. Just start!

Journal page

> *"You just have to have the guidance to lead you in the direction until you can do it yourself."* Tina Yothers

- Have you decided to get help from a coach/mentor? If so, why?
- What sort of help do you feel you need? List some of the benefits.
- Have you considered who could be a good mentor/coach for you and why?
- Who has been a good mentor for you so far, and why?
- If you were giving others guidance, what would be one or two pieces of advice you feel could help someone in business or life in general?
- Start listing some people you could mastermind with.
- What do you believe the benefits of masterminding will be for you?

Guidance

Abundance

A lack of money isn't the problem

Most men who to come to me for coaching want to earn more money. They believe that with more money, they'll be happier, more fulfilled, more confident, and it will give them more stability. Beyond that, there are perceived societal expectations and the ability or lack thereof to fulfil their role as a provider.

Some men think it's just about *how* to earn more money. They want me to teach them what to do to make more money; to show them what I'm doing or help them discover ways to bring in more income.

Other men have insight a little beyond this. They do realise that it's not really about the "how" or the "doing" – they know a mindset shift will be required to reach their financial goals, but they're still looking outside themselves. They think there is something they're not seeing, and by working with me, they will suddenly discover the secret. They want me to simply point them in the right direction and after that, the money will flow.

Remember, these men are smart, capable, hardworking men. There is nothing "wrong" with someone just because their bank balance isn't currently reflecting the abilities they know they have. Equally, there is nothing wrong with asking for help.

And in a way, it is a simple mindset shift, but at the same time, it's so much more than that.

The issue here is that so many men – so many people – are still looking *outside themselves* for the key. That if they just tweak something they're doing, something they're not doing, or approach it with a different attitude, that all their problems will be solved, and money will no longer be an issue.

Their focus is on what they don't have and how they're limited in some way. They blame situations or other people – or the world around them. What kind of job they have, what they're doing in their career or business, where they live, what they look like. These are external factors, and while they can contribute to our financial situation, they are not why we got there, and changing them won't make any difference if we don't go deeper.

They will say things like, "I would love to earn more money, but I'm already earning in the top bracket of my industry," "I'd love to earn more, but that would mean getting another qualification or learning something new, and I don't have the time for that with the kids and everything else ..." or "I definitely want to make more money, but first I have to focus on paying off some debt ..."

Do any of these sound familiar? Have you said something similar to yourself or someone else?

Don't worry, you're not alone.

Ultimately, all these things are excuses – but when we say them to ourselves (or others), we believe that they are facts. They *feel* like legitimate reasons, but in reality, everything is changeable.

Even when men are ready for coaching, it's usually not going to be the journey they think it will be. They *will* earn more, but not by doing what they think they need to do.

Delving into your own money story will unearth a whole range of limitations you didn't even know you had been placing on yourself.

My client Brendan came to me in a place of severe financial struggle. His wife was the primary breadwinner, as his income was totally erratic and mostly very low. Brendan felt like the key to his success lay just around the corner with the next idea, the next qualification, the next course. Nothing he tried or invested in seemed to achieve its full potential, and he was beyond frustrated.

Brendan was from a middle-class American family with strong family values. He felt like he was letting down his wife and children by not earning more. He was driven by the need to provide and to "be a man". He was so focused on the "things", the external factors, and "how" to best achieve his goals (which vehicle, which program, which qualification). He hadn't examined what was going on for him at a deeper level.

When Brendan started working with me, I could feel his frustration deeply. I recognised it in myself, and how I had previously operated in my own marriage and life. I knew that if Brendan was anything like me, he'd need to have quiet time, and to go deeper, to ask the universe for what he wanted, and then be open to receiving.

"Brendan, I want you to take half an hour of quiet time every day this week," I said. "I just want you to quiet your mind. Don't think about the current situations or circumstances, and just allow any positive guidance or ideas to come to you. Take note of them, but it's not about you doing something. It's about just being with yourself."

He wasn't giving himself any mental space to breathe, and to allow ideas and thoughts to come to him. He was too busy trying to control everything that was happening outside and gave no energy to the inside.

Our conscious mind is reported to operate at 40 bits per second (bps), in comparison with our subconscious mind, which races ahead at 40,000,000 bps. Trying to control your outcomes by addressing exterior forces using your conscious brain, or your "will", is much like trying to break into a government agency's computer mainframe using your Nintendo. It's powerless to achieve the outcome you desire.

Working with me for a few months, Brendan finally realised he had been fighting the wrong battle.

He let go of trying to physically make things happen. He stopped trying to control things. Instead, he started quietening his mind. He listened to his inner voice and became open to receive. He reprogrammed the old, unhelpful paradigms which had not been serving him, by writing down his goals, repeating affirmations, and really feeling into the life he wanted.

A couple of key people came into his life who created new and exciting opportunities for him in his previously flailing business, and then new ideas seemed to crop up out of nowhere, which created even more opportunities. He also took action because he felt inspired, rather than because he was desperate.

None of this is coincidence, as this is how the Universal Laws operate.

Your money patterns

How did you get where you are now?

First, let's look at your earnings history. What do you currently earn or what's the most you've ever earned in a year?

Look back over the past 5 to 10 years, write down those figures, and then average it out ... Are there any obvious patterns in your earnings related to the average? Namely, have you ever had a year where you earned, say, $100k, and in the previous year, you earned $50k and then had an adjustment the following year, so that really, your average was closer to $75k? I did. In 2006, I earned $50k, 2007 was close to $100k, and 2008 dropped back to $75k. I convinced myself it was because of the Global Financial Crisis and moving cities, but my income had been erratic for years.

These earning patterns are not really to do with the money itself. We have to think about money as an energy, not the paper it's printed on or the gold coins that represent it. The higher your energy is around your own self-worth, the higher your stock goes up; when you internally have a higher view of yourself, you can earn more money and live a better life.

Get clear on why you want more

Get clear on your "why". Why do you want to earn more money? What does it mean to you? What will more money create in your life? What will it give you?

If your answer was something like, "a Porsche," or "a new house", or "regular holidays", then dig deeper. If you had those things, how do you think you'd feel?

Happier, more confident, more free ...?

Create a vision of what money means to you and what you believe it will bring you.

When Jonathan started working with me, he had a goal of earning $10 million a year. He'd been dreaming about it for years and with his salary in the five-figure range, he was far, far from this goal. When speaking about his current progress towards his goal, I could see the deflation written all over his body.

The next question I asked him was, "What does $10 million represent for you?"

Jonathan's eyes immediately lit up. "It would mean we'd have no mortgage, we'd have savings, we'd be able to invest in property, and be able to easily pay for our children's education."

With that response, I could see that he was already a step closer to achieving his goal.

Jonathan had been really focused on his goal, which was great, and had started various businesses to achieve the goal, but hadn't really connected with what this money would bring him. Besides that, his businesses had "failed", and he hadn't forgiven himself for putting his family through the financial and emotional stress of his near-bankruptcy. So, there was also a lot of emotional turmoil wrapped up in his financial situation.

The key to moving towards new goals is getting clear on why you want this goal and what it would mean to you.

Millionaire traits

When you are clear on why you want more money, how do you bridge the gap?

When you think about it, you got to where you are because of a certain set of beliefs and resultant actions.

"What got you here will not get you there," Abraham Hicks is famous for saying.

In order to reach an amount of money or achieve a lifestyle you've never had, you need to be prepared to approach things differently, and essentially "be" a different person. The key is to identify as someone who earns that much. You need to think and act like someone who is a $10 million earner (or however much you want). You must adopt the habits of someone who does earn that much and get into the mindset of someone who is already there.

What characteristics does a millionaire typically have?

This answer is many and varied, but generally they will get out of bed early; they work on their mind and goals first thing in the morning by doing affirmations, journaling, goal setting, and practising gratitude. They will also usually workout or move their body in some way.

Millionaires are often, although not always, focused and disciplined. If they make the decision to do something, they will stick to their word – not just to others, but to themselves.

More than likely, a millionaire with a successful business will be positive and happy. Not false, pretend happy, but more focused on things that make them feel good and bring about positive results, rather than focusing on what doesn't work, and what makes them feel bad, stressed, or worried.

Of course, there are always moments and situations where you'll immediately react by feeling bad, but it must be temporary. Your overall mindset and focus need to be more on what makes you feel good, what is going right, and what you can learn from any situation in order to progress and grow.

"Feeling the feelings" is key to the universal Law of Attraction. It means conjuring up the feeling of happiness (or abundance, or confidence, or whatever you seek) from any situation or thought that you can. The more you feel a certain way, the more you will bring situations towards you that create those same feelings.

One of the hardest things at first can be to feel the way you want to feel, based on your goals and desires, rather than constantly feeling based on what currently IS. When you keep your energy focused on what IS, rather than what you WANT, you get more of what is.

Therefore, in order to start feeling the way you want to feel, earning the money you'd like to earn, and reaching the success you'd like to reach, you need to start with exploring what's happening on the inside and then shift your thoughts and actions accordingly.

In Jonathan's case, connecting with his why enabled him to think creatively about how to achieve his $10 million goal.

He came up with a consultancy business based on his decades of experience in customer service. He narrowed down to a niche where the market wasn't competitive for his ideal clients, and customer service would set them apart. Aware of the difference it could make, businesses were prepared to invest heavily in Jonathan's support.

A year later, his business, and his finances, are flourishing; and it's only the beginning. Jonathan has plans for licensing his system and expansion is on the cards.

"I can't afford it"

Another common hurdle in the path of achieving our goals is saying that you can't afford things.

The first time I spoke to a sales consultant from the Proctor Gallagher Institute, I was excited to hear about the 13-month Bob Proctor Coaching Program.

Of course, the first question I asked was, "How much is it?".

"$10,000," he said.

My heart sank because I knew it was out of my reach. "Oh mate, there's no way I can afford that," I said.

He suggested an alternate program for $440, which was exactly the amount I had saved. I signed up.

A couple of years later, when I had progressed in leaps and bounds in my life and business, I became the person on the other side of the phone.

Jack was a client who abandoned his program, and hadn't finished paying it off either. However, I saw great potential in him, and reminded myself of why I became a coach in the first place, and how I was here to serve others. I had made the commitment to never give up.

A few months after he'd left my program, I spoke to Jack to check in and see how he was travelling and to offer a discussion about joining one of my new mastermind client groups. His first response was, "Thanks for reaching out. I can't afford to do that. I have to buy a new car and I've got kids' schooling to consider. I'm on a strict budget."

I recognised that response from myself in years gone by, always using my current reality and sets of conditions as to why I couldn't possibly consider doing "this" or "that."

Hearing this response and considering the types of clients I admit to these groups, I thanked Jack for his response and said, "No problem, Jack. I hear what you're saying and I can appreciate it because I've been there myself. However, at the moment, you're only looking at it based on your current reality, and making your decision based on what you can or can't do today, rather than making your decision on what you *want* to do. The more you keep accepting your current reality about why you can't do something, the longer you're going to stay there. So, the decision you need to make today is whether you're prepared to be open to looking at a new way to move forward, or to simply say no and just accept the current reality the way it is."

Several of my other clients had been in similar financial situations when they joined me, but had been ready to receive significant change and were open to looking for ways to make it happen. They found financial support where they could, and invested in themselves and their desired future. Taking the action inspired more action and the subsequent change. I could tell from Jack's response that he wasn't ready yet.

Jack mulled it over for a few moments. "I see what you're saying, and I do want to change my situation. What do I need to do?" he said.

"You need to make the decision that you want to do it, and then find a way to make it happen. I suggest you read Chapter 3 of *Think and Grow Rich*, which is about faith. Then write out an affirmation along the lines of, "I am so happy and grateful now that I have the money to be in Brett's mastermind group, and am working towards my goals."

I didn't want to push Jack to join if it wasn't the right move for him. But I did want him to see the ways he was limiting himself, and keeping himself exactly where he was already stuck.

Jack joined the group.

The transformation was incredible. Jack upped the ante and made the decision to pay his program ahead of schedule. Money started flowing to him from his side business, from foundations he'd put in place previously but hadn't materialised yet; and within a month, he paid off the program in full.

The key is in making your decisions based on what you want, not what currently is. Where you are now is a sum of all the decisions and actions you've taken up until now. If you want something different, you must do something different.

Other common blocks and pitfalls

My poor relationship with money was perhaps my biggest downfall. I partially attribute this to the habits of the role models available in my life (and the role models of my role models before them), and it was also a matter of developing poor money habits of my own.

I always wanted that next best thing, and it started to become more of a coping mechanism for the other aspects of myself that weren't working. Bob Proctor says there is a direct correlation between your relationship with money and your self-image or how you feel about yourself. My image was very poor. I had an unhealthy obsession with getting rid of money as quickly as possible.

When I was in real estate, I was offered a phenomenal deal on a townhouse in Brighton (Melbourne) Australia. It's one of the wealthiest areas of Melbourne, right near the beach, and it was where I worked and sold property. My wife and I put a deposit down and applied for a loan. After anxiously waiting the few days it took to get a response, we were really disappointed to hear that the loan wasn't approved.

"Elissa, let's go to Dunk Island for a holiday," I said, five minutes after hanging up the phone to the bank officer.

Elissa looked up from her coffee, her brow furrowed in confusion. "What? Shouldn't we try and sort out the loan first?"

What I hadn't told her was that our knockback was certainly the result of my very poor credit history. Because I was in the habit of concealing some of the deeper truths from my wife, she knew I'd had some money issues, but not how deeply they ran.

"Oh, I think the universe is showing us that it's not the right house. Maybe we need to step back for a while and see what happens," I said, immediately deflecting my focus away from our financial strife. They were returning our deposit, and I needed to spend it.

I didn't want to face the truth about my situation. I had feigned optimism when applying for the loan, but now the gig was up. There was clearly no point in me addressing or facing my issues, and I didn't even realise I was avoiding it. Everything about money was short-term for me. I wouldn't have a shiny new house to focus on, so I needed another fix.

Did I know the value of a long-term strategy? Hell, yes. But I was hypnotised by my spending spree mentality – always looking for short-term satisfaction. Buying "things", going out drinking, partying, never truly focused on a strategy for the future.

My wife was much more sensible and future focused. She had great ideas and the personality and commitment to implement them, but I was good at distracting her, or at times, simply lying to her. She never truly knew the depth of my distraction*.

(*Elissa was a truly great wife and even better friend. I'm lucky I've repaired or restored part of that trust back with her since our son Orlando was born. It took me a solid few years, but I got there and was grateful to have made our friendship work, as I'm positive it helps my son having that sort of stability between two parents.)

If we only examine our spending decisions, we're only treating the effect. We're not looking at the underlying cause. Our money habits don't come from nowhere.

Our childhood role models do have an initial part to play, although this isn't about blame. Looking back at my childhood, I had to forgive both the adults in my life, and myself. I also had to let go of some stories in order to see the effects dissipate when it came to spending money.

Growing up, my mum moved us around a lot. I went to seven different primary schools. We never had a lot of money, but my mum always made sure I had what I wanted. We lived by the principle of surviving week to week and getting a treat on special occasions. Perhaps that's where part of it stemmed. I also recognise not having my dad or a father figure impacted me, especially as a teenager. I was a great candidate for juvenile detention with my shoplifting, breaking and entering, graffiti, and stealing cars, and I often felt a yearning for that male influence. Every time I would reach out to my dad, I wouldn't get what I was hoping for.

I had to forgive my dad, my mum, and myself, for the past. While those many crazy and sometimes outrageous and dangerous experiences have made me what I am today, it doesn't mean I want to repeat them.

In addition to the money stories I dismantled, there were other benefits I realised from my past. My dad was not present in my life, and through this, he actually gave me a gift unknowingly. He wasn't equipped to be a hands-on father, and by not being there, he created a desire in me to be an amazing inspiration to my own son. I believe I've been doing that from the day he was born and I'm not slowing down.

The point of talking about the past is simply to recognise that we all have a history. Who we are today is a sum of that history, but we don't want to carry it around forever. You need the awareness of what's not working in your life, and what isn't serving you; and then it's time to go through a process of recognising where it came from, forgiving yourself and others, and then moving through it. It's like unblocking yourself and allowing yourself to break free from your old stories.

Take the time to look back and ask yourself ...

"Am I holding on to crap that doesn't serve me?"

Creating a new self-image

Most of us are going through life wanting to be happy. We are looking for things on the outside which we believe will make us happy. It will never happen, or at least not to the depth we want it to. The truth is that true happiness comes from the inside. It's from loving ourselves unconditionally and accepting ourselves that we can begin to find what we need – from within.

How do we know where we're lacking in our self-image, and what do we need to do in order to change it?

Ask yourself these questions and carefully consider your answers. You may want to write them down.

What is some of the negative self-talk you're engaging in?

Do you say things to yourself like, *I'm not good enough ... I'm not as young and energetic as I used to be ... I'm not smart enough ... I'm too ... I can't do this because ...*

The more you focus on what you don't want or what you don't have, you will stay in lack. You are reinforcing what you don't want to think, feel, or do, and giving yourself more of the same. You can't get to a place of abundance from here. The Laws of Attraction and Vibration say that you can't make a huge jump – from complete negativity to overwhelming positivity – but what you can do is slightly improve your thinking, one step at a time.

You receive a phone call from the bank and someone has spent $3,000 of your savings, yet that was this months bill payments and the bank doesn't know when they'll get the return of funds, as it can't yet be proven as stolen. You start to spiral into depression. "I'm going to receive a default on my credit history." "I don't have anymore income for another month, how will I eat." "I can't borrow from anyone and my credit cards are maxed, probably gonna get kicked out of our rental."

These feelings are natural, but they are absolutely unhelpful. So how do we change the inner dialogue? First of all it starts with the awareness that you can change your situation. Next step is to start focusing on how it feels to have this problem resolved quickly. How does it make you feel getting another call from the bank stating "Mr Scott, we have great news. Video footage of a woman using your card has been sourced and the police know who she is. We have updated your account with the $3,000" Do you feel elation? Relief? Which bill do you pay first? It's a satisfying feeling right?

Lastly, it's writing out ideas of how you could possibly solve the situation. But not necessarily how 'YOU' would do it. Look at this issue from someone else's point of view. What would Tony Robbins do in this situation, not taking into account his current lifestyle and back balance, his personality. What ideas do you think Tony might have? Or perhaps someone like Henry Ford. He was well known for having a desk with push buttons attached, each button would call to an employee who would come in and answer any question he had. After all, Henry barely attended school at all.

Focus on solutions. Always know, there is often a way to change the situation and it doesn't start by picking up the phone or going straight into action. Often I've fixed situation simply by increasing my mood, but taking myself for a walk in nature. Raising my vibration has completely solved situations for me, more than a few times.

Do you lack energy or enthusiasm for things you used to enjoy?

If so, when you think about it, where does that come from? I used to identify as a major extrovert, yet over the years I increasingly disliked crowds, parties, or any social event. I dismissed it as just getting older and becoming more introverted. Looking back, I know that it was just me "showing up", unconsciously putting on a mask and looking happy and bright. It was a way of avoiding people seeing the real me – the me who had no idea what I was doing and how to get out of the rollercoaster shit storm I'd been living in.

Have you experienced a big change in personality or habits?

Do you love what you do, or do you hate it?

If you feel drained and frustrated by your daily activities, whether that be in business or a job, you might think, "Yes, but if I keep going, eventually I'll get the result and then I can move up."

It actually has the opposite effect. Doing work which drains or frustrates you will cause more angst, stress, and anxiety, and you'll end up burning out and losing energy altogether. It doesn't enable you to make the progress you desire.

There will be "things" you don't enjoy doing, even in your dream business or job, but overall, if you're doing something you truly love doing, your self-belief and self-esteem will skyrocket.

Do you look for validation from others to feel good?

Humans crave interaction, affection, and validation. It's fair to say that all people seek a certain amount of validation from others, although some people are much more evolved in terms of not allowing the opinions or words of others to affect them at a deep level.

Do you crave phrases like, "You're so smart," "You're so handsome," "I couldn't have done this without you," or similar?

Does attention from your romantic partner make you swell with pride, but a lack of it makes you look elsewhere for the same? Do compliments from business partners fuel you to succeed and criticism have you tempted to call quits on the partnership?

Looking for validation from others is an endless and very unsatisfying game. It's human nature to take people for granted, and the saying, "familiarity breeds contempt" is fairly true. The longer somebody is in your life, the less likely they are to feed you with the constant stream of compliments you require to feel appreciated. This means you'll always be chasing the next best person, activity, or venture to fuel your ego.

This is why it's imperative to sustain your own needs by recognising and feeling good about your self-worth.

Do you avoid speaking to groups?

If you're a coach or entrepreneur, do you avoid situations where you need to speak to groups, such as live videos, speaking to others at networking events, or presenting? If so, do you find that you're fine speaking one-on-one?

This can be a sign of low self-confidence, based on a fear of what the group will think of you. In a one-on-one discussion, it's easier to read the body language and reaction of the other person. That can make it more comfortable to speak your mind or share your feelings, without as much concern for how it will be received. In a large group, however, you can't keep track of everybody's reactions or impressions, so dealing with potential reactions can be overwhelming. The bigger the group, the more concerning it can be for people who are lacking in the confidence to just do and say what they feel, regardless.

I'm not saying that you need to disregard what anybody thinks of us, because as humans, most of us still do care a certain degree, but if you have true inner belief and confidence, you can share your message more courageously.

I used to act confident in front of a group, but internally I was suffering. I wasn't aware of my barriers at the time, but I did know that I was feeling fear and I passed it off as a fear of public speaking. Looking back, I was so lacking in self-belief that I was worried how people would see me and what I might say, which would make me look stupid. I was able to put on a brave face, but it was all for show.

Ask yourself these questions:

- How do you remove these barriers?
- How do you go from this to making more money?
- Ask yourself if you're wearing a mask? Is that the "real" you?

- What would happen if you didn't change your self-image?
- Who are some people that have self-images you like? Could you start to "act" like them?
- What is one thing you could implement today to change how you internally view yourself?

Start reading more on topics relating to the Universal Laws and people who've used them to earn more money than they'll ever need. If you're like me, and struggle to keep your attention on a book, go to YouTube, Audible or somewhere else that you can listen to a book or watch a video related to the topic. Look for recommended or popular books and authors, and then see who you feel connected to, so that you can go deeper.

Making money can't be motivated by greed, because the satisfaction is generally short-lived. Make more money so you can help more people. Help your family and friends, help people that you personally would like to help. Share the wealth. Teach others.

Keep learning. One of the other great lessons Bob Proctor teaches is, "There's only two ways to make money." When I first heard this, I thought, *That's not true, I've been offered half a dozen different ways just this week!*

However, he's right.

You're either working for money or money is working for you.

So, when you're ready to start earning the money you truly desire, remember – it's got to be you in charge of money; you're the boss. Choose some strategies or ways you can build your wealth via multiple sources of income, ideally including some passive income streams. I believe most successful people have at least 8 to 10 different ways. That way, if one stops working, you've got backup and the income you "work for" is no longer the revenue you depend upon to pay bills and live.

Money management

After getting through some of my worst financial moments, I decided to hire a financial adviser. At the time I made the decision I wasn't earning much, but I knew that my success was inevitable, and even when you get stronger at earning money, it doesn't always translate into knowing how to look after or grow it. Adam Kennedy of Ethical Financial Advice also became a friend and trusted confidante, and his support and knowledge has highlighted the money areas I used to be completely oblivious to or in denial about.

My advice is to find someone you trust to give you some great advice about understanding budgets, investing money, handling super, and creating a nest egg. Even if you earn ten times the amount of money, you could easily find ten more ways to spend it. Bob Proctor often tells people that even when he earned $1,000,000 the first time, it disappeared quickly, and that was back in the early 60s when things were much cheaper. He often advises getting good quality financial advice. Do it before you make your millions, because you'd hate to get too busy and carried away and then wake up one day realising you should have and could have.

Handling money poorly is a paradigm; it's a habit. You can change it, but you've got to reprogram it and put things in order, so you don't need to think about it. Have it automated in a system. Set and forget.

The book *The Richest Man in Babylon* by George Clason states these seven timeless principles.

- **Start thy purse to fattening.** This principle outlines putting aside 10% of all you earn as savings, even if you're paying off debt. It's about being consistent and preparing for your future starting from today.

- **Control thy expenditures.** Don't allow your expenses to become overly inflated as you earn more. Resist the temptation to continually up the ante with your lifestyle spending.
- **Make thy gold multiply.** You don't get wealthy by working. You get wealthy by having your money earn money. Invest wisely and take advantage of time and compounding interest.
- **Guard thy treasures from loss.** While investment is essential for financial growth, it's important to remember that in almost all investments, there is the potential for loss. Balance your investments so that risk is mitigated. Essentially, don't put all your eggs in one basket and ensure you understand the risks involved with every investment.
- **Make of thy dwelling a profitable investment.** While Clason meant for this to be encouragement to own your own home, and allowing your family to thrive in it (therefore creating a feeling of abundance), these days this point is the most debatable, because many financial advisers recommend buying investments and renting, rather than buying, your own home. I'll sit this one out!
- **Insure a future income.** This point is related to preparing for unforeseen future circumstances and protecting yourself and/or your family for retirement or other financially negative situations which could come your way. In today's terms, this refers to retirement planning and income insurance.
- **Increase thy ability to earn.** You are paid what you are worth to the market (and the world). Educate and enrich your knowledge with continual learning and you will reap the rewards.

While you are fulfilling these financial goals, you will learn so much more in the process. It's not just about the money. The skills you acquire along the way will enrich you in many other ways.

Are you ready to earn more and keep growing it? I am!

Journal page

> *"Abundance is not something we acquire. It is something we tune into." Dr Wayne Dyer*

- How are you with money? What's your relationship? Does it control you, or are you in charge?

- Do you feel as though you may have a money-block or does it flow? If blocked, what do you think may be the root cause?

- What does Abundance mean to you? Is it just money? Or are there other elements for you? If so, what are they?

- What is the most you've ever earned? What's the average? Often, we can earn more money and then the following year or period, we have a correction. How about you? And how much would you love to earn?

- Often, a lack of abundance is attached to our internal self-image. How is your own self-belief, self-worth, and self-confidence?

- What other sources of revenue do you have, or would you like to have? Investments? Property? Stocks? Other businesses? MSIs (multiple sources of income)

- Millionaire traits are: Focus, Discipline & Decision-making. How do you stack up? What else do you think a millionaire does to be successful and is this a status you'd like to achieve?

Super-Charged Freedom

Abundance

Super-Charged Freedom

Self-Care

"We can't practise compassion with others, if we can't treat ourselves kindly," says Brené Brown. She goes on to say, "If walking a mile in someone else's shoes is a way to describe the concept of empathy, then self-compassion is almost like learning how to tie them in the first place. Self-compassion is the key to practising empathy for others. You need to learn how to do one before you can truly do the other."

"I'm so busy"

Modern society celebrates busyness. "I'm so busy," is one of the most heard phrases today. People are hustling, working 60-70 hours a week, pulling all-nighters, pushing themselves to burnout, all to try and "make it work".

If you live like this, like many other men on the planet, it's important to understand that this has an impact, not only on you, but on your families and those around you. If you are constantly pushing and hustling, you don't allow time to dream and create visions of something better for yourself. Besides, who wants money and "success" if you're just too damn tired to enjoy it?

Giving yourself time and space allows you time to decide if what you have been working towards is actually important. Many of the things we are working towards – cars, houses, boats – will not make us happy. People desire them because they believe the having of those things will make them happy, but it is far from true. I'm yet to meet a person who has been fulfilled by their material possessions, and in fact, those who do focus on the attainment of these things will always want the next shiny new thing immediately after. Once they buy the items, their incessant desire for new objects kicks in again, and they want just one more thing. The pursuit of material objects is insatiable.

When you get clearer on doing the work for yourself and become more focused on improving your internal self-image, you may find that your need to buy things starts to dissipate. As a recovering shopaholic myself, I have more recently found myself walking out of shops without purchases, because I've asked myself some tough questions about what was driving me to pull out my wallet in the first place.

For example, if you desire a Porsche, what do you feel the car would give you? Status, confidence, power, happiness, thrill, or excitement are pretty common desires. People believe that by having the car, they will feel these things. And to be sure, driving a flashy car can be lots of fun – but you might be surprised to learn that many people who drive these cars are just as fucked up as the rest of us. They have all the same issues and all the same worries as a guy driving last century's Hyundai. The people driving those cars who *are* happy found the key to

Self-Care

happiness elsewhere – inside themselves – and the car was just a fun thing for them to drive around.

The lesson here is that allowing yourself time and space to just "be" is integral to going to the next level in your life. It might seem counterintuitive to get more by doing less, but I assure you it's true. I recently saw a quote from George Monbiot that said, "If wealth was the inevitable result of hard work and enterprise, every woman in Africa would be a millionaire."

So, if hard work doesn't get us there, what will?

Self-care will go a long way to getting you started. It's no coincidence that all your best ideas pop into your head in the shower, during a run, or in the pool. Our mind is zoned out or focused on something which is primarily a physical activity and not taking up valuable thinking and creative space.

This is where the magic happens.

If you spend time in nature, relaxing, taking part in hobbies and sports you love, or even just daydreaming, ideas and inspiration about how you want to live your life, and what you can do to get there, ideas will appear. These ideas happen when you least expect it, rather than when you schedule 20 minutes into your day for "brainstorming good ideas".

Feel grateful for what you have, enjoy your surroundings, appreciate your loved ones, see the beauty in small things ... and the more you feel relaxed, happy, and grateful, the more you will attract things, people, and situations into your life which inspire more relaxation, happiness, and gratitude.

What I do to relax

Mountains, beach, movies, playing with my son. There are many things I enjoy doing, but most of all I love getting outside and enjoying fresh air and exercising. It's hard to not feel grateful when you're activating endorphins.

One of my favourite things to do in summer is to pair a mountain climb with a beach swim. The contrast between the effort of walking up a mountain in the heat, followed by a swim in cold ocean water is invigorating, and I usually come away with a rush of new ideas and inspiration.

When I was running a fitness facility, I used to offer to take members on hikes and climbs once a month. After one climb up Mt Cooroora in Queensland (where I've competed in the King of the Mountain race, three years' running), we drove to Noosa and walked through the National Park, finishing up with a splash around in the Fairy Pools, which are connected to some beautiful cliffside scenery and stunning turquoise waters.

It was a great day and everything went to plan. We brought kids along too and they loved it; in fact, many of the young ones were able to climb quicker and easier than the adults. At the end of the day, when we were walking through Alexandra Bay to get to the Fairy Pools, I forgot to warn everyone that it's a nudist beach, and not the uber-cool, sexy type you might discover in Europe. It's generally frequented by overweight men in the company of other men. I think it's great that people have somewhere to go and not get arrested for their naturalist preferences, but the kids couldn't stop pointing and yelling, "I can see his willy!" and all the parents were completely floored with laughter.

These unexpected, funny moments don't happen when you are chained to your computer and focusing all your energy on chasing the next dollar.

Why is time out important?

Think of taking a break as a form of turning your computer off and on — that secret fix for when your computer is not working properly. The same goes for you.

When you start to feel fogged or blocked or overwhelmed or burnt-out, stop what you're doing and do something that helps you have a release from this pressure or stress. I'm not saying you need to quit for the day – although that can be a good idea at times – I'm suggesting you just have a breather. Go for a walk. Watch a TV show or movie that makes you happy (not a doco about serial killers.) Read a book that uplifts you. Catch up for a coffee and a quick chat with someone who inspires you. Essentially, I want you to replace those negative feelings with positive ones.

To help you really understand the importance of taking time out, some of the top producers I know, including my old bosses (Brad and Jason of Trainer HQ) would book their holidays in advance and schedule in time for breaks. This is in addition to weekend getaways. This does a few things. Firstly, it says "I matter" and it also gives you a target that you don't need to do anything else for. It gives you a sense of enjoyment knowing that this is an event to look forward to and reward yourself for all the energy and effort you're putting into the business or job.

If you want more happiness and fulfilment in your life, take more time off. Book holidays and breaks in advance. Doing this means you've always got something to look forward to, and you're ensuring that you will take time to recharge your batteries.

Some self-care ideas

It's not uncommon for people to lack ideas of how to enjoy time off. They are so used to working the grind, getting by, pushing themselves, that true relaxation time is few and far between. I've asked clients what they would do in their spare time, if they could do anything or go anywhere, and many will respond, "I don't know. I haven't thought about it, and I never have time anyway." If you can relate to this, here are a few suggestions for what you could do during some downtime.

- Yoga/Pilates/stretching.
- Exercise; walking, running, gym, HIIT, weights.
- Water sports like stand-up paddle boarding, snorkelling, jet-skiing.
- Hiking/mountain climbing.
- Coffee/drinks.
- Lunch/dinner.
- Beach/swim.
- Movies/TV shows (uplifting).
- Massage/spa treatments.
- Shopping (to a budget).
- Holiday (locally or overseas).

Journal page

> *"Talk to yourself like you would someone you love."* Brené Brown

- What excuses do you use for yourself to not have a self-care routine? List them out, then decide which ones you will not accept.
- Do you understand the importance of timeout? What does it mean to you? What things would you like to do?
- You can't pour from an empty cup. List some self-care ideas you'd like to try and choose one of these to start doing today.
- Are you booking in holidays ahead of time every year? Where would you like to go, what would you do and who would you like to do it with, and why?
- Time is your only commodity, not money, not things. If time was of the essence, what would you choose to do for yourself?

Super-Charged Freedom

Self-Care

Super-Charged Freedom

Freedom

This is what I've learned so far

A friend who worked in merchant banking in London for many years shared a story about her manager. An ambitious, driven guy, he burned the candle at both ends as an Analyst for three years, then an Associate, and later, a Vice President. He was well-known – like many of his colleagues – to indulge in certain illegal powdery substances, to give him the stamina he needed.

His goal was to be the youngest Senior Vice President in history. On the day of his promotion, he celebrated by taking his entire team out to a fancy restaurant for lunch. After a few hours of eating, drinking, and celebrating – no doubt on the expense account of a client – they returned to the office.

An hour later, his secretary walked in to find him slumped over his desk, dead at the age of 30.

He was working towards riches, status, and power, but did he have freedom?

Freedom is imperative to humans. Everyone has a different view of what freedom is. To me, it's being able to do what you want, when you want, and being able to help people by donating or helping out causes I believe in, on a regular basis.

Freedom is important to me, and with what I've been through and learnt on my way, I've developed a great grasp on it. That's why I decided to call my coaching company "Freedom Coaching".

As a twenty or thirty-something, I would often imagine my impending wealth and all the time I would have to relax and do whatever I desired; yet the behaviour and habits I was displaying were anything but those of someone who understood how to obtain this. I knew "consciously" how to imagine and daydream, but these were hopes and wishes that I managed to thwart every time. I was either not emotionally committed to them, or I made an initial decision to pursue something, and would immediately hit the infamous "terror barrier"; the invisible wall that shows itself anytime we decide to change a paradigm and replace the old program with this new idea. We start hearing all the doubts, worries, fear, and excuses.

As soon as I earned decent money or moved towards achieving my goals, I would run. That analogy we've been using as our caveman instinct – the fight or flight – is just as real in our mind as in the physical world. These days, rather than sabre-tooth tigers, we're running from obstacles, personal challenges, and perceived emotional threats. If you have set out to achieve big goals you haven't reached, then I'm sure you've done it, too.

When you try something new – like sticking to your plan and persisting despite perceived obstacles – your confidence may be drowned out by that loud, critical, inner voice, trying to talk you out of the awesome decision you've made. Don't let it. Stand your ground. Ask for help. Get someone to hold you accountable.

Freedom is so close for any person who decides it's time to take action. Freedom doesn't come from money and things. People with financial wealth can be just as miserable and trapped as somebody with a negative bank balance. Freedom actually comes from becoming the person you need to become, enjoying the ride, and opening yourself up to emotional abundance so that you can enjoy the financial freedom you create.

Creating this freedom requires patience. This doesn't mean sitting back and taking it slow. It means accepting that it will take time and practise to shed your old habits and embrace your new way of being, and the bigger and broader your goals are, the more small adjustments you will need to make. Growing into your more evolved self will take time – how much time depends on how quickly you can get yourself into the state of assuming belief of your future self as already here.

There will be tests, there will be people trying to bring you back to reality, there will be naysayers, there will be all sorts of tests, but this is YOUR life and for the purposes of these lessons, let's say that you only get one crack. I waited way too long to really understand and apply Bob's lessons. I don't plan on EVER going back to the old life. Why? Because it wasn't living; it wasn't freedom. I'm not saying my life was bad, it just wasn't truly serving me, my son, my mum, or my future girlfriend/wife.

"The cave you fear to enter holds the treasure you seek"

This is far more than just my favourite quote.

For the many years I've loved it, I didn't always understand what it really meant. For me, it represented a big, scary goal that somebody was afraid to tackle, such as starting a business or reaching for a significant promotion. My focus was always on something outside of myself, and the quote gave me confidence that if I just faced my fear of doing something new, that something magnificent would come out of it.

What I didn't realise was that the cave was never outside of me. The cave is inside. It's your own limitations or shortcomings, the part of yourself that you are afraid to examine and tackle head-on. For me, that was my dishonesty. Dishonesty primarily with myself, which resulted in not facing where I wasn't showing up in life, or where I was letting myself down. Dishonesty always towards others, when I didn't want to speak my truth out loud in case they reacted negatively. I didn't admit to myself where I was ignoring growth opportunities and instead, was hiding in bravado and bullshit. I was too scared of facing my damaged self-image. I was too scared to enter my internal cave and break through the terror barrier of change.

Today, I'm metaphorically in a different world. Diving into my internal cave has resulted in uncomfortable yet spectacular growth as a person, and the treasure I have found is valuable beyond measure. If you go headfirst into your own "cave" I can assure you there is only joy when you break through. It may not be comfortable going in at first – it wasn't for me – but it definitely gets easier, especially when your subconscious realises you're not going to quit this time; you're all in.

Are you getting ready for the adventure?

Ideas of how to free yourself

My journey is unlikely to be the one you want to emulate, so let's look at some possibilities and how you can obtain your version of freedom.

Starting with the action points from Chapter 1, let's set a goal.

What do you want? I mean, what do you truly want? Remember, you need to be excited at the prospect of achieving it and also scared by the fact it feels so big and outrageous.

Once you've made that "committed" decision, you need to make a list. I'll give you some ideas:

- What will I need to give up to be the person I need to be in order to reach my goal?
- What paradigms or poor/negative habits will I need to replace?
- Am I willing and able? (If not, maybe it's the wrong goal.)
- Do I have all the necessary knowledge to get me to my goal?
- If the last answer is no, then who can help me? Find a coach or a mentor! Even if you have a coach in your life, successful people hire different coaches and mentors for different areas of focus.
- Start creating a plan. It won't be a complete plan, because if it is, your goal is too small. Make it bigger.
- Create your goal as an affirmation and state in detail what you want, when you want to complete it by (date), and also what you're prepared to give in return. This could be the fabulous service rendered, it could be donating to charity, it could be anything that gives

value to others. You can't expect to receive something without first giving – it's impossible.

- Keep a positive mental attitude by reading daily, listening to positive material, sharing with likeminded people, join a mastermind, get someone as an accountability partner.

This is not an exhaustive list, and you may want to add some of your own ideas, but those above have served me well so far and I'm sure they will for you too.

What's next?

ACTION! You have the learnings and now you know that what you want is possible. Follow the above steps; remove those paradigms that aren't serving you (in fact, they are probably controlling you, like they were me).

It may be difficult to start, and you might want to quit, multiple times. But don't just take my word for it – hundreds of others I've worked with, studied with, and spoken to, have blasted through terror barriers, stripped away unhelpful paradigms, and smashed the ceilings which previously held them in.

When you make the decision to FINALLY be successful, an immediate wall can appear before you. Why? It's the battle of your conscious and subconscious that occurs when you decide to commit to an idea. You start emotionalising, and the feelings inside can trigger fear and resistance.

The great news is, you will get used to it and you'll keep reminding yourself, "I am growing." It's the growing pains of you strengthening your mind. Just like building muscles in the gym, it follows that this process is "no pain, no gain". If at some point it's not a struggle, you're probably not growing. It won't all be uphill, but you will certainly encounter some uncomfortable moments.

Let's all build mental muscle together!

Remember, I'm only a few steps ahead of you. Reach out to me. I'd love to help you. If you've read this book and it's inspired you, maybe it's time we talk?

Email brett@brettdscott.com
Website www.superchargedfreedom.com

Journal page

> *"The great revolution in the history of man, past, present and future, is the revolution of those determined to be free."* John F Kennedy (35th President of the United States)

- What does freedom look like for you? How will you know when you've got it?
- Do you know what beliefs, habits and other characteristics you'll require to set yourself free? List them here.
- What will life look like once you've reached your "freedom"? Draw a picture. Where are you living? What do you do with your days? Do you travel? Are you doing exciting hobbies?
- Often what holds us back from living a life of Freedom is something that's inside our cave that we fear to enter. List out some possible internal triggers, past traumas, or limiting beliefs that could be that for you.
- How long have you been wanting Freedom? How important is it? Will you take action to live your very best life?
- What is your plan of attack? How are you going to get started? What do you need to ensure your success? Start the plan and then move into inspired action.

If part of your plan is to hire a coach or a mentor, perhaps it's time you reached out to me to discuss your desires and if I believe I can help, I will give you the game-plan.

Freedom

Super-Charged Freedom

AFTERWORD

I've known Brett the past few years and have been blessed to be a guest expert for him in his mastermind programs, helping his clients understand my own perspective on Freedom by sharing the very real journey I've had in discovering the true meaning for myself.

When Brett asked me to write the afterword for his new book, I immediately said yes. Not just because he asked, but for the fact that this book is meant to help people understand a recipe for success that he has implemented for himself and many hundreds of his own clients.

Freedom means different things for all of us, but for me it means balance between what others deem as our professional and personal life. I like to differentiate these a bit, I divide everything into two categories: activity I get paid for and activity I do not get paid for. What I have learned to do often is overlap these activities, such as bringing my wife with me to an international speaking engagement or bringing my son on our company trip to The Masters in Augusta, and ensure that I am never losing sight of the "non-negotiables" in my calendar. Not everyone agrees with my idea of a weighted balance in terms of priorities, but this approach allows people to better understand their personal, experiential, giving, and receiving values, and make key decisions according to those values.

Before the global financial crisis of 2008 I had amassed a personal net worth of more than $100 million dollars. Due to surrounding myself with the wrong people, ideas, and decisions, I lost touch with the values that had brought me success. It resulted in losing all of that money and I was eveon on the verge of losing my wife, as well. When I finally came to terms with what had transpired and took accountability for what had happened, I understood that my ego had been Edging Goodness Out of my life. Being forced to take stock in who I was and who I wanted to become has led me to living a values-based existence. Now, I live in a world of more than enough, where there is more than enough of everything to make everyone happy, healthy, wealthy, and worthy.

That experience has not only helped me to recoup my wealth, but discover my true calling of empowering over 1 billion people to be happy. That is my version of Super Charged Freedom.

My advice to you going forward is re-read this book, take notes in the pages provided to remember, recollect, and reengineer some of all of the ideas shared. Most importantly, create a plan of action for yourself in order to take your purpose to the next level. Create positive habits and invest in your own potential. Find coaches or mentors who sit in a position you want to be in and ask them for help or directions in getting there. Freedom comes from consistently and persistently enjoying your pursuit of your potential, so go out there and pursue it.

David Meltzer

Co-founder of Sports 1 Marketing, best-selling author, and top business coach

ABOUT THE AUTHOR

Brett D. Scott is a multi award winning, metaphysical mindset coach, bestselling author & TEDx Talk speaker who has discovered success, true success and freedom at an older age. Older than he was expecting to be, when having worked it out. Probably like many others in the world and hence why Brett began and continues to pursue this mission by delivering this book. The book he was guided to write almost 8 years prior, during his biggest breakdown moment of his life.

Since Brett started his own journey of self discovery, personal healing and decision to pay it forward and positively impact others to experience the same, he has had one main focus. Genuinely, truthfully, vulnerably help others.

Since 2019, Brett has been doing just that. Focusing on his own improvement consistently and persistently and ensuring he's sharing that with his audience and clients daily.

Brett has just upgraded his business Freedom Coaching to take on the trading name 'Super Charged Freedom', yes, the title of this book. He now has a team of people helping his clients with their breakthroughs and numerous incredible transformations. that those individuals who've experienced them would attribute part of that success to Brett's help or involvement.

Such accolades and outcomes as; Emmy & Hollywood Music in Media awards. Rookie of the Year award in business (change of careers.) Sporting MVP & Best&Fairest. Double, Triple, TenX incomes. First & upgraded homes. The list goes on...

You can reach Brett at **www.superchargedfreedom.com** or **info@brettdscott.com** directly, if you're inspired to continue your journey, after reading this book.

THE GARDEN (Poem by Wendy A. Scott)

There is this most beautiful garden. It has been nurtured and loved, well maintained, healthy and glowing. The colours of the flowers are rich and vibrant. When one enters this garden they are filled with peace and love. It is a place of calm, one where you are filled with the magic of being alive.

One day, the one who has been nurturing this wonderful garden, leaves. Slowly weeds start to come up. Over time, they take over and the garden disappears. It is now totally neglected and forgotten.

The owner has decided to go on a journey to see what is on the outside of the garden. As he gets further and further away, he begins to forget where he started. Over time he becomes so very weary from his experiences and travels, he becomes despondent and unhappy.

A memory stirs somewhere deep within him, of a beautiful place where he once lived.

One day he walks past the place he started from and as the wind blows, it parts the weeds, and he catches a glimpse of flowers growing. He walks toward the weeds, pushes his way through and sees before him a wonderful garden, amidst all the debris and begins to remember what it was like.

He now decides to get some tools and start clearing away the weeds and debris, as he does this work, he feels the peace and contentment filling up inside him, he has now realised; he is the garden and he's begun to bloom in the light.

So please all of us remember, the flower that we are, the garden that we are, for we are the light and the beauty of all that is there.

We are 'The Garden of Eden'

www.ingramcontent.com/pod-product-compliance
Lightning Source LLC
Chambersburg PA
CBHW020322010526
44107CB00054B/1943